Modernism as Institution
On the Establishment of an Aesthetic and Historiographic Paradigm

Hans Hayden

Translated by Frank Perry

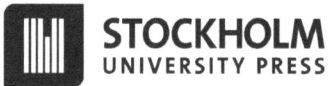

Published by
Stockholm University Press
Stockholm University
SE-106 91 Stockholm, Sweden
www.stockholmuniversitypress.se

Text © Hans Hayden 2018
License CC-BY
ORCID: Hans Hayden
ORCID: orcid.org/0000-0002-0487-0666
Affiliation: Stockholm University

Supporting Agency (funding): Riksbankens Jubileumsfond (The Swedish Foundation for Humanities and Social Sciences) and STINT (Swedish Foundation for International Cooperation in Research and Higher education)

First published 2018
Cover Illustration: Armory Show, International Exhibition of Modern Art, Chicago, 1913. The Cubist room
Cover License: By Anonymous photographer. Shot 100 years ago.
[Public domain], via Wikimedia Commons
Cover Design: Karl Edqvist, SUP
Translator: Frank Perry (from Swedish to English)
Original version in Swedish: Hayden, Hans, *Modernismen som institution. Om etableringen av ett estetiskt och historiografiskt paradigm*, Östlings bokförlag Symposion, Eslöv 2006.

Stockholm Studies in Culture and Aesthetics ISSN: 2002-3227

ISBN (Paperback): 978-91-7635-071-3
ISBN (PDF): 978-91-7635-068-3
ISBN (EPUB): 978-91-7635-069-0
ISBN (MOBI): 978-91-7635-070-6

DOI: https://doi.org/10.16993/bar

This work is licensed under the Creative Commons Attribution 4.0 Unported License. To view a copy of this license, visit creativecommons.org/licenses/by/4.0/ or send a letter to Creative Commons, 444 Castro Street, Suite 900, Mountain View, California, 94041, USA. This licence allows for copying any part of the work for personal and commercial use, providing author attribution is clearly stated.

Suggested citation:
Hayden, Hans. 2018. *Modernism as Institution: On the Establishment of an Aesthetic and Historiographic Paradigm*. Stockholm: Stockholm University Press. DOI: https://doi.org/10.16993/bar

 To read the free, open access version of this book online, visit https://doi.org/10.16993/bar or scan this QR code with your mobile device.

Stockholm Studies in Culture and Aesthetics

Stockholm Studies in Culture and Aesthetics (SiCA) (ISSN 2002-3227) is a peer-reviewed series of monographs and edited volumes published by Stockholm University Press. SiCA strives to provide a broad forum for research on culture and aesthetics, including the disciplines of Art History, Heritage Studies, Curating Art, History of Ideas, Literary Studies, Musicology, and Performance and Dance Studies.

In terms of subjects and methods, the orientation is wide: critical theory, cultural studies and historiography, modernism and modernity, materiality and mediality, performativity and visual culture, children's literature and children's theatre, queer and gender studies.

It is the ambition of SiCA to place equally high demands on the academic quality of the manuscripts it accepts as those applied by refereed international journals and academic publishers of a similar orientation. SiCA accepts manuscripts in English, Swedish, Danish, and Norwegian.

Editorial Board

Jørgen Bruhn, Professor of Comparative Literature at the Centre for Intermedial and Multimodal Studies at Linnaeus University in Växjö
Karin Dirke, Associate Professor of History of Ideas at the Department of Culture and Aesthetics at Stockholm University
Elina Druker, Professor of Literature at the Department of Culture and Aesthetics at Stockholm University
Johanna Ethnersson Pontara, Associate Professor of Musicology at the Department of Culture and Aesthetics at Stockholm University
Kristina Fjelkestam, Professor of Gender Studies at the Department of Ethnology, History of Religions and Gender studies at Stockholm University

Christer Johansson (coordination and communication), PhD Literature, Research officer at the Department of Culture and Aesthetics at Stockholm University
Jacob Lund, Associate Professor of Aesthetics and Culture in the School of Communication and Culture, Aarhus University
Catharina Nolin, Professor of art History at the Department of Culture and Aesthetics at Stockholm University
Ulf Olsson (chairperson), Professor of Literature at the Department of Culture and Aesthetics at Stockholm University
Sonya Petersson, Postdoctor of Art History at the Department of Culture and Aesthetics at Stockholm University
Meike Wagner, Professor of Theatre Studies at the Department of Culture and Aesthetics at Stockholm University

Titles in the series

1. Rosenberg, T. 2016. *Don't Be Quiet, Start a Riot! Essays on Feminism and Performance.* Stockholm: Stockholm University Press. DOI: https://doi.org/10.16993/baf. License: CC-BY 4.0
2. Lennon, J. & Nilsson, M. (eds.) 2017. *Working-Class Literature(s): Historical and International Perspectives.* Stockholm: Stockholm University Press. DOI: https://doi.org/10.16993/bam. License: CC-BY 4.0
3. Tessing Schneider, M. & Tatlow, R. (eds.) 2018. *Mozart's* La clemenza di Tito: *A Reappraisal.* Stockholm: Stockholm University Press. DOI: https://doi.org/10.16993/ban. License: CC-BY 4.0
4. Callahan, S., Holdar, M., Johansson, C. & Petersson, S. (eds.) 2018. *The Power of the In-between: Intermediality as a Tool for Aesthetic Analysis and Critical Reflection.* Stockholm: Stockholm University Press. DOI: https://doi.org/10.16993/baq. License: CC-BY 4.0
5. Hayden, H. 2018. *Modernism as Institution: On the Establishment of an Aesthetic and Historiographic Paradigm.* Stockholm: Stockholm University Press. DOI: https://doi.org/10.16993/bar. License: CC-BY 4.0

Peer Review Policies

Stockholm University Press ensures that all book publications are peer-reviewed in two stages. Each book proposal submitted to the Press will be sent to a dedicated Editorial Board of experts in the subject area as well as two independent experts. The full manuscript will be peer reviewed by chapter or as a whole by two independent experts.

A full description of Stockholm University Press' peer-review policies can be found on the website: http://www.stockholmuniversitypress.se/site/peer-review-policies/

Recognition for reviewers

The Editorial Board of Stockholm Studies in Culture and Aesthetics applies single-blind review during proposal and manuscript assessment. We would like to thank all reviewers involved in this process.

Special thanks to the reviewers who have been doing the peer review of the manuscript of this book.

Contents

Illustrations   ix
Acknowledgements   xi
Introduction   xiii

PART I. THE REGIME OF AUTHENTICITY   1
The Modernity of Modernism   3
The Tradition of the New   3
True and False Modernity   16
Metaphoric Displacements   20

Conflicting Truths   36
The Antithesis of Modernism   36
A Space of Transformations   48
The Mirror and the Lamp   61
Critical Margins   88

Endnotes for Part I   101

PART II. THE NORMALISATION OF THE AVANT-GARDE   133
The Struggle for Interpretive Privilege   135
Complex Settings   135
The Criteria of Normalisation   149
The Issue of the Function of Modern Art   156

The Aesthetic and Ideological Criteria of Normalisation   164
The Dictates of the Antitheses: The Cold War Cultural System   164
The Production of Identity as *Realpolitik*   173
The Model of Indirect and Symbolic Interpretation   181

The Modernist Metanarrative 188
    Between History and the Present 188
    Institution and Narration 190
    Alfred Barr's Diagram 200

Endnotes for Part II 213

PART III: TRANSFORMATION/TRANSMEDIA/TRANSFUSION 243

Realities Around and Underneath the Sign 245
    Approaches in Post-war Visual Cultures 245
    The Reactivation of an Old Relationship 255
    Trespassing on Common Culture 265

Open Aesthetics 272
    Paradigmatic Reinterpretations 272
    The Play of Opposites 283
    Endgame 301

Endnotes for Part III 307

Illustrations

1. Pablo Picasso, *Guitar and Wine Glass*, 1912, collage and charcoal on board, 47,9 x 36,5 cm, Collection of the McNay Art Museum, San Antonio, Bequest of Marion Koogler McNay, 1950.11. Copyright: Succession Picasso, License CC BY-NC-ND 22

2. Johann Heinrich Füssli, *The Artist's Despair Before the Grandeur of Ancient Ruin*, 1778/80, red chalk and brown wash on paper, 42 x 35,2 cm, Kunsthaus Zürich, Wikimedia Commons, License CC-0 (Public Domain) https://commons.wikimedia.org/wiki/File:Johann_Heinrich_F%C3%BCssli_013.jpg 32

3. Henri Meyer, *Le Triennal. Le Grand Salon Carré avec les portraits des peintres et des sculpteurs principaux*, illustration i *Le Journal Illustré*, sept. 30, Paris 1883, Photo and copyright: Uppsala University Library, License CC-0 CC BY-NC-ND 37

4. Jules Lefebvre, *La vérité*, 1870, oil on canvas, 110 x 226 cm, Musée d'Orsay, Paris, Photo and copyright: Reunion des musées nationaux/ IBL, Wikimedia Commons, License CC-0 (Public Domain) https://commons.wikimedia.org/wiki/File:La_V%C3%A9rit%C3%A9,_par_Jules_Joseph_Lefebvre.jpg 62

5. José Maria Mora, *Vanderbilt Ball, Mrs. Cornelius Vanderbilt as the electric light*, March 26 1883, fotografi, The New York Historical Society, New York (Department of Prints, Photographs, and Architecture Collections: Costume Ball Photographs Collection, PR-223, Series V, Box 3, Folder 34), Photo: The New York Historical Society, Wikimedia Commons, Licence CC-0 (Public Domain) https://commons.wikimedia.org/wiki/File:Mrs_Vanderbilt_ElectricLight.jpg 76

6. Anonymous, Trademark of Allgemeine Elekrizitäts-Gesellschaft (AEG), Germany, 1894, Photo and copyright: The Archives of the National Museum of Science and Technology, Stockholm, License: CC BY-NC-ND 78

7. Advertising poster for Philips TV, 1958, Photo and copyright: The National Library of Sweden, License: CC BY-NC-ND 246

Acknowledgements

This book was originally published in Swedish in 2006. Two years later, I received the *Pro Lingua Prize*, which was awarded by Riksbankens Jubileumsfond (The Swedish Foundation for Humanities and Social Sciences) and STINT (Swedish Foundation for International Cooperation in Research and Higher education), in order to fund a translation in to English. Prior to the translation, the original text was revised and in certain areas rewritten. This rather lengthy process has resulted in an obvious dilemma: Since the outlines and the issues of this study are quite extensive, a lot of new research has been produced since the book was originally published. For me, the only reasonable solution to this problem was to stick to the existing text, but in some cases – based on the helpful comments made by peer reviewers – supplementing the text with reference to current research. During the course of this work, a number of people have read, discussed, criticized and helped me in other ways; Persons without whose support this text could never have been completed. First of all, I would like to address my thanks to Frank Perry who undertook the extensive task of translating this text, always with an encouraging attitude and a willingness to discuss the subtle nuances of language and meaning. I am also most grateful to Lena Johannesson, who in various contexts showed her support and interest in this project, and without whom I would not have had the opportunity to begin nor finish my work. She also played a key role progressing the translation of the book. In the earlier stages of work, the late Anders Åman's and Lars Hjelmstedt's dedication and critical comments were of great importance. So too was the contribution of Kathryn Boyer, who generously entrusted me with her research material and knowledge of American and European art of the Post War era. A number of distinguished researchers undertook the task of proof reading my text in different phases of the work: Emilie Karlsmo, Annika Öhrner, Charlotte Bydler,

Dan Karlholm, Håkan Nilsson, Annika Olsson, Jeff Werner and Magdalena Holdar. Your critical and constructive views have been an invaluable help for me to finally formulate the goals and limitations of the study and I would like to warmly thank all of you. I also would like show my gratitude to Vetenskapsrådet (The Swedish Research Council) for the funding of the original project, as well as Riksbankens Jubileumsfond and STINT for funding the translation and publication of this study. Also, I am most grateful to everyone at Stockholm University Press for this edition. Finally, I would like to thank Anna for your love, inspiration and support.

Introduction

The German artist Thomas Struth has established himself in the art world with a cycle of large-format color photographs depicting visitors in famous museums throughout the world. These so-called 'Museum Photographs' show in a seemingly unmediated (albeit aesthetically extremely conscious) way people viewing artwork in different rooms. On one level these pictures are hardly particularly remarkable; photos of people performing various routines or watching something exist in a plenitude of variations. Yet, something strange and alienating rests over Thomas Struth's images.

The actual situation, considering a work of art at a museum, is of course a familiar act for a lot of people. One strolls through empty halls or jostles through crowded spaces, hastening past a number of works or stopping and reflecting for a long time before something of interest. But what are we actually doing? How do you stand, how do you move, how do you relate to the artworks, to the room and to other viewers? The subject-position, the general other or the 'one' that the anonymous crowd in Struth's photos pose, might as well be considered as an individual 'I'; the border between the ideal and the real viewer stands out as indistinct or liquid. Reception as a theoretical problem, and 'the encounter with the work' as a mystical conception, are placed into a physically tangible, yet impersonal social situation. And this situation as a depicted phenomenon is becoming the subject of a new work of art—ready to be exhibited and experienced in precisely the same place depicted. The aesthetics and the large scale of the photograph reinforces, in turn, a distance to the documentary

---

How to cite this book chapter:
Hayden, Hans. 2018. Introduction. In: Hayden, H. *Modernism as Institution: On the Establishment of an Aesthetic and Historiographic Paradigm* Pp. xiii–xx. Stockholm: Stockholm University Press. DOI: https://doi.org/10.16993/bar.a. License: CC-BY

feature of the images, as well as the everydayness of the action of the beholder of art. But what the pictures also do is visualize a part of a discursive practice: the world where art exists as 'art'.

One example is *Museum of Modern Art, New York 1994*, a study of observer of Jackson Pollock's *One: Number 31, 1950*. By accident, I visited MoMA myself for the first time a few months after Thomas Struth took his photograph. I was absolutely mesmerized by Jackson Pollock's huge painting. And as I walked through the collections, where each room contained key works, I felt like I was moving through the history of art, as though my own physical movement through the halls corresponded with reading a handbook on 20th century art or taking art history lectures at the university. It was probably the immensely high level of the collection that made me, a visitor from one of the semi-peripheries of Northern Europe, estranged of an otherwise familiar situation— and thus made me recognize the close relation between display and narrative.

What I'm trying to describe is the moment when a rift emerges between yourself and something familiar, when the real but unconscious conditions for something you do every day suddenly emerge. When one suddenly is able to observe an otherwise invisible pattern.

The pattern in this case means the notion of modernism as *the* art of the modern era, which became fully institutionalized sometime during the 1900s. Thus modernism emerges as the historical standard against which all other forms of art and visual codes are measured. This idea can be described as normalized in the sense that it has been a hidden condition rather than a thesis that requires arguments. Since that moment of realization at MoMA, I have observed the same basic pattern in numerous exhibitions, catalogues, handbooks, review papers and special studies. This led to an urge to study this phenomenon, the meta-narrative of the modernist art history. The problem of such a task was to find a way to recognize the duality of the word historiography—to write history and to write about history-writing—in a way similar to how Thomas Struth's photographs make it possible both to contemplate art and study the contemplation of art.

* * * *

When, where and how did modernism become synonymous with modern art? The question may seem preposterous, but it highlights that something taken for granted may not be quite so obvious. If one were to write a chronicle of the visual arts between 1850 and 1950 from a purely historical perspective, without any aesthetic considerations, the picture would be radically different from those conveyed in the vast majority of the exhibitions, textbooks and special studies. Other contexts and other images would appear that, in their historical situation, were judged to be the most important and essential works of art but were disregarded or completely excluded in the modernist historiography. Thus, the triumph of modernism in the West after the Second World War was not just a case of institutional acceptance of radical art, it was a victory that established a historic narrative based on a certain aesthetic paradigm.

This survey stems from a desire both to understand modern art—and modernism—from a broader perspective than what the matrix of modernist historiography offers and to understand how and in what historical context this matrix was framed and on what implicit criteria it rests. Therefore, this objective is examined from a position that goes beyond a purely art historical story in order to analyze the historical and institutional situations in which the story was formulated and subsequently normalized. In this respect, the title *Modernism as Institution* refers not only to a social historical or sociological analysis of the art world institutions, but also to an analysis that combines social, aesthetic, historical and historiographical perspectives. This perspective is close to Griselda Pollock's definition in 'Feminism and Modernism' (1987):

> Modernism can be understood as an institution, composed of and realised in a series of practices –painting, sculpting, writing art criticism, curating exhibitions, marketing pictures and careers, lecturing on art history courses, collecting and so forth. These practices circulate an ideology for the making, consuming and ratification of art . . . It [modernism] also refers to a *representation* of twentieth-century art practices which select some as significant (advancing, avant-garde), while marginalising others as residual, reactionary or historically irrelevant. Modernist criticism and art history have become the shaping and 'selective' tradition of and for twentieth-century culture in the West.[1]

Here, modernism is not only understood as a certain aesthetic approach or a contiguous cluster of artistic strategies, but also as an ideological matrix for interpretation, selection and evaluation. The very concept of modernism (and the theoretical perspectives that it historically has included) stands by itself as an interesting and problematic phenomenon, with its own history of establishment, operations and transformations during the 1900s.

It is possible to emphasize a couple of disparate purposes for such an analysis. One aim is to make visible alternative historical empirics (works of art, groups of artists, events, ideas, networks, contexts) that were perceived as obsolete or excluded from the modernist historiography. Another is to establish theoretical positions and analytical instruments in order to visualize the historically specific criteria and strata that the modernist narrative was resting upon and, at the same time, made invisible (by making them universal, ahistorical and 'normal'). These two objectives are not in any way mutually exclusive but can be seen as necessary and mutually supportive strategies; if the main purpose has been to investigate the very canonizing modernist narrative *itself*, its omissions and blind spots have made it possible to catch sight of the narrative as part of a discursive practice.

Thus the aim has been to articulate a distance towards the object of study in order to obtain an understanding of modernism that differs from its own historiography. This reinterpretation is in no way uniform but consists of a huge amount of divergent issues and starting points, which all in one way or another can be described as critical. The keyword in my application of this critical perspective has been *ambivalence*: an active effort to visualize cracks in and to deconstruct the apparently stable and uniform structure established by modernist historiography. This theoretical framework is to a large extent informed by the work of Michel Foucault. *L'archéologie du savoir* (1969) and *L'ordre du discours* (1971) have been of particular importance, not as a direct methodical influence, but rather as a motivation to ask certain kinds of questions, to call in a certain kind of context and to make visible certain kinds of patterns. The perspective presented here involves creating a distance from categories that have been taken for granted in previous historiography in order to find possible contexts and patterns beyond established narratives and to reconcile a historical and metahistorical analysis.

But to clarify my theoretical stance, I would like to make a distinction between discourse theory and discourse analysis. In his own characterization of discourse analysis (what he called 'archeology'), Foucault states that this is not a new method of interpretation, but rather an analysis of a historical stage in the form of an episteme: the aim is not to ask what has motivated a singular statement or what kind of meaning it expresses, but rather to try to 'define specific forms of articulation'.[2] My primary purpose, however, is to write history in terms of an interpretation of the contexts and content of statements and events. For this purpose, discourse theory has had the function of a theoretical reference point to provide a distinct rigor in how the questions are asked and how the contexts are described.

The concept of discourse is, in other words, used as an instrument to distinguish certain kinds of contexts where meaning is produced: an institutional and/or socially conditioned regular structure that creates a certain order and maintains the limits for acceptable representations, choices, actions, identities and transformations and, thereby, regulates both what can be said and how it can be said. The limit for a statement or an artistic representation is in this respect not only on an aesthetic or theoretical positioning within or opposed to other positions, but also part of a larger social, structural, intellectual and institutional context ('the archive').[3]

Based on this fundamentally structural determination, my purpose is to perform a closer examination of unique historical situations: of events; of social, political and aesthetical contexts; of institutional structures, as well as the production of historical, aesthetical and ideological identities. The concept of modernity has, in that regard, been used as an interface between the aesthetic and the social; it is a concept whose ambiguity reveals different connections, contexts and interpersonal relationships, which allow an analysis that does not stick to a specific schedule of causal relationships. In this purpose I do not differ from a tradition of social art history (Marxist or not); although, my combination of historical and metahistorical perspectives gives my study a rather different structure than most other works in this tradition. This also suggests that despite my deep impression of poststructuralist theory, not least in terms of a skeptical stance towards essential, absolute and stable constants, I basically still write from a hermeneutic perspective.

The reason for this is my interest in directing interpretation towards the object, which I have elsewhere described as the possibility of holding an iconological paradigm—although significantly modified.[4] As such, this perspective presents an antithesis against the tendency in some semiotic and poststructuralist theories to delegitimize the interpretation of a work of art as a central task in humanistic research, a tendency where the question of *how* a work means is set in opposition to the question *what* it means.[5] My point is that these issues do not need to be understood as mutually exclusive; to the contrary, it is precisely in the critical relationship between the how and the what that interpretation is activated and also where it is possible to establish a relationship between the then and the now. In this context, the interpretation is activated both as part of a meta-understanding of the formation meaning in a certain context and as an identification and interpretation of possible meanings within that context.[6] The purpose has been both to understand images as the primary sources of an individual (and historically specific) horizon of meaning and to use images as intersections in the overall analysis in order to concretize a theoretical or historiographical argument. In the latter case, one can understand the concept of image in relation to Douglas Crimp's use of it in his essay 'Pictures' (1979): as a critical tool for relating the production of aesthetic objects to mental and ideological conceptions.[7] It is in this context that the formulation of modernism as the essential modern art can be understood as a constitution of a specific picture or trope (an ideologically saturated representation).

*****

Part one, the Regime of Authenticity, consists of a thematic interpretation of some of the key tropes of modernism: modernity, authenticity, presence, originality, truth, historical necessity. The aim here has been to differentiate and deconstruct certain fundamental patterns of crucial importance in the interpretation of modern art in order to present a more complex and multilayered understanding of modernism and modern art. The key starting point in this regard has been to analyse the era of modern art on the basis of a larger context (modernity) than that offered by a purely art-historical study so as to uncover the contours and anchor points in a narrative that has served as an interpretive template underlying modernist historiography. This theoretical and epistemological investigation of modernity has been augmented by an analysis of the changes to the institutional structure of the art world and the establishment of a particular sphere of value. Using this approach, I attempt to identify some key nodes in the vast and all but incomprehensible pattern constituting modernism as an institution.

Part two, the Normalisation of the Avant-Garde, is more an historical and chronological study. The key premise here is that the period following the Second World War brought with it a fundamental change in the way modern art was understood and described and that it was at this time that Modernism was normalised and institutionalised in the prevailing normative systems of the West. As is made readily apparent in the application of concepts such as normalisation and institutionalisation, the postwar period brought with it social, discursive, intellectual and historiographic shifts in the conditions of modern art. What became institutionalised were not only a set of aesthetic criteria and stylistic idioms, but also a considerably more extensive and more authoritative interpretation of the art of the modern era—both in contemporary and historical terms. Moreover, what normalisation means in this context is that not only was a particular way of seeing entrenched in the system of norms of the dominant culture, but also a certain form of representation/narration was also gradually adopted as a premise whose ideological criteria and historically specific circumstances were concealed behind a notion of its universal applicability. These intellectual and ideological aspects of the institution are just as important as its social, economic and material infrastructure.

Part three, Transformation/Transmedia/Transfusion, considers the changes that have affected the normalised historiography and narrative of modernism from the end of the 1950s onwards.

It was then that the conflict over the right to formulate the nature of the problem became acute once more in the art worlds of Western Europe and the United States. A struggle in which the established view, which emphasised to a great extent the boundary between art and the surrounding world, was opposed by various open strategies aimed at bridging this very cleavage. This analysis leads to a concluding argument concerning the paradoxical position of the avant-garde as an institutionalised counterculture and the extent to which the alternative aesthetic and epistemological viewpoints labelled postmodernism have managed to call into question and to delegitimise both this position and the institutionalised narrative of modernism. This challenge did not involve a simple dismissal but should be understood instead from two diametrically opposed viewpoints: one attempted to demonstrate how the new forms of pluralism within the art world meant that the phenomenon of the avant-garde had become impossible, while the other sought to reestablish the oppositional and antagonistic position of the avant-garde in contemporary society. Both sides of this discussion may, however, be considered as the logical outcomes of the dilemma that is the hallmark of the historical process in this study: *what happens when a counterculture becomes integrated into the dominant one?*

PART I
THE REGIME OF AUTHENTICITY

The threshold between Classicism and modernity . . . had been definitely crossed when words ceased to intersect with representations and to provide a spontaneous grid for the knowledge of things. At the beginning of nineteenth century, they rediscovered their ancient, enigmatic density; though not in order to restore the curve of the world which had harboured them during the Renaissance, nor in order to mingle with things in a circular system of signs.[1]

Michel Foucault, *Les mots et les choses* (1966)

Modernity is a polemical tradition which displaces the tradition of the moment, whatever it happens to be, but an instant later yields its place to still another tradition which in turn is a momentary manifestation of modernity. Modernity is never itself; it is always *the other*. The modern is characterized not only by novelty but by otherness. A bizarre tradition and the tradition of the bizarre, modernity is condemned to pluralism. . .[2]

Octavio Paz, *Los hijos del limo* (1974)

The Modernity of Modernism

The Tradition of the New

Understood as a question, the subtitle to Kirk Varnedoe's book *A Fine Disregard* (1990) poses a problem that may appear puzzling: What Makes Modern Art Modern.[3] Remarkably, what Varnedoe has made it his task to explain has not just been taken for granted but appears to be a contradiction in purely semantic terms—for if modern art is not modern, what is it? Put briefly, the answer as developed in Varnedoe's study is based on the idea that the very modernity of modern art (and implicitly of modernism) lies in a decision by certain artists to rethink the traditional goals and methods of visual art in a manner that was only made possible by the changes to social and cultural systems that took place in the late nineteenth century.[4] In a nutshell, the modernity of modernism is to be found in the striving of the individual to remodel the rules of tradition and produce something radically new within the framework of that same tradition. This explanation may seem entirely plausible, but it remains far less perplexing than the formulation of the problem itself: the very modernism of modernity as a matter taken for granted, a premise rather than an open question.

Kirk Varnedoe's account has recourse to a theme that has been central both to the avant-garde discourse of the twentieth century and the historiography of that period: the relationship of visual art to the modern and the new. In *Aesthetic Theory* (1970), Theodore Adorno describes how this relationship has become burdened by an element of compulsion or of an almost a priori necessity:

How to cite this book chapter:
Hayden, Hans. 2018. The Modernity of Modernism. In: Hayden, H. *Modernism as Institution: On the Establishment of an Aesthetic and Historiographic Paradigm* Pp. 3–35. Stockholm: Stockholm University Press. DOI: https://doi.org/10.16993/bar.b. License: CC-BY

Yet since the mid nineteenth century and the rise of high capitalism, the category of the new has been central, though admittedly in conjunction with the question whether anything new had ever existed. Since that moment no artwork has succeeded that rebuffed the ever fluctuating concept of the modern.[5]

The concept of modernism itself involves a radicalisation of this theme: a movement that not only stands in a specific relation to the modern, but which by its very nature affirms the new without reserve, attempting at any cost to go beyond the utmost boundaries of modernity in this process of affirmation. In this context, Ezra Pound's celebrated battle-cry 'Make it new!' may be understood as both a condensation and a radicalisation of the demand for contemporaneity that the realist avant-garde of the late nineteenth century sought to impose on art ('il faut être de son temps'). Obviously, this insistence on newness and contemporaneity had not only a descriptive, but also a powerfully normative aspect. Sooner or later, however, this cross-boundary pursuit of perpetual newness was bound to find itself in an uncomfortable position, as the change was interpreted in relation to history. This apparently paradoxical situation has been aptly described by Harold Rosenberg when referring to 'the tradition of the new'.

If Pound's and Rosenberg's formulations are placed side by side, an interesting dislocation is revealed in which the aesthetics and identity of the avant-garde have become a norm for historical classification. Furthermore, when the dates of these phrases are compared, 1934 and 1959, respectively, a period of time is marked out that would in many ways come to redefine modern art.[6] Certain definitive changes can also be detected during this period in the use of a concept such as modernism when applied to the way in which modern art is defined.

According to Matei Calinescu, the concept of modernism was first used relatively recently, during the 1920s, as a collective term for various radical, at first literary and subsequently artistic, movements.[7] The term modernism is conspicuous by its absence from the period before the Second World War, irrespective of whether art criticism, manifestos or historicist writings about modern art are being studied. It would prove much more useful at a later stage: towards the end of the 1930s, when an epochal concept was required as part of the intensifying efforts to chart, distinguish, evaluate and classify historically the hodgepodge of various avant-garde movements that had arisen from the late nineteenth century onwards. Modernism would provide the term required to circumscribe these heterogeneous movements, managing to inject an element of uniformity into their radical disunity, while also putting it in relation to modern life. Attempts to chart the terrain in this way had also been made as part of the art history and exhibition activity of the early nineteenth century, but then it was more a matter of establishing and legitimising new movements ('-isms') in relation to one another, to history and to contemporary society. The need to produce an overall map did not, in fact, become topical until later: once avant-garde art had become increasingly institutionalised as part of the cultural life of Europe and the United States. A further change both in meaning and usage can be identified a few decades later, from the end of the 1970s onwards, when the concept of modernism was used as a collective term for the art and aesthetics that had just been declared anathema and which postmodernists wanted both to transcend and negate.

The decisive change in this regard is not to be found in the historicisation of the avante-garde during this period, but in the shifting of the position of the avant-garde from the margins to the centre of discourse: with the normalisation of the logic of perpetual change that would now define contemporary cultural life. The historical interpretation of modern art—and the interpretation of modernism *as* modern art—thus constitutes both a historically transient category and an understanding from which our own self-image has developed in one way or another, positively or negatively. The image of the dominant position of modernism in the art and visual culture of modernity still provides a matrix for what is considered historically normal in the art history of the twentieth century.[8]

*****

The relationship between modernism and modernity has been characterised in general terms by many authors. One example is the historian Louis Dupeux, who thinks that modernism amounts to 'the systematic valuation' (la valorisation systématique) of modernity.[9] A similar formulation can be found in the work of Charles Harrison and Paul Wood, who write that modernism involves 'the deliberate reflection' on modernity.[10] These formulations may appear entirely plausible, but they are nevertheless too vague to provide any kind of answer as to the nature of the relationship. Nor do they succeed in identifying anything typical about modernist art in comparison with other aesthetic approaches; instead, they presuppose a connection that is at once too general and too specific to be characterised: general in the sense of self-evident and specific in that it can only be described on the basis of each individual example (in the form of particular statements or works of art.)

Marshall Berman, on the other hand, manages to be considerably more detailed when describing the connection between modernity and modernism in *All That Is Solid Melts into Air*:

> To be modern, I said, is to experience personal and social life as a maelstrom, to find one's world and oneself in perpetual disintegration and renewal, trouble and anguish, ambiguity and contradiction: to be part of a universe in which all that is solid melts into air. To be a modern*ist* is to make oneself somehow at home in the maelstrom, to make its rhythms one's own, to move within its currents in search of the forms of reality, of beauty, of freedom, of justice, that its fervid and perilous flow allows.[11]

Throughout this work, Berman succeeds in highlighting the significance of contradiction in the modern and within modernism, as, in particular, in his quoting of Marx's celebrated phrase in the title. He describes the link between base and superstructure from a historically materialist viewpoint as a multifaceted and occasionally contradictory dialectical process. It is the paradoxical unity, the risk, the transformation, and the pain and the dangers, too, that are focused on, while 'the maelstrom of continual dissolution' evokes bold, energetic, almost futuristically charged images and metaphors. Rather than present us with the humdrum greyness of the everyday in modern society, its routinisation of social life and increasing alienation, Berman's account paints a picture of heroic struggle and confusion in which the individual launches himself unflinchingly into the maelstrom of dissolution of futurity.

Although this perspective is somewhat modified in the rest of his presentation, (particularly when describing Robert Mose's planning/devastation of the Bronx as an image of the more brutal and technocratic aspects of modernism), the idea of modernism itself retains its heroic nimbus. It still conveys, in his eyes, a creative, radical and even revolutionary potential that needs to be affirmed—despite all the evils that can be attributed to the process of modernisation. This condensed account succeeds in situating the various forms of the word modern in a self-evident and transparent relation to one another: modernity, modernisation, modernism. A value judgement is also being made here, in which the capacity for relating to the modern in a particular way—of 'being modern'— is a positive characteristic on the part of a group or an individual living in the modern world. For Berman, modernism as a collective term encompasses rather more than a particular aesthetic canon; although, particular linguistic qualities and artistic devices are considered in terms of an essential value and thus given a privileged relation to the contemporary: modernism is not primarily presented as a style but as a zeitgeist in the old and idealistic sense of the word.

This judgement can no doubt be traced back to Charles Baudelaire's description of the specific aesthetic value of contemporary art in 'Le peintre de la vie moderne' (1863), where the ephemeral aspects of the contemporary world are seen as a specific quality of the art of the modern period:

> By 'modernity' I mean the ephemeral, the fugitive, the contingent, the half of art whose other half is the eternal and the immutable. Every old master has had his own modernity; the great majority of fine portraits that have come down to us from former generations are clothed in the costume of their own period. They are perfectly harmonious, because everything – from costume and coiffure down to gesture, glance and smile (for each age has a deportment, a glance and a smile of its own) – everything, I say, combines to form a completely viable whole. This transitory, fugitive element, whose metamorphoses are so rapid, must on no account be despised or dispensed with. . . . . Woe to him who studies the

antique for anything else but pure art, logic and general method! By steeping himself too thoroughly in it, he will lose all memory of the present; he will renounce the rights and privileges offered by circumstance – for almost all our originality comes from the seal which Time imprints on our sensations.[12]

It is a total immersion in the present, which is described by Baudelaire as the essential task of contemporary art (whose fate is inevitably to become part of history and thus lose its most crucial quality). Part of Baudelaire's argument may, of course, derive from the very ancient and long-established notion of the superiority of one's own time over the past: that because we stand on the shoulders of giants, we can see further than they could. But he emphasises the specific beauty of the contemporary (of the present) without necessarily rejecting the efforts of previous ages to find general (eternal) beauty. What he is actually formulating is a paradoxical relationship between the transient and the eternal, which does not involve a simple polemic against tradition, but rather an analysis of the contemporary that serves as an exhortation to establish a dynamic connection with history.

Baudelaire's definition entails a revaluation of the dynamic variability of modern society, which also introduced a new sense of time and a different way of reflecting on the particular identity of contemporary society in relation to the past. But where Baudelaire highlights a diffuse phenomenon in his own society as reflecting a comprehensive change, Berman affirms instead the entrenchment of that phenomenon in a particular aesthetic canon. These authors also speak to us from two diametrically opposed historical positions. Between these texts lie not only just over a century of changes in aesthetic pronouncements and historical selections, but more importantly a normalisation of a certain kind of pronouncement and selection. For it is, of course, not as simple a matter as Charles Harrison, for example, would have us believe: that modernist art theory has proved better able at capturing the concepts and views that have turned out to be definitive of modern artistic practice.[13] Once modernist art theory is afforded this privileged position, what it actually does is establish the preconditions for what may be understood and defined as modern art.

The concept of modernity that emerges here is not only multivalent, but also applied in a wealth of diverse and, occasionally, contradictory areas of usage in which it fulfils different functions. In order to illustrate the complexity of these interconnections, Fredric Jameson has distinguished two distinct uses and meanings of the concept of modernity: one linguistic and one epochal.[14] In the former sense, the concept has an ostensive function, identifying a phenomenon as modern. Here the concept remains constant in terms of form but completely empty in terms of content, like a personal pronoun alternating between different tenses and individuals, like the 'I' that is used by different people in a conversation and identifies the particular person using it. The phenomena of his contemporary world Baudelaire would so enthusiastically describe as modern belong nowadays to history; the characteristics I attribute to the modernity of my own time are contradicted by other interpretations and selections. In an academic context, this process of exclusion and inclusion involves both the choice of an interpretative horizon and an affiliation to a subject area: an art historian will presumably emphasise different matters than a sociologist or an economist. In the second sense, which could be said to be a function of the first, the concept of modernity is used to characterise a particular age or epoch.[15] The concept of modernity is usually considered to encompass a historical period that had its beginnings in post-feudal Europe and is therefore associated with industrialisation and technological change, with the advent of a capitalist commodity market and a systematic division of labour, with continually increasing economic growth and the trans-national flow of money and information, with the rise of the bourgeoisie as the dominant social class and the establishment of the nation state, with the philosophy of the Enlightenment and the scientific revolutions that introduced a greater degree of rationalisation and a demystification of existence, with a greater differentiation of the functions of society as reflected in new forms of administration, jurisprudence and the exercise of power, with urbanisation and the establishment of new patterns of social life.

Together all these shifting uses and attributes may be condensed into a single historical perspective in which a particular historical change (modernisation) is combined with a new intellectual orientation (the Enlightenment) and in which the formulation of a post-traditional world view is interwoven with an emancipatory idea of human liberation. A number of key tropes can thus be discerned connecting the various, divergent theories about modernity that were produced in the twentieth century; all of these tropes may be traced back to the idea that modernity is not just a concept or a representation, but is also, or perhaps above all, a narrative category. What this tells us is that knowledge *about* the modern has also been produced *in* the modern, an apparently banal statement that succeeds nevertheless in highlighting the close connection between descriptive and normative criteria—between the production of knowledge and of ideology—because the formulation of the contemporary is crucial to the formation of the political.[16] Fredric Jameson has described this relationship in particularly apt fashion:

> 'Modernity' then, as a trope, is itself a sign of modernity as such. The very concept of modernity, then, is itself modern, and dramatizes its own claims. Or to put it the other way around, we may say that what passes for a theory of modernity in all the writers we have mentioned is itself little more than the projection of its own rhetorical structure onto the themes and content in question; the theory of modernity is little more than a projection of the trope itself.[17]

The essential aspect of this argument is that the descriptive identification also encompasses a meta-level, which is not only based on a particular judgement, but also follows a set dramaturgy. This means, first, that a hyper-complex and boundless context is reduced to a limited set of themes, and second, this thematic arrangement is based on a narrative structure, on various rhetorical figures and on images and metaphors that are more or less integrated. Put simply, it involves discursive representations that condense a vast and contradictory context into a comprehensible (and ideologically effective) form, into images that have been produced, translated, projected and reproduced in every conceivable context. This is a process that has no space for deviations and doubt but which seeks to shape history with regard both to the needs of the current age and to the aims of the future.

This could be said to be the standard version of the modern narrative of modernity; it is a version of the story that produces a relatively coherent image of modernity. What Berman is attempting to bring to light is its critical and even revolutionary potential—a way of thinking and being that blows apart the standardised image. Contradiction is a crucial factor in this enterprise and one that must be continually affirmed and renewed in order to wrest the modern project away from the technocrats of modernisation. The problem with his account is not so much its heroic ambitions for contemporary society but the way it establishes a horizon for historical analysis *from within* modernity as an overarching system. Contradiction becomes an ideological weapon, rather than a tool, for illuminating and analysing the premises of his own historiography: the words modernity and modernism are used as a means of defending particular ideological and existential values rather than as the starting point for an analysis of the premises of established historiography. But to describe or analyse this context *from without*—so as to demonstrate both its rhetoric and which tropes it takes for granted—is no easy task. Even if we accept the idea that we could be said today to stand outside modernity and are thus capable of observing its beginning and end, its factual preconditions and ideological tropes, every aspect of this modernity has served to create the very foundations on which our own age, our own ideological narratives and historical blind spots have been constructed.

A good place for such an investigation to begin might be to take Octavio Paz at his word when he asserts that modernity is always another, all the values, functions and forms of experience, that is, which arise between and beyond all its apparently obvious and clearly defined attributes. We might formulate a strategy in this regard that has certain similarities with a Derridean deconstruction: where Jameson distinguishes modernity as a trope formulated in and by the modern, Paz points out the necessity of discovering and investigating the cracks in this undifferentiated image. Instead of simply adding together a series of attributes in order to produce an apparently objective and factual equation of the modern, we could choose, like Zygmunt Bauman, to describe modernity as something more than a general pluralism, as something that is fundamentally ambivalent. According to Bauman, ambivalence is a normal phenomenon of linguistic practice and has its origins in one of the key functions of language: naming or classifying. Classification is an act of inclusion and exclusion that divides the world in two, thus creating a stable structure of binary polarities. Ambivalence may be understood as a by-product of this process, a bugbear that directs attention to phenomena and values outside the range and norms of the system and, in so doing, demonstrates its arbitrary and unstable nature:

> Ambivalence, the possibility of assigning an object or an event to more than one category, is a language-specific disorder: a failure of the naming (segregating) function that language is meant to perform. The main symptom of disorder is the acute discomfort we feel when we are unable to read the situation properly and to choose between alternative actions.[18]

Because the goal of rational modernity is to create a stable and symmetrical order within all its practices and areas of operation, every form of ambivalence presents a threat that has to be eliminated. But as no language provides an unambiguous and stable structure, ambivalence cannot, in Bauman's view, be eliminated—on the contrary, it appears to be a fundamental attribute of all linguistic construction and communication. If modernity is considered as a discursively produced phenomenon, ambivalence would constitute a basic component of its defining characteristics and classification: a persistent ontological fault line running through the forms of experience and representation that the modern has given rise to.

Elsewhere, Bauman has described this ambivalence of modernity as a split between ability (what I may do) and wanting (what I wish to be done), which has brought about a state of permanent disharmony.[19] This rift may also be considered to be a function of the intersection of these two heterogeneous patterns of movement, the dynamic of continual change and novelty as opposed to the equilibrium of rational order and the system. Attempts to eliminate ambivalence of this kind—by reproducing, for example, the idea of a uniform and consistently rational modernity—would involve not only a normalisation of particular selections and evaluations, but also a potential threat to modernity's fundamental, cross-boundary dynamic. This idea of uniformity may be countered by a motley and contradictory combination of scepticism and deferral of a more philosophical and epistemological kind, a combination that has frequently been dismissed as the product of nostalgia or of lingering premodern forms of experience.

One of the most resolute and simultaneously heart-wrenching examples of a stance that is critical of both modernity and progress is found in Walter Benjamin's posthumously published *Geschichtphilosophische Thesen* (1940), where he inscribes his doubts about the present and the future in a painting by Paul Klee:

> A Klee painting named 'Angelus Novus' shows an angel looking as though he is about to move away from something he is fixedly contemplating. His eyes are staring, his mouth is open, his wings are spread. This is how one pictures the angel of history. His face is turned towards the past. Where we perceive a chain of events, he sees one single catastrophe which keeps piling wreckage upon wreckage and hurls it in front of his feet. The angel would like to stay, awaken the dead, and make whole what has been smashed. But a storm is blowing from Paradise; it has got caught in his wings with such violence that the angel can no longer close them. This storm irresistibly propels him into the future to which his back is turned, while the pile of debris before him grows skyward. This storm is what we call progress.[20]

This short text contains an array of suggestive metaphors: from the eyes of the angel (the gaze of the historian) and the storm out of Paradise (the development of history) to ruins that form a veritable Tower of Babel (the ultimate consequences of this development). What Benjamin is formulating here is an attitude critical of civilisation that is particularly reminiscent of the Primitivist trope, which characterised so many of the various avante-garde movements of the early twentieth century. In opposition to the maelstrom of change, the storm of progress emerges as an alternative image of how historical change has driven human beings further and further away from their original condition while also driving the Enlightenment ever further away from the original idea of the liberating and life-affirming force of rational thinking. The melancholy and despair evoked by the Biblical metaphors are, of course, connected with the real-life circumstances in which Benjamin found himself: fleeing from the German Nazi-regime, whose war machine at that time seemed impossible to stop, while deeply disillusioned at Stalin's betrayal of world communism in the signing of the nonaggression pact with Hitler. This pessimism was not restricted to the acute situation that obtained at the beginning of the 1940s but encompassed the developmental process of history as a whole in that it considered change and progress to be a story of continually repeated catastrophes. It is in this context that he would impose a fundamental moral requirement on historiography: not to pass on blindly the history of the victor, but to allow the depiction of the past to become a commemoration and rehabilitation of the victims of the triumphal march of the generals and of 'development'.

This lack of trust in progress might well have been shared by anyone who managed to live through the years immediately following the war in the bombed-out metropolises of Europe. The political, social and economic problems confronting the countries affected were enormous, and this would be particularly true following the Second World War. The image of growing piles of ruined buildings was no metaphor but an extremely tangible form of reality for millions of people. They were also faced with the moral and existential reevaluation forced on them by the Holocaust and the mass destruction created by modern warfare. How could the image of the modern project as a process of perpetual progress and liberation be sustained when it seemed that it was this very progress that had forced human beings into the most extreme forms of barbarism? And what was the role of the individual in this process of development; what moral responsibility could be laid on him or her? Modernisation and the idea of progress contained within themselves consequences that were as unavoidable as they were appalling, or so it might seem.

Voices critical of progress and development are therefore to be found within the modern; there is, in fact, a long tradition of such critical voices, which includes several of the greatest thinkers and interpreters of modernity (Marx, Weber, Nietschze, Sprengler). It should nevertheless be pointed out that the fundamental value inscribed in the image of modern society, particularly after the Second World War, was created not through doubt and criticism of various kinds but primarily by trust in the emancipatory potential of technology, social planning and science. This would be particularly evident when the chaos and crises of the late 1940s transformed into the powerful economic recovery of the 1950s, the period when the welfare state would increasingly become a reality in Western Europe and the US. In the ideological context of the Cold War, the real threat was not provided by a vague internal enemy (the negative consequences of modernism), but by a very specific external one (the expansion of the Soviet empire). This was also a period in which private consumption was continually growing, while various innovations in technology and the media made it possible to travel and to acquire information, culture and entertainment on a far greater scale than ever before. Although the notion of progress might be subject to criticism in a particular context, the growing rise in living standards appeared to demonstrate its incontrovertible validity in another. In antithesis to the criticism of civilisation, a growing sense of trust in the rationality and inherent reasonableness of science and democratic society became established now that political reforms and a socially adapted market economy appeared to create better conditions for the freedom and existence of the individual than ever before in history. In consequence, criticism was not aimed at the idea of enlightenment in itself, but against what was seen as the utopian and metaphysical delusions of totalitarian ideologies.

It would appear, therefore, that a new need was felt in the postwar period to employ a genuinely or supposedly rational form of scientific analysis as a foundation not only for the understanding of society, but also for its planning, which inevitably involved other sciences, such as economics, political science, urban studies, psychology, mathematics. And this would also have applied, of course, to other disciplines and discourses that treated or analysed modernity in various ways. What was problematic here, however, was both the choice of perspective and the selection of the level of abstraction. Even though different sciences could provide a diversity of viewpoints in the analysis of modernity, in many cases this involved the taking for granted of certain categories and premises in the transfer between different disciplines.

In order to focus on the ambivalences of modernity and modernism in this context, fault lines have to be made visible that, in many ways, run entirely counter to the values and identities that are reproduced within the modern. It is, therefore, of crucial importance that any such interpretation should encompass a description of not only what modernity means, but also of how and in which contexts its normative values have been produced.

True and False Modernity

The analogy drawn by Marshall Berman between modernity and modernism may appear both more specific and more normative than an unconsidered view of the relationship as being obvious or unproblematic (modernism as a conscious form of reflection or a systematic evaluation of modernity). And yet both these viewpoints are actually embedded within each other to the extent that the explicitly formulated notion is simply a codification of something that would otherwise be taken for granted. However, when manifestos, specialist studies, monographs, essays, surveys and other texts are read anew with this relationship in mind, a particular pattern emerges that makes the analogy manifest, albeit in various ways and with dissimilar aims. And if it is the origins of the analogy that are being sought, they can also be discovered in some of the manifestos, programmatic writings and statements of the avant-garde.

The most celebrated are, of course, the Futurist paeans to the speed, harshness and mutability of the modern age. Or as the 'Manifesto dei pittori futuristi' of 1910, devised by Umberto Boccioni and signed by Carlo Carrà, Luigi Russolo, Giacomo Balla and Giovanni Severini, has it,

> Comrades! We declare that the triumphant progress of science has brought about changes in humanity so profound as to dig an abyss between the docile slaves of the past and us who are confident in

the shining splendor of the future.... The only living art is that which finds its distinctive features within the environment that surrounds it. Just as our forbears took the subject of art from the religious atmosphere that enveloped them, so we must draw inspiration from the tangible miracles of contemporary life, from the iron network of speed which winds around the earth.... Waiting to contribute to the necessary renovation of all artistic expression, we resolutely declare war on all those artists and institutions that, even when disguised with a false costume of modernity, remain trapped in tradition, academicism, and above all a repugnant mental laziness.[21]

Even though all these ideas may be familiar from the modernist canon—the notion that there is an absolute gulf separating the present and the past—the phrase referring to a false modernity is noteworthy. This can only be taken to mean that these Futurist painters were claiming to be creating in their art a true modernity, a language and a value that have their origins in the changes occurring in the contemporary world and are, therefore, authentically in relation to the essence of modernity.

The bombast and self-glorifying rhetoric of the Futurists might appear to be a rather facile example, an unintended parody almost of the attempts by the avant-garde to legitimize their art to their contemporaries. But if one disregards the rhetorical façade, an intellectual construct becomes apparent that recurs in a range of similar contexts and in which the modernity of a particular artist's work is presented as the ultimate criterion of its legitimacy: why something appears as it does and why it has to look that way as a matter of necessity. While it would of course be possible to stick to the old ways, art that is striving for authenticity and to be in harmony with its own age must embody the changes of the modern age.

And yet it is striking how seldom explicit analogies were formulated in the discourse of the historical avant-garde between the work of a particular artist and the modernity of his or her contemporary world. The main reason presumably being that the analogy runs counter to one of the key tropes of the avant-garde: the individuality and autonomy of art and the artist. Instead, the key argument in the avant-garde manifestos was the formulation and legitimation of the modernity of new art by means of negations. This was reflected in a continually recurring antagonism toward the art of previous ages, the dominant culture of the contemporary world and tradition as such. It also involved, as Theodor Adorno put it, establishing more or less specific registers of taboos that could not be transgressed. As a result, the definition of the art a particular artist practised was, equally, a definition of what was no longer possible:

> Art is modern when, by its mode of experience and as the expression of the crisis of experience, it absorbs what industrialization has developed under the given relations of production. This involves a negative canon, a set of prohibitions against what the modern has disavowed in terms of experience and technique; and such determinate negation is virtually the canon of what is to be done. That this modernity is more than a vague Zeitgeist or being cleverly up to date depends on the liberation of the forces of production.[22]

The cultural identity of the avant-garde is expressed here through a demarcation of the limits of aesthetic and social autonomy in relation to the bourgeois normality of the modern age. Adorno, indeed, asserts that modernism, unlike previous artistic practice, not only negates preceding aesthetic forms, but also the very tradition *per se,* which serves to integrate, in a manner of speaking, the pursuit of change by bourgeois modernity within artistic practice.[23] Modernism could be seen in this context as a mainly negative trend, which—like Walter Benjamin's angel—observes and illuminates the misery of modernity and whose form of representation could even be described as a kind of anti-modernity.[24] But this negative dialectic should be interpreted, rather, as a form of antagonism towards the aspects of bourgeois culture, which failed to keep pace with the dynamic changes of the modern age. It is in this sense that Boccioni's remark about false modernity becomes so important: it marks the point at which a descriptive statement is transformed into a normative identification.

Instead, it is in the historical interpretation and legitimation of avant-garde art that the analogy between modernity and modernism has come to play a crucial role. Its practitioners, in contrast, were more preoccupied with the detail of describing and explaining their aesthetic starting points and artistic devices and, above all, with their contempt for the conventions of bourgeois modernity. Both the use of the term modernity and the need it fulfilled may be seen as a symptom of the shift in the status of the avant-garde: from marginalisation, autonomy and antagonism to acceptance, historicisation and institutionalisation. Two general phenomena can be distinguished in relation to the changing circumstances in the Western democracies during the twentieth century. On the one hand, the 1920s and the 1930s witnessed the gradual acceptance and institutionalisation of various avant-garde movements (when the notion of the avant-garde began to be formulated in terms of modernism); on the other, modernism became a more or less standard way of describing modern art *per se* in the decade following the end of the Second World War. A particular paradigmatic image of the nature of modernism and modern art is thus being constituted during this period. Although this image obviously encompassed a number of divergent interpretations, it would nevertheless define a distinct horizon for what was both possible and legitimate. And it is as part of this process that the analogy becomes necessary.

What this also demonstrates is the necessity of making a distinction between the concepts of the avant-garde and modernism. Although not (as some have done) in order to distinguish a different essential content, but because the use and meaning of both terms have different histories. While the concepts may not be considered synonymous, there is a tangible proximity, historically speaking, between the phenomena both terms are usually associated with.[25] When this closeness is borne in mind, the history of modernism and the avant-garde emerges as a perpetual conflict or crisis within the modern. The most esoteric movements within the avant-garde and those most critical of civilisation may also be understood in this light—as a utopian pursuit of a different form of modernity: a new order and a new human being which could transcend the established culture of the West.[26]

Here were have the contours of a specific historical process: a concept is introduced at a certain point because it meets a particular need; the concept is then widely disseminated through various institutions; certain interpretations are privileged and a somewhat simplified image of a complex historical situation becomes established (essential developmental perspectives and analogies, canonical selections and collections of examples, a process of exclusion and inclusions). The temporal (historical) change in function and value must also, of course, be taken into account, because it marks a number of different historical positions that determine the relevance and significance of both the aesthetic criteria and the theoretical legitimacy of a particular interpretation. Seen from an art historical perspective, the establishment of a discursive and epistemological boundary between the modern and the postmodern is of particular relevance here as it allows for a degree of distance from the object of research (in this case, modernism). Instead of understanding this boundary line as separating the criteria deemed legitimate and illegitimate aesthetic in one's own contemporary period, it may be used to differentiate a number of historical situations in which descriptions of the contemporaneity of particular periods have taken place. This is an issue that calls for both a historical and a historiographic perspective.

Metaphoric Displacements

When modernism is understood to be a direct and simple reflection of modernity, the image in the mirror appears distorted. However, like Renato Poggiolo, we could also view modernism as an exceptionally polysemous reflection of and on the distortions of modernity:

> [T]he nature of modernism in general is anything but timid, moderate, or discreet; it naturally leads to exaggeration and disequilibrium and must even be defined as an unconscious parody of modernity, an involuntary caricature. Modernism leads up to, and beyond the extreme limits, in the modern spirit which is most vain, frivolous, fleeting, and ephemeral.[27]

At issue here is an experience of distortion—as both reflection and judgement—which is expressed, in particular, in the negative rhetoric of contempt for tradition and the criticism of civilisation. Matei Calinescu, for his part, has attempted to explain this phenomenon by maintaining the existence of two modernities: one connotes a stage in the history of Western culture and is associated with scientific and technological progress; the other is an aesthetic concept (the avant-garde).[28] These two modernities appear to be locked in a dialectical struggle, continually repelling and attracting one another, the former rationalist and competitive, the latter critical and focused on demystifying the established values of the former.

> Literary modernism, to take one quick example, is thus both modern and antimodern: modern in its commitment to innovation, in its rejection of the authority of tradition, in its experimentalism; antimodern in its dismissal of the dogma of progress, in its critique of rationality, in its sense that modern civilization has brought about the loss of something precious, the dissolution of a great integrative paradigm, the fragmentation of what once was a mighty unity. To go beyond the all-too-obvious conceptual difficulties raised by the vocabulary of modernity, I have spoken metaphorically of the "faces" of a constitutively double – dual, ambiguous, and duplicitous – modernity.[29]

The problem of the essentialist connotations of the analogy remains, however, in these negative or contradictory explanations. And yet the possibility emerges, in Calinescu's argument, of an entirely different interpretation of the relation between modernity and modernism in that he succeeds in demonstrating a multiplicity of aesthetic forms of representation not only *of* but *within* the modern, which is explicitly alluded to in his title: *Five Faces of Modernity*. Included among the faces of modernity here are areas that clearly lie outside the self-image of modernism, such as kitsch (the antithesis of modernism) and postmodernism (the transcendence of modernism). This makes it possible to describe the various artistic manifestations of modernism as a continuous, critical, parodic, antithetical, serious and contradictory process of evaluating a particular contemporary period—without having to understand the problem on the basis of a direct analogy, a specific consciousness, an inherent meaning, a particular view of the world or an essential spirit of the times.

In order to make this argument more specific, we might consider an individual work with the following question in mind:

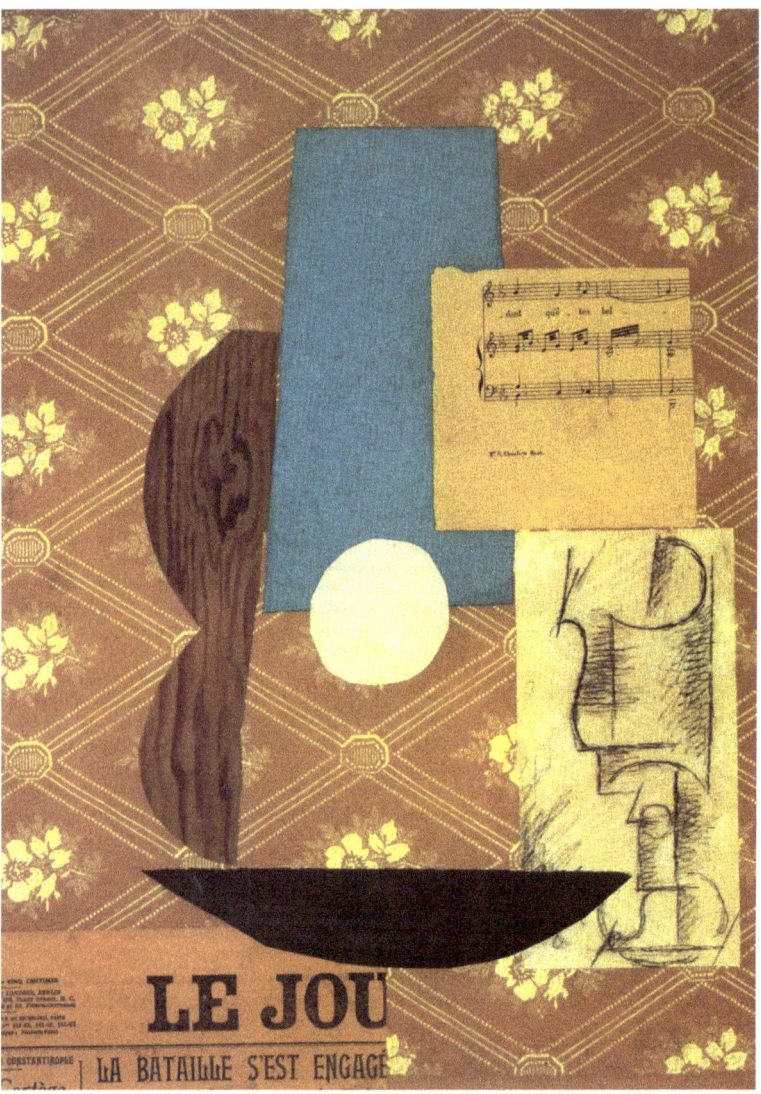

Figure 1. Pablo Picasso, *Guitar and Wine Glass*, 1912, collage and charcoal on board, 47,9 x 36,5 cm, Collection of the McNay Art Museum, San Antonio, Bequest of Marion Koogler McNay, 1950.11. Copyright: Succession Picasso, License CC BY-NC-ND.

what would such a proposition about the ambivalence of modernity mean in practice? Pablo Picasso's *Guitar and Wine Glass* of 1912 may serve our purpose in this regard.

This collage may be said to be one of the standard examples of modernist art. While there is no doubt that it is a modernist work (in terms of current linguistic usage), the interesting question concerns the different ways in which it is modern.

The picture is apparently simple. Various visual elements have been assembled on a surface covered by fairly ordinary patterned wallpaper: cut-out pieces of paper, a fragment from a newspaper, part of a music score and the drawing of a glass. The pieces of paper have been shaped and composed into what might be perceived as an iconic sign for a guitar (its throat, frame, sound-hole, and the indication of overall volume provided by the shading). This was one of Picasso's first *papier collés* and may be inscribed, in historical terms, in a multiplicity of different contexts: in a tradition of still-life painting, in relation to Cezanne's aesthetics, as part of Cubism's transitional phase, as belonging to the period in which modernism became definitively established, at the beginning of the collage tradition and so on. The selection of this particular image as representative of the change in stylistic and linguistic conventions brought about by modernism is, of course, not a matter of chance. On the contrary, it could be said to reproduce a very widely held view of Cubism as the principle hub and engine of modern art, whose idiom has come to be seen as identical with the idiom of modernism and whose centrifugal power would influence, in one way or another, almost the entirety of the remaining art of the twentieth century (or rather: the modernist art of that century).[30]

When describing Picasso's Cubist phase, John Berger locates its aesthetic in a larger context of alterations to the circumstances of production and living conditions, of technological innovations and a new form of scientific thinking, and in a period (prior to the First World War) when these enormous changes—modernity— were still capable of instilling people with hope: they were painting 'the good omens of the modern world'.[31] Berger's thesis is that during his Cubist phase Picasso was working in harmony with the revolutionising (or revolutionary) potential of modernity, while in his later career he lost this essential connection and became the victim of his own myth. What the Cubists were painting was, therefore, not simply the good omens of the modern world, but above all the original, progressive and emancipatory core of modernity.

But in order to avoid the evolutionist (and/or) nostalgic notion that underpins both the assertion that Cubism was a crucial phase in the history of modernism and that its function was to reflect the lost progressiveness of modernity, the idiom of Cubism could be said instead to concentrate and condense a new form of linguistic analysis and examination that would prove to be one of the major themes of modernism. While Picasso's collage may seem unproblematic to us because it forms part of such a familiar art historical context, his contemporaries would have perceived it as extremely strange. To describe the picture simply as a modern representative of the tradition of the still-life genre would, of course, be to miss its most obvious attribute: the way it plays with the iconicity of its subject matter. Guillaume Apollinaire would describe Cubist painting as follows:

> If painters still observe nature, they no longer imitate it, and they carefully avoid the representation of natural scenes observed directly and reconstituted through study. Modern art rejects all the means of pleasing that were employed by the greatest artists of the past: the perfect representation of the human figure, voluptuous nudes, carefully finished details, etc. . . . The young painters of the avant-garde schools, then, wish to do pure painting. Theirs is an entirely new plastic art. It is only at its beginnings, and it is not yet as abstract as it would like to be. The new painters are in a sense mathematicians without knowing it, but they have not yet abandoned nature, and they examine it painterly. A Picasso studies an object the way a surgeon dissects a corpse.[32]

All forms of idealism, naturalism and good taste were being abandoned here as part of an assertion that the painter's sole task was to create an entirely new plastic art—an art whose purity was to be found in its formulation of an immanent linguistic logic, transcending any reference to the surrounding world or to tradition. And to the extent that a relation to the surrounding world might still exist ('art is not yet as abstract as it would like to be'), this should involve an almost scientific examination of objects on the basis of the laws of geometry. The apparent verisimilitude generated by the meticulous rendering of detail in realist art was to be replaced by a higher degree of truth. The simile between Picasso and a surgeon evokes the radical nature of an art in which the artist has cut away all unnecessary props and is fully engaged on forcing his way into the objects that remain. The simile also signals a logic of change, because it involves a metaphor and not a factual description—Picasso analyses his motifs the way a surgeon does (objectively, impartially, unsentimentally, accurately), and this leads him to find an entirely new truth that is no longer based on a tradition of interpreting the knowledge and language of past ages.

The question that remains, however, is what the collage's specific form of representation actually means. A whole array of answers have been provided in response: that it is a technique for further accentuating the surface of the painting (Clement Greenberg); that it is the logical consequence of the Cubist view of the work as an autonomous, self-reflexive and constructed object (John Golding); that it is a way of problematising the relationship between the internal logic of the pictorial surface and the depiction of objects from the surrounding world (William Seitz).[33] All these interpretations inscribe collage as a passage in the development of the medium-specific aesthetic of avant-garde art, in which the subject matter appears to serve primarily as a temporary and, in itself, not particularly significant starting point for the formal study. These interpretations were, moreover, formulated in a period (between 1959 and 1961) when the abstract and self-referential criteria of visual art appeared to be definitive both of the understanding of contemporary art and of the history of modern art as such. Seen in this light, Picasso's collage would serve as an example of modern art's very deliberate transformation of both subject matter and tradition, in which the primacy of form and pictorial surface would increasingly come to inhabit the centre ground—in which the quality of the image as surface is, to use Greenberg's words, a more or less direct function of that altered view of history, which can be called modernity.

To inscribe this transformation directly into an analogy between modernism and modernity without further delimitation would, however, miss an important point, namely, that the issue of the modernity of contemporary art has itself been subject to a number of historical changes that occurred between Baudelaire's writing and the questions raised by Cubism. By 1912, reference to the modernity of visual art was distinctly old hat, an echo for the most part of the attempts made in the previous century by realist and impressionist art to break free from the conventions of the academy. It was at this time, however, that the issue of modernity and the representation of the modern in pictorial art were to assume an entirely new relevance. Two definitive turns took place that pushed in diametrically opposed directions: on the one hand, the inheritance of the symbolism of the 1880s and its intensified interest in the linguistic function of visual art and, on the other, a new interpretation (not to say distortion) of Baudelaire's old notion of 'modernité' as embodied in the Futurists' heralding of the modern age.

The linguistic turn meant that the focus was directed at visual art as an examination of the relationship between inner and outer worlds, where the key issue was the nature of the visual sign and its reference to the object.[34] Large parts of the renewed interest in 'the primeval' and 'the primitive' and the associated move away from the social iconography of modern life at the dawn of the twentieth century can be traced to this turn.[35] One consequence would be that more traditional motifs became essential in the most advanced avant-garde art of the period: recurring depictions of mountain landscapes (Cezanne), views of the German countryside (Kirchner), silent Algerian landscapes (Matisse) or monotonous series of still lifes (Picasso). The Futurist turn did not involve stylistic influences from the Futurists, but rather the desire to inject something of the dynamism of modern life into fine art. The first Futurist exhibition in Paris at the Galerie Bernheim-Jeune in 1912 met with considerable suspicion; what was seen as the Futurists' preoccupation with the content of art—and as a result their incomplete emancipation from the academic tradition—would be the crucial factor in explaining its negative reception by the avant-garde.³⁶ This was a sin against the pictorial logic described earlier: within the context of Cubism, the picture was not intended to be a reconstruction of an anecdotal fact but a construction of a new, pictorial fact.³⁷ However, there was also some ambivalence towards the radical stance of the Futurists, as many perceived it to be, which meant that while their art could be dismissed, their ideas could not. A key example is provided by the change in Apollinaire's attitude to Futurism when he proved quick to realise how their ideas could be transformed to form part of that general pursuit of lyrical and abstract dynamism he referred to as 'Orphism'.³⁸ Although this movement, which encompassed several of the leading artists of the French avant-garde, derived its energy from the dynamics of the surrounding world, it transformed these impressions into a purely visual (non-figurative, non-allegorical) representation.

The modernity of *Guitar and Wine Glass* may be understood in terms of the work being situated at the intersection of these two turns. Even though Picasso, too, was strongly antipathetic to Futurism, there was an ambivalent streak to his distaste.³⁹ The issue of the pictorial subject was not quite such a taboo matter for him, because he never accepted Apollinaire's evolutionist thesis that advanced art should pursue abstraction. The subject of the work, he maintained, is always a 'source of interest' for the individual with the eyes to see it and a mind open to his or her surroundings.⁴⁰ The Italian Futurists had presumably touched on a sensitive point for the French avant-garde of the time: its self-referential involvement with the formal or expressive problems of pictorial art as transcending the dynamic and transient impressions of the urban environment. The problem was how to reestablish the relationship between art and society, to combine in a sense the internal and external criteria of the work without renouncing one side or the other. Theodor Adorno has described this as a source of tension in modern art: 'The unsolved antagonisms of reality return in artworks as immanent problems of form. This, not the insertion of objective elements, defines the relation of art to society.'⁴¹ The issue would also appear to have been an acute problem for Picasso at this time, a dilemma to which the collage technique provided a particular solution.

If we choose to look beyond the generic constraints imposed by the term still-life, it becomes clear that the pictorial elements in *Guitar and Wine Glass* do not represent only objects and environments; neither do they constitute simply an examination of the representative nature of visual art. The work appears, instead, to dramatise representation itself: the relationship of the score to the music; the relationship of written language both to events and to the medium itself (the Crimean war, the daily newspapers); the relationship of the pieces of paper to the iconicity of the objects and the relationship of the drawing to the glass itself and to the medium-specific type of representation (a Cubist picture of a glass). This interplay of signs is made possible by a linguistic peculiarity of the collage technique: that the sign is both a representation and identical with the referent. In his study *Painting as Model* (1990), Yve-Alain Bois draws parallels between this linguistic and sign-oriented change in Cubism and the state of linguistic research at the time. The point of his interpretation is not to demonstrate any direct influences between art and linguistics, but to attempt to shed light on how the interpretation of certain African masks (primarily from Gabon, Liberia and the Ivory Coast) would lead to a similar realisation of the arbitrary nature of the visual sign:

> The syntax is "arbitrary" in that it no longer relies on anatomical knowledge, and therefore on the pictorial illusionism that always springs from this knowledge (the face and hair can be separated in two equal volumes, disposed on one side and the other of a cylindrical neck – an example to which we can add the protuberant quality of the Grebo mask's eyes). The vocabulary is arbitrary and, in consequence, extends to infinity because the sculptural elements no longer have need of any direct resemblance to their referent. A cowry can represent an eye, but a nail can fill the same function. From this second type of arbitrariness unfolds the third (that of materials), as well as a complete range of methods that we might now call metaphoric displacements.[42]

The mutations and metaphoric displacements of the signs are not simply a form of playing with the rules, but rather a kind of perception (albeit an intuitive one) in which the function of the sign and its variation within a particular context appear more important than its morphology. What is crucial is not that Picasso allowed himself to be inspired by the formal vocabulary of African or Iberian masks as a kind of naive gesture that was both critical of civilisation and in praise of the 'primitive', but that he was able to interpret this art as a means of redefining the sign function of the picture.

The question might be asked at this point what *Guitar and Wine Glass* actually represents? It might seem redundant as the subject matter is indicated in the title: a guitar, a sheet of music and a glass. But the key issue here is not simply what the subject is, but what it does. Observe the accumulation of objects against the background in the upper half of the work, and, after a while, the pattern no longer appears to be a form of superficial decoration (a wallpaper), but a faceted roof. A similar illusion emerges in the lower half of the image. Here, the image of flat paper fragments against a level surface is contrasted with the image of objects in space. In *The Picasso Papers* (1998), Rosalind Krauss has described what she calls the 'polyphonic spaces' of collage and its 'circulation of signs' when referring to Bakhtin's interpretation of the dialogic function in Dostoevsky's poetics.[43] Applied to *Guitar and Wine Glass*, this is an evocative characterisation of how each pictorial fragment and each voice are doubled and then split up in a game played with the interpretation of the sign and its referentiality. The perception of the work oscillates between surface and depth, between facticity and transparency, while the function of particular pictorial elements shifts in similar fashion between what is immediately observable and what is hermetically abstract.

The pictorial elements do not, however, refer simply to a number of objects that just happened to be at hand in Picasso's studio; they also provide clear connotations to a specific context. They appear to be poetic and transient reflections of the world and life outside the frame, while also serving as a more specific index of the kind of environment (a café or a bar), which still served, for the most part, as the social arena of the avant-garde at the time. Apollinaire was among the first to interpret Braque and Picasso's use of letters and textual fragments directly in relation to the symbols, signs and advertisements of the urban visual environment, which he saw as having such an important role to play in modern art.⁴⁴

Jeffrey Weiss has described this relationship in terms of an intricate game between sign and referent, which he locates more specifically in the rise of the music hall. This was an extraordinary, ostentatious, ironic and ultramodern form of entertainment, a mix of seriousness and superficiality, which many of the representatives of the avant-garde were very interested in both attending and observing. In analysing the role played by daily newspapers, Weiss takes as his starting point one of the central elements of music hall: allusion. *Le Jou* represents both a specific newspaper and the medium of the press as such; the fragmented word is at the same time a pun on the French word for play (both game and theatre) and an allusion to the actor's change of costume and character in accordance with the dictates of the role.⁴⁵ Here the circulation of signs serves not just as a game with the phonetic qualities of words, as in Mallarmé, but as a means of referring to modern life as it is lived in the world.

The point, however, is not the illustrative effect of the visual references or that this mundane and apparently banal form of entertainment is inscribed in the hermetic language of Cubism; it is, instead, that music hall's particular mixture of different motifs, genres and languages—in which various events and tableaux are jumbled together in a succession of fragments rather than in a coherent linear narrative—provided a model for the syntax of the collage. And, crucially, it is through this encounter that the inward motion of symbolism (towards the fundamental qualities of language) is turned outwards (towards the dynamism of modern life). The collage did not simply provide a new set of rules to play by; it was by its very nature a form of playing with the rules.

Interpreted in this way, the subject matter of Picasso's collage would refer both to the world around it and to its own language system: a fateful leakage, so to speak, is occurring both between different sign systems and between the picture and the surrounding world. The work oscillates between several levels of meaning as a result, in which the various voices are duplicated and where fleeting but profound encounters take place between art (between genres, composition, the formal logic of Cubism) and the wider world (allusions, the collage fragments) and where none of the levels can be understood without reference to any of the others. This interplay of unstable references and directions is, however, made to cohere within the strict uniformity of the composition. The work should not, therefore, be described as dissonant, but as contrapuntal, with each reference, each voice and each point of view being disciplined by the harmony of the whole. Its unity might best be compared to a force field in which the movement of the individual particles is kept in equilibrium while nevertheless remaining visible *as* motion in its stillness, to borrow Adorno's phrase.[46]

This is also a key point for understanding the metaphorical displacements of the collage: as an interplay between the affirmation and the denial of every outward and inward movement. Although the discipline of the composition and its generic connotations serve to anchor it in an ancient tradition that is far removed from the noisy, urban and futuristic modernity of the music hall, the metaphorical displacements and the manner in which the collage plays with arbitrary signs radically violate the rules of the same tradition at the same time. This allows the play—the game—with signs, motifs and allusion to operate within the framework of the serious (of Art), while the logic on which that framework is structured is simultaneously being redefined.

*****

Picasso's *Guitar and Wine Glass* provides an example of how modernism's centrifugal and centripetal forces are able, paradoxically, to collaborate in one and the same work: the collage refers both inwards and outwards, forwards and backwards in time. This is also a crucial aspect of its modernity. The work appears to radicalise the particular ambivalence of Baudelaire's definition of the modernity of modern art as 'the ephemeral, the fugitive, the contingent, the half of art whose other half is the eternal and the immutable.' It is modernity itself that constitutes the particular polyvalent coding of the transient and the eternal in this collage, in which the artist's reflection on this paradoxical situation necessitates a continual reexamination of its pictorial language. The circulation of signs in the subject matter may be seen in this light not only as a possible solution to the problem of relating the internal linguistic game of art to an external reality, but also as a metaphor for the alteration in the conditions and displaced function of the artistic process.

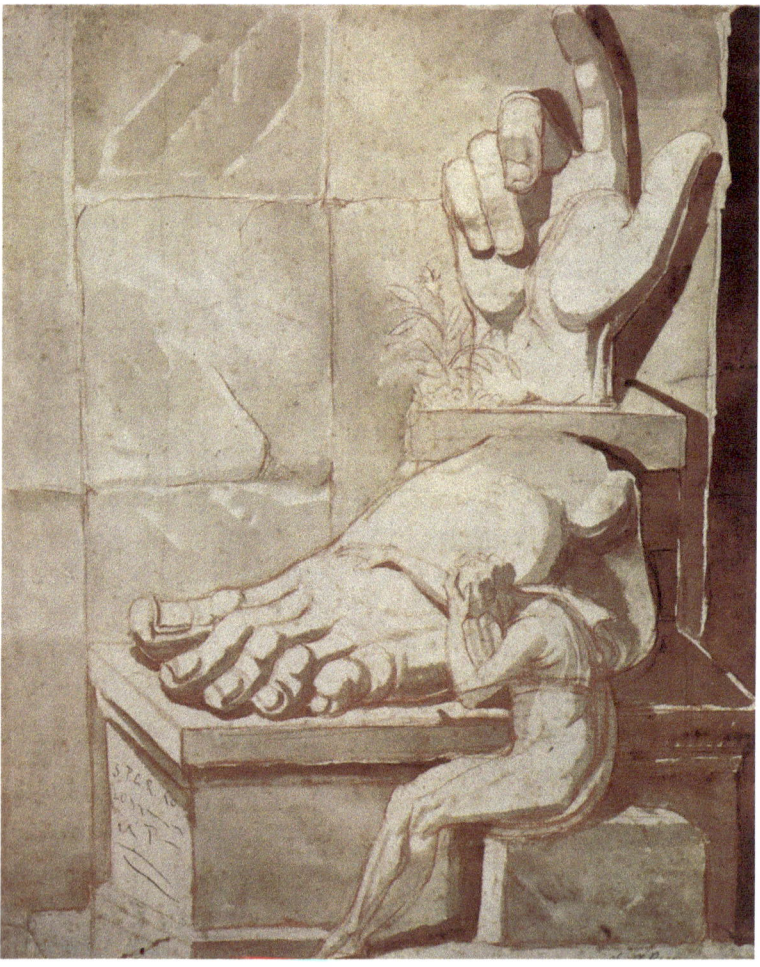

Figure 2. Johann Heinrich Füssli, *The Artist's Despair Before the Grandeur of Ancient Ruin*, 1778/80, red chalk and brown wash on paper, 42 x 35,2 cm, Kunsthaus Zürich, Wikimedia Commons, License CC-0 (Public Domain) https://commons.wikimedia.org/wiki/File:Johann_Heinrich_F%C3%BCssli_013.jpg.

This is not, however, an exclusive or unique attribute of the art of modernism, but a much larger phenomenon and one that Linda Nochlin has aptly described in terms of the sense of distance, nostalgia and fragmentation expressed in Johann Heinrich Fuseli's *Der Künstler verzweifelnd vor der Grösse der antiken Trümmer*: the artist is not simply portraying himself as being overwhelmed by the dignity of antiquity, but also as being crushed by the ruins as a symbol of the contemporary world's loss of wholeness and coherence.[47]

The discrepancy in size between the hand and foot of the Emperor Constantine and the artist is interpreted as a metaphor for modernity's relation to antiquity and to the increasing fragmentation of the artist's own age. This relation is, however, not simply one of longing and nostalgic tragedy: 'Out of this loss is constructed the Modern itself. In a certain sense, Fuseli has constructed a distinctively *modern* view of antiquity-as-loss – a view, a "crop", that will constitute the essence of representational modernism'.[48] My point here is not to compare fragmentisation as such as a device in Fuseli and in Picasso (even though this is an interesting subject), but to understand the issue of the modernity of visual art as a conscious process of reflection at finding oneself irretrievably lost on the other side of the boundary to the past (the premodern). At issue is a position capable of encompassing both nostalgia and futurism and of shedding new light on the question of the linguistic nature of the visual. Precisely because it presented a change in the function of the sign, Picasso's collage may also be understood in this context: providing one possible answer to the question that had been posed as early as the end of the eighteenth century as to the possibility or impossibility of the truth and authenticity of the sign—it is an answer, however, based on entirely different aesthetic, social and intellectual premises. Picasso sheds no tears over his fragments, setting them in motion instead as a springboard from which to raise new questions about the possibilities of visual art.

Lastly, Picasso's posture in this regard might also be considered in terms of Charles Baudelaire's designation of the particular point at which the contemporary and the past intersect, where the work transcends both history and the present—which would subsequently be identified as the paradoxical condition of modern art. In the 1910s, however, this would not by any means have been an obvious posture for an avant-garde artist to adopt, whose identity would, in many cases, be characterised by a desire to cast off all that belonged to the past and to arrive at a point of departure, which signalled a new direction forward. With reference to Nietzsche, Paul de Man has described how this form of progressive striving has, as a matter of necessity, consciously or unconsciously, entered into a pact with history:

> Modernity and history relate to each other in a curiously contradictory way that goes beyond antithesis or opposition. If history is not to become sheer regression or paralysis, it depends on modernity for its duration and renewal; but modernity cannot assert itself without being swallowed up and reintegrated into a regressive historical process.[49]

One aspect of this remarkable pact is, as we have seen, that the pursuit of modernity has a very long history. Another is that the changeable logic of modernity also brings with it an accumulation of yesterday's news: an archive, if you like, of artifacts, which may be ordered—and always will be ordered—according to a historical chronology. What de Man means, rather, is that the creative process contains both original and reflective elements and, as part of this process, the writer (or the artist) inevitably functions in his text as both actor and observer. In order to cross the boundaries separating us from the past, one would presumably have to possess a memory in which every text emerges in relief against the historical context of previous texts. The polysemous relationship between history and modernity is thus already inscribed in the production of every single work of art, even though it may not necessarily constitute a conscious part of the self-image and intentions of the modern artist.

What this interpretation of artistic modernity offers is the understanding that modernism constitutes a vital part of the visual culture of modernity, although in a rather different sense than the one-sided insistence of the analogy on a progressive forward/outward movement. It also runs counter to the analogy's implicit definition of modernism *as* the modern art. It would be useful at this point to return to Matei Calinescu's argument concerning the various faces of modernity, as this provides a form of differentiation that points not only to the multiplicity of forms of aesthetic expression and values existing within the modern, but also to a means of overcoming the orientation imposed by the analogy towards realistic definitions and the consequent normative identification of what constitutes the essential form of representation of the modern age and of modern art.

The issue here is the need to pay serious attention to what is fragmentary in the representation of the contemporary and the historical and to understand the differences between representations as symptoms both of an increased differentiation within the world of art and of a profound crisis in the perception of the authenticity of the sign. The fragment sets up a structure that is capable of taking ambivalence seriously; it leads to a provisional selection of detail and, possibly, to an open question mark, rather than to an all-embracing system whose answers are followed by an authoritative full stop.[50] This is, in my view, perhaps the most important consequence of Octavio Paz's notion that modernity is condemned to pluralism.

Conflicting Truths

The Antithesis of Modernism

There is a remarkable illustration by Henri Meyer in the September 1883 issue of *Le Journal Illustré* that depicts an interior from the Triennale exhibition held in Paris in the same year, in which hang portraits of the most famous of the participating artists.[51]

At that time, the Triennale was the only official art exhibition held in France, the government having previously awarded control of the Salon to artistic organizations that were independent of the Académie des Beaux-Arts. This was a change of no little consequence. Since the eighteenth century, the Salon had been both the real and symbolic site for the public demonstration of the operations of the Academy—and for the more or less critical reception of its work.[52] This shift would mark a new era of public competition within the art world: the Salon was the first recurring, publicly accessible exhibition of contemporary art in Europe and proved, as such, to be one of the most popular public events in Paris.[53]

The Salon provided a spectacle without any real peer in the visual culture of the period, filling a number of the halls of the Louvre (and later the Palais de l'Industrie) with thousands of paintings and sculptures, colorful depictions of mythological and historical subjects, portraits, genre paintings and still lifes.[54] The context in which the Salon functioned would appear to have been a complex one in which the financial and social interests of the artists were dependent on the willingness of the Academy and the authorities to show aesthetic representations they deemed

How to cite this book chapter:
Hayden, Hans. 2018. Conflicting Truths. In: Hayden, H. *Modernism as Institution: On the Establishment of an Aesthetic and Historiographic Paradigm* Pp. 36–132. Stockholm: Stockholm University Press. DOI: https://doi.org/10.16993/bar.c. License: CC-BY

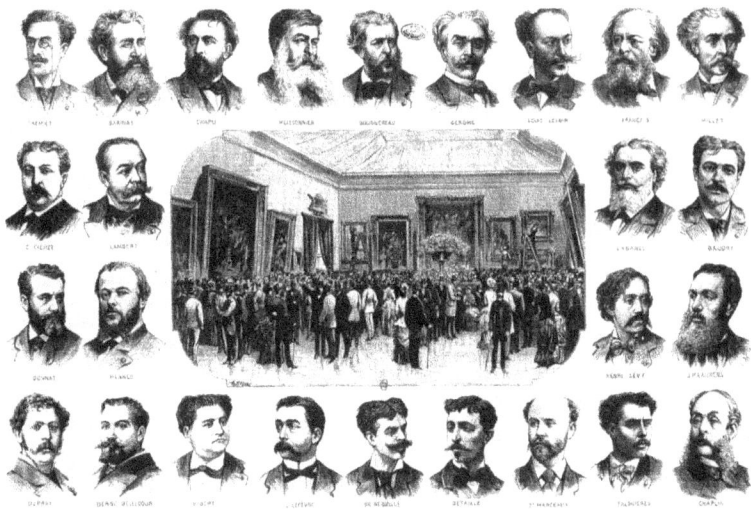

Figure 3. Henri Meyer, *Le Triennal. Le Grand Salon Carré avec les portraits des peintres et des sculpteurs principaux*, illustration in *Le Journal Illustré*, sept. 30, Paris 1883, Photo and copyright: Uppsala University Library, License CC-0 CC BY-NC-ND.

acceptable. Its public nature made the Salon into a kind of index of the various possible and acceptable positions within the art world: controlling the Salon during the eighteenth and nineteenth centuries was tantamount, therefore, to controlling a major part of the official art world. And this control had slowly but surely been passing into the hands of individuals who either had no entrenched position in the official institutions or were directly opposed to them. The introduction of the Triennale can therefore be described as a last (though ultimately stillborn) attempt on the part of the conservative forces within the Academy to retain power and influence in a changing art world.

But Henri Meyer's illustration also bears witness to the artists who formed the establishment at this time: William-Adolphe Bouguereau, Jean-Louis-Ernest Meissonier, Jean-Léon Gérôme, Jean-Jacques Henner, Alexandre Cabanel, Jules Lefebvre, Léon Bonnat, Paul Baudry, Henry Lévy. These are the names of powerful and influential individuals who are today all but forgotten and whose works have either become invisible to art history as a whole or may, conceivably, still be studied with a kind of appalled delight as part of that cabinet of curiosities usually and disparagingly termed 'Salon art'. Of interest here, however, is that this art forms a key part of the visual culture of modernity, which not only existed in parallel with the early history of modernism, but also dominated the art world of that time. What separates 'us' from 'them' is not just modernism's history of radical experimentation, its insistence on the need for reconsideration and revision and on making a fresh start, but also an extensive process of normalization, which has rendered invisible large parts of the historical context within which modernism became established.

In 'The Allegorical Impulse: Towards a Theory of Postmodernism' (1980), Craig Owens describes how modernism may be understood in a historical context as a parenthesis between the different conceptions of the allegorical image in classicism and in postmodernism; this theory also helps to explain the taboo placed on allegorical aesthetics by modernism.[55] Although Owen's aim was polemical (and by now, perhaps, somewhat dated) the distinction itself is interesting because it appears to isolate an age or epoch with a distinct beginning and end, in which the contours of an idea that has otherwise appeared diffuse can be more clearly distinguished by means of thematic interpretations clearly situated outside the period in question. The outlines can be discerned here of a fundamental shift that started with Romanticism and encompassed a change in the way the formation of meaning, interpretation and historiography functioned: a reinterpretation of the very nature of the artistic image (the work of art as expression/essence), its forms of representation (how and to what the sign refers) and also its interpretation (the development of a formalist tradition). This is a change, moreover, that extends far beyond the context of the avant-garde and which, in the twentieth century, has come to affect large parts of the modern discourse on visual art.

Baudelaire's definition of modernity, to take one example, can be understood within this framework. His formulation of modernity as 'the ephemeral, the fugitive, the contingent, the half of art whose other half is the eternal and the immutable' may be considered a symptom of a fundamental change in the way the nature and function of art were seen during the nineteenth century, a change which found its own catchy formulation in Realism's demand that art should be of its own time ('il faut être de son temps'), instead of reproducing (and possibly revitalising) the ideals of previous ages.[56] A fundamental idea was emerging here that would transcend the ideals and definitions of the academic code. 'To be of one's own time' also meant a change in the way the work of art was seen: a shift, in metaphorical terms, from serving as a reflection of a metaphysical ideal (truth/beauty) that could be appraised using an external yardstick to becoming a creation that embodied the truth and could only be judged on the basis of its own premises. As a result, an alternative discursive order became established in the art world of the West during the nineteenth century, which was characterised by notions of creativity, uniqueness, originality, authenticity and integrity. As we have seen, this order arose in antithesis to bourgeois modernity in general and to academic discourse in particular; its hallmarks were variation, individuality and pluralism, as opposed to the continuity, generality and traditionalism of the academic code.

But is it at all possible in such a disparate and pluralist context to refer to an order? This cannot, of course, be done in the same way as would apply within academic discourse—as a more or less established matrix of possible interpretations and actions—but rather as a network in which the ideals serve as its nodes, all of which seem to be connected, all of which presuppose one another and so constitute the boundaries for what is possible within the discourse. These ideals may be gathered together under the overall concept of the regime of authenticity. Authenticity is understood here, in the words of Jürgen Habermas, as a fundamental form of legitimation: a basic idea that, ultimately, legitimates each disparate (although approved) activity within a discourse.[57] This form of legitimation might be said to constitute the internal code that creates a factual or fictitious continuity—a distinct narrative—by means of the unstable and mutable context that developed alongside academic discourse: as an antithesis to its notion of ideal beauty.

Although this antithetical relationship would characterise the late nineteenth and early twentieth centuries to a considerable extent, the former of its two poles—the academic—has largely vanished from history. It is remarkable that the academic discourse that was so dominant in its time has ceded the field and been erased, more or less, from art historical awareness, like a sunken continent or an unconscious layer whose fragments and splinters occasionally rise to the surface as the remnants of the nightmare of modernity's unhappy and meticulously repressed childhood. What this demonstrates is how one discursive practice (the avant-garde) becomes defined in opposition to another and then, once an interpretive privilege under the heading of modernism has been established, excludes it.

*****

The increasing significance accorded to modernism and its subsequent acceptance and eventual dominance of the art world of the West should not, of course, be described simply in terms of a conflict between two opposed viewpoints, as a battlefield from which one of the parties emerged triumphant. Instead, this was a wide-ranging historical process whose contours are much less clearly defined, but which nevertheless involved the establishment of one particular way of seeing as opposed to another and which at a certain point acquired the right to privilege its interpretation and could thus make its own position the self-evident one. For the most part, this is not a process that can be read about in the survey literature or even in specialist studies, but one that requires some effort even to discern.

One way of shedding light on a process of this kind is to trace its roots back to a time when that interpretive privilege had not yet been acquired, when a particular statement could not be presented as self-evident but had to be formulated in opposition to the other: when the thesis could still be seen in relief against its explicit antithesis. The relevant question as far as this work is concerned is, therefore, when and how modernism acquired its interpretive privilege within the discourse of the visual arts. When did its aesthetic and historical position emerge as the natural and self-evident precondition for any statement about modern art? In order to answer this question, the primary antithesis of the self-image of the avant-garde needs to be isolated and its various historical strata have to be examined in a manner that might be likened to an archaeological process of excavation.

A useful starting-point is provided by Richard Wrigley's *The Origins of French Art Criticism* (1993) in which he identifies the reaction against the academic tradition as a crucial aspect of the way art history has come to define the tradition of modern art:

> Art-Historical accounts of eighteenth and nineteenth-century European art have been overwhelmingly predisposed to seek out and celebrate innovation. In such progressive narratives, longer-term continuities of art practice and their associated habits of thought are included only as a necessary but *retardataire* evil.[58]

Here, Wrigley has put his finger on a key point not only for the twentieth-century understanding of its own contemporary art, but also for its interpretation of previous epochs. A whole range of celebrated examples can be found for what this reappraisal meant in terms of bringing historical figures to light who had previously been overlooked or marginalised (as in the transformation of Francesco Goya into 'Goya'), but what is important here is that the process of reevaluation also risks obscuring significant historical relations and connections. In consequence, the image of the art of the modern age has, in many instances, been so refined and simplified as to diminish the significance of the academic tradition entirely. This tradition has become a diabolic antithesis that is invoked whenever someone has to be scared off by the appalling alternative to the hermetic and abstruse experiments of contemporary art.

This view has, in fact, continually reappeared as a fundamental tenet throughout the entire history of modernism, while also being handed down as a constitutive element of the identity of both modernism and the avant-garde. At the beginning of the 1960s, the American art critic Thomas B. Hess described the extraordinarily negative connotations of the academic tradition in the art criticism and art history of the twentieth century as follows:

> Academy, Academic, Academism (or Academicism) – these words mean "bad" in the conversations of the art community, much

worse than "pretty" or "decorative" or even "sentimental" – they are about as dirty as polysyllables can get. They do not refer to a category, like "Neo-Classic" or "Cubist", which are tags on rather specific, more or less homogeneous, bodies of material, but rather indicate areas where something unsettling has gone on, in any time, in any place.⁵⁹

Not just bad, therefore, but about as bad as it is possible to be! Hess' comment may seem exaggerated but is, to all intents and purposes, an accurate description of the value modernism assigned to art of this kind. The same view is reflected, for example, in Clement Greenberg's characterisation of the official painting of the nineteenth century in his influential essay 'Towards a Newer Laocoon' (1940):

> There have been academies before, but for the first time we have academism. Painting enjoyed a revival of activity in 19th century France such as had not been seen since the 16th century, and academism could produce such good painters as Corot and Theodore Rousseau, and even Daumier – yet in spite of this the academicians sank painting to the level that was in some respect an all-time low. The name of this low is Vernet, Gérôme, Leighton, Watts, Moreau, Böcklin, the Pre-Raphaelites, etc., etc.⁶⁰

Greenberg's analysis produces an interesting (and, for him, rhetorically necessary) conflation of academy and academism so that what had been the neutral name for a certain type of institution was transformed into a highly charged term of abuse. The distinction involves not only a change in taste, but also a radical redefinition of what art is and should be. This preoccupation with criteria pertaining to the innovative, creative and original aspects of art developed out of an opposition and would reproduce, in turn, the image of a cleavage running through the art world of the most recent centuries. This is explicitly described in Lionello Venturi's *History of Art Criticism* (1936), where the author describes how an abyss had opened up between the accommodating, eclectic and reactionary art of the academy and that of the avant-garde, the authentic expression of the progressive and creative spirit of the age.⁶¹

A similar separation can be found a decade or two earlier in Clive Bell's essay collection *Art* (1914). In what is an extremely summary historical presentation of Western art, Bell shows how the gradual decline of art during the eighteenth century would, in the course of the subsequent one, generate a complete collapse of all aesthetic values to the extent that the visual arts could be all but declared dead—during the heyday of the academic doctrine that is. According to Bell, the artefacts produced under the name of official art during this period fall entirely outside any conceivable definition of art:

> But the mass of painting and sculpture had sunk to something that no intelligent and cultivated person would dream of calling art.... It is not until what is still official painting and sculpture and architecture gets itself accepted as a substitute for art, that we can say for certain that the long slope that began with the Byzantine primitives is ended. But when we have reached this point we know that we can sink no lower.... Except stray artists and odd amateurs, you may say that in the middle of the nineteenth century art had ceased to exist. That is the importance of the official and academic art of that age: it shows us that we have touched the bottom.[62]

Bell's work was, it should be said, produced in a context in which the avant-garde scene had still to be legitimated theoretically and historically in opposition to an official artistic tradition, which may go some way to explain the pitilessness of his judgements. Both Bell and Greenberg describe the academic tradition as constituting the aesthetic ruins from which the authentic art of the avant-garde arises. In both instances, history is used to distinguish an authentic artistic trend from a tradition of pictorial creation under the aegis of the official academies and salons, which was as perfunctory as it was superficial. The wheat can, therefore, be sifted from the chaff and the artists who proved essential to the development of (modernist) history distinguished from those who constituted both a degenerate species and a blind alley—despite that fact that they were all operating largely within the same historical and institutional context.

This kind of historiography emerges in its turn from the programmatic writings and manifestos of the avant-garde itself, where the front against the established art world was defined above all by a savage criticism of everything the art academies represented.

This may be seen, almost without exception, as the other side of the manifestos' rhetoric: the indispensability of their own form of modernity is asserted in terms of the equally unconditional necessity of the destruction of the academic ideal. One example among the many available is found in Wassily Kandinsky's *Über das Geistige in der Kunst* (1911), where, in the opening paragraph, he presents his assessment of the retrospective tendency that characterised the canonisation of Ancient Greece by the academic tradition:

> Efforts to revive the art-principles of the past will at best produce an art that is still-born. It is impossible for us to live and feel, as did the ancient Greeks. In the same way those who strive to follow the Greek methods in sculpture achieve only a similarity of form, the work remaining soulless for all time. Such imitation is mere aping. Externally the monkey completely resembles a human being: he will sit holding a book in front of his nose, and turn over the pages with a thoughtful aspect, but his actions have for him no real meaning.[63]

According to Kandinsky, the error of academic doctrine lies in that it made the repetition of the past—of a dead language—into its very core, with the effect that the empty gesture became the rule at the cost of losing touch with the contemporary world and the ruin of artistic authenticity. The apparently paradoxical consequence is that academic art in its search to recapture eternal verities through the past simply recreated an external appearance without any engagement with the trans-historical necessity/truth that characterises all authentic art in every age and culture. Kandinsky is enrolling himself here in an established tradition critical of academic art, which can be traced at least as far back as the romantic movements of the early nineteenth century.[64] Kandinsky's description of the simultaneous and paradoxical relationship of artistic modernity to the transience of the present and the eternity of the historical mediates an insight that had, in principle, already been expressed by Charles Baudelaire in 'Le peintre de la vie moderne', even if there is a vast gulf between Baudelaire and Kandinsky's interpretations of how this relationship might best be manifested in artistic practice. The necessity of a connection between modern art and the contemporary world, and thus to the immanent workings of history, appears to have been a key issue in the entire tradition of implacable criticism of academic discourse. It is, moreover, on this point that the crucial distinction between academism and modernity is drawn.

This journey back in time helps to reveal not only a critical context, but also a change in the position from which criticism was formulated, as the antagonistic attitude of the avant-garde was gradually codified by radical art criticism and the judgements and selections made by such art critics were incorporated over time, surprisingly fast, within the historiography of the visual arts. Another index of this change may be found, for example, by studying how art-historical survey literature treated the visual arts of the late nineteenth century. From around the turn of that century and into the 1930s, although academic discourse is mentioned in the image mediated, it increasingly appears as a decadent phenomenon, the last outgrowth of an already withering branch of the development of art.[65] After the Second World War, academic discourse more or less disappears from the historical picture and an evolutionist trend emerges instead in which each work, each artist and each grouping is legitimated in terms of the significance of their influence on future generations.[66]

The logic of change Harold Rosenberg so aptly characterized as 'the tradition of the new' would thus become an authoritative description of modern art in general. The process of rendering the academic art of the late nineteenth century invisible had finally been normalised by this point, while what once constituted a marginal area for critical attention had been transformed into the mainstream of history.

This does not, of course, mean that art history underwent a process of radicalisation during the twentieth century, increasingly embracing the aesthetic ideals of the avant-garde. Rather it is a function of what Hans Belting described as the late nineteenth century separation of art history (as a university discipline) from art criticism, which meant that the former no longer constituted an authoritative or autonomous voice in the interpretation and conceptualisation of modern art and was obliged to place its trust in the gradual reevaluation of the avant-garde by the art world.[67] What were once radical and antagonist positions would in this instance become entirely internalized and institutionalized over time. The reason for this was that the normative study of the art historical disciplines was so extensively directed at ancient art. For the interpretation, evaluation and historiography of the contemporary—when this became necessary in teaching, for example, or in the production of survey literature—art history was more or less obliged to call on expertise in the field, on modernism's own historiography in effect.

If a narrower definition of the historical framework for this process is desired, the decades immediately prior to and following the Second World War can be considered to be a first breakpoint. It was then that modernist art was incorporated and institutionalized within the established system of cultural norms in Western Europe and the United States—as an aspect of the unified rational and progressive modernity, which at that time became a cornerstone of the ideological structure of the modern welfare state. There is a chronological agreement at this point between the establishment of a particular unified image of modernity and a similarly unified image of modernism as the essential artistic form of modernity. It is also at this time that the separation between modern art and academic art became so self-evident that it no longer needed to be made explicit and salon art would finally be hidden away in the cellars and storerooms of the major museums. The other breakpoint can be traced back to the end of the 1960s when theoretical and ideological perspectives were formulated within a range of different fields that sought to go beyond the established understanding of modernism and modernity.

The dialectic between both these breakpoints can be observed in a multiplicity of areas, the art world in particular, in which the formulation of postmodernism was based largely on the negating of the values that had been accentuated by post-war modernism. Let me provide a single example here that may also serve as a coda to this archaeological excavation. This is the American art critic Hilton Kramer's violent reaction to the altered display of late nineteenth century European art at the Metropolitan Museum of Modern Art in New York in 1980 (as a result of a donation by André Meyer), in which a more unorthodox selection was exhibited:

It is the destiny of corpses, after all, to remain buried, and salon painting was found to be very dead indeed. But nowadays there is no art so dead that an art historian cannot be found to detect some simulacrum of life in its mouldering remains. In the last decade, there has, in fact, arisen in the scholarly world a powerful sub-profession that specializes in these lugubrious disinterments. . . . So long as the modernist movement was understood to be thriving, there could be no question about a revival of painters like Gérôme or Bouguereau. Modernism exerted a moral as well as an aesthetic authority that precluded such a development. But the demise of modernism has left us with few, if any, defences against the incursions of debased taste. . . . What we are given in the beautiful André Meyer Galleries is the first comprehensive account of the 19th century from a post-modernist point of view in one of our major museums.[68]

The intentions of the Metropolitan Museum of Art (an institution which might very well have been accused of being culturally conservative rather than postmodern in any more radical sense) in showing this selection are not the object of discussion here, but rather the impertinence of the museum at even entertaining the idea of showing 'the dead' alongside 'the living'—under one and the same roof. The crime committed by the curators would appear to have been a kind of cultural necrophilia, the bare fact of the presence of these dug-up and mouldering corpses being enough to sully the truth of deathless Art.

It would, of course, be easy to incorporate Kramer's verdict within the tradition discussed above. However, my point is not to extend further the unbroken chain of academic criticism, but rather to identify a historical threshold: the fact that by this time the need was felt once more to mount a rhetorical defence both of modernism and of good taste. The true crime committed by the curators involved was that they had acted as historians, and their selection, deliberate or not, had made visible the standard (i.e., the invisible) presuppositions of established historiography. What so upsets Kramer is, fundamentally, that the discourse he has been operating so unselfconsciously within is being questioned from without and that a theoretical and temporary boundary for the scope of modernist discourse is being established. If Clive Bell's censure was motivated by the attempts (on his part and by others) to establish an interpretive privilege, Kramer's statement corresponds to that point in the story when this privilege has been lost. Modernism's paradigmatic criteria for judgement and selection were being transformed from a tacit presupposition into the object of debate, a debate, moreover, in which all parties were obliged to present openly their arguments and their underlying reasons.

Hilton Kramer's real position (and that of modernism) in 1980 therefore corresponds more closely with that of the academic establishment at the time of the Triennale a hundred years earlier. What these interconnections also demonstrate is that the various historical positions of the pictorial arts within the visual culture of modernism involve a conflict, not simply between different aesthetic ideals, but also between different kinds of truth, and that each acceptable formulation of truth actually takes place in a particular and delimited space.

A Space of Transformations

Paul Oskar Kristeller has described how a modern system that encompassed the various artistic genres developed in the mid-eighteenth century. Although the function and definition of art in this system were still linked to a much older tradition, they nevertheless displayed a number of specifically new features.[69] In this study, he reinterprets the implications of the old *paragone* debate and shows how the continual process of comparison between the various art genres during the first half of the eighteenth century led to a gradual change in the content of the traditional concept of the liberal arts. This shift was codified in Abbé Batteaux's formulation of the term the fine arts (les beaux arts) in 1749 and in Alexander Gottlieb Baumgarten's *Aesthetica* of 1750. Not only were the fine arts seen as sharing an essential definition and a set of values, which meant they could be considered in relation to one another, they were also understood as a category separate from other realms of human experience and knowledge. According to Kristeller, Kant's *Kritik der Urteilskraft* (1790) was a key text in this context. Partly because it was the first study in which aesthetics and art theory were treated as an integral part of an advanced philosophical system, and partly because the different genres of art were presented as separate forms of experience while aesthetic judgement was also considered to be a specifically subjective perception beyond any practical function.[70]

However, unless grounded in institutional practice, these distinctions would in themselves be of limited importance. It is, nevertheless, possible to see how they are linked together in time with an extensive change in the social and institutional structure of aesthetics and the visual arts, which would result in their codification both through the establishment of particular aesthetic disciplines at many of the universities of Europe and through the publication of encyclopaedias and specialist tracts that served to reproduce the system.[71] The considerable significance the new system of the arts would actually acquire reflected the fact that it bore such an obvious relationship to social, political and artistic contexts and practices: it became definitive of the constitution of the identity of artists in the modern era and for the specific function of art in modern society. It is, however, necessary to distinguish between the subjective perception of aesthetic judgement and the specific social and ideological functions that the visual arts also established. What these two aspects of the modern system of the visual arts actually make clear is that, on the one hand, the work of art was increasingly seen as an autonomous value (that an autonomous category of Art was being established) and, on the other, that an ever-more-specialised institutional apparatus for the administration and circulation of this value was being organised.

A number of structural shifts took place at the end of the nineteenth century whose effect as a whole was to constitute the art world as a somewhat different type of discursive space than before. One such shift can be observed in the power and significance of the official institutions: it was at this time that the art museum took on ever-greater importance as a setter of norms in the art world, while the university increasingly took over the role of the art academy as the producer of art theory (of rules for the definition and interpretation of art).[72] Another major shift saw the art world gradually become secularised, despite the continuing significance of the church as both actor and commissioning body throughout the nineteenth century. As part of a further change, the role of the state became defined much more clearly in relation to an evolving bourgeois public sphere, in which both the official institutions and a private sector simultaneously acquired greater significance for the financial and social situation of the artist, primarily in the major European metropolises and capitals.[73] The historian Daniel M. Fox has characterised this state of affairs as follows:

> At the end of the eighteenth century patronage came from the middle class as well as the aristocracy. Painting had a social function: as decoration, an index of sophistication and prestige, a luxury to be enjoyed aesthetically or materially and as an investment of potential financial value. Perhaps for the first time in the history of art men were painting more often in anticipation of a market than on commissions. By the end of the nineteenth century, government buildings, town halls, and public squares were full of paintings and statues. The artists who received these commissions were the men who had captured the market by best anticipating the taste of the members of official committees.[74]

What makes this description so interesting is that it reveals the ambiguous situation of the art world within the bourgeois public realm: on the one hand, a process of individualisation through private initiatives was occurring in which the position of the artist as subject was increasingly transformed from an employee with craft skills (and with varying degrees of classical education) into an individual market-orientated *Artiste*; on the other, the organs of the state were taking on an ever-greater role in the institutionalisation of the art world. The dynamic within this system had a major effect on the aesthetic foundations of the visual arts and on the institutional structure of the art world. The modern art world could be said to have evolved in the tension between both these areas, in which changes in art, ideals and identities were matched by various movements between the public and the private spheres.

This meant that the ties connecting the arts to the church, the aristocracy and the court that had existed previously were gradually transformed into a form of representation and commodity within a general public sphere. This is, of course, not the same as saying that visual art had previously lacked public functions; what it indicates, rather, is a shift occurring on several levels, where the previous functional values of art are increasingly differentiated and specialised such that the functional value comes largely to be overshadowed by purely aesthetic ones. Kant's distinction of aesthetic experience from other forms of experience and knowledge may be understood as part of this comprehensive institutional and social dislocation. While artistic practice was not obviously transformed overnight, discussion of art was increasingly determined by partially different theoretical and discursive premises. It also meant that a similar institutional infrastructure would be established in a majority of European states during the nineteenth century. This would make it possible to produce and maintain a more or less coherent system of codes, norms and ideals—a hierarchical and normative order that laid down the boundaries for the possible and legitimate production of meaning and value in the art world. The art world was establishing a particular and distinctive logic that would set the norms for the definition of art and the boundaries for its interpretation. Reference may be made here to "a specific discursive practice", to borrow a phrase from Foucault, a set of written or unwritten rules, which, in a given period and in a given social, economic, geographical and linguistic circle, determine the conditions for various kinds of statements, representations and actions.[75] This practice takes place at specific institutionalised sites that constitute the nodal points, so to speak, of the discourse and where the order stipulated by the archive is codified, put into practice and demonstrated.

In order to describe this relationship in greater detail, let us return to the fundamental issue of the differentiation in modern society of different spheres of value. In terms of the scale and speed of change, the modern epoch would seem exceptional in this regard as well: with changes occurring to many aspects of human existence within the course of a single generation. In many instances, this involves a gradual process of change within already existing institutions, which are assigned either partially or entirely new meanings and functions. This process of differentiation can be seen both as the result of the new requirements of industrialised urban society and as a function of a rational view of knowledge and social life. In his *Theorie des kommunikativen Handelns* (1981),

Jürgen Habermas has described how Max Weber understood the process of differentiation in terms of a lost wholeness, such that what were formerly coherent spheres were split into more or less distinct sectors and areas of operation with specific functions and forms of legitimation.[76] Weber contrasts science and art here with the value sphere of ethics and shows how they mediate their specific claims to universal validity through the fundamental order of their own spheres. This would mean that the modern subject is capable of adopting different fundamental attitudes to various parts of the same world, all of which may be described as rational in relation to their specific organising principles.

Working with Weber's distinction, Habermas has portrayed cultural modernity as consisting of three autonomous fields with varying kinds of legitimacy: science (truth), morality (normative law) and art (authenticity and beauty).[77] The separation of the spheres does not mean that visual art can be understood and interpreted in a context that transcends society, economy and politics. On the contrary, it serves to indicate how a sphere that manifests its own autonomous logic may nevertheless be inscribed within a social and political space.[78] Habermas' distinction identifies two determining factors for how visual art functions in the modern world: differentiation leads, on the one hand, to the development of a heterogeneous context of dissimilar spheres or discursive structures while, on the other, the production of knowledge and value within each and every one of these spheres does not constitute a cumulative, universal and uniform process, but rather a paradigmatic one.[79] At issue here is the development of different systems of norms, rather than the existence of fully autonomous spheres. The establishment of particular epistemological, theoretical and social regulatory systems thus creates a particular order or horizon of understanding, which influences and, in many instances, determines the production of knowledge and values in each of the various spheres, and it is the power of the discursive framework itself that sets the limits for which statements and representations are possible within a specific sphere.

Even if this admittedly general (not to say generalising) proposition needs to be interpreted in terms of specific historical, cultural and national situations, it serves to indicate the development of relatively autonomous spheres within various social sectors that demonstrate more or less distinct patterns and regularities. It would be possible, for example, to describe how the value sphere of the visual arts in Europe and elsewhere during the second half of the nineteenth century established not only a particular institutional order, but also a particular kind of space for the transformations that took place. At a fundamental level, this involves what Arthur Danto portrayed in 'The Artworld' (1964) as the manner in which the art world defines and regulates each object produced or incorporated in this context by means specifically identifying something as a work of art, which he refers to as 'the *is* of artistic identification'.[80] Here we have a space that opens on one side to a wealth of interpretations that would otherwise not have been possible (everything that a particular sign may signify in the art world), while the horizon of meaning, in contrast, closes off this space by defining the category that both makes possible and sets limits to every interpretation (art/the art world). This idea, when transferred to the sphere of the visual arts, appears to furnish a key insight into both the art world and how various kinds of interpretation and transformation function within this world: what was recently a bottle rack has now become a work of art, the mirror in an allegorical representation of *veritas* is also a symbol for the reflection of light/the truth, et cetera.

The archive, however, not only regulates what is possible within this space—what may exist at all, on what conditions and within which horizons of meaning—but also how values and meanings may be related to the surrounding social world. In contrast to what certain theoreticians have sought to make valid, the autonomy of art must be perceived as relative. This open/closed space might best be described in terms of an economy of signs: a system for regulating symbolic transactions that possess a relative autonomy in relation to the society around them. Autonomy is relative because the transactions of information, meaning and value that take place in this economy of signs are always reversible and compatible with the world around them: they can move in opposing directions from, and are (in certain respects) consistent with, one another. What happens within the confines of the art world is, therefore, not a game that is completely without any kind of obligations whatever, but an activity that—together with other kinds of sign economies—interacts with the surrounding world and constructs a particular image of reality. Ultimately, an appropriately sanctioned aesthetic value may not only affect the wider society but may always be exchanged for hard cash. The fact that the notion of an artistic avant-garde should have shown itself to be so productive was the primary test that determined it was possible for the modern system of the arts to be applied in full in an always-changing capitalist (and to varying degrees democratic) world order. The parenthesis between classicism and postmodernism described by Craig Owens is actually only a part of a far more complicated and profound social and institutional change.

* * * *

According to the Oxford English Dictionary, the word authentic is derived from the Greek *authentikos* and embraces a range of different meanings:

> Of authority, authoritative . . . Legally valid, having legal force . . . Entitled to acceptance or belief, as being in accordance with fact, or as stating fact; reliable, trustworthy, of established credit . . . Original, first-hand, prototypical; as opposed to *copied* . . . Real, actual, genuine . . . Really proceeding from its reputed source or author; of undisputed origin'. . . [81]

These various levels of meaning all relate to how truth and certainty can be attained and demonstrated in a context where this is not obvious, in order to constitute an authoritative interpretation of something in a particular situation. The concept establishes both a distinction and a certain direction between two or more phenomena, one of which can only be considered authentic in relation to something else. An authentic document can (in contrast to a dubious one) be traced back with certainty to a particular event or individual and serves, by virtue of its authenticity, as proof or evidence of something: the wording of a peace treaty, for example, whether a painting was really executed by the individual whose signature it bears, or the extent to which it is a matter beyond any reasonable doubt that a particular person carried out a murder. The manner of determining the authenticity of a document varies but is always directed at testing and eliminating any conceivable doubt. It is in this sense that the concept of authenticity has acquired key importance in a range of fields—in the historical sciences in particular—as an interface to the true (in the sense of the term within the natural sciences, mathematics or metaphysics).

But when Jürgen Habermas calls attention to authenticity as a fundamental criterion for the legitimation of art in the modern world, he is, of course, referring to a phenomenon that extends far beyond the determination of the genuineness and historical reliability of a document. Ultimately, it provides a principle with which to underpin the nominalism that characterises those aspects of the modern art world to do with constant change and the way in which the individual artist serves as the yardstick of his or her own work. This should not, however, be taken to mean that the word authenticity was used or played any significant role in the historical discourses under discussion. Instead, the concept can be used today as an instrument with which to identify ideas and ideals that have emerged in the course of historical interpretation as being of key importance in a particular historical and discursive context. The cluster of different meanings to which the concept of authenticity relates can be derived from its two-fold root: truth and origin. This duality points to specific differences in relation and direction: what something is authentic in relation to. Different levels of meaning in the concept of authenticity may be identified here: the authenticity of the work in relation to time/change (true modernity), in relation to the autonomous, self-reflexive subject (the originator), in relation to form and language (the work as an organic whole), and in relation to history (the work's developmental logic and/or place in a canon of authentic works).

Primarily as a function of modernity's altered view of history, reflexivity and subjectivity, the crucial relationship has become the one that establishes an authoritative connection between truth and origin, between the work and the originator. Within this horizon, an authentic work of art can mean a genuine and a unique expression both of the artist's subject and, as a direct consequence, of the contemporary world as interpreted by this subject. Or, in the terms used by Rosalind Krauss, the self as origin makes possible the idea of an experience of the contemporary as absolutely pure and uncontaminated by a past weighed down by tradition, which forms the basis for the claim made by the avant-garde of the need for change and originality.[82] In this context, authenticity has to do with how a certain understanding is established within a social and intellectual community that regulates the relation of the work both to a specific origin and to the wider world. The notion of origin is transformed here from a purely descriptive statement (X executed this work) to a normative interpretation (this work is an essential expression of X and his/her contemporary world). Alternatively, the descriptive horizon might be said instead to merge with the normative as two inseparable parts of a fundamental value: the idea of the inherent truth of the work of art. When referring to an origin, this would, therefore, mean keeping these two levels apart in order to analyse wherein the subjective dimension of this authenticity lies. And even though this transformation may be interpreted from an array of different perspectives—ranging from the work of art as an individual or existential expression to the work of art as a product on the market—it signals a change both in the perception of what art means and how the function of art is defined in the modern world. Here, art, irrespective of the medium, has become an almost symbolic representation of the idea of the reflexivity of the modern subject.

This understanding comes close to what Jacques Derrida has described in another context as a metaphysics of presence: the ancient idea that the linguistic or visual sign always possesses a given centre of meaning, which, ultimately, can be traced back to the presence of an absolute origin, which has served as the foundation for what he calls the tradition of Western metaphysics:

> Its matrix ... is the determination of Being as *presence* in all senses of this word. It could be shown that all the names related to fundamentals, to principles, or to the center have always designated an invariable presence – *eidos, archè, telos, energeia, ousia* (essence, existence, substance, subject) *aletheia*, transcendentality, conciousness, God, man, and so forth.[83]

Derrida derives this view from the logocentric hierarchy between speech and writing, which served as one of the cornerstones of this tradition from Plato to Saussure and onwards, in which the former is always privileged at the cost of the latter owing to its greater proximity to the origin (the referent). A written text is always marked by a greater degree of distance to its origin because it can be read and reproduced independently of (in the absence of) the referent. Whereas articulated speech involves a primary sign whose absolute origin is its referent, writing serves instead as a supplement or a secondary sign—a sign of the sign.[84] In this tradition of ideas, the subject constitutes not only the origin of the sign and the immanent centre to which all parts of the system (language, utterance, image) can be traced back, but also that which transgresses the boundaries of the system—the subject who speaks exists prior to and, in principle, independently of language.

Now it may, of course, be objected that what Derrida is describing is an ancient tradition of ideas primarily derived from a philosophical context that has nothing specifically to do with the changes in the way art was seen during the latter part of the nineteenth century to which we are referring here. Another fundamental difference between the linguistic distinction (speech/writing) and the praxis of the visual arts is that the latter appears to lack any counterpart to speech—that the whole content of the visual arts is writing and, therefore, consists of secondary signs. Derrida's distinction nevertheless helps to pinpoint an important aspect of the change of the form of legitimation under discussion here, and at least two dimensions of this change can be distinguished that involve a metaphysics of presence. First, there is the change in the perception of the nature of art, which took place at the end of the eighteenth century when the ontology of the work was interpreted by analogy to botany as an organic whole.[85] Second, there is the change in the evaluation of the linguistic function of the visual arts, which led, during the nineteenth century, to an increasing emphasis on the autonomy and intrinsic value of the graphic sign as both form and content.

The central importance accorded discussion of the creative act in the theoretical formulations of both romanticism and modernism can be traced back to a perception that the genesis of the work appears to be a creative process that originates in the unconscious of the individual, rather than a rational consummation of a complete idea. A revaluation of the function of the sketch and individual brushwork as factors of significance in the finished work would become increasingly evident as a result. In some instances this process would lead in the twentieth century to a view that the interpretation of handwriting, graffiti and the brushstroke could serve as the royal road to an understanding of the aesthetic essence and source (the subject) of the work. From such a perspective, the image would only emerge as writing at the moment it becomes a signifier, which means that at least one level of the artistic sign (below its referential and iconic layer) would share with speech the claim to originality.

There was, however, considerable interest in the artist as individual within academic discourse as well, an interest that verged at times on a cult of original genius to which the view of the originator as the absolute source of the work was, naturally, a far from alien idea. The relevant difference had more to do with an alteration in the centre of gravity: a dislocation rather than a change in meaning, which brought with it a considerably greater emphasis on the significance of presence/authenticity for the existence of the work as a work of art. And it was the accentuation of this particular aspect of the concept of authenticity that is of interest here: the extent to which the development of a field of competition within this discourse also entailed a change in the form of legitimation such that the artist and the individual qualities of art were emphasised in an entirely different way—in theory, in practice and on the market.

One example of this initially gradual but eventually distinct change is provided by the growing importance of the sketch. While the sketch also played a very significant part in understanding the creation of art in academic discourse, it was not, in itself, an acceptable final aim for the finished work.[86] Winckelmann's celebrated advice to the artist to 'sketch with fire, and execute with phlegm' bears witness to this, but it also highlights the division between these two elements, which reflects, in turn, the distinction discussed earlier between craft and theory in the academic code. The function of the sketch within the academic system was utilitarian rather than aesthetic: the sketch was considered to be a preliminary stage in the artistic process, or an embryo from which the trained eye could determine the potential of the finished work at competitions.[87] The specific qualities (warmth, individuality, spontaneity, originality) of the sketch in the introductory stages of the creative process may have been clearly perceived, but, as Albert Boime pointed out, these qualities were not seen as definitive, or even acceptable, aesthetic criteria for the finished work of art:

> The Artist's verve had to be governed by his judgement, and ultimately his spontaneity had to be modified by ethical thought. To achieve this content, a work demanded reflection and finish; the casual brush technique of the sketch required an austere drawing in the translation, appropriate to the norm of classical themes. . . . Throughout the history of the Academy, the generative phase was identified with idiosyncratic genius and originality, while the executive phase was identified with skill and scientific ability. Critics rightly observed the polarization of the two stages, the one often operating to the detriment of the other. But in the mind of the Academician the two stages balanced each other; impulse and free hand were checked by careful control and reflection.[88]

The gradual revaluation of the intrinsic value of the sketch and of the significance of free brushwork that took place during the beginning of the nineteenth century thus involved a shift in the underlying aesthetic criteria. It also led to an ongoing art-critical discussion of the relationship between the sketch and the finished work (a discussion which, in France at least, would also signal the establishment of more less officially sanctioned artistic positions outside the influence of the Academy).

To consider, as Boime does, the particular importance assigned to the sketch as the point at which an academic tradition would continue within the discourse of modernism is, therefore, partially correct, although a statement of this kind neglects the evident shifts this interest would undergo. While it is possible to maintain that the accentuation of artistic genius, indeed its mythogenesis, can be traced at least as far back as Ancient Greece, the mythologisation of the artist that occurred during the Renaissance and afterwards introduced a different emphasis, as a kind of emancipation of the divine act of creation. This satisfied a variety of aims, one of which has survived into the modern age: the promotion of the social status of the artist and of art.[89] The emphasis in romanticism, and subsequently modernism, on the value of individual expression and originality as being of crucial importance did not, therefore, constitute a break with this tradition, but rather it served to lend greater weight to a mystical and quasi-religious narrative of emancipation surrounding the identity of the artist. Instead, the key change that took place was the way the originator was identified as/through the work, which led to a new and fundamentally different interest in the specific qualities of the sketch and, by extension, of the spontaneous brushstroke.

One of the most extreme and influential formulations of this value can be found in Harold Rosenberg's article 'The American Action Painters' (1952), in which he describes how the new art cannot be understood as an image in the traditional sense, but as an event:

> The painter no longer approached his easel with an image in his mind; he went up to it with material in his hand to do something to that other piece of material in front of him. The image would be the result of this encounter. . . . The act-painting is of the same metaphysical substance as the artist's existence.[90]

According to Rosenberg, the painting as act cannot be distinguished from the biographical facts of the artist's life. The brushstrokes thus become traces: indexical signs not just of the vitality and transience of the creative act but, above all, of the presence and the transcendence of an artist and a sensibility in the painting. This formulation can be inscribed in a historical process in which the very spontaneity of the sketch as expressed in its brushwork would be transformed into a fundamental transcendent and aesthetic criterion for the appraisal of the finished work. But this revaluation would also introduce a new form of representation. Rosalind Krauss describes, for example, how Claude Monet's work was praised by certain critics for the qualities of immediacy and spontaneity his brushstrokes conveyed while, in fact, the pictorial staging of this spontaneity might require several weeks to achieve.[91] What this demonstrates is how the brushstroke served not only as an indexical sign of the action of the artist, but also as an iconic representation of a particular quality—the spontaneity of the creative process—irrespective of whether the work took two weeks or two seconds to execute.

Even though this quality may be considered an ancient tradition in the art of the West, Harold Rosenberg's formulation and the works of Willem de Kooning or Jackson Pollock were, of course, concerned with a radically different practice than would have been possible or desirable for painters such as Eugène Delacroix or Claude Monet. The brushstroke itself would become charged in the context of Abstract Expressionism (as a result of Rosenberg's extraordinary significance as an art critic) with an aesthetic and existential import that extended far beyond the notions of contemporaneity, spontaneity and originality cherished by the Romantic and Impressionist traditions.[92] We can see the principle of the pivot at work here, where a difference in degree (a gradual change in the interpretation and evaluation of the graphic sign) over time becomes a difference in kind, one that, on certain key points, represents a diametrically opposed view of the ontology and aesthetic value of the work.

The Mirror and the Lamp

The development of a value sphere specific to the visual arts during the nineteenth century should not be seen simply in terms of an empty discursive practice. On the contrary, this sphere would be characterised by continual conflict and revolt, as any art-historical survey can testify. But the accepted narrative in which the academic ideal was excluded from the 1850s onwards and replaced by an unbroken line of (proto-) modernist pioneers starting with Courbet may appear somewhat insubstantial and one-dimensional. The academic ideal would be replaced by the narrative of modern art. And yet what happens if we fail to take the exclusion of academic art seriously and put together, instead, an interpretation that considers the academic and avant-garde discourses as two historical aspects of modernity's possible forms of representation? In order to provide at least one possible answer to this extraordinarily wide-ranging question, let us start with a single example from outside the modernist canon: Jules Lefebvre's painting *La Vérité* (Truth) dated 1870.

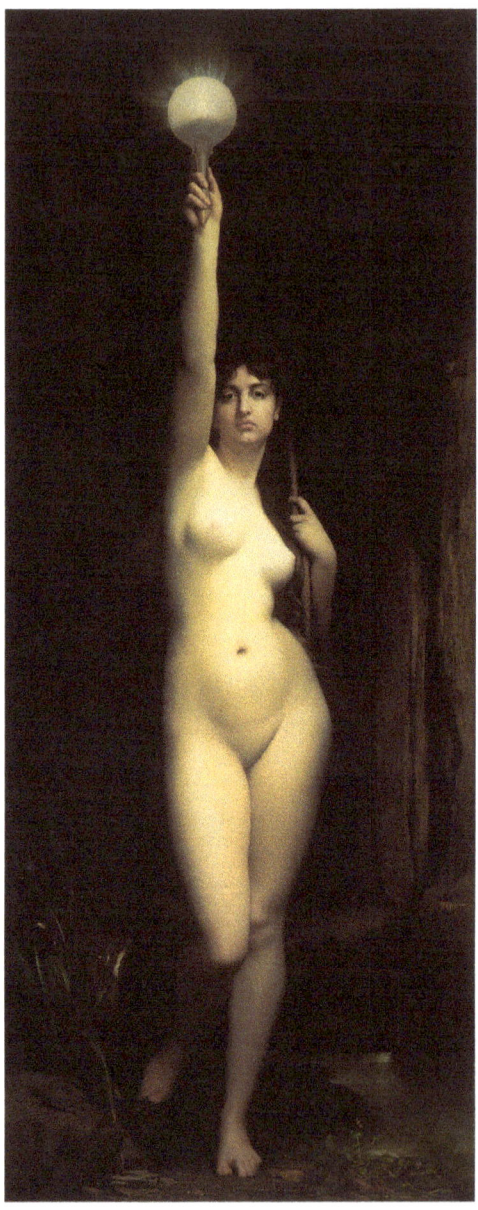

Figure 4. Jules Lefebvre, *La vérité*, 1870, oil on canvas, 110 x 226 cm, Musée d'Orsay, Paris, Photo and copyright: Reunion des musées nationaux/ IBL, Wikimedia Commons, License CC-0 (Public Domain) https://commons.wikimedia.org/wiki/File:La_V%C3%A9rit%C3%A9,_par_Jules_Joseph_Lefebvre.jpg.

This painting has been chosen because of its considerable oddness. I first saw it in a book by the Swedish historian of ideas Sven-Eric Liedman and was dumbfounded when he described the painting as a representation of Truth holding a light bulb.[93] I showed the picture to various colleagues who reacted in different ways, from aversion, pure and simple, to gales of laughter. I felt, nevertheless, that Lefebvre's picture was saying something essential, something that might be able to deepen a historical understanding of the art and visual culture of modernity.

What are we actually looking at here? The representation is in keeping with an established convention that can be found exemplified in Cesare Ripa's *Iconologia* (1593), where Truth is personified by a (partially) naked woman holding the sun in her right hand, a book and a quill in her left, with her right foot placed on a globe of the world.[94] She is naked because simplicity is natural to her, and the sun lends her the joy of clarity; she is the strongest of all the things of this world and, therefore, has the globe (i.e., the world) beneath her foot. This pictorial formula both recurs and is transformed in many subsequent representations of Veritas in which the source of light, for example, may change from a burning torch to a mirror that reflects the light, although not all the other attributes need be present.[95] Lefebvre's work complies with this basic scheme, and his image satisfied all the technical and aesthetic requirements established by the discourse of academic painting,

The mixture of heightened idealism and eroticised nakedness may seem comical to us; this was the very combination that would give Salon art such a poor reputation as being pompous, vulgar, pornographic and bad theatre, rather than authentic art. If Lefebvre's painting seems comical to us today, its comedy may perhaps be found primarily in the date of its genesis: the viewer of today would in all likelihood expect quite a different portrayal of truth in a picture produced in 1870. It was created when Courbet's thematic claims to truth were yesterday's news, five years after Manet caused a scandal at the Salon with *Olympia*, at a time when books, periodicals and newspapers were increasingly furnished with documented illustrations, when the Impressionists were first formulating the necessity for optical truth in their paintings and when photography was being established as the pencil of nature, particularly in the genre of portraiture and in various scientific and documentary contexts. As far as the official academic art world of Paris was concerned, however, the truth claims of the Realists and the Impressionists (not to mention those of the photographers) were delusions that had nothing to do with Fine Art. But this difference in interpretation has more to do with a difference in the historical perspective of our own time: the extent to which we understand Lefebvre's image in the light of its modernity or its traditionalism, the extent to which we can see beyond the stylistic categories of historicism in order to understand the difference that actually exists between this image and previous classical representations. The painting was, in fact, much praised by the artist's contemporaries when exhibited at the Salon of 1870, where it received the Jury's prize, and it was bought the following year by the Musée du Luxembourg, the most prestigious museum of contemporary art at the time.[96]

If we leave all aesthetic considerations aside and take this painting seriously, as was apparently done when it was first shown, we might begin by asking ourselves what kind of truth the title of the work refers to. The image has been interpreted as an allegory for the new conceptual universe of the Enlightenment, with the mirror reflecting the naked light of Truth that would 'drive lies and shadows out of the world'.[97] Such an interpretation of the allegory would, however, seem rather odd because the Enlightenment and science are being portrayed through a mythologizing motive, while the primary claim to legitimacy of modern science is its criticism of myth. Neither, apparently, can Lefebvre's painting be said to be making a claim for truth in the sense of being a naturalistic depiction, complying as it does with a convention that the visual arts should portray ideal beauty. The female figure is, to use Kenneth Clarke's distinction, not naked but nude, dressed in art.[98] If the mirror of the goddess of truth is reflecting the light of truth, the composition and the representation of the female body reflect a particular notion of the absolute truth content of ideal beauty. This does not mean that Veritas is a stylised form: she appears to be an individual, although endowed with classical or classicist features, both in the design of the body and the face. This would also apply to the composition as a whole, whose chiaroscuro testifies to a kinship with a painterly tradition, rather than the linear approach of the rigid neo-Classicism of the early nineteenth century. The interplay of light and shadow creates the illusion of a three-dimensional space in which it is the body of the goddess and her reflection of the Light (in her person and in the mirror) that are accentuated.

Irrespective of what stylistic connections one chooses to make, this is a painting that could justly be accused of being traditional—and one that, in its traditionalism, points to a different kind of concept of truth than the one embraced by the natural sciences of the late nineteenth century. Interpreted in this way, the painting would appear to be an allegory almost of the classical tradition's definition of both truth and beauty, in which light had a crucial symbolic significance. One example of the way in which this ideal could be expressed is found in the work of the librarian and theologian Antonio Ludovico Muratori, who wrote these words at the beginning of the eighteenth century:

> Beauty, which delights and moves us with its sweetness, is nothing other than the radiant light of truth. This light is revealed in brevity, or clarity, or evidence, or force, or novelty, or honesty, or utility, or magnificence, or proportion, or arrangement, or verisimilitude, or in the virtues which may accompany truth.[99]

Aesthetic beauty is intimately linked to truth in this definition because it corresponds to and reflects a divine world of ideas beyond the imperfect and transient appearance of the material world.[100] The mirror may be said to have served as a general metaphor in classical doctrine, both for an ineluctable distance from the ideal (the light or the source of the light) and for the materialisation of the ideal through the reflecting process of art. A similar connection between light, beauty and truth was made at the end of the eighteenth century in the work of Friedrich Schiller, for whom art, while not serving as a surrogate for science or philosophy, nevertheless signified a particular form of knowledge in the service of human enlightenment:

> Even before Truth's triumphant light can penetrate the recesses of the human heart, the poet's imagination will intercept its rays, and the peaks of humanity will be radiant while the dews of night still linger in the valley.[101]

In Lefebvre's painting, this classical (and possibly pre-Romantic) conception of Truth and Beauty is directly represented in the subject and should not be confused with a scientific, positivist concept of truth. Here, the mirror has become a metaphor for the capacity of the work of art to reflect the light of Beauty/Truth like a mirror.

The idealism that characterised academic aesthetics also entailed the canonisation of a particular historical ideal: classical Greek art. The art of the ancient world was considered so important in that it was believed to provide the best guide as to how such an idealised portrayal of reality should appear and how the artist, on the basis of a meticulous study of this art, might find a path to the understanding of the beautiful form behind nature's endless supply of accidental variations and defects. It would be a mistake, however, to see academic doctrine simply as the expression of a particular artistic style. It was rather an institutionalisation of an ancient art tradition in the theory of art of using an image to make visible an idea: the ideal truth behind the objects of the sensory world.[102] In artistic practice, what the interpretation of this idea involved was a clarification or refinement of the theory of selection, in which the nature study was combined with a particular conception of ideal forms. Studying at an academy of art involved a systematic initiation into the discursive order of academic doctrine, in which the rationality of the modern age was interwoven with (a particular interpretation of) a very ancient ideal.[103] The process of legitimation through science and philosophy allowed both aspects to emerge as the two sides of an underlying truth.

The art academies would thus appear to have been intellectual rather than practical institutions (in ideal terms at least), whose aim was to teach art as a form of knowledge through the disciplining of drawing and the sign, but not through the practical skills of painting or sculpture.[104] This form of knowledge also made possible the classification and evaluation of the type of subject matter on the basis of the established hierarchy of genres, which, at a superficial level, provided a system for the assessment of different types of subject matter while also serving at a fundamental level as a matrix for interpretation and debate.[105] The hierarchy of genres also defined relative criteria for the appraisal of every type of genre, which also entailed a division into different types of art.[106] Despite the existence of this strictly rational order, there was an obvious discrepancy between the representation of the ideal, as prescribed by the regulations of academic discourse, and the pragmatism that frequently characterised its application. For even if practical skills were variously described as secondary in relation to theory (idea), it was a key tenet that both aspects had to be woven together in order to perfect the work.[107] The production of the mature artist was, and was supposed to be, an interpretation whose hallmarks were his (or more rarely, her) temperament and genius.[108] And becuase the value sphere in which this interpretation was produced must be considered partially autonomous, neither the academic ideal, nor its aesthetic practice may be understood as absolute, ahistorical norms, but rather as an approach that was gradually adapted to a changing social situation.

It may be observed in this regard that although the changes undergone by the hierarchy of genres, despite its continued considerable significance during the nineteenth century, had some extent to do with alterations to the political landscape, they were primarily the outcome of the development of a bourgeois public sphere and its transformation of the social structure of society. This meant, furthermore, that the dividing line between the genres (and for what was acceptable) was constantly shifting during this period. History painting increasingly became the province of erotic fantasies or bloody dramas inscribed in historical or mythological tableaux. This particular shift can perhaps be more readily interpreted on the basis of the increased importance of the bourgeois public sphere and its need for sensory realism, greater historical detail and subjects that fired the imagination, rather than for an abstract scheme of ideal beauty.

The significance of the ambivalence manifested in Lefebvre's mythological motif applies not only to single artwork or a particular individual, but also it also reflects a crisis phenomenon, what might be described as a linguistic and ontological insecurity in the art world of the late nineteenth century. The unintended comic effect of the image may be more revealing of our own one-sided relation to this culture than any failure on the part of the academic tradition.

****

Although Jules Lefebvre's *La Vérité* can be interpreted both in terms of its traditionalism and its modernity, it is not my aim to assert or cultivate either one or the other. The issue, rather, is to understand how these two perspectives point to an unresolved ambivalence in the art world of the late nineteenth century Europe, where neither the rational concept of truth cherished by science or the metaphysical notion cherished by idealism could be taken for granted.

At the beginning of the twentieth century, Max Weber characterised modernity in terms of rationalisation and disenchantment: the definitions provided by the enlightenment/modernity of knowledge, the human being and society had not only proven superior to those provided by the traditional connections to the church and an older social structure, those very connections were also being called into question on a more systematic basis for the first time.[109] As a result of this shift, social actions and theories about the world could increasingly acquire legitimacy through the application of a rational and secularised form of knowledge, in which the world could no longer be understood as a unity whose ultimate ontological foundation was constituted by religion or by mystical forces. At the same time, however, modernity should not be seen as a uniform movement away from the forms of experience of the past, even though the traditional significance for society of religion and the church had been undermined, they were not necessarily in a state of opposition to the modern. Neither did rationalisation mean the same thing in every value sphere, but it should be seen as an overarching process that led to a range of different contexts being incorporated and institutionalised within the framework of the modern now that religion had come to constitute a separate value sphere and the church was seen as merely one institution among others.[110]

So how should we understand the effects of this multivalent process of disenchantment on the art world? Even though the reception of antiquity constituted a key part of academic doctrine, a fundamental precept of that doctrine was the distinction between the ancient world and the contemporary one. The abilities of the artists of ancient Greece were likened to those of someone speaking their native tongue; whereas, modern artists had to acquire this extinct foreign language by artificial means.[111] The metaphor of a dead language also tells us something interesting about the emancipation of idealist art during the nineteenth century: the dualistic representation of the relation between the world and the world of ideas was extinct. Applied to Jules Lefebvre's *La Vérité*, this idea might be understood in terms of the painting representing the uncertainty of the contemporary world when confronted with the tradition of classical art and of the idealist nude, rather than as expressing Truth or reflecting it in itself. Although the greatness of that tradition remained undimmed at this point and it was still seen as providing a guiding light for the contemporary world, the cleavage between the idealism of the classical tradition and the materialism of the modern age inevitably entailed an awareness of loss.[112]

Historical reflection on greater awareness of change in the ahistorical notion of beauty had been a feature of the aesthetic discourse of the recent past. Friedrich von Schiller, for example, described the phenomenon in *Briefe über die ästhetische Erziehung des Menschen* (1795) as a consequence of the process of civilisation, in which progress had fractured the organic unity between feeling and reason that had still existed in Ancient Greece.[113] This fundamentally nostalgic view was to characterise the work of many theorists during the second half of the eighteenth century and reached it most significant formulation in Johann Joachim Winckelmann's *Geschichte der Kunst des Altertums* (1764). For Winckelmann, the authority of the ancient Greeks was founded on favourable external factors, such as climate, nature and constitution, all of which had created the circumstances that endowed the character of the ancient Greeks with a superior notion of truth in life and in art.[114] The concept of truth involved was, however, not relative or culturally determined, but absolute and universal; it was the inner essence of things and in tune with a God-given harmony, which could be recreated by the artist as 'ein aus der Material durchs Feuer gezogener Geist'.[115] Although the artist of the modern age had to strive to comprehend this harmony and portray it in his art, he could hardly be expected to succeed as well as the ancient Greeks.

There was, however, considerable variation in the kind and degree of authority accorded the art of antiquity. The entire problem complex may be inscribed in the debate between the ancient and the modern, which had been going on since the seventeenth century. Matei Calinescu has described how the modern camp assigned a normative role to the ancients in terms of the ideal of beauty, while assuming that the contemporary world was superior to all past epochs in terms of rational argument and religion.[116] What this discussion reveals, however, is a growing insight into the peculiarity of the modern age during the nineteenth century, when an increasing degree of historical awareness could lead both to nostalgia and a belief in progress. A particular aesthetic trend could, after all, not be legitimated solely on the basis of utilitarian rational argument, but had to be weighed in the balance with notions of morality and beauty. A chasm was opening in this regard, as well between the aesthetic and epistemological functions of art, to the extent that fewer and fewer people viewed the world of ideas as a divine and transcendental order, even though idealist doctrine still clung on to legitimacy by dint of convention and tradition.

For Schiller, art offered a unique opportunity to bridge this chasm by conveying a sense of harmonious equilibrium between reason and feeling, which the viewer was able to perceive intuitively through aesthetic contemplation.[117] Schiller's approach may be considered a version of the modern belief that art—precisely because it now comprised a semiautonomous sphere within modern society—transcended the general trend towards fragmentation and alienation. This was a view that became largely institutionalised through the academic system of the early nineteenth century, a view in which the dualism of classical art would be overshadowed by confidence in the quintessential nature of art, which was an emancipated belief in the capacity of aesthetics to mediate an understanding of a unity of existence that was both hidden and lost.

One indication of this comprehensive social, epistemological and linguistic turn is the change in the reception of Ancient

Greece and Rome during the second half of the eighteenth century when the notion of antiquity as a natural order was replaced by the image (or myth) of antiquity as both a rhetorical trope and a code that clearly marked the historical difference between us (the moderns) and them (the ancients).[118] A similar change in the reception of the antique world during the Enlightenment has been characterised by Maiken Umbach in terms of an ambivalent process of mediation and deliberate detachment:

> It is true that archaeological excavations in this period opened up new perspectives on classical culture. Yet paradoxically, the more enthusiastic eighteenth-century writers became about the physical contact with the classical world, the more remote this world also became. What has so often and somewhat confusingly been dubbed 'neo'-classicism was rarely an exercise in recreating the classical world in a literal sense. Ancient Rome and Greece became an 'other'; they were remembered in quotation marks. Classical notions of order and reason quoted them, retold them – and turned them into fiction. These fictions were ambiguous and multiple – and in this multiplicity lies the 'modernity' (or post modernity) of the Enlightenment.[119]

As Umbach indicates, this altered awareness was not only a defining characteristic of the neo-classical and academic reception of antiquity, it also provided a foundation for ideas that would, in the long term, lead beyond academic doctrine and the dualism of allegorical aesthetics towards a Romantic view of the authenticity of the work of art, its organic unity and mythical origins. And, later even, towards a series of Utopian models (the avant-garde) that would overtrump, overthrow and replace one another at an ever increasing pace. Though the language may have become extinct, it still retains its relevance, albeit in a new form, because art is capable of *re-presenting* that lost unity, of conveying the idea of ideal beauty as part of the mutable, fragmented and materialist way of life of the modern age. It is here, too, that the foundations were laid for the way in which modern art would be formulated within academic discourse.

The element of the modern in the neo-Classicist view of contemporary art did not, of course, entail a potential revolution; it was more a matter of a gradual shift that occurred as a response to the institutionalisation of a change in the way time and history were seen. Although the debate/dialectic between the moderns and the ancients is longstanding, at issue here was a new type of awareness, a historic shift, which became the impetus for notions of the demystification of the contemporary world that understood it in terms of a fundamental social and linguistic loss (of unity and natural connection). I would maintain that the idea of this shift has had far greater significance than simply providing the spur for various forms of early nineteenth century nostalgia. Rather, it has served ever since as a fundamental premise for the various aesthetic, functional and ontological formulations of the visual arts and for their position in modern society.

Meyer Howard Abrams has described how the shift from classicism to what is called romanticism can also be deciphered from changes in the metaphors used to describe the ontology of the work of art at the beginning of the nineteenth century: increasingly, it was the expressive value of the work (the work as lamp) that was accentuated, rather than, as before, its imitative function (the work as mirror). The light was seen, therefore, as emanating, so to speak, directly from the work of art, while the truth of the work was increasingly considered to be a reflection of its originality and authenticity, rather than its capacity to reflect the objects of the surrounding world or an abstract ideal.[120] A gradual change in emphasis, selection and focus may thus be perceived that would, by extension, herald a decisive difference in the way art was seen:

> Even though the characteristic patterns of romantic theory were new, many of its constituent parts are to be found, variously developed, in earlier writers. By shifting the focus and selecting the examples, we can readily show that romantic aesthetics was no less an instance of continuity than of revolution in intellectual history. In the course of the eighteenth century, some elements of the traditional poetics were attenuated or dropped, while others were expanded and variously augmented; ideas which had been central became marginal, and marginal ideas became central; new terms and distinctions were introduced; until, by gradual stages, a reversal was brought about in the prevailing orientation of aesthetic thinking.[121]

Not only did this change in metaphors involve the use of new images to describe a particular phenomenon (a work of art), it was also a symptom of a more profound change in the way the nature of art and its manner of representation were understood.

The combination of a gradual and radical change might be described in metaphorical terms as a historical pivot: that point at which the conditions for the production and interpretation of art undergo a shift by a number of degrees. Initially, this shift would only involve small-scale deviations from a prevailing ideal, but, over time, it would lead to an entirely different perception of art and of the foundation for its legitimacy.[122] The kind of change referred to here could also be described as a dispersed historical process that would produce a deep-seated and substantial change in the course of several decades: the establishment of an alternative paradigm for the understanding of what art is and how art should be perceived.

It is within the extensive context of effects created as part of this shift that a broad range of phenomena may be understood, ranging from the traditionalism of academic art and the condemnation of traditionalism as such by the Futurists, from Romantic notions of the authentic expression of the subject to the Postmodernist dramatisation of the thesis on the death of the subject. In all cases, this involves ideas about a radical position on the other side of the boundary to something that had either existed before or been taken for granted, about the way in which the loss of something that had previously seemed self-evident would provide the impetus for new ways of formulating a particular artistic practice. What is at issue here is not a linear tradition, but the existence of a specifically modern premise—a shared intellectual construct—which would give rise in various theoretical and social contexts to a range of different interpretations and patterns of reaction that, taken as a whole, serves to characterise what might be called the episteme of modern art.

* * * *

The question nevertheless remains, what is Veritas actually holding in her hand? Although convention tells us that it has to be a mirror, it has also been suggested that she is grasping a light bulb.[123] The fact that the painting was produced in 1870—nine years before Edison's patent of the incandescent bulb—would make this truly remarkable. In itself, however, this would not refute the attribution, because there had been ideas about electric light and indeed demonstrations of it throughout the nineteenth century.[124] But no contemporary or subsequent description of the picture mentions anything about a light bulb.[125] Moreover, it would have been unthinkable, in principle, for a painting that was not only accepted by the Salon jury but also awarded a medal to have so punctured the academic ideal as to incorporate a modern and worldly detail such as a light bulb in a mythological subject. The absence of naturalistic, individualistic and material signs was the very foundation of the increased importance accorded the nude at the end of the 1860s, in which the academic tradition's synthesis of idealism and abstraction was considered to demonstrate a value that transcended the triviality of modern life (and the potentially pornographic connotations of the subject matter).[126] The crossover between the general and the specific would seem, in fact, to have been at once a risky, subversive and pleasurable zone in the academic art of the late nineteenth century.

But even if the proposed attribution is not correct, this does not make it irrelevant. For there can be no doubt that a connection exists between the pictorial formula and iconography of Lefebvre's work and various attempts to establish visual codes to do with electricity and electric light a decade or so later. In her fascinating book *When Old Technologies Were New* (1988), Carolyn Marvin describes the visual culture that developed in tandem with the electrification of modern society during the 1880s and 1890s, when the problem was not just a matter of making visual a new (and rather abstract) technology to the general public, but also (for a particular social group of experts) of displaying knowledge and authority in the form of dramatic demonstrations:

> In the perceived novelty of its high-drama public role, the electric light also expressed the sense of unlimited potential that was a staple of nineteenth-century discourse about the future of electricity. For if electricity was the star of the nineteenth-century show, its most publicly visible and exciting agent was certainly the electric

light. It was present in exhibitions, fairs, city streets, department stores, and recreation areas. It was physically and symbolically associated with whatever was already monumental and spectacular. It appeared in grand displays, processions, buildings and performances. It borrowed from every established or dramatic cultural self-promotion.[127]

Although electric light proved a spectacular event in itself, its merits were not only demonstrated in practical demonstrations, but also as extravagant displays in the form of stellar constellations, illuminated bunting, fountains lit up with coloured light, signal lamps, illuminated department store fronts, projections on clouds, light in the shape of emblematic figures, and so on. The use of light in public demonstrations of this kind formed a significant part of the visual culture into which this technology was inscribed. It may be observed here how the visualisations and metaphors employed in both the specialist and popular press to describe the new technology were extremely varied and oscillated between diametrically opposed connotative poles: from apocalypse, utopia or magic to rational science and the utilitarian pragmatism of the everyday.

However, this culture and, indeed, the use of the new technology as a whole involved a form of translation between new signs and codes, on the one hand, and older conventions, on the other, which meant that the discourse that developed around electricity as a technology and as a mass medium only became possible within certain accepted cultural and social systems of norms.[128] The same pictorial formula on which Lefebvre's painting was based also recurred in images that alluded more directly to electricity and electric light and were produced for popular, commercial and private contexts. One example is provided by a photograph from 1883 of Mrs. Cornelius Vanderbilt as 'The Electric Light'.

Wearing an evening gown, the woman in the picture is holding aloft an electric bulb. The motif would appear to be a direct translation of Lefebvre's formula, albeit rather more clumsily executed. Any direct application of the classicist nude would have been impossible in terms of the conventions of this particular medium (photography): such a photograph would definitely have

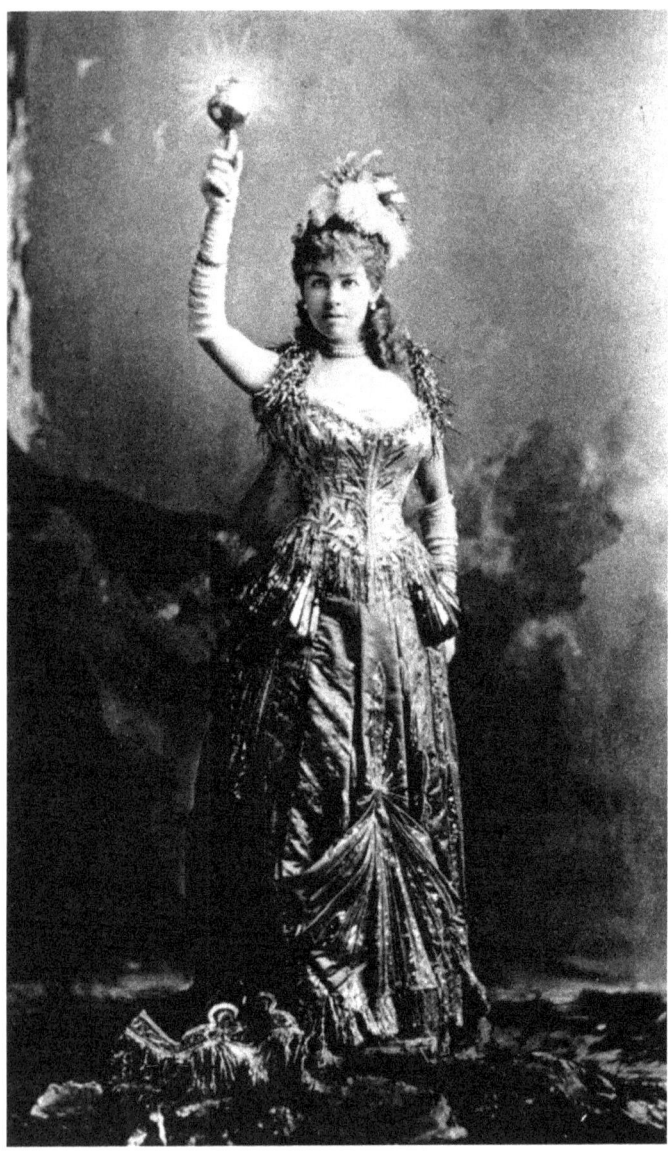

Figure 5. José Maria Mora, *Vanderbilt Ball, Mrs. Cornelius Vanderbilt as the electric light*, March 26 1883, fotografi, The New York Historical Society, New York (Department of Prints, Photographs, and Architecture Collections: Costume Ball Photographs Collection, PR-223, Series V, Box 3, Folder 34), Photo: The New York Historical Society, Wikimedia Commons, Licence CC-0 (Public Domain) https://commons.wikimedia.org/wiki/File:Mrs_Vanderbilt_ElectricLight.jpg.

crossed the boundary to the pornographic. It is difficult to determine the particular aims of this photograph, but considering that the model belonged to the very summit of New York's social and financial elite, it may reasonably be supposed that the image was intended as a fashionable and/or humorous tableau for private consumption. The really interesting aspect from our point of view, however, involves paying attention to what the translation and transformation of the motif are actually doing: combining the classical ideal of truth with one that is scientific and technological; light-as-truth is being transformed into electricity-as-truth.

This combination of convention and innovation would presumably have been a key incentive for the commercial companies that had invested in the new technology and were keen to convert it into cash by selling it to the general public. As described by David E. Nye, the crucial issue for electric companies was to be able to dramatise the superior benefits of their own products while simultaneously downplaying the utopian/apocalyptic connotations. By placing an electric bulb in a traditional, premodern environment, the technology was presented as harmless and in keeping with tradition.[129]

A variation on this theme can be found in the trademark of the German electrical company AEG from 1884, in which the attributes of Truth are combined with those of Fortune, and the resultant goddess is seen holding an incandescent bulb.[130]

A company such as AEG would appear to have felt the need to transpose a widespread but diffuse perception of this extraordinary novelty into a traditional and, therefore, more comprehensible figure. The combination of visual codes gave rise, however, to a particular communication problem in that the emblem had to mediate a specific iconography while remaining comprehensible to anyone not versed in iconographic and allegorical matters. The same kind of competence is, in principle, at issue here as was essential, in Arthur Danto's view, for creating an aesthetic identification in the art world of the 1960s. But the problem is both a more ancient and more wide-ranging one in that it applies not only to the confused visitors confronted with Andy Warhol's Brillo boxes at the Stable Gallery in New York in 1964, but also, and in a more general sense, to the art world that was constituted

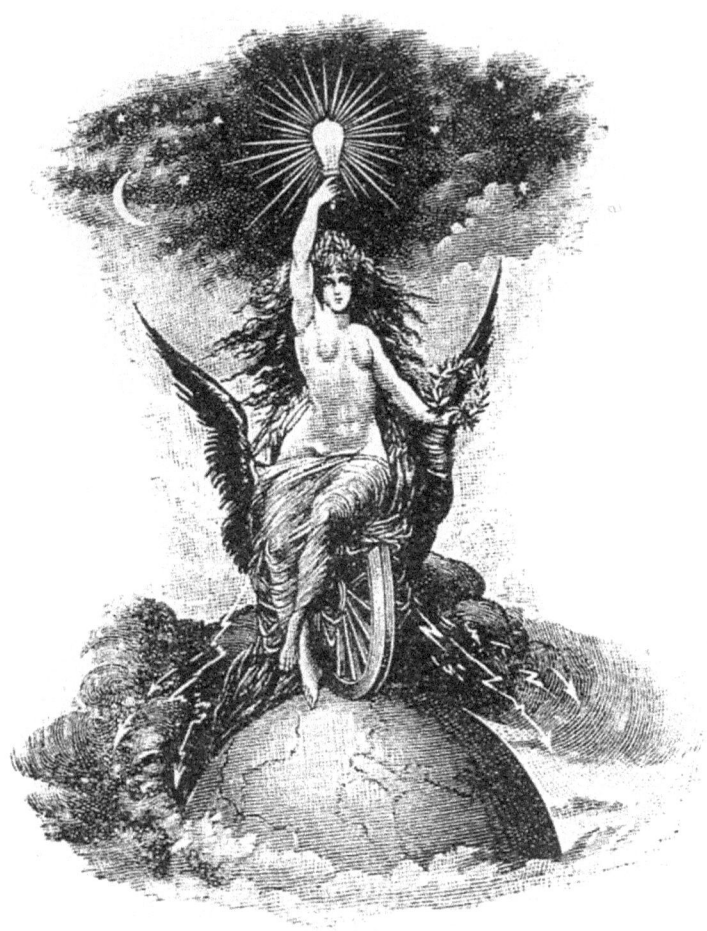

Figure 6. Anonymous, Trademark of Allgemeine Elekrizitäts-Gesellschaft (AEG), Germany, 1894, Photo and copyright: The Archives of the National Museum of Science and Technology, Stockholm, License: CC BY-NC-ND.

as an autonomous value sphere during the nineteenth century and to the broader visual culture that was oriented towards the general public. A new need was emerging to mediate the codes of the visual arts to the public as a whole, while greater competence was being required of that same audience at deciphering various forms of visual communication (from official art to different kinds of advertisements, trademarks, labels, items of political propaganda, etc). To a target group that was either entirely or partially unfamiliar with allegorical matters, the trademark delivered a more general connotation of the union of the old and the new, in which a mythological figure of some kind is seated on a wheel (modern communications), which rests on a globe of the world (world dominion, universality), while holding a light bulb (modern technology). To be on the safe side, the goddess of light is also strategically draped in cloth to prevent uninformed observers from confusing the different and distinct connotations of nudity. The way of reading inscribed here is allusive rather than descriptive, with the text serving both as an anchorage (leading potential interpretations in a particular direction) and as a relay (shifting the category of the motif from the field of art to that of the trademark).[131]

Unlike this commercial and popular cultural use of the convention, Lefebvre's picture served an entirely different function, in which two aspects that were both typical and definitive of the artistic practice of academic discourse could be said to converge: the interplay between doctrinaire and rational classification and the necessity of individual interpretation and pragmatism. What becomes apparent here is that the hierarchy of genres operated within a field whose boundaries were explicitly defined against other fields, a field in which the Fine Art that Lefebvre's painting exemplified was regulated and assessed on the basis of quite different norms than those governing the applied art represented in this instance by AEG's trademark. AEG, for its part, was able to profit from what was conventional in academic visual culture as a source of a particular value. But it also tells something else, namely that neither of these images—or categories of image—can be considered in isolation from a much more extensive process of social change.

Certain mythical and religious views were, as we have seen, included in the differentiated repertoire of both compatible and contradictory contexts found within the modern. Demystification in this regard should, therefore, be understood as a more complicated process than the differentiation of particular activities and values to specific domains. Various generally disseminated ideas of the consequences of the scientific revolution could even be considered to constitute a new and secularised form of mythology.[132] Within the bourgeois public sphere, modernisation was the economic and financial prerequisite for the new social life of the middle class. That life would, however, be characterised by an ambivalence between the upholding of traditional social hierarchies and moral values and an almost blind, spellbound even, trust in the future potential of science and the process of modernisation. However, as Carolyn Marvin has shown, the boundary between science and myth was much less clearly defined in the late nineteenth century than it is today:

> Although an express mission of science was to kill magic and myth, electrical experts were deeply implicated in the production of both.... The occasional appearance of sensational stories about the occult at the fringes of scientific and professional literature was usually legitimized by the suggestion that science was absorbing and taking over disreputable magical modes and replacing them with benign scientific ones. Stories of this kind dramatized the heroic encounter with the unknown, and the contest of power against power. As in any thrilling story, the plot of scientific proof and verification revealed what was authentic and legitimate in the eternal drama between good and evil.[133]

Here we see emerging the outlines of a position that would encompass an almost mystical faith in the material rationality of science, on the one hand, and a merger of occult and rational criteria and narratives in the public understanding of scientific innovation on the other. This extraordinarily ambivalent situation (which was in no way unique to the turn of the century) was, to some extent, a reflection of the sheer pace of change. Although political power structures can be swiftly altered and new technology may rapidly change the conditions of everyday life, changes within social structures and thought patterns usually occur much more slowly.[134] Various forms of mysticism, tradition and convention seem to have been entirely necessary criteria for the social context in which the public understanding of scientific innovations took place in the decades either side of the turn of the century. This would also serve to explain, in part, the shifting function of the visual arts in this period.

As Jonathan Crary has so convincingly demonstrated, the nineteenth century can be described in terms of a comprehensive change both in the organisation of visual forms and in the position of the observing subject; this change would, in turn, entail the development of new technologies, instances of social control, fields of knowledge and forms of linguistic representation:

> Rather than stressing the separation between art and science in the nineteenth century, it is important to see how they were both part of the single interlocking field of knowledge and practice. The same knowledge that allowed the increasing rationalization and control of the human subject in terms of new institutional and economic requirements was also a condition for new experiments in visual representation. Thus I want to delineate an observing subject who was both a product of and at the same time constitutive of modernity in the nineteenth century. Very generally, what happens to the observer in the nineteenth century is a process of modernization; he or she is made adequate to a constellation of new events, forces, and institutions that together are loosely and perhaps tautologically definable as 'modernity'.[135]

At the beginning of the nineteenth century, the fixed and stable visual regime on which both classical art and visual technologies, such as the *camera obscura,* depended was broken up. The varying foundations of visual truth on which it was based (idealist and scientific, respectively) were not only called into question by alternative ideas, but also were challenged and outmanoeuvred over time by a spectrum of various interchangeable and mutable visual values and forms of experience. The reception of the photographic image as a visual medium at the time of its breakthrough provides a striking example: the photograph was understood and promoted both as a spectacular technical innovation and, through the references it made, as a more highly evolved form of older visual media (graphic art, drawing).

From this perspective, a comparison of Jules Lefebvre's painting, the photograph of Mrs Cornelius Vanderbilt and AEG's trademark would have to involve not only the identification of various metaphors for truth or various media and image genres, but also the understanding of an intellectual and experiential context that meant these diverse forms of representation would all become possible within the framework of the modern. This shift also had an influence on the change in the visual language and types of representation of the academic visual arts. As Linda Nochlin has pointed out, the superficiality of academic art and the dissolution of the hierarchy of genres reflected not only the poor taste of the middle class and its passion for the spectacular and the sentimental, but also the more detailed knowledge and altered view of history introduced by the science of the modern era:

> As the treatment of historical subjects became more factual and mundane towards the mid-century, so the chronological range available to artists was expanded. The limits of time itself were being gradually pushed back from Archibald Ussher's judicious starting-point in 4004 B.C. The fluid relativism of a perpetually revised scientific hypothesis replaced the story of Creation and the metaphysical absolute it implied. History and value, history and faith, which had been inseparable since the earliest creation myths and integrated in the doctrine of the Christian Church, were irremediably torn asunder by the Higher Criticism and the New Geology. What was left was history as the facts, in a vast landscape extending from the mists of prehistoric times to the Comtean precincts of present-day experience.[136]

In light of this change, it is possible to see Lefebvre's painting as located at the crossroads between different conventions for the artistic representation of objects and abstract ideas, where a scientific ideal of truth comes up against an aesthetic one and where various forms of legitimation are simultaneously at work within the modern. In which case, the painting would not be a peculiar exception, but extremely representative of large parts of the visual world of the nineteenth century. However, this overall change in the organisation of visual forms should not, in my view, be considered solely as a coherent continuity, but must also be read and understood within the framework of every type of discursive practice. The ambivalent quality of the work of an artist such as Lefebvre actually involved a state of tension within the value sphere specific to the visual arts, a tension that was the hallmark of the late nineteenth and early twentieth century: while incapable of being considered in isolation from the wider social world, it nevertheless developed a particular pattern of inflection based on the order that regulated the definition and discussion of art within established discourse.

We only have to move a few decades forward to study how this intricate interplay between tradition and modernity is expressed in quite different ways in a form of visual art that made the same claims to ultimate value that the academic had done, but which embraced a diametrically opposed concept of truth. One such example is Sonia Delaunay's painting *Prismes électriques* of 1914. By this time, even though the technological innovation of electric lighting had already reached the living rooms of town-dwellers, it was considered sufficiently new to appear both evocative and dynamic. Consequently, this form of light also served as an appropriate starting-point for an avant-garde that was attempting to capture and transpose the dynamism of the modern age in its pictures.

Stanley Baron describes an episode when the Delaunay couple, while walking along the Boulevard Saint-Michel in Paris that same year, found themselves amazed at the newly installed electric lights.[137] It was that impression that impelled Sonia Delaunay to start work on a set of sketches in which she attempted to capture the dynamism of that light by gradually reducing all the incidental, figurative elements in the street scene in order to distil from it an abstract composition of circles in shining colours. It was not only the mythologisation of the academic tradition that was being excluded as part of this compositional process, but also the social iconography of realism and impressionism: visual art was no longer intended simply to depict modern life; it had to be true, in itself, to the modern. Delaunay's painting is an attempt to portray the perception of electric light directly in the language of images: two circular coloured prisms, both separate and interconnected while expanding across the surface of the image like an optical distillation of the transformations of energy and matter. The composition of the colour field is based on Michel Eugène Chevreul's theories about the interaction of simultaneously contrasting colours, with the aim of evoking the perception of the visual effect of light.

While the picture obviously exists in relation to the realist tradition and to Claude Monet's attempts, for example, to depict a particular light at a particular time and place, Delaunay's painting is making more general claims: light is not being depicted solely as an effect, but is being employed equally as a metaphor for the energy-saturated and kaleidoscopic dynamism of modern life. In its pursuit of a radical present, the painting is deliberately turning its back on the tradition and the attitude to life that had given rise to both Lefebvre's painting and AEG's trademark.

What this comparison demonstrates first and foremost are two diametrically dissimilar forms of representation. John Berger uses, at one point, a couple of metaphorical models to highlight linguistic or rhetorical differences on the part of various historical epochs: Lefebvre's painting would correspond most closely in this scheme to the model of 'the theatre stage'; whereas, Delaunay's corresponds to that of 'the diagram'.[138] In terms of the former model, the subject matter is presented as a tableau, while art is seen as an artificial language; in the latter model, the image constitutes a directly observable, symbolic rendering of invisible processes. It is noteworthy in this context that Delaunay's depiction avoids any suggestion of a staged tableau; all the props and all the actors have been erased in order to accentuate the portrayal of the dynamism of electric light.

Michael Fried's characterisation of the element of theatricality in academic painting may be understood as a function of the hierarchy of genres, which served not only as a simple taxonomy of types of subject, but also as a manifestation of a specifically new way of perceiving the image.[139] He describes this altered perception in terms of a change in the appreciation of the dramatic effect of the image, an accentuation of its essential unity and a new relationship between the image and the viewer. The theatre stage served, therefore, not only as a metaphorical model (for the composition as a static tableau), but also as a paradigm, both for the perception of the genre of visual art (as genre) and its communicative function. And it is in its obvious transgression of this tradition that Delaunay's painting inscribes itself so strikingly in a radically different definition of the ontology and truth criteria of visual art.

This changed definition also points to a changed way of reading. As we saw earlier, Lefebvre's painting served as a codified form of representation, in which the presumption of a varying degree of familiarity on the part of the public with the code would determine its significance in a particular context. Delaunay's painting is also, of course, a coded representation, but here, the interpretation—in its original context—appeared more indirect and intuitive: the specific iconography of the former work has been transformed in the latter into more general allusions. This meant that the need for conventional linguistic skills in the case of the former work was replaced by a more general requirement for an imaginative sensibility in the latter. At issue here is a changed relationship between image and narrative that is indicative of the increased focus on the purely visual and the formal in the modern discourse of the visual arts. The idea of the exclusively visual nature of art would appear to be a distinct, historically specific and relatively recent construction. Many of the visual cultures of the nineteenth century were not intended to be understood exclusively as visual cultures but in terms of a more or less clearly-defined textual and narrative framework.[140]

This text-based way of reading is, of course, not new to the modern era but part of an ancient tradition of mythological allegories and religious iconography. The allegorical aesthetic would, in this sense, establish at least one common criterion within the visual cultures of the late nineteenth century: the close connection between image and story. Here, the allegory may be likened to what Kant called the *parergon*: an element, or layer, which exists both alongside and inside the work (ergon), like the frame of the painting, the drapery of a statue or the columns of a building.[141] In neo-classicism, a distinction was, in fact, made between substance and ornament, with truth/beauty being constituted by the former, although the latter (in the form of myth and history) was deemed equally necessary to adorn, as it were, the ideal and to uphold the intellectual level of the work.[142] The allegory appears to have served rather as an interface between the work's external and inherent qualities. While its various linguistic levels created a duality, they also interacted and displaced one another. How this interaction and its reception function is entirely dependent on convention, but even though the meaning of the allegory may be fixed by a particular iconography, a gap nevertheless exists between idea and image. A gap that meant, according to Walter Benjamin, that the allegorical idiom had to be understood as dialectical and, thus, in principle, open-ended.[143]

The distinction between allegory and symbol may seem peculiar at first because both terms appear to be so closely related in many ways. Even though the concept of allegory has its origins in a rhetorical practice, Hans-Georg Gadamer has described how both concepts clearly relate to a philosophical and religious context in which they function as a means to understand and make visible a concealed meaning/truth:

> Both words refer to something whose meaning does not consist in its external appearance or sound but in a significance that lies beyond it. . . . The allegorical procedure of interpretation and the symbolical procedure of knowledge are both necessary for the same reason: it is possible to know the divine in no other way than by starting from the world of the senses.[144]

The semantic problem is made all the more intricate by the existence of so many different definitions. Although both allegory and symbol may be defined as the representation of something in the guise of something else, and although an allegory may also contain symbols, there are nevertheless some crucial differences. First, there is the unity and closed nature of the symbol, as opposed to the allegory's syntactical merging of discrete entities and its openness and, second, the sense in which the symbol communicates by means of an immediate insight, as opposed to the reflexive and postponed reading of the allegory.[145] The distinction between symbol and allegory that was drawn in the late eighteenth century also entailed a redefinition and transformation of the meanings of the terms, and this led to a shift in the intuitive (aesthetic) connotations of the allegory and the rational (scientific) connotations of the symbol; they changed place, so to speak: the symbol was now presented as an intuitive and occasionally irrational fusion of the sensual and the transcendental in contrast to the way in which the allegory maintained a meaningful, although artificial, relation between these two levels.[146] From the end of the eighteenth century, this change in the way art was perceived also entailed a relatively explicit criticism of the cold rationalism of classical doctrine, both in terms of its forms of education and the increasingly abstract and bloodless allegorical tableaux that resulted from its aesthetics.[147]

The shift in meaning reflected a broader current of ideas that not only affected the distinction between allegory and symbol, but also brought about a revaluation of the former at the cost of the latter. Ernst Gombrich has aptly described the new value assigned to the symbol:

> [T]he implication that the Great and the Beautiful provide the mind with a symbol through which we can grasp a hidden truth certainly led back to Platonism. And while German classicism had thus taken the upward path on the ladder of analogy through the image of harmonious forms to the idea of harmony, Romanticism re-discovered the Areopagite's alternative, the power of the mysterious and the shocking to rouse the mind to higher forms of thought.[148]

What emerges here is not simply a change in aesthetics and in artistic ideals, but a change, too, in the way the nature of art and its linguistic identity and function were seen. In the work of Goethe and Schelling, for example, this distinction was formulated in terms of a critical polarisation between two forms of presentation, an idea to which Friedrich Creuzer would return somewhat later in *Symbolik und Mythologie der alten Völker, besonders der Griechen* (1810–12). In this work, the allegory is presented as a general concept or an idea separate from itself; whereas, the symbol constitutes the very incarnation and embodiment of the idea. The mediation of the idea by the symbol takes place not through a conventional reading of its syntactically arranged attributes, but through an immediate and intuitive insight, and this constitutes, in Creuzer's view, the very ground of 'the nature of pictorial expression'.[149] This would suggest that these defining characteristics were not being identified on the basis of a neutral desire to classify categories of images of rhetorical figures, but from an already existing need to draw a distinction between two fundamental approaches concerning the essence and communicativeness of art. Interestingly, one of the basic tenets of classicism—the idea of the unity of the work of art—would appear to have undergone a transformation, from forming part of an aesthetic ideal to becoming a defining characteristic of the nature of art, the work of art, that is, seen as an organic whole integrating form and content.[150] As part of this process, the function of the symbol would alter, from serving as a pictorial element to being a definition of the art work in itself.

Critical Margins

Modernity may be described as a phenomenon that encompasses both an extensive historical process and a definitive change. In this sense, it calls to mind Norbert Elias' description of the process of civilisation itself: an interweaving of individual human plans and actions whose outcome is quite different from what anyone planned, creating a particular kind of order that is both more powerful and more compelling, but also more diffuse, than any purpose or formulation on the part of an individual or a group.[151] The break between the modern and the premodern should not, therefore, be seen as absolute, but understood, instead, in terms of both continuity and discontinuity. The specifically new context created as a result of the change in social and experiential patterns introduced by modernity may have broken with tradition, but the resulting forms of experience were far from unambiguous. On the one hand, the present and the future were described in many contexts as a process of continual expansion in all fields, which, in its most extreme form (the discourse of the twentieth century avant-garde), would lead to historical memory, as such, being declared superfluous or even reactionary—a notion that, in some instances, would result in a cult of the future.[152] On the other hand, reference may also be made to a modern cult of the past.[153] In both cases, modernity introduced a situation in which a particular relation to the past was established: a sense of circumspection and loss that created a need to bridge the gulf to the past—not in the sense of a real return, but in the form of various means of reexperiencing (and thus transforming) what had come before.

An array of ideological and institutional changes may be identified with modernity, which constituted and characterised the development of the value sphere of the visual arts in the Western world during the nineteenth century, with Paris as its more or less accepted centre. Let me focus here on three of these changes: (1) the expansion of the art academies, (2) the interaction between the public and the private and (3) the development of a system based on competition within and around a critical margin. All these structural changes affected the relation of the visual arts to what Jürgen Habermas has called the 'bourgeois public sphere': an expanding and increasingly significant public arena in which the middle class gained a role in the formation of opinion and in economic and social exchange. It was in this arena that new forms of economies of the sign in the world of art were established as part of major structural transformation. This change was not perceived as linear and unidirectional in the world of art or in social life as a whole; on the contrary, a broad range of trends can be identified that worked both in its favour and against it. It thus provides a classic example of the pluralism, contradictoriness and ambivalence of the modern era.

By the beginning of the century, the system of art academies had become increasingly specialised while also expanding in unprecedented fashion: from only a score or so art academies in Europe at the beginning of the eighteenth century to well over a hundred by the start of the following one.[154] The significance of the art academies thus appears to have gradually increased by the start of the modern era. Nikolaus Pevsner explains this expansion both in terms of the ever greater emphasis on the social, political and national-economic benefits of the dissemination of knowledge brought about by the Enlightenment and a new realisation of the commercial value of art and design on the part of manufacturing industry.[155] The demands on the administrative agencies to maintain the political, administrative and normative continuity of society were an additional factor. Despite the growing scale of political conflict, as exemplified in the various revolts of the nineteenth century, the overriding function that the Art Academy fulfilled to the satisfaction of every regime was to meet a requirement increasingly experienced during the modern age for a stable organisation of various areas of administrative responsibility.[156] Academic discourse was thus an integral part of the growth of a normative scheme for mediation, discipline and control within the fields of both production and consumption. While the didactic, economic and political explanations correspond in this regard to various kinds of needs within the modern public sphere, they also provide a pattern-card of the way the old and the new interacted in modernity, allowing us to observe how some traditional institutions and ideals continued to survive while undergoing changes in a number of crucial respects.[157] It was, of course, essential for any regime that was not completely authoritarian to create a certain (acceptably large) space for new movements and changed ideals within the art world, as in other fields.

An academic code could, nevertheless, be said still to exist that embraced a range of distinctions—both in practice and in principle—affecting the various parts of the art world: the definition of art and the value of art, the way the function of art was seen in society, the practise of artistic education, the definition of the social and professional identity of the artist as subject. In broad terms, the academic code may also be considered to have been a means of determining the boundaries between various fields within the visual culture of modernity.[158] This differentiation corresponded both to a change and a need that affected all the fields of the art world. Having constituted a boundary between various genres of subject matter (history and genre painting), the distinction between high and low—which had, of course, been codified within the hierarchy of genres—would later be transformed in Romantic/Modernist aesthetics into a universally applicable definition of a difference in kind within visual culture. This difference in kind did not, however, necessarily entail a distinction between the fine and the applied arts but, rather, that Art should be understood as a transcendent attribute of a particular type of artefact (the work of art).

What this makes clear is that the order of the academic code should be understood in relation to the gradually more autonomous position of the art world within the bourgeois public sphere. It was becoming increasingly evident at the same time, however, that this autonomy was dependent on public life, because the influence of the public sector encompassed not only the production but also the distribution and consumption of art. Applying

Jürgen Habermas' distinction between the public and the private, the structural change that occurred from the middle of the 1850s onwards may be described both in terms of the general development of different types of institutions within the art world and in terms of a greater and more complex exchange between the public and the private sectors. While the power base of the art academy was still very influential at this point, two other public institutions were becoming increasingly significant: the art museum and the university. The role of leading producer of art theories increasingly shifted to the university, while the art museum was developing into an ever more important arena for the encounter between the art world and the public sphere.[159] Perhaps the most crucial aspect of the position of the art world in the late nineteenth century was not, however, the roles played by the institutions within the system when seen as a static entity, but rather the interaction between the public and the private.

This was not a new phenomenon. For an artist working in mid-eighteenth century Paris, this dynamic would, in many cases, have been a prerequisite for survival. While the official sanction of the *Académie royale de Peinture et de Sculpture* through the awarding of commissions and prizes provided vital status, in order to survive financially, an artist had to obtain private commissions, mainly in the form of portraits. Just over a hundred years later, however, and as a result of a gradual process of change, the definition of the order of the discourse itself became the subject of a debate formulated largely within the bourgeois public sphere.

The initially problematic position of art criticism—private opinions on the works of the Salon were published in pamphlets and, subsequently, in the press—may be seen as emblematic of the changing nature of this dynamic. The general debate about art was taking place neither in private isolation, nor in the studio or the house of a collector, nor in closed sessions of the Academy, but in an open arena aimed at a literate general public— and thus beyond the sanction and control of the Art Academy. The definition and interpretation of the relevant issues, the establishment of aesthetic ideals and the evaluation of artistic devices was increasingly transferred into the private sphere during the second half of the nineteenth century. Thus the Art World was increasingly subjected to a fundamental form of institutionalised doubt that, according to Antony Giddens, may be understood as an all-pervasive feature of the critical reasoning of the modern age.[160] The rhetorical and occasionally self-glorifying presumptuousness that characterised many of the theoretical and critical pronouncements of the modern era could, therefore, be seen as a consequence of such a form of doubt. Modern institutions, too, may be defined on the basis of the particular dynamic created by this form of doubt, such that a particular order may at times be stubbornly and aggressively defended as the ultimate truth, while nevertheless always (in principle at least) remaining open to revision and rejection. Similarly, a concept that has become established in a particular field may be challenged and even ousted without the institutional structure of the discourse collapsing.

In this sense, the private world may be seen as interacting with globalising trends and official institutions to create a dynamic interplay in which specific rules can be described for the possible extent of transformation within the art world. This interplay affects individuals in their choices (of career and artistic practice), but it also means that an officially sanctioned pronouncement may be challenged and flouted by the individual. A degree of democratic freedom that allows for the development of competition within a critical margin is, however, a precondition for a dynamic interaction of this kind between the public and the private.

This transformation corresponds to what Pierre Bourdieu has described as the development of an autonomous field. The specific meaning Bourdieu attributes to this phrase is not simply concerned with a process of successive position-taking within a permanent order, but describes rather an unstable state characterised by continually occurring competition for positions and by open conflict over the power to define the legitimacy and fundamental *nomos* of the field:

> This relatively autonomous universe (which is to say, of course, that it is also relatively dependent, notably with respect to the economic field and the political field) makes a place for an inverse economy whose particular logic is based on the very nature of symbolic goods – realities with two aspects, merchandise and signification, with the specifically symbolic values and the market values remaining relatively independent of each other.[161]

The ways in which the field and the various orientations of artists are differentiated generate a wealth of variables, by which they are also evaluated: pure (intellectual) production as opposed to that on a large-scale (commercial), different political positions, the degree and significance of economic gain, the degree and type of consecration (initiated, sanctified, recognised). A key point of Bourdieu's concept of the field is that it makes visible a structure that is both fundamental and dynamic. Even if the structure of the field remains constant over time, the reciprocal relationships between the actors are subject to change, as are the values represented by the different positions. The private sector served as the main driving force for the field at the end of the nineteenth century, with the official institutions found above it (or rather in the background). An inverted economic structure provided one of the cornerstones of this arrangement, reflecting the lack of importance attached to financial matters in the self-image of avant-garde artists, while also serving as a reminder of how various types of capital are actually interdependent—the economy of signs of the avante-garde served as a reflection and function of the capitalist market.

In the decades both before and after 1900, a development may be observed that proved fundamentally similar throughout Europe with the expansion of subcultural infrastructures, whose focal points consisted of private galleries, periodicals, manifestos, theoretical writings, private art schools, social coteries. This infrastructure lacked the very features that provided the foundation for the expansion of the system of art academies during the nineteenth century, namely uniformity and continuity. However, this lack proved the key to its success: unlike the academic system, an informal, temporary and pluralist infrastructure was capable of adapting relatively quickly to changes in aesthetic, economic and social conditions.

These were the circumstances in which the idea of a cultural avant-garde was established, both then and subsequently, as a cornerstone of the historiography of this period. Such an occurrence would have been unthinkable without the profound structural change we have been discussing. The problem here, however, is that this phenomenon—the avant-garde—eclipsed the scale of this transformation precisely because it so pointedly dramatised and heroicised the outsider status of art and the artist. Given its military connotations, the word avant-garde should never be understood as a purely descriptive or empty social category.[162] Applied to the cultural sphere, the constituent parts of the term (an avant and a garde) encompass a range of diverse attributes: a temporal aspect (being part of, or ahead of, one's time), a social dimension (a restricted circle that espouses a divergent viewpoint), an ideological aspect (opposition to the prevailing values) and an aesthetic one (unconventional forms of artistic expression and approaches). According to Matei Calinescu, the avant-garde would have been inconceivable without a modern consciousness in which the various attitudes and forms set up by the avant-garde appeared to serve as a kind of kaleidoscopic distorting-mirror, which showed fragments of modern life that were amplified, exaggerated and taken out of their context.[163] It is in this sense that the avant-garde appeared not simply dependent on modernity for its intellectual *raison d'être* but, rather, a dramatisation of modern society, in which every comment or judgement on the surrounding bourgeois culture can only ever remain a gesture because the avant-garde is dependent on this culture for every aspect of its existence. Within the framework of the economy of signs referred to above, however, this gesture is not empty but, in fact, of crucial importance.

In his critical analysis of the contemporary art world, Bourdieu describes a principle crucial to the modern value sphere of the visual arts: the necessity for different strategies to create both economic and symbolic capital. He also describes how these incompatible interests give rise to remarkable and ritualised patterns of behaviour for various types of actors as an interaction between symbolic and physically concrete factors: the different symbolic values/charges of the private institutions and their geographic distribution in Paris, for example. This led to a situation in which the artists of the avant-garde were able to (or were obliged to) create a matrix for the interpretation of their own art and its rules and forms of legitimacy. This mixture of reality and fiction, of collective identity and individualism, of pragmatism and utopia and of the historical and the contemporary may, in fact, be considered to have constituted a particular narrative concerning the notion of an aesthetic avant-garde—a story that would, in certain cases, be refashioned into romantic myths about 'the misunderstood genius' or 'the starving artist'.[164] For the most part, however, this narrative was produced retroactively in history books.

Let us return once more to the example of Jules Lefebvre in order to examine what the career of a successful academic artist during the second half of the nineteenth century was like. He was awarded a place at the École des Beaux-Arts in 1853 and made his debut at the Salon three years later. In 1861, he won the Prix de Rome, which made it possible for him both to live and to work during the following five years. In the 1870s, he worked as a teacher of drawing at the Académie Julian, a private art school with close connections to the Académie des Beaux-Arts, of which he was made a member in 1891. Despite this unimpeachable career within the official art world, it was primarily as the supplier of portraits and sensual female nudes to the middle classes that Lefebvre made a living. He appeared to have opted at an early stage for these genres, which were much less celebrated by the Academy, than for history painting. Although he was awarded few official commissions, he enjoyed all the more success as a result in the private market.

To compare this career path with that of an artist of the same generation as Lefebvre, such as Edouard Manet, elicits not only a different story but a different type of story. Manet, who never gained a place at the École des Beaux-Arts, was educated privately at Thomas Coture's studio (1850) and at the Académie Suisse (1861). He made his debut at the Salon in 1861 when he showed two portraits (after a failed attempt two years before) that, although given an honourable mention, made little impact. In the years that followed, he increasingly distanced himself from the academic ideal he had learnt under Coture and developed what might be called an increasingly complex form of realism. He failed in his attempt to get three works entered in the Salon of 1863 but was given the chance to show them at the officially sanctioned *Salon des refusés* instead. Although his 'Olympia' caused an outcry when it was shown at the Salon two years later, Manet continued to send in works to this institution throughout his working life, while also exhibiting at various private galleries.

That is about the full extent to which Manet's career was involved with the official institutions. It is worth pointing out the alternative direction he followed and the entirely different events that marked his future path, whose significant milestones included the following: his visits to the Café Guerbois in 1865 and his meetings with the younger Impressionists, the transfer of his loyalty to the Café de la Nouvelle Athènes in 1872, the rejection of his work for the World Exhibition in Paris in 1867 and his consequent decision to show fifty or so of his paintings at a private gallery instead, becoming close friends with Emile Zola at the end of the 1860s, the marriage of his brother to Berthe Morisot in 1874, his various travels, his relationship with the regime during the Paris Commune of 1870, his professional links with the art dealer Durand-Ruel, the changing nature of his social life, his interest in graphic prints and, above all, his development as an artist. Manet's career would be accorded a rather unexpected official finale when his friend Antonin Proust was installed as minister for the fine arts in 1881 and awarded him the rank of chevalier in the *Légion d'honneur* that same year.

Although this comparison could, of course, be fleshed out in greater detail, it reveals not only two different artistic careers, but also, more significantly, two distinct patterns of movement in the French art world of the later nineteenth century. An artist emerges, in the case of Lefebvre, who was able to move between the private and public sectors and for whom, even though success in the one did not necessarily mean success in the other, these sectors were not opposed in principle. Despite these movements, social and aesthetic interconnections were established in Lefebvre's career that were determined by the discursive practice of the Academy. These provided him with an identity that allowed the artist access to specific opportunities within both the sectors referred to above. For Manet's part, his failure within the official institutions meant that his career took a different route and led to acceptance within quite different circles. The entire institutional framework took on a different guise in his case. While it is entirely possible that Lefebvre visited the Café Guerbois in the mid-1860s, these premises played no role in his career, neither in terms of the narrative of an artist's *oeuvre* as a form of social identity, nor, presumably, in terms of actual networks or social contacts. The narrative form Manet's career subsequently generated in art-historical writing became, in fact, normative of the social and aesthetic identity of the artist in general. According to this narrative, which relies on tropes regarding the exclusion and individuality of the artist, his social agony and aesthetic autonomy, the originality and authenticity of the work and the connection between the artist's oeuvre and his life, not only would Lefebvre's irreproachable career have been a failure, but also all but impossible to integrate within the confines of such a story.

Thierry de Dueve has described Manet's artistic activities in the period 1860 to 1870 as heralding a radical change in the discursive standardisation and classification of officially exhibited works of art. Furthermore, the shift in question also applied to the narratives that legitimised this altered situation, both for Manet's peers and posthumously.[165]

This shift encompassed not only movements within an institutional framework, but also, ultimately, a change in the concept of truth in art as well. Although the requirement for originality and individuality in execution and concept were also emphasised within a classicist tradition regulated through the discursive practice of the academy, authenticity in that instance referred to the credibility of the image as a representation of a transcendent (historical/metaphysical) ideal. The artist was expected to work in a rational manner and meticulously calculate each step in the process, starting with the sketch. This ideal might perhaps be better described in terms of the distance and the absence that characterised how the artwork was seen—the distance in time from both the historical/mythological models and the canonical art of the Hellenistic period and by genre from the realm of the Ideal. In terms of this approach, the work of art seemed to be a language that might describe the truth and, at best, even approximate it by means of its form, iconography and dramaturgy, but it could never, in itself, be anything other than a reflection or a trace of the Absolute. The Romantic aesthetic was a different matter. Here, the issue was no longer the acquisition and mediation of a foreign/extinct language—to attempt to reflect the connection between the natural and the ideal that had been lost by modern man by means of a rational analysis of the composition and by the use of allegorical stagings—it involved, instead, the creation of an organic whole in which the authenticity of the sign was understood in terms of proximity to and presence in a specific origin (the artist/the contemporary world). It is this shift in particular that is indicated by the change in metaphorical language from describing art as a mirror (representation) to a lamp (expression).

This approach meant that truth appeared to be manifested directly in the authentic work of art as both meaning and aesthetic value. The transcendental or prelinguistic meaning was fused with the linguistic (conventional) reference to the surrounding world and relocated to a higher sphere of eternal values. While the artist was free, in principle, to create his or her own interpretation, it was evaluated on the basis of a new requirement that the image be a representation of an integrated subject. In contrast, the requirement formulated within the discursive practice of modernism was for the uniformity and continual development of an artist's *oeuvre*, which could, ultimately, be evaluated in the form of representation provided by the retrospective exhibition, because the authentic image had to bear the hallmarks of an inner necessity rather than any external factors.[166] The discursive context used to legitimise what were, in their time, the extreme forms of transgression represented by some of the key works of modernism may be understood on the basis of this form of legitimation through authenticity.

A gradual process of adoption meant, however, that a particular tradition and hierarchy were established over time and that the legitimation of the avant-garde occurred at the cost of its fundamental openness. It might be said, in this regard, and to paraphrase Foucault, that in order for an utterance to appear to be true it must be uttered 'in the true': the various transformations of the avant-garde could only be inscribed as representations in the value sphere of the visual arts within a discursive system of norms that emphasised the interaction between 'change' and 'authenticity'.[167] However, the development of this position—both with regard to its linguistic transparency and the critical legitimation of that openness—involved a radical reformulation of what the concept of Art might encompass.

The change we are referring to here did not, however, involve the kind of definitive break that results in the fracturing of the discursive structure at a particular moment but, still in the words of Foucault, in a process that brought about a shift:

> To say that one discursive formation is substituted for another is not to say that a whole world of absolutely new objects, enunciations, concepts, and theoretical choices emerges fully armed and fully organized in a text that will place that world once and for all; it is to say that a general transformation of relations has occurred, but that it does not necessarily alter all the elements; it is to say that statements are governed by new rules of formation, it is not to say that all objects or concepts, all enunciations or all theoretical choices disappear. On the contrary, one can, on the basis of these new rules, describe and analyse phenomena of continuity, return, and repetition: we must not forget that a rule of formation is neither the determination of an object, nor the characterization of a type of enunciation, nor the form or content of a concept, but the principle of their multiplicity and dispersion.[168]

A mistake that is often made is to consider the most aesthetically radical groups as providing the pattern for this process. This risks obscuring both the true scale of the process and the variation in its artistic effects. The avant-garde movements of the late nineteenth century could be said to have revealed the development of a field within the discourse of the visual arts. These movements signalled the presence of radically different aesthetic perspectives but did not, in themselves, define the existence of the field. The advent of the avant-garde was incorporated, rather, as part of a larger institutional and aesthetic process of differentiation, whose consistent theme was defining a position outside the order of academic discourse as such. Even during the first half of the nineteenth century, an increasing measure of pluralism was an ongoing feature of the official art world as well.[169] The complex and disparate course of art history of the modern age may be understood within this context, which extends from the ever-greater acceptability of Romantic art to the increased significance of landscape and genre painting at the Salons to the establishment of various kinds of *juste-milieu* painting to the more radical groupings that were called avant-garde (by their contemporaries or posthumously).

An array of alternative codes were established in turn within the value sphere of the visual arts, which stipulated different types of aesthetic ideals and different kinds of identities to those that had been approved and mediated by academic discourse. The approximate timeframe for this conflict over interpretive privilege extends from the mid-nineteenth century to the mid-twentieth century. A decisive shift took place in the course of these hundred years that redefined what art is and what it may be, what form of legitimation a work of art must espouse in order to be accepted within the discourse and what types of transformation the discursive space will allow. Or to put it another way, it was a shift that created a context in which Duchamp's bottle rack would become a possible utterance; whereas, Lefebvre's mirror would not.

Endnotes

1. Michel Foucault, *The Order of Things. An Archeology of the Human Sciences*, (Trans. Alan Sheridan) London/New York 2003 (1966/1970), p. 331.

2. Octavio Paz, *Children of the Mire. Modern Poetry from Romanticism to the Avant-Garde*, (Trans. Rachel Phillips), The Charles Eliot Norton Lectures 1971–72, Cambridge (Mass.) 1991 (1974), pp. 1–2.

3. Kirk Varnedoe, *A Fine Disregard. What Makes Modern Art Modern*, New York 1994 (1990).

4. Ibid, p. 22.

5. Theodor W. Adorno, *Aesthetic Theory*, (Trans. Robert Hullot-Ketnor), London 2009 (1997), pp. 25–26.

6. Both these phrases also served as titles, see Ezra Pound, *Make it New*, London 1934 and Harold Rosenberg, *The Tradition of the New*, New York 1959.

7. According to Matei Calinescu, although the term 'modernism' was used as a term of invective as early as the beginning of the 18th century (in the work of Jonathan Swift), it was not until the 1920s— and then mainly in the Spanish-speaking world—that the term was employed on a more systematic basis (and with more neutral or even positive connotations) to characterise a rather broad spectrum of different avant-garde or nonconformist literary movements (*Five Faces of Modernity: Modernism, Avant-Garde, Decadence, Kitsch, Postmodernism*, Durham 1987, (1977), pp. 68–85).

8. Although this general, and to some extent unproblematic, relationship between modernity and modernism can be traced far back into the past, it should not, for that reason, be considered simply a residue of the historiography of older ages, but a feature of contemporary revisionist settlements with modernism/modernity. One example of this was provided by the symposium on 'Modernism and Modernity' held in Vancouver in 1979 (see Benjamin Buchloh, Serge Guilbaut & David Solkin (ed.), *Modernism and Modernity. The Vancouver Conference Papers*, The Nova Scotia Series Source Materials of the Contemporary Arts 14, Halifax 1983). The

overarching theme of the conference was the need for a reinterpretation of modernism as a historical phenomenon when reconsidered from a postmodern position. And while the published anthology contains a range of brilliant contributions, the problematic nature of the relationship between modernism and modernity was completely overlooked—apart from in purely passive terms. To the extent the issue of modernity was touched on at all, the term was used as a keyword for the rather one-dimensional social, political and economic backdrop against which modernism was defined. The only thematic analysis of modernity contained within the published proceedings is an extract from the study *Introduction à la modernité* (1962) by the French philosopher Henri Lefebvres. This text, however, fails to deal with the relationship between art and society in any way and provided, instead, an introductory philosophical and ideological reference point, which freed the remaining speakers from having to deal with the relationship actually referred to in the title of the conference. The rubric and the lack of problematisation meant that here, too, a direct and self-evident relation between modernism to modernity was simply taken for granted.

9. Louis Dupeux, "'Revolution conservatrice' et modernité", *La révolution conservatrice allemande sous la republique de Weimar*, (Ed. Louis Dupeux), Paris 1992, p. 19.

10. Charles Harrison & Paul Wood (ed.), *Art in Theory 1900–1990. An Anthology of Changing Ideas*, Oxford/Cambridge (Mass.) 1992, p. 126.

11. Marshall Berman, *All that is Solid Melts into Air. The Experience of Modernity*, NewYork 1983 (1982), pp. 345–346.

12. Charles Baudelaire, "The Painter of Modern Life" (1863), in *The Painter of Modern Life and Other Essays*, (ed. Jonathan Mayne, trans. Jonathan Mayne), New York 1986 (1964), pp. 13–14.

13. Charles Harrison, "Modernism and the Transatlantic Dialogue", in Francis Frascina (ed.), *Pollock and After: the Critical Debate*, London 1985, p. 217.

14. See Fredric Jameson, *A Singular Modernity. Essay on the Ontology of the Present*, London/New York 2002, p. 19.

15. Two extremes may be observed in this regard: Henri Lefebvre, on the one hand, who uses the concept of modernity to characterise the modernisation of the twentieth century (Lefebvre, "Modernity and Modernism", in Buchloh, Guilbaut & Solkin, pp. 3–12), and Matei Calinescu, on the other, who traces back the intellectual foundations of modernity to a fifth-century Christian reinterpretation of the concept *modernus* as opposed to *antiquus* (Calinescu, pp. 14–15.). What most writers and thinkers seem to be agreed on (explicitly or implicitly), however, is that modernity as an epochal term encompasses a post-feudal and post-traditional order with its origins in the social, economic and intellectual revolutions of the late eighteenth and early nineteenth centuries.

16. A distinction may be drawn here between descriptive and normative theories: the former describes how and why things are, the latter how they ought to be. But what this actually entails is a distinction of a more operative kind between different levels within one and the same theory. We have, in fact, already seen how this applied in Marshall Berman's account of the relationship between modernism and modernity. Although the most obvious example might be the contemporary analysis provided by Marx and its prognosis of the classless society, the more specialised and scientific (positivist) theories of modernisation produced in the post-war period also contained a powerful normative element. The scientific perspective merged here with the reproduction of ideals, with the apparent aim of taming the maelstrom, so to speak, of identifying the logic of its laws and the strategies required to adapt social change to those laws or of steering the development of society towards a desirable goal.

17. Jameson, 2002, p. 34.

18. Zygmunt Bauman, *Modernity and Ambivalence*, Cambridge 1991, p. 1.

19. Zygmunt Bauman, *The Individualized Society*, Cambridge 2001, p. 58.

20. Walter Benjamin, "Theses on the Philosophy of History" (1940), in *Illuminations* (ed. Hannah Arendt, trans. Harry Zorn), London 1999 (1955), p. 249.

21. Umberto Boccioni, Carlo Carrà, Luigi Russolo, Giacomo Balla, Giovanni Severini, "Manifesto of the Futurist Painters" (1910), in Lawrence Rainey, Christine Poggi & Laura Wittman (eds.) *Futurism. An Anthology*, New Haven & London 2009, pp. 62–63.

22. Adorno 2009, p. 45.

23. Ibid, p. 27.

24. Jameson, 2002, p. 143.

25. Two fundamental distinctions may be noted between these concepts. The first involves the difference in the terms' lexical significance. The two parts of the concept of the avant-garde ('avant' and 'garde') actually encompass a social or temporal positioning: a group that goes ahead, which is in advance. How this frontal position should be understood obviously depends on the context in which the term is used. In cultural contexts, its metaphorical meaning usually refers to a group that is ahead of the dominant culture in an aesthetic sense. A second distinction based on ideological and/or theoretical grounds creates a greater difference in principle between the two terms. The German literary theorist Peter Bürger, for example, considers modernism to represent an attempt at preserving the autonomy of art and thus as a form of continuity in established discourse; whereas, the avant-garde is defined as that which has deliberately taken up a position outside that discourse and attacked it—as that which has transgressed the boundaries of anything that might be called art. For Bürger, the prime example of the avant-garde work of art is provided by Marcel Duchamp's readymades, which rebelled against the institutional order of the art world and subsequently undermined it. (Peter Bürger, *Theory of the Avant-Garde*, (Trans. Michael Shaw), Minneapolis 2002 (1974), pp. 51–54) He contrasts the medium-critical revolt of modernism with the avant-garde's critical attitude to institutions. He also identifies and classifies the avant-garde work as 'non-organic', in that it was based on the compositional principles of the montage (allegory), chance and the fragment and, thus, no longer complied with the modernist idea of the work of art as an organic whole (Bürger, pp. 68–70). This distinction amounts to an attempt to isolate and save, so to speak, the ideologically and aesthetically radical aspects of modern art from the institutionalisation modernism

underwent during the post-war period. For a discussion of the relationship between modernism and the avant-garde, see also Håkan Nilsson, *Clement Greenberg och hans kritiker*, (Diss. Stockholms universitet 2000), Stockholm 2000, pp. 31–39.

26. The notion of the new man is connected with the romantic and occasionally apocalyptic idea that modernism represented the last, doomed stage of an age for which the art of the avant-garde would serve as a signpost to a new era. German Expressionism, in particular, cherished an, at times, almost messianic notion of the role of the artist, who was considered not only to have an intuitive connection to spiritual forces, but also was capable of acting outside the established moral and aesthetic norms of bourgeois society (see, e.g. Douglas Kellner, "Expressionist Literature and the Dream of the 'New Man'", Stephen Eric Bronner & Douglas Kellner (ed.), *Passion and Rebellion. The Expressionist Heritage*, New York 1988 (1983), pp. 166–200). A similarly Utopian ambition can be discerned in most of the avant-garde movements, even though this might take on very different forms of expression. It is in this regard that modern art, despite its extremely individualistic notions of art and man, was considered capable in itself of producing (or at least providing the catalyst for) social change. This is the somewhat obscure context in which the temptation felt by certain representatives of the avant-garde to seek out extreme political movements (both fascism and communism) may be explained, though not explained away. It is here, too, that the state of tension may be observed that existed between the belief of the aesthetic avant-garde in the socially transformative role of art and the view held by the political avant-garde that art had to be subordinated to political leadership.

27. Renato Poggiolo, *The Theory of the Avant-Garde*, (Trans. Gerald Fitzgerald), London/Cambridge (Mass.) 1968 (1962), p. 218.

28. Calinescu, p. 41.

29. Ibid, p. 265.

30. T. J. Clark , *Farwell to an Idea. Episodes from a History of Modernism*, New Haven/London 1999, p. 175.

31. John Berger, *The Success and Failure of Picasso*, New York 1989 (1965), p. 71.

32. Guillaume Apollinaire, "The New Painting: Art Notes" (1912) in Leroy C. Breuning (ed.), *Apollinaire on Art:Essays and Reviews 1902–1918* (Trans. Susan Suleiman), London 1972, pp. 197–198.

33. Clement Greenberg, "Collage" (1959), *Art and Culture. Critical Essays*, Boston 1984 (1961), p. 74, John Golding, *Cubism. A History and Analysis 1907–1914*, London/Boston 1988 (1959), and William Seitz, "The Liberation of Objects", *The Art of Assemblage*, Museum of Modern Art, New York 1961, pp. 22–25.

34. See W Clark, 1999, p. 79 and passim.

35. An obvious symptom of this turn is provided by the historical genealogies of expressive art, set out in some of the writings and manifestos of the avant-garde. A prime example is *Die Blaue Reiter Almanach* of 1912, in which a manifesto by Franz Marc described how modern art was revealing 'spiritual treasures' in history and in other cultures; the same perspective also permeates the rest of the anthology (Franz Marc, 'Spiritual Treasures', in Klaus Lankheit (ed.), *The Blaue Reiter Almanac*, The Documents of 20th-Century Art, London 1974 (1965), pp. 55–60). This search for the sources of authentic art outside the norms of modern civilisation encompasses two of modernism's favourite narratives, to use the terminology of Kirk Varnedoe: visiting distant places and visiting museums (Varnedoe, 1994, p. 183). Peter Selz makes the important point that this interest involved both domestic traditions and exoticism, history and escapism, which was made possible in particular by museum exhibitions and the general dissemination of reproductions (*German Expressionist Painting*, Berkeley/Los Angeles/London 1974 (1957), pp. 12–16 and passim).

36. See e.g. Guillaume Apollinaire "Art News: The Futurists" (1912), in Breuning, pp. 202–203.

37. Georges Braque, "Thoughts on Painting" (1917), in Edward Fry (ed.), *Cubism*, London 1966, p. 147.

38. In a review dated 1912, Apollinaire dismissed the artistic products of Futurism as lacking originality and as pale and unfinished reflections of the French avant-garde in general and Cubism in particular ("The Art World: the Italian Futurist Painters" (1912), in Breuning, p. 199). But Apollinaire approved of their boldness and their general aim of depicting shapes in motion and, in 1913, wrote a manifesto of

his own with the title 'L'antitradition futuriste' that clearly travestied the typography and slogan-like phrases of the Futurists (see Folke Edvards, *Den barbariska modernismen. Futurismen och 1900-talet*, Malmö 1987, p. 247). The key turning point came in the same year when Apollinaire enrolled Futurism in the Orphist movement in an article published in German in Herwald Walden's periodical Der Sturm ('Modern Painting' (1913), in Breuning, p. 270).

39. An interesting analysis of Picasso's relation to Futurism is found in Rosalind Krauss, *The Picasso Papers*, Cambridge (Mass.) 1999 (1998), pp. 83–84 and footnote 58, pp. 251–252.

40. Pablo Picasso, "Statement to Marius de Zayas" (1923), in Fry, 1966, p. 168.

41. Adorno, 2009, p. 7

42. Yve-Alain Bois, *Painting as Model*, Cambridge (Mass.)/London 1995 (1990), p. 83.

43. Krauss, 1999, pp. 47–48 and passim.

44. Apollinaire (1913), in Breuning, p. 269.

45. Jeffrey S. Weiss, "Picasso, Collage, and the Music Hall", in Kirk Varnedoe & Adam Gopnik (ed.), *Modern Art and Popular Culture. Readings in High and Low,* The Museum of Modern Art, New York 1990, p. 93.

46. Adorno, 2009, p. 233.

47. Linda Nochlin, *The Body in Pieces. The Fragment as a Metaphor of Modernity*, The Walter Neurath Memorial Lecture 1994, London 1994, p. 7.

48. Ibid, p. 8.

49. Paul de Man, "Literary History and Literary Modernity", *Dædalus. Journal of the American Academy of Arts and Sciences*, vol. 99, Spring 1970: 2, p. 391.

50. See Horace Engdahl, *Stilen och lyckan. Essäer om litteratur*, Stockholm 1992, p. 57.

51. See Patricia Mainardi, *The End of the Salon. Art and the State in the Early Third Republic*, Cambridge 1993, p. 90.

52. Richard Wrigley, *The Origins of French Art Criticism. From the Ancien Régime to the Restauration*, Oxford 1993, p. 12.

53. Thomas Crow, *Painters and Public Life in Eighteenth-Century Paris*, New Haven/London 1986 (1985), p. 3. Richard Wrigley has estimated the number of visitors to the Paris Salons at the end of the 1780s at around 35,000, while the corresponding figure during the 1840s was just over 1 million. (Wrigley, pp. 78–80.) There are no exact figures available for the number of visitors at the end of the eighteenth century, which have instead been calculated on the basis of the number of catalogues sold. The fact that these figures should be taken with a pinch of salt—or that the number of visitors fluctuated over time—is demonstrated by Jules Claretie's calculations that the number of visits made to the Salon of 1880 was 680,000 (*La Vie à Paris 1880*, Paris 1881, pp. 97–98, reproduced in Mainardi, p. 72).

54. Crow 1986, p. 1. The exhibitions of the Paris Salon were opened to the public in 1725 and were held regularly every, or every other, year, which set the pattern for the rest of Europe. During the nineteenth century, the Salon developed into by far the most important stage for the art world. While there were other opportunities for artists to exhibit outside the Academy, they were usually occasional and received much less attention (Wrigley 1993, p. 38). Initially, the exhibitions of the Salon were restricted to artists connected with the Academy, but following the Revolution, they were open not only to independent artists, but also to those of every nationality, which served to cement the central role played by Paris on the contemporary exhibition scene (Elizabeth Gilmore Holt, *The Expanding World of Art, 1874–1902. Vol 1: Universal Expositions and State-Sponsored Fine Arts Exhibitions*, New Haven/London 1988, p. 173). Once participation in the Salon was no longer linked directly with the Academy, the jury system (which was established in 1848) became the key to control. In the increasingly divided French art world, the composition of the jury and the selections it made were the source of (now almost legendary) controversies. At the end of the 1870s, Edmond Turquet, the minister of the republic responsible for cultural matters, initiated a number of reforms that loosened the dominant grip of the Academy on the selection of jury members and also led to the works being hung thematically—which meant alternative art movements became increasingly visible (Mainardi, pp. 74–89). In 1872, a quarter of the jury

were appointed by the administrators of the Salon, while three quarters of the artists chosen were linked with the Academic establishment (its members, laureates, recipients of its medals and honours). Turquet's reform of 1879 meant that the jury had to include all the artists who had exhibited in the three previous Salons, which increased the number of artists entitled to vote in the painting section of the jury from 711 to 2219. The following year, he set up two separate jury groups within painting, one for historical and figure painting and one for the lower categories (genre, landscape and still life). Conflict over the composition of the Salon jury and the role of the Academy in the public art world should be seen in the light of an increasingly lively formation of political and social opinion during the second half of the nineteenth century. In Mainardi's view, the forces in conflict may be inscribed on a political value-scale, with the conservative groups in favour of greater centralised control through the Academy, while the republicans called for a liberalisation of the structure of the art world (Mainardi, p. 82). Irrespective of the merits of the arguments of the opposing sides, the very intensity of the conflict demonstrates that the Salon was considered a vital arena in both political and aesthetic respects: being able to control this arena was also a means of influencing the formation of opinion.

55. Craig Owens, "The Allegorical Impulse: Toward a Theory of Postmodernism. Part I" (1980), *Beyond Recognition. Representation, Power, and Culture* (ed. Scott Byron, Barbara Kruger, Lynne Tillman & Jane Weinstock), Berkeley/Los Angeles/London 1997 (1992), pp. 52–53.

56. Nochlin, 1976, p. 104. This notion was not an invention of the Realists, according to Nochlin, but an idea with deep roots in the world view of Romanticism and its conception of art.

57. Habermas (1981), 1998, pp. 7–8.

58. Wrigley, p. 285.

59. Thomas B. Hess, "Some Academic Questions", in Thomas B. Hess & John Ashbery (ed.), *Academic Art*, London 1971 (1963), p. 2.

60. Greenberg (1940), 1988 a, p. 27.

61. Lionello Venturi, *History of Art Criticism*, (Trans. Charles Marriott), New York 1964 (1936), p. 254.

62. Clive Bell, *Art*, Oxford 1987 (1914), pp. 178 f. and 192.

63. Wassily Kandinsky, *Concerning the Spiritual in Art*, (Trans. Michael T.H. Sadler), New York 1977 (1911), p. 1.

64. See e.g. Nicolaus Pevsner, *Academies of Art. Past and Present*, London 1940, pp. 190–245, concerning the reactions of the romantic movements for and against the academic training of artists.

65. Although different in some respects, the image of this century that emerges in Richard Müller's comprehensive three-volume work *Geschichte der Malerei im XIX. Jahrhundert: I-III*, München 1893–94, is not unfamiliar. The enormous amount of text is structured according to different types of genres, problem areas, nations and styles. The result may be a little confusing, but it provides a fascinating insight into a body of historical material before it became incorporated into a dominant narrative—and before that narrative was taken for granted. While, unsurprisingly, academic art is accorded a significant amount of space, this applies to the second half of the century and is under the rather charged heading 'Die Epigonen' (Müller, s. 355–381). A couple of decades later in a general survey work by Karl Woermann, *Geschichte der Kunst aller Zeiten und Völker. Bd. 3: Die Kunst der christlichen Völker vom 16. bis zum Ende der 19. Jahrhunderts*, Leipzig/Wien 1911, the art of the nineteenth century is presented to a considerably greater extent in terms of the linear narrative that subsequently became so familiar. Here, too, it is academic art of the second half of the nineteenth century that is dealt with, although it is treated to an even greater degree as a historically subordinate and qualitatively inferior part of the art history of the epoch when compared with the various representatives of Realism. (Bastien-Lepage just as much as Courbet och Manet). The restriction of narrative and selection is further consolidated in Helen Gardner's *Art Through the Ages. An Introduction to its History and Significance*, London 1927. While the academic tradition is summarily referred to in Gardner's study (without naming the artists concerned), it is defined as the antithesis of the 'spirit' of the new age (p. 369): the great developmental line, that is, from Romanticism onwards. The same image appears even when one turns to contemporary French survey literature, such as André Michel's work on the nineteenth century in the huge eighteen volume compendium *Historie de l'art. Tome VIII :2, L'art en Europe*

et en Amérique au XIXe siècle et au début de XXe, Paris 1926, or to the depiction of that century in Louis Réau's three-volume *Historie universelle des arts. La renaissance l'art moderne*, Paris 1936.

66. In *The Story of Art*, London 1967 (1950), p. 381, Ernst Gombrich refers to a gulf opening up between 'official artists' and 'nonconformists' during the nineteenth century and how this gulf subsequently led to a shift of historical focus and to the exclusion of late academic art from the art-historical narrative. Whereas art historians of today may be rather unfamiliar with the official art of that period, Gombrich is convinced that it actually surrounds us, although in areas outside the domains of serious art and art history: as public monuments in urban space, as mural paintings in town halls, as stained-glass in churches, as the decor of hotel foyers. What is interesting about this relatively minor comment of Gombrich's is the fact that it is even included in his text. This historiographic segment is missing from the original edition of 1950. It is, of course, impossible to provide any unambiguous answer as to why he chose to reflect on the disappearance of the academic tradition in subsequent editions. But perhaps the classically trained Gombrich, who always adopted a sceptical attitude to modernism, was perturbed by the fact that the tradition of nineteenth century academic art had been so completely excluded from the image of that century presented in the survey literature. This process of rendering the academy invisible while normalising the avant-garde is also a dominant feature of such works as H. W. Janson's *History of Art. A Survey of the Major Visual Arts from the Dawn of History to the Present Day*, New York 1962, which is probably, in international terms, the most influential art-historical handbook of the post-war period. Here, the presentation is based exclusively on a number of epochal concepts (romanticism, neo-classicism, realism, impressionism), and the narrative is driven forward by an almost exclusive focus on a few artists and on the stylistic comparisons drawn between them. Art (with a capital A) is presented as an autonomous phenomenon, without any real links to economic and social circumstances or to a context of intellectual history. No traces of alternative forms of representation are to be found in this survey since the aesthetic and historical selection criteria have been woven together to create an impenetrable whole, under the aegis of a notion of (stylistic) innovation.

67. Hans Belting, *The End of the History of Art?* (Trans. Christopher S. Wood), Chicago/London 1987 (1984), pp. 12–15.

68. Hilton Kramer, "Does Gérôme Belong with Goya and Monet?", *New York Times*, 1980-04-13, section 2, p. 35.

69. Paul Oskar Kristeller, "The Modern System of the Arts. A Study in the History of Aesthetics", Part II, *Journal of the History of Ideas*, vol. 13, No. 1, January 1952, pp. 17–24.

70. Ibid, pp. 42–43. See Immanuel Kant, *Critique of Judgment*, (Trans. Werner S. Pluhar), Indianapolis/Cambridge 1987 (1790), particularly § 56–59, pp. 210–224.

71. The dissemination and normalisation of the defining features of the system to a broader social stratum of interested laymen, academic functionaries and professional artists occurred primarily through the publication of general encyclopaedias and specialist reference works in which this approach was expressed in various articles. Marta Edling has demonstrated the considerable significance of Johann Georg Sulzer's *Allgemeine Theorie der schönen Künste* (1771–1774) and Claude-Henri Watelet's & Pierre-Charles Levesque's *Encyclopédie Méthodique. Beaux-Arts* (1788–91) for the dissemination of this view, not least in terms of their influence on the second edition of Diderot's and d'Alembert's general *Encyclopédie* (1777–1779), which was widely circulated throughout Europe (Edling, pp. 33–37.).

72. Maria Görts, *Det sköna i verklighetens värld. Akademisk konstsyn i Sverige under senare delen av 1800-talet*, (Diss. Stockholms universitet 1999), Stockholm 1999, p. 195.

73. For an exhaustive discussion of the nineteenth century bourgeois public sphere and its private and official dimensions, see Jürgen Habermas, *The Structural Transformation of the Public Sphere. An Inquiry into a Category of Bourgeois Society*, (Trans. Thomas Burger & Frederic Lawrence), Cambridge (Mass.) 1991 (1962), pp. 141–159.

74. Daniel M. Fox, "Artists in the Modern State: The Nineteenth-Century Background" (1963), in Milton Albrecht, James Barnett & Mason Griff (ed.), *The Sociology of Art and Literature*, London 1970, p. 371.

75. Michel Foucault, *The Archeology of Knowlege*, (Trans. A. M. Sheridan Smith) London 2001 (1972), p. 117.

76. Jürgen Habermas, *The Theory of Communicative Action*, vol. 1, London 1984 (1981), pp. 235–236.

77. Jürgen Habermas, "Modernity – An Incomplete Project" (1981), in Hal Foster (ed.), *The Anti-Aesthetic. Essays on Postmodern Culture*, New York 1998 (1983), pp. 7–8.

78. Habermas' 'separation' should not be taken as either self-evident or objective; it has, in fact, been the object of fairly extensive criticism. Fredric Jameson describes, for example, how the autonomy of aesthetics served as a key tenet of the historicising ideology of modernism after the Second World War, which may be understood as criticism in indirect form of the description of the separation of the spheres as portrayed by Habermas. (Jameson, 2002, p. 161). In his turn, Richard Rorty has explicitly criticised Habermas' system both because it sets up boundaries between the spheres that are far too rigid and because it takes seriously Kant's extremely arbitrary (and fundamentally metaphysical) philosophical division (Richard Rorty, "Habermas and Lyotard on Postmodernity", in Ingeborg Hoestercy (ed.), *Zeitgeist in Babel. The Postmodernist Controversy*, Bloomington/Indianapolis 1991, pp. 88–90). But even though Habermas' distinction may be criticised, it is a useful means—bearing the objections cited above in mind—of highlighting and defining that area of modern social life where ideas about Art and aesthetics have their place.

79. In the work of Thomas Kuhn, the concept of the paradigm is used exclusively to explain developments within various areas of the natural sciences such that the search for knowledge may no longer be considered as the continual pursuit of ever-greater understanding of the world, irrespective of the social and political context of the production of knowledge. Instead, certain scientific conquests emerge at a particular point as 'model problems and solutions to a community of practitioners' (Thomas Kuhn, The Structure of Scientific Revolutions, Chicago/London 1970 (1962), p. viii). Those periods of 'normal science', in which the scientific cohort 'know what the

world looks like' and in which the production of knowledge is, in principle, aimed inwards in order to supplement the dominant paradigm, will over time and as a result of an ever greater accumulation of anomalies shift into a 'period of revolution', when the paradigm can no longer be revised but has to be replaced by a different one in order to provide a theoretical scheme capable of encompassing the observations and calculations that have been made. In our context, however, the term paradigm should be understood in a more general sense in keeping with its fundamental linguistic sense of a social framework that constitutes and regulates the production by the art world of knowledge and value. Understanding a process of change as paradigmatic would therefore mean that it is governed by particular local and arbitrary (discursive) norms, rather than by universal laws for the development of Art and its ends.

80. Arthur Danto, "The Art World" (1964), *The Journal of Philosophy*, Vol. 61, No. 19, American Philosophical Association Eastern Division Sixty-First Annual Meeting (Oct. 15, 1964), p. 577.

81. *The Oxford English Dictionary*, Second edition, (Ed. James A. H. Murray, Henry Bradley, W. A. Craigie & C. T. Onions), Vol. 1, Oxford 1989, pp. 795–796.

82. Krauss (1981), 1991, p. 157.

83. Jacques Derrida, "Structure, Sign, and Play in the Discourse of the Human Sciences" (1966), *Writing and Difference*, (Trans. Alan Bass), London/New York 2001 (1967), p. 353.

84. See Jacques Derrida, *Of Grammatology* (Trans. Gayatri Chakravorty Spivak), Baltimore/London 1997 (1967), pp. 6–26 and passim.

85. For a history of the metaphor of the organism and its effects, see Abrams, p.184–225. Particular mention should be made here of Edward Young's distinction in *Conjectures on Original Composition* (1759) between 'the growth process of the organism' and 'mechanical production' as a symptom of a change of perception, which, in terms of aesthetics, would subsequently become common property.

86. Hugh Honour describes, for example, how many researchers have been perplexed by the discrepancy between the spontaneity of

Canova's sketches and the coolness of their execution, although this difference was, in fact, a particular feature of an established artistic practice in which the *bozzetti*, rather than being an autonomous form of artistic expression, represented an initial attempt to capture the ideal form of the subject matter (see Hugh Honour, *Neo-Classicism*, Harmondsworth 1984 (1968), p. 101–102).

87. Albert Boime, *The Academy and French Painting in the Nineteenth Century*, London 1971, pp. 82–87.

88. Ibid, pp. 85–87.

89. Ernst Kris & Otto Kurz, *Legend, Myth, and Magic in the Image of the Artist. A Historical Experiment*, (Trans. Alastair Lang & Lottie M. Newman), New Haven/London 1979 (1934), p. 52.

90. Harold Rosenberg, "The American Action Painters" (1940), *The Tradition of the New*, Chicago/London 1982 (1959), pp. 25 and 28.

91. Krauss (1981), 1991, p. 167.

92. Although this approach was not, it should be said, based solely on the words of Rosenberg, it took on a new topicality as a result of the dramatic force of his judgements and the enormous influence he exerted over the American art world of the 1950s. This was made clear to me when perusing a number of the annual volumes of *Art News* (vol. 54–62, 1955–1963), which was, under the editorial control of Thomas B. Hess, far and away the most influential periodical at that time in American art circles. What I found confirmed in these pages was not only the extent of the dominance of Abstract Expression, but also that the manner in which this art was interpreted, written about and understood was based on Rosenberg's aesthetics in various forms. But instead of his radical notion of the primary significance of the creative act over the material appearance of the work, what most critics focused on was the work as an autonomous structure of signs and on the value of the brushstroke as the expression of the artist's sensibility and the authenticity of the work. Now the objection may of course be made that this was only one of many sources and that, despite the significance of this particular periodical, it cannot be assigned any absolute authority. But, in my view, the vast amount of

articles and reviews involved serve as a quantitative confirmation of an image that is frequently mediated by other sources (specialist studies, monographs, survey works) and which, interestingly, were still so dominant well into the 1960s when a new generation of critics began taking over and when attention was increasingly devoted to other art forms, such assemblage, environments, junk-art, happenings and pop art. The transition period between Abstract Expressionism and Pop Art may, in fact, be considered a key resource for understanding the actual significance of the idea of the value of the brushstroke in the American (and to some extent the European, as well) art world. Both by studying the rather laborious process almost all Pop artists went through in order to free themselves from the 'idiom of the brushstroke' (see Peter Schimmel, "The Faked Gesture: Pop Art and the New York School", in Russell Ferguson (ed.) *Hand-Painted Pop. American Art in Transition 1955–62*, The Museum of Contemporary Art, Los Angeles, New York 1993, p. 19) and through a consideration of the more or less ironic representations of this idiom in Pop Art during its established phase, as in Andy Warhol's rhetorical and practical use of the silkscreen technique as a mechanical antithesis to the brushstroke or Roy Lichtenstein's gigantic paintings representing 'authentic brushstrokes', painted by copying the raster artwork of the comic.

93. Sven-Eric Liedman, *I skuggan av framtiden. Modernitetens idéhistoria*, Stockholm 1997, p. 452.

94. See Cesare Ripa, *Iconologia*, (facsimile of the 1618 edition), Milano 1992 (1593), pp. 463–464.

95. Among the immediate predecessors of Lefebvre's composition of a naked woman holding up a mirror was Pierre-Jules Cavelier's sculpture ' La verité' of 1849–53 (see T. J. Clark, *The Absolute Bourgeois. Artists and Politics in France 1848–1951*, London 1973, p. 40).

96. See F-G Dumas, *Livret Illustré du Musée du Luxembourg*, Paris 1884, p. xxxvi and p. 153, and *The Musée d'Orsay*, Paris/New York 1987 (1986), p. 153. While Lefebvre may have been feted by the official art world, his works and academic methods of instruction were the object of contempt in more radical and avant-garde circles (see e.g. Emile Zola, "Une exposition de tableaux á Paris" (1875), *Salons*, Société de publications romanes et francaises LXIII, Geneve/

Paris 1959, p. 165, and John Rewald, *The History of Impressionism*, Museum of Modern Art, New York 1946, p. 330).

97. Liedman, 1997, p. 453.

98. Kenneth Clark, *The Nude*, Harmondsworth 1960 (1956), pp. 1–25. Clark's distinction, which largely reproduces the ideal of academic art, obscures the fact that all portrayals (including the naked) are culturally coded, while the idea of the nude also serves to conceal the proximity of this kind of painting to an area beyond the confines of the socially acceptable. It was, in fact, this very distinction and the way that the naked body could be used to mediate higher values that long allowed this motif to be a source of aesthetic pleasure (see Lynda Nead, *The Female Body. Art, Obscenity and Sexuality*, London/New York 1997 (1992), p. 25). Not only the naked body but also the sexual gaze was therefore dressed in (disciplined through) Art.

99. Antonio Ludovico Muratori, "Della perfetta poesia italiana" (1706), as quoted in Wladyslaw Tatarkiewicz, *History of Aesthetics. III. Modern Aesthetics*, (Trans. Chester A. Kisiel & John F. Besemeres), Haag/Paris/ Warszawa 1974 (1967), p. 447.

100. The presentation of human beings and human actions was a key aspect of academic doctrine since the human being in action was considered to be the purest and most visible means of portraying the human soul. The human form, therefore, not only had to be anatomically credible, but also had to represent an abstract concept of ideal beauty and a personification of an abstract content. Under the generic constraints of history painting, this action was supposed to serve as a carefully considered interpretation of a historical, mythological or religious subject whose details had to be in harmony with the whole. The dramatic, epic and narrative effects also had to be weighed against the ideal harmony of the composition and the elevated dignity of the subject matter.

101. Friedrich von Schiller, *On the Aesthetic Education of Man. In a Series of Letters* (1795), English and German Facing, (Trans. Elizabeth M. Wilkinson & L. A. Willoughby), Oxford 1982 (1967), p. 57.

102. Erwin Panofsky has described this tradition as being based on Plato's distinction between art as the depiction of material (imperfect)

reality and art as an attempt to make visible a higher (perfect) understanding, which the Greek philosopher referred to as an idea (Erwin Panofsky, *Idea – Ein Beitrag zur Begriffsgeschichte der älteren Kunsttheorie*, Berlin 1960 (1924), pp. 1–2). Even during antiquity, Plato's negative view of the function of visual art as purely representational was subjected to reinterpretation, however, and made part of an approach in which art served as one possible (or perhaps even the best) means of depicting the ideal order of the world and of objects: the order in which the variation of nature has its origin. One consequence of this was that during the Renaissance it was believed that the rules of art theory could be derived from a system of universal laws, which were applied primarily in the principles of perspective (geometry, mathematics) and proportion (anatomy). However, a notion of the beauty of art was not necessarily based on any speculative, neo-Platonic theory and, during the High Renaissance, was often described in terms of a 'spiritualised' selection theory, notions of a higher reality and the perfection of nature (Panofsky, p. 35).

103. The idealist view of art created specific notions both about the inherent value of art and about the methods used to teach it. The training offered by the art academies, however, encompassed both practical skills and theoretical knowledge: from the study of drawing to the teaching of the principles of perspective and proportion; from history, mythology and anatomy to geometry, philosophy and art theory. Every aspect of art had to be studied separately while also forming part of a systematic progression: the student began by learning how to draw parts of the body before being allowed to portray the body as a whole; the body was studied bone by bone, muscle by muscle, before the student was taught how to draw the posture and movement of the body through the study of antique plaster casts, anatomical preparations or live models. Torsten Weimark has described the crucial role played in this training by the systematic study of anatomy, which ranged from theoretical studies to the practice of dissection, and is characterised in his words as lacking 'clearly defined boundaries between academic and anatomical drawing, drawing, that is, from living and dead models' (*Akademi och Anatomi. Några aspekter på människokroppens historia i nya tidens konstnärsutbildning och ateljépraktik, med särskild tonvikt på anatomiundervisningen vid konstakademierna i Stockholm och Köpenhamn*

fram till 1800-talets början, Stockholm/Stehag 1996, p. 123). The relationship between anatomy and antiquity was fluid in the same way: although the former involved the study of a real phenomenon (a corpse), the knowledge gained from this study was aimed at creating the familiarity needed to form the basis for the artistic interpretation of ideal beauty.

104. The art academies long taught only drawing, as it was considered to be that part of the artistic process that could, in fact, be taught. Learning to draw from other drawings, plaster casts and living models did indeed involve training in practical skills but also—and above all—the capacity to see, assimilate and apply ideal forms. In order to learn the crafts of painting and sculpture, students were sent to the private studio of a master, which would be outside the organisational reach of the Academy (in formal terms at least). This situation gradually changed during the second half of the nineteenth century, however, when painting and sculpture became increasingly integrated into academic teaching. In some of the more progressive German academies, a significant shift had taken place by the mid-nineteenth century, when the teaching of painting was introduced and the student was given the choice of attending the master classes of various teachers (Pevsner, pp. 218–219). In France, however, the established system of teaching painting in the studios of master painters outside the teaching programme of the Academy remained intact long after the mid-century. This circumstance led to the development of an increasing number of private or semi-official art schools in Paris and elsewhere, such as the Académie Julian. In 1863, however, the authorities made three studios available to each professor at the École des Beaux Arts, where students were trained instead of in the teacher's private studio (Pevsner, p. 226).

105. See Görts, p. 55. The hierarchy of genres was established in academic discourse at the end of the 1660s and codified in André Félibien's *Conférences de l'Académie Royale de Peinture et de Sculpture pendant l'année 1667* (1669). The force of this fundamentally classicist system of norms was, however, by no means self-evident and was further diminished by the preoccupation of the Rococo with intimate and elegant genre motifs that were often lighthearted and carefree. The renewed focus on the hierarchy of genres during

the second half of the eighteenth century may also be considered a reaction in part to Rococo painting (see e.g. Michael Fried, *Absorption and Theatricality. Painting and the Beholder in the Age of Diderot*, Chicago/London 1988 (1980), pp. 72–76). Even though the hierarchy took on different guises and also underwent significant changes (or rather dissolution) during the nineteenth century, its fundamental ranking was that history painting was placed highest, followed by genre, portrait, landscape and still life. The supreme position of history painting within this hierarchy was partly a result of this genre being considered the most demanding (it brought together all the different aspects of the visual arts) and partly because it provided the most profound aesthetic and emotional form of representation: history painting speaks to the soul, where others only offer pleasures for the eye (Fried, 1988, p. 74, quotation of La Font de Saint-Yenne, *Réflexions sur quelques causes de l'état présent de la peinture en France*, Paris 1747). It was in history painting that the cherished tenet of academic doctrine, which demanded a fusion of epic and allegorical (literary) content with an ideal (visual) form, was manifested. This approach to painting was based on the Renaissance theory of epic poetry, in which the action and the structure of the narrative were intended to encompass an inherent higher meaning (Rensselaer W. Lee, *Ut Pictura Poesis: The Humanistic Theory of Painting*, New York 1967 (1940), p. 19). History painting also entailed an extraordinarily complex and multifaceted form of representation with various overlapping levels of meaning, in which the viewer was expected to be able to decipher the different layers of the work by means of the other layers. Despite their multiple legibility, these paintings were not considered fragmentary or partitioned in any sense because the classicist ideal prescribed that all parts of the whole should come together to form an organic whole. In similar fashion to the insistence of classicist doctrine on the unity of time, action and place in drama, the Aristotelian doctrine of the unity of action served as the guiding principle in the visual arts for the harmonisation of the different elements of time and action in painting (Lee, p. 63).

106. Marta Edling, *Om måleriet i den klassicistiska konstteorin. Praktikens teoretiska position under sjuttonhundratalets andra hälft* (Diss. Stockholms universitet 1999), Stockholm 1999, p. 87. The boundaries set by the hierarchy of genres also imposed a definition

of the ideal and autonomous functions of art as opposed to its representative and ideological ones. Both these poles were the subject of continual debate during the nineteenth century, particularly during turbulent historical periods, such as in the wake of the French revolution of 1789 and after the insurrections of 1848. Making a direct link between the (general) value of the visual arts and the (particular) demands of politics could be hazardous. An interesting example is provided by the disputes about the continued survival of both the hierarchy of genres and the academy of arts following the French Revolution, when radical groups proclaimed the necessity of eliminating these remnants of the old society (Wrigley, pp. 287–290). The problem then arose that the framework for the definition and interpretation of art would also have been dissolved and the function of art in society made unclear, which might have led at worst to the visual arts becoming a subversive element in the new republic. The continued crucial role played by the hierarchy of genres in both Republic and Empire, as well as during the Restoration, demonstrates the common need felt by these different regimes for stability. While history painting in the form of battle scenes was explicitly employed during the Napoleonic era to glorify the military efforts of the regime, the tendency during the Restoration was to tone down the political role of painting and emphasise instead its autonomous and ideal meanings (Wrigley, p. 332 and pp. 339–340).

107. The aesthetic and communicative implications of academic doctrine were to do with scope—the artist, quite simply, being expected to express as much as possible with the least possible means. Simplicity and refinement may be considered the two key virtues in this regard, not only as a result of a fixed aesthetic ideal, but also in order to retain the concentrated focus of the image while extending its capacity to affect the viewer.

108. An example of this approach can be seen in Joshua Reynold's third 'Discourse' (1770), in which he describes the educational course to be followed by the artist, from the introductory mechanical copying of objects in the surrounding world to the necessity of developing an individual form of interpretation and the capacity to correct nature in order to achieve both maturity as an artist and beauty of style, no matter how difficult it was to capture the nature of this grand style

in words (see Reynolds, "Discourse III. Delivered to the Students of the Royal Academy on the Distribution of the Prizes, December 14, 1770" (1779), *Discourses on Art*, (ed. Robert R. Wark), New Haven/London 1981 (1959), pp. 41–53).

109. This theme had already been discussed in Weber's study *Die protestantische Ethik und der Geist der Kapitalismus*, Tübingen 1934 (1904–05) and was raised in his posthumously published work *Wirtschaft und Gesellschaft. Grundriss der verstehenden Soziologie*, Tübingen 1980 (1920).

110. The continual expanse of rationalisation in science and social life during the twentieth century may also be deemed to have resulted in periods that witnessed an upswing both in the practice of traditional religion and the development of new spiritual and esoteric movements. Neither did demystification lead to an absence of the mystical dimension in general; mention need only be made here to the increased significance of the nation state, nationalism and regionalism during the twentieth century, all of which frequently made allusion to mystical narratives about historical origins and ethnic/national identity.

111. Weimark, 1996, p. 134. The linguistic metaphor has been drawn from Mathias Duval's and Édouard Cuyer's *Histoire de l'anatomie plastique* (1899).

112. Alison Smith, *The Victorian Nude. Sexuality, Morality and Art*, Manchester/New York 1996, p. 17.

113. Schiller, pp. 31–32.

114. Johann Joachim Winckelmann, *Geschichte der Kunst des Altertums*, Wien 1934 (1764), pp. 128–131. One example mentioned by Winckelmann is how artists were able to study the perfect bodies of young men at Gymnasia and the other places, where the latter trained in order to take part in games and sporting events, and, by doing so on a daily basis, artists could acquire a superior understanding of the structure of beauty (Winckelmann, p. 151).

115. Ibid, p. 149.

116. See Calinescu, pp. 26–35. As early as the seventeenth century, in the work of writers such as Charles Perrault, the compilation of

rules brought about by rational and scientific thinking for the field of aesthetics as well provided the stimulus not only for a greater and more informed awareness about the nature of beauty, but also for the production of works of superior quality. This was lent added force by the self-evident moral superiority of the absolute truth of Christian doctrine demonstrated by contemporary understanding when compared with the pagan cultures of antiquity.

117. Schiller, p. 57.

118. Sabrina Norlander, *Claiming Rome. Portraiture and Social Identity in the Eighteenth Century*, (Diss. Uppsala universitet 2003), Uppsala 2003, pp. 6–9.

119. Maiken Umbach, "Classicism, Enlightment and the 'Other': Thoughts on Decoding Eighteenth-Century Visual Culture", *Art History*, vol. 25, June 2002: 3, p. 333.

120. Meyer Howard Abrams, *The Mirror and the Lamp. Romantic Theory and the Critical Tradition*, Oxford 1971 (1953), pp. 51–52.

121. Abrams, p. 70.

122. The use of the term pivot (*cheville* in French) is derived from Jacques Derrida, *The Truth in Painting*, (Trans. Geoff Bennington and Ian McLeod), Chicago/London 1987 (1978), p. 18. I use the terms, however, in a different sense: not as a metaphor for how Kant succeeded in turning philosophical investigation towards his own premises, but as a much simpler image of how a particular intellectual shift can create a new and different paradigm over time.

123. Liedman, 1997, p. 453, the paperbook edition of the same book, respectively (Stockholm 2000), p. 453.

124. The history of electric light runs parallel to that of the electric generator. Edison's patent, both of a particular type of electric bulb and of a system for the provision of electric current, heralded rather the start of the practical and commercial use of electrical lighting (see Thomas P. Hughes, *Networks of Power. Electrification in Western Society, 1880–1930*, Baltimore/London 1983). Although rudimentary forms of apparatus for the production of electricity were already in existence in the seventeenth century, access to a continuous form of electric current only arrived with Alessandro Volta's pile (a battery)

in 1800. By 1802, the English chemist Sir Humphrey Davy used electricity from the Voltaic pile to make threads of platinum glow, and in 1808, he demonstrated an electric arc lamp to the Royal Institution of Great Britain. Practical operation of the arc lamp became possible from the 1850s but only on a very limited scale. Various attempts to develop more practical forms of incandescent bulbs were made during the first half of the nineteenth century. Ideas about electricity and electric light were prevalent throughout the entire nineteenth century and were not just the province of obscure laboratories but increasingly formed part of public awareness through various types of demonstrations and events, such as the first use of the arc lamp as a stage prop at the Paris Opera in 1836, when the electric light it produced was, presumably, as much a matter of dramatic extravagance as a practical source of illumination. References to electric light can also be found in the fiction of the period, particularly in Jules Verne's novels *A Journey to the Centre of the Earth* (1864) and *Twenty Thousand Leagues Under the Sea* (1869–70), in which electric light serves as a symbol that underpins the theme of both works: the combination of fear and fascination at the effects of the (prospective or Utopian) achievements of modern technology.

125. See, e.g., Louis Énault, *Paris-Salon 1881*, Paris 1881, p. 26, A. M. Belina, *Nos Peintres dessinés par Eux-Mémes*, Paris 1883, p. 267 and Jules-Antoine Castagnary, "Année 1870 ", *Salons*, Paris 1892, pp. 420–421.

126. Smith, pp. 104, 115.

127. Carolyn Marvin, *When Old Technologies Were New. Thinking About Electric Communication in the Late Nineteenth Century*, New York/Oxford 1988, p. 158.

128. Ibid, pp. 232–233.

129. David E. Nye, *Image Worlds. Corporate Identities at General Electric 1890–1930*, Cambridge (Mass.)/London 1985, p. 122.

130. A comparison of the presentation of the Veritas motif in academic art and the recycling of the same motif in various trademarks can be found in Jan Garnert, *Anden i lampan. Etnologiska perspektiv på ljus och mörker*, Stockholm 1993, pp. 150–159. For AEG's

trademark and its ideological context, see Tilmann Buddensieg, "Behrens und Messel. Von der Industriemythologie zur 'Kunst in der Produktion'", in Tilmann Buddensieg (edit.), *Industriekultur. Peter Behrens und die AEG 1907–1914*, Berlin 1980 (1979), pp. 21–23.

131. See Roland Barthes, "Rhetoric of the Image" (1964), *Image, Music, Text*, (Trans. Stephen Heath), London 1977, p. 38.

132. Nochlin, 1976, p. 41.

133. Marvin, pp. 56 and 59.

134. Daniel Bell, *The Cultural Contradictions of Capitalism*, New York 1976, pp. 7–8.

135. Jonathan Crary, *Techniques of the Observer. On Vision and Modernity in the Nineteenth Century*, Cambridge (Mass.)/London 1992 (1990), p. 9.

136. Linda Nochlin, *Realism*, New York/Baltimore 1976 (1971), p. 25.

137. Stanley Baron, *Sonia Delaunay. The Life of an Artist*, London 1995, pp. 51–52.

138. John Berger, "The Moment of Cubism" (1969), *Selected Essays* (ed. Geoff Dyer), New York 2002 (2001), pp. 84–85.

139. Fried, 1988, pp. 75–76.

140. Lena Johannesson, *Den massproducerade bilden. Ur bildindustrialismens historia*, Stockholm 1978, p. 243.

141. Kant, § 14, p. 72. See also Derrida, 1987, pp. 17–147.

142. Abrams, p. 269.

143. Walter Benjamin, *The Origin of German Tragic Drama*, (Trans. John Osborne), London/New York 2003 (1928), p. 160 and passim.

144. Hans-Georg Gadamer, *Truth and Method*, (Trans. Joel Weinsheimer & Donald G. Marshall), New York 1995 (1960), pp. 72–73.

145. In various publications Paul de Man has analysed the allegory as a particular form of reading, see e.g., "The Rhetoric of Temporality" in *Blindness and Insight. The Rhetoric of Contemporary Criticism*, Minneapolis 1997 (1971).

146. For a historical survey of this change, see Götz Pochat, *Symbolbegreppet i konstvetenskapen*, Kungl. Vitterhets Historie och Antikvitets Akademins Handlingar, Antikvariska serien 30, Stockholm 1977, pp. 3–35.

147. See Gombrich, 1978, p. 183.

148. Gombrich, 1978, p. 187.

149. Friedrich Creuzer, *Symbolik und Mythologie der alten Völker, besonders der Griechen*, Bd. I, Leipzig 1819 (1810), p. 80. See also Walter Benjamin, *The Origin of German Tragic Drama*, (Trans. John Osborne), London/New York 2003 (1928), pp. 164–165.

150. See Benjamin, 2003 (1928), p. 160.

151. Norbert Elias, *The Civilizing Process. Sociogenetic and Psychogenetic Investigations*, (Trans. Edmund Jephcott), Oxford 2000 (1939), pp. 376–379. The notion of modernity as a post-traditional idea nevertheless presupposes a process of change of vast proportions, which could obviously not be understood simply through causal explanatory models. The fact alone that the various phenomena which characterise the modern as an epoch range in time over a hundred or so years, and that they also vary between different cultures and even exist, on occasion, in a contradictory relationship to one another, disqualifies explanations of this kind.

152. This view reflects, perhaps, both a general desire for change (the desire of the aesthetic avant-garde to seek out and constantly shift the frontline between the present and the future) and the pursuit of a particular kind of future (the utopian goals cherished by the political avant-garde for the society to come). The utopian ideal would, however, seem paradoxical in terms of modernity's approach to time, because it defines the goal of development as a state that transcends all change. Were the utopia of art to be realised, change would no longer be possible and art would die. It was for this reason, in the view of Theodor Adorno, that art had avoided this catastrophe by continually altering and postponing utopia. This would also mean that the disavowal of a historic purpose on the part of the avant-garde appeared legitimate as long as it was the new itself, which served as its sole aim. (Adorno, 2009, p. 41).

153. An illuminating example of this can be found in the work of the historian of ideas Karin Johannisson. In *Nostalgia. En känslas historia*, Stockholm 2001, she describes how nostalgia, in the course of the modern epoch, has changed from being a medical diagnosis to a social symptom and how this feeling has, in some instances, acquired meanings that are critical of civilisation while, in others, is channelled into a modern and rational view of society.

154. Pevsner, pp. 140–141. Although this expansion occurred primarily in France and the German and Italian states, a similar trend may be observed in the rest of Europe. In terms of organisation, exhibitions and the institution of competitions and prizes, the structure of almost all of these art academies was based on that of the Académie royale de Peinture et de Sculpture in Paris. The comprehensive nature of the expansion makes it possible to refer to the development of a particular discursive order and process of standardisation in relation to the public administration of the art world, even though the establishment of these academies would also have to be considered from the perspective of the different national contexts.

155. Pevsner, pp. 149–152.

156. One example is the changes in France during the First Republic. As a royal institution, the Académie royale de Peinture et de Sculpture was the target of fierce criticism. From 1791, the Salon was open to all French artists, and the exhibition was no longer under the monopoly control of the members of the Academy; its members formed, in fact, a minority on the jury appointed to evaluate the works submitted (Daniel M. Fox, "Artists in the Modern State: The Nineteenth-Century Background" (1963), in Milton Albrecht, James Barnett & Mason Griff (ed.), *The Sociology of Art and Literature*, London 1970, pp. 375–376). The aesthetic ideals of the Academy were also called into question, but this proved to be a sensitive issue: the new regime did not want the standard of the art exhibited to fall and so undermine the reputation of the republic (Wrigley, p. 44). The aesthetic requirements were thus upheld, even though the ideological guidelines were changed. In organisational terms, however, the entire system of the academies was changed in 1791 when a majority of the established institutions were amalgamated and subordinated to the

Institut de France. Its art section was given a name more in keeping with the times: the Académie des Beaux Arts. Under its aegis, artistic education was carried out at the École des Beaux Arts (Pevsner, pp. 199–200). The fundamental role played by the Academy within the art world and public administration nevertheless remained intact, and it even gained in importance during the Empire and was confirmed during the Restoration.

157. Various political upheavals, particularly in France, also influenced the composition, influence and ideology of the Academy. T. J. Clark describes, for example, how the revolution of 1848 created a vacuum in the art world, which was confronted with the major issue (as was, indeed, the case after the 1789 revolution) of what approach to art the new republic should embrace (see Clark 1973, pp. 31–71). The problem was there was no accepted aesthetic model with which to replace the established academic code. More reform-minded forces wanted to provide greater scope for Romantic or Realist artists, such as Eugene Delacroix, Honoré Daumier, François Rude and Auguste Préault, while others were intent on upholding the established values. The politicisation of the art world during the Empire and the rapid change of course that took place after the Restoration deterred many, no doubt, from defining themselves too explicitly in terms of a particular political orientation. In this phase, the Academy appears to have been made up of what was, in ideological terms, a relatively heterogeneous collection of individuals whose unifying characteristic, nevertheless, was that they had invested their careers in a particular system. Demolishing academic doctrine in its entirety would not only have risked creating aesthetic uncertainty or even decline (which the rulers of the republic were determined to avoid at all costs), also it would have demonstrated that the investments made by many of the key actors had been a failure. Moreover, the aesthetic preferences that prevailed in the developing private art market (which admittedly suffered a major decline during the period following the revolution) were based on particular norms defined by the academic code. Although the art policy of the Second Republic could not be said to have introduced a revolution of any kind, alternative aesthetic approaches were established during the four years it lasted, which would, in the long term (several decades later), undermine the monopoly position of the academic code together with its general legitimacy.

158. Although the increased economic importance of the visual arts provided a major incentive for the expansion of the academic system at the turn of the nineteenth century, when art schools and schools in the applied arts were, in many cases, amalgamated, an entirely opposite trend was also affecting the entire art world at the same time. Perhaps the most distinctive feature of nineteenth century art teaching was the segregation, rather, of these kinds of schools. In the case of some of the art academies, this meant that although elementary courses were set up in commercial art and design, the more advanced lessons were only open to those in training to become creative artists: a process that eventually laid the foundations for a more explicit separation between colleges of fine arts and those teaching craft and design (Pevsner, pp. 228–229). Although the cause of this change was primarily practical in nature, rather than an administrative matter, and reflected a growing social need for certified professional skills, this differentiation may also be considered in terms of the problem of the artistic identity in the new public sphere of the art world. In this new social and professional landscape, the distinction between fine art and applied art became increasingly important. The need for this distinction did not, however, involve a one-sided and patronising form of exclusion from the fine art establishment but was instead emphasised by both sides. By the mid-nineteenth century, there was a growing demand for the provision of a more practical and realistic form of training within the applied arts. However, education within the applied arts long remained influenced by the academic ideal, centred as it was on drawing. Growing dependence on machinery in manufacturing industry nevertheless entailed the end of the craft skills of previous epochs, and the need for better and more practical training within the design industry became increasingly pressing. The Great Exhibition held in London in 1851 may be considered a watershed in this debate to the extent that the first major international exhibition of the state of the applied arts led to criticism and reconsideration within both established and more radical circles. Referring explicitly to this exhibition, Gottfried Semper, for example, observed that the solution to the problems of the day lay in changing the taste and approach to art of the general public on the one hand, while raising the level of education on the other, by entrenching it in practical requirements through the introduction of on-site training and the creation of a better foundation for

aesthetic judgement by reconnecting education in Art with that in the applied forms (Gottfried Semper, *Wissenschaft, Industrie und Kunst. Vorschläge zur Anregung nationalen Kunstgefühles bei den Schlusse der Londoner Industrie-Ausstellung*, Braunschweig 1852, pp. 37–40 and pp. 61–62). A similar, if politically more radical, view of the social problem of the art industry was formulated somewhat later by William Morris, when he maintained that the commercialism and competitiveness of modern society were the cause of the decline of both the intellectual and the applied arts (for several key texts on these issues, see William Morris, *On Art and Socialism*, (Ed. Norman Kelvin), New York 1999).

159. Görts, p. 195. Tony Bennett interprets the development of the exhibitionary complex as a parallel to what Michel Foucault described as the modern society's apparatus for apportioning punishment ('the carceral archipelago'), which was designed at the same time, with both systems being seen as responding to a need on the part of the authorities for differentiation, control and order. With the considerable difference, however, that the direction of the disciplinary apparatus of the exhibitionary complex was the reverse of the modern prison's panopticon: instead of control by an invisible watchman, it provided control by making the ideals, principles and extent of the powers that be visible to the public. Surveillance in this case involved the legitimation by the official institutions of particular types of knowledge, codes and representations (see Tony Bennett, *The Birth of the Museum. History, Theory, Politics*, London 2002 (1995), pp. 59–69).

160. Anthony Giddens, *Modernity and Self-Identity. Self and Society in the Late Modern Age*, Cambridge 1991, pp. 2–3.

161. Pierre Bourdieu, *The Rules of Art. Genesis and Structure of the Literary Field*, (Trans. Susan Emanuel) Cambridge 1996 (1992), p. 141.

162. As a general metaphor, the concept of the avant-garde first entered use at the beginning of the nineteenth century in political and cultural contexts. Subsequently, both these contexts frequently appeared in such close proximity that the radical aesthetic vanguard was able to derive its forms of representation, rhetoric and legitimacy from the political and vice versa. A key etymological aspect, which lingered on from the military origins of the metaphor, was the idea

that a battle had to be fought against some form of enemy. According to Renato Poggioli, the notion of an avant-garde movement in France in the years prior to the Revolution of 1848 had a general, but nevertheless distinctly political, connotation, as part of which art was seen primarily as an instrument of social change; not until after 1870 was the concept used in a specifically cultural sense (Poggioli, p. 9). Nevertheless, the concept was not definitively separated into two distinct areas of meaning, and it would long embrace a link between art and politics. From then on, however, it was interpreted in various ways depending on which side employed it. As Matei Calinescu has convincingly demonstrated, the crucial distinction was that the aesthetic avant-garde emphasised the independent revolutionary potential of art whereas the political avant-garde saw art as being subordinate to the needs of politics (Calinescu, p. 105). These two diametrically opposed interpretations of the function of art in society were a source of confrontation throughout the nineteenth century wherever the political avant-garde (of left or right) managed to seize power.

163. Calinescu, p. 95.

164. The combining of descriptive and normative criteria in which the self-image of the avant-garde is interwoven with the characterisation of a historical reality is a recurrent problem in every analysis of the avant-garde. One example is provided by the four fundamental attitudes shared, in Renato Poggioli's view, by all the different avant-garde movements to a greater or lesser extent: activism (the pursuit of the unknown), antagonism (its counter-cultural position), nihilism (the desire to break with established norms) and agonism (heroic suffering) (see Poggioli, pp. 25–40, and pp. 61–77). Poggioli's survey helps to make comprehensible many of the apparently paradoxical phenomena within the different representations of the avant-garde, but it also creates a blueprint for the definition of the aesthetic avant-garde that is based entirely on its own self-image. The values that underpin a particular discursive position are simply taken for granted in the historical analysis of that position. A similar, though slightly different, problem arises with Peter Bürger's description of the avant-garde, in which he employs a highly restrictive definition of what the avant-garde is based on certain ideological criteria: the avant-garde equlans anti-aestheticising movements that are critical of institutions

and whose ideal model are the attacks by Dadaism (and Duchamps in particular) on the autonomy of the art work in bourgeois society (Bürger, pp. 47–54). Here, too, although the selection is more restrictive, particular historical values and identities are being taken for granted. As such, certain criteria are deduced from an empirical material and then allowed to form an *a priori* matrix for the interpretation of this material. As part of this process, exclusions are made (A is avant-garde, but not B), gradations arise (A is more avant-garde than B) and a vicious circle of descriptive and normative statements is allowed to determine the historical analysis. There is a clear need, in my view, for a sociological and historiographical analysis of this problematic context in which the issue of how a historical situation may actually be described is linked to the displacement of meaning between the concepts used and to the gradual normalisation of the judgements involved.

165. Thierry de Duve, *Kant after Duchamp*, Cambridge (Mass.) 1996, pp. 264–265.

166. For a discussion of the retrospective exhibition as a key 'language game' within modernism, see Clark, 1999, pp. 55–56.

167. Michel Foucault, "The Order of Discourse", (Trans. Ian McLeod) in Robert Young (ed.), *Untying the Text. A Post-Structuralist Reader*, Boston (Mass.) 1981, p. 60.

168. Michel Foucault, *The Archeology of Knowlege*, (Trans. A. M. Sheridan Smith) London 2001 (1972), p. 173.

169. Boime, s. 14 ff.

PART II
THE NORMALISATION OF THE AVANT-GARDE

The rise and fall of modernism does not . . . simply tell us something of what we have become. It does, in a way, but it also tells us how we have come to understand or interpret ourselves, and so it introduces a question as well as a historical event. The question concerns the potential fragility or distortion of the narratives that generate these "grand categories". [1]

Robert B. Pippin, *Modernism as a Philosophical Problem* (1991)

Benjamin's "aura" may wither away in the age of mechanical reproduction but authenticity remains. What is made more explicit, more transparent, by the so-called "dematerialization" of the object, is that *the production of authenticity requires more than an author for the object; it exacts the "truth" of the authorial discourse*.[2]

Mary Kelly, 'Re-viewing Modernist Criticism' (1981)

The Struggle for Interpretive Privilege

Complex Settings

Distinguishing the particular moment or event that constitutes a definitive turning point is a problem in many historical accounts. Frequently, the attempt to pinpoint the exact cause and date of comprehensive and complex changes appears to be essential to the analysis and, on occasion, even its goal. The need to distinguish such critical junctures is linked to some extent at least to the desire to explain a complex phenomenon by means of a coherent and effective account whose linear structure requires a fixed beginning and end. An event derived from empirical historical data that exemplifies in startling fashion something whose impact extends far beyond its factual determinants is fixed on—and transformed into—a metaphor with an extraordinary rhetorical force. Such widely disseminated mythical notions as the birth of Renaissance Man with Petrarch's ascent of Mont Ventoux in 1335, the beginning of the modern era with the outbreak of the French Revolution in 1789, and the start of the First World War with the shots in Sarajevo in 1914 may be considered to form part of this intellectual pattern. Charles Jenck's description of the death of modern architecture with the demolition of Minoru Yamasaki's 'Pruitt-Igoe Housing' in St. Louis on 15 July 1972 at 3.32 pm could also serve as an extreme (and, it must be hoped, ironic) example.[3]

How to cite this book chapter:
Hayden, Hans. 2018. The Struggle for Interpretive Privilege. In: Hayden, H. *Modernism as Institution: On the Establishment of an Aesthetic and Historiographic Paradigm* Pp. 135–163. Stockholm: Stockholm University Press. DOI: https://doi.org/10.16993/bar.d. License: CC-BY

A revolutionary or apocalyptic narrative of this kind risks, however, becoming a violation of history by historiography, with the need for simplification and distillation excluding more gradual processes and interconnections that are inevitably polysemous and harder to understand. The problem is one that is ever-present in this study as well. How is one to distinguish and describe the institutionalisation of modernism as a distinct historical phenomenon without falling into the trap of the revolutionary narrative? The simple, if rather unoriginal, answer—although the appropriate one in my view—is to emphasise that aspect of the phenomenon to do with process in order to compose a story that develops out of a number of different but reciprocally determined fragments, perspectives and nodal points, rather than as a linear structure with a fixed beginning and end. To risk abandoning the effectiveness of the revolutionary narrative in favour of an attempt to formulate a connection between continuity and discontinuity is of crucial importance here. To that end, I would like to highlight two different periods that were of decisive importance for the process under discussion: the 1930s until the Second World War and the post-war period until the second half of the 1950s.

This process should not, however, be seen as a straightforward chronological course of events that encompassed the gradual acceptance of modernism and was only interrupted by World War Two. As stages in this process, the pre- and post-war periods were quite different in kind, while the experience of both the war and the terror practised by the dictatorships clearly played a significant role in the institutionalisation that took place in the post-war period. That difference may, of course, be described solely as an aesthetic matter, but it can also be understood in political terms. In *After the Great Divide* (1986), Andreas Huyssen has analysed how the divide reconfigured the relationship between the avant-garde and mass culture and how, under the influence of the general political situation of the 1930s, it generated a need for an elitist and exclusive cultural discourse:

> I would suggest that the primary place of what I am calling the great divide was the age of Stalin and Hitler when the threat of totalitarian control over all culture forged a variety of defensive

strategies meant to protect high culture in general, not just modernism. Thus conservative culture critics such as Ortega y Gasset argued that high culture needed to be protected from the "revolt of the masses". Left critics like Adorno insisted that genuine art resist its incorporation into the capitalist culture industry which he defined as the total administration of culture from above. And even Lukács, the left critic of modernism *par excellence*, developed his theory of high bourgeois realism not in unison with but in antagonism to the Zhdanovist dogma of socialist realism and its deadly practice of censorship.[4]

The gradual institutionalisation of the avant-garde served, in other words, as a link between the decades before and after the Second World War. However, the situation in the post-war period was qualitatively different in that the historical avant-garde was no longer presented as a marginal phenomenon but as the unquestioned art-form of the twentieth century. This multifaceted process involved not only a codification of the avant-garde as modernism and the widespread inculcation of the essential difference between Art and popular culture, but also a greater emphasis on the development of modernism *qua* the development of modern art. The course of this process, its rhetoric and gradual shifts, is crucial to understanding the institutionalisation of modernism. Before analysing the process of institutionalisation in the post-war period, I begin by setting out two different perspectives on the situation of modernism and modern art during the second half of the 1930s. The first is based on one of the last major world exhibitions before the outbreak of war, the second on two minor texts published on the margins of the established culture.

****

The *Exposition Internationale des Arts et Techniques dans la Vie Moderne* held in Paris in 1937 has gone down in history, perhaps primarily, as a symbolic showdown between the two major European dictatorships. Like two menacing monoliths, the pavilions of the Soviet Union and Nazi Germany stood facing each other at the very centre of the Fair, between the Eiffel Tower and the Palais de Chaillot. In the light of subsequent history, the image of their location opposite one another has been considered an omen of the dreadful acts of war that would characterise the relationship between these countries a few years later. The German and Soviet pavilions were, in fact, constructed at the very time negotiations were being conducted to create a nonaggression pact between the two states.[5] Such posthumous symbolism, however, also encompassed the small, and in terms of its relation to those of the other two countries, somewhat overshadowed, Spanish pavilion. Represented here by the Republican side, Spain, which had been so afflicted by civil war, was making its final international appearance before Franco's seizure of power and had chosen to show a painting that has become the stuff of legend for many reasons: Pablo Picasso's 'Guernica'. In this scenario, what history later proved one of the most important art-political tropes of the post-war period—modernism as the symbolic champion of liberty in the face of repression and dictatorship—was manifested in a single painting.

The extensive exhibitions of historical and modern art mounted by France, the host nation, have been all but eclipsed by this fateful and dramatic image. Nonetheless, the fair provides a number of interesting clues to the situation of modernism prior to the outbreak of war. The most prestigious exhibition, *Chefs-d'œuvre de l'Art Français*, was arranged by the French state and shown at the Palais de Tokio. It comprised some 1300 works of art and objects spanning two millennia of French art history, concluding with the Impressionist and post-Impressionist painting of the late nineteenth century. The show emphasised the great tradition of French art and its universal and authoritative value with nationalist bravura.[6] Attention had been drawn during the planning phase to the fact that this comprehensive exposé came to a stop just before the contemporary period, and this led the government to arrange an additional art exhibition in the Petit Palais entitled *Les Maîtres de l'Art Indépendant, 1895–1937*, which was made up of over 1500 works. Shown here—and with the emphasis on the movements based on Fauvism and Cubism—were works that eventually came to be seen as constituting the accepted canon of modernist art, although now the majority of the 117 chosen artists are not considered to form part of the representative and canonical selection of modernism.[7]

In the entrance hall, the visitor encountered a pair of sculptures by Emile-Antoine Bourdelle and a large collection of plaster-casts and bronzes by Charles Despiau (52 works) and Mateo Hernandez (26 works). He or she then proceeded around an inner circle of galleries, which alternated the showing of works by a group or by a single artist. Those apostrophised as modern masters, inasmuch as they were accorded a room of their own with space for 30 or so works, included Maurice de Vlaminck, André Derain, Georges Rouault, Maurice Denis and Pierre Bonnard, while Henri Matisse (61 works) and Aristide Maillol (60 works) were accorded one large and three smaller halls, respectively. Having toured the inner galleries, visitors found themselves in a room in one of the wings, where some relatively radical works, or perhaps ones that were simply harder to categorise, were on show. The artists on display here included Auguste Herbin, Jacques Villon, Francis Picabia, Giorgio de Chirico, Gino Severini, Max Ernst, Chaim Soutine and Marc Chagall. From this room, the visitor was then led into an outer sequence of galleries made up of somewhat smaller halls in which the leading names of Cubism were exhibited: Roger de la Fresnaye, Georges Braque, André Lothe, Fernand Léger, Maria Blanchard, Pablo Picasso, Juan Gris, Ossip Zadkine, Henri Laurens and Jacques Lipchitz. The tour was not simply an innocent stroll through the world of modern art; it involved a carefully calculated and normative choreography of the visitor's route: from the post-Impressionist and Fauvist traditions toward more or less experimental variants of Cubism. Movements, that is, which could all be inscribed within the great School of France.

Although its selection was also geared towards French art, the rhetoric of *Les Maîtres* was of a very different kind to that of *Chefs d'œuvre*. In the former exhibition, Paris was asserting its cosmopolitan character as a city by highlighting the independence of the modernist tradition from the official establishment. This was emphasized even more clearly at the exhibition *Origines et développement de l'art international*, mounted at the Jeu de Paume, which described the development of the international avant-garde in terms of various movements (Fauvism, Cubism, Dadaism, Surrealism, Constructivism, Abstraction), while accentuating the significance of Primitivism for modern art in particular. Taken together, the exhibitions and the various national pavilions provided what would have been at the time an unequalled opportunity to acquaint oneself with modernism in all its guises.

It was *Chefs d'œuvre* and *Les Maîtres*, however, that jointly established a paradigm for the national programme of France at the World Fair. Despite their obvious differences, a continuity between the exhibitions can be discerned on a more abstract level: at the point where the two selections meet in the late nineteenth century. The compatibility of the two chronologies made it possible to assert the existence of an evolutionary trend that underlined the importance of France in various ways for the development of art in general and modern art in particular. This meeting point could also be described in terms of continuities: with the older canon representing the continuity of tradition, while the contemporary selection revealed a continuity of individualism. James Herbert has described this complex interplay as stemming from two different standpoints, both of which tended to marginalize the academic tradition:

> Where the Chefs-d'œuvre de l'Art Français gave no real play to the old chestnut about the battle between hackneyed academic technique and fresh artistic innovation – indeed, its defenders tended to discount the importance of the Academy in the development of true French art over the centuries – the chief organizer of the Les Maîtres de l'Art Indépendant resuscitated that distinction in order to declare the city of Paris the defender of novel and important work produced since 1895.[8]

By this time, the academic tradition had disappeared from both the official version of the art history of the modern age and the somewhat less official one as well. To point to the disappearance of the Académie des Beaux-Arts from the historical narrative of modern art is not, however, the same as saying that its role as an institutional centre of power in the French art world had been played out; rather, academic discourse had for various reasons been gradually excluded from the historiographic record. This took place at the same time various forms of modernist art were becoming an increasingly accepted part of the official art world, a state of affairs emphasised by the architecture and exhibitions of art on display in many of the other national pavilions.

The open functionalist building and exclusively modernist art of the Spanish pavilion was not, however, representative of the rest of Europe: although modernism had been accepted, it was not the dominant element on show at the World Fair. The works chosen for exhibition in *Les Maîtres* provoked fierce criticism from politically conservative circles and from what was at that time the still influential academic establishment. In their view, the one-sided apostrophe of modernism was tantamount to a betrayal of the fundamental values represented by the noble French tradition.[9] In this respect, the particular selections made for these two exhibitions could also be seen as a key indicator of the way in which the French state was apparently unwilling to engage with the complexity and potentially subversive nature of modern art; whereas, the city of Paris considered *avantgardiste* contemporary art and cultural life to be one of the most important components of its identity.

While the avant-garde as a phenomenon may have been considered a positive symbolic value, this should not be taken to mean that this value encompassed all parts of the avant-garde subculture. After all, the works selected for *Les Maîtres* excluded not only academic art, but also the more ideologically and aesthetically aggressive (not to say transgressive) movements within modernism: Futurism, Dadaism and Surrealism. The exclusion of Surrealism in particular sent an unmistakable signal in the arena of art politics, because this movement was a vital and high-profile force on the contemporary French art scene.[10] These movements were not entirely censored, however: they could be included in an international event but not serve as representations of the great French tradition. Although the clearly official nature of this signal might be considered a failure for the Surrealist movement, it was entirely in keeping with the anti-bourgeois attitude of André Breton and his compatriots, an attitude on display in Paris just a few months after the closure of the World Fair at the *Exposition Internationale du Surréalisme* in 1938.[11]

The increasing acceptance of the art and theory of modernism did not amount to its integration as a self-evident component of the normative political and cultural structures of the western democracies in the years leading up to the outbreak of war. Like open and democratic society as a whole, modernism was confronted with the immediate and very real threat posed by the two totalitarian blocks. The exposed position of the Spanish pavilion was a metaphor not just for the heroism of modern art, but also for the reality of the political situation.

It was this particular state of affairs that provided the background to Walter Benjamin's 'Das Kunstwerk im Zeitalter seiner technischen Reproduzierbarkeit' (1936) and Clement Greenberg's 'Avantgarde and Kitsch' (1939). Both essays were written from ideological standpoints informed by a Marxist analysis of society and culture, and both may be considered reactions to what many perceived to be an acute crisis in the cultural life of the time. This was a crisis with political and aesthetic consequences and one that came about as a result of changes in the nature of the perceived threats, domestic and foreign. The external and most tangible threat was the triumphal progress of European fascism and Nazism, but another kind of threat existed, too, from within the mechanisms of capitalist society, which meant that the avant-garde had to legitimate and reformulate its art in line with a changed social reality. The problem both these essays describe was the risk of eradication facing the tradition of progressive art as it had existed to this time. But their respective solutions to the problem appeared to be diametrically opposed.

Benjamin describes how the techniques of reproduction in the modern age, photography and film in particular, have introduced a potentially subversive and substantive change in the perception of the unique nature of the work of art, of its aura, which in turn calls into question its traditional authority and authenticity.[12] This change is linked to a transformation in the social and perceptual patterns of the modern age, as part of which, perception has increasingly shifted from the observation of the unique to a sense of the similar. The sacrosanct connection of the aura and a unique here and now has been replaced by a secularised function, everywhere and everywhen as it were. In this situation, film appears to be a much more relevant medium than the ancient art of the easel:

Magician and surgeon compare to painter and cameraman. The painter maintains in his work a natural distance from reality, the cameraman penetrates deeply into its web. There is a tremendous difference between the pictures they obtain. That of the painter is a total one, that of the cameraman consists of multiple fragments which are assembled under a new law. Thus for contemporary man the representation of reality by the film is incomparably more significant than that of the painter, since it offers, precisely because of the thoroughgoing permeation of reality with mechanical equipment, an aspect of reality which is free of all equipment. And that is what one is entitled to ask from a work of art.[13]

Unlike the unique work of art, film (like the mechanical reproduction of images) offers a social context of collective consumption, a new form of social participation that has to be affirmed by progressive forces but is continually under threat from the manipulations of fascism and capitalism. The metaphor of the magician and surgeon is used by Benjamin to highlight the need for a radical break with tradition in particular, as the definition of modern art can no longer be contained within the regime of authenticity. Although he cites Dadaism as an example of painting still being able to fulfil a function even within this changed situation, that function, as he sees it, requires an acceptance of the necessity of the technology of reproduction if it is to respond to the changing needs of the modern age. The Dadaist artist, therefore, deliberately obliterates one of the key characteristics of the tradition, (the aura of the work), by 'branding' his work as 'a reproduction' by dint of its 'means of production.'[14]

Clement Greenberg, too, was fully aware of these altered circumstances. As we saw earlier, he describes the avant-garde as a specific territory within cultural life. He saw it as the only area, in fact, that remains unaffected by the harmful consequences of modernisation and still characterised by an authentic form of expression.[15] It is in this sense that the history of the avant-garde can be described as a kind of critical awareness, a function almost of modernity's progressive and emancipating tradition of ideas. Greenberg draws a distinction here between the educated elite (which supports progressive culture) and the great masses (which have always been indifferent to it); this parallels his most important distinction between the avant-garde and kitsch. For Greenberg, the difference between these domains was not just a difference of degree, between good and bad art, but a distinction in kind: whereas avant-garde art imitates artistic processes, kitsch imitates their effects.[16] The avant-garde, defined as the higher critical awareness of bourgeois culture, must constitute a preserve set off from the rest of the culture, in which the efforts made by artists to investigate the specific preconditions of their own media inevitably result in an art that is cut off from the society around it and the unpredictable chaos of popular culture. An interesting conflation also occurs in Greenberg's text when the description of the historical situation shifts to the contemporary scene: this concerns the adaptation of the superficial and rigid eclecticism of the academic tradition to the demands of the market and modernisation and its transformation into an equally false and mechanical version of the parasitisation of the forms of the living culture perpetrated by industrial popular culture.[17]

Greenberg is entirely in agreement with Benjamin that the new ways of using images introduced by popular culture constitute a threat to authentic art. This is not a situation Greenberg embraces, however. He focuses instead on the essential duties of the elites in relation to modern society: the educated economic elite has to shoulder its responsibility and support the tiny elite of artists who are still working beyond the influence of capitalist culture and its dumbing-down of key values. Advanced avant-garde art can only be identified by its qualities as a unique work of art and by its capacity to reflect critically on the conditions of its own medium. His view of modern art actually involves an even greater emphasis on the necessity of authenticity.

Benjamin's and Greenberg's essays represent two possible approaches to the state and future development of the contemporary visual arts at the end of the 1930s. These two texts could hardly be more dissimilar in the way they formulate the problem: where the former expands the domain of the visual arts so as to abolish the boundary between different media and between Art and art, the latter shrinks the definition of avant-garde art to an extremely restricted area within visual culture, drawing clear distinctions between it and both other media and mass culture. Although neither essay was widely read in its own time, both have since emerged as key texts in the art debate of the twentieth century. In terms of their reception in the last few decades, Walter Benjamin's essay is considered to be one of the most important historical documents concerning a change in the perception of art and one that still possesses an astonishing and almost prophetic topicality for the art world of today. Clement Greenberg's text, in contrast, serves as one of the key documents for an approach to aesthetics and history from which postmodernist theorists have been keen to distance themselves. How are we then to explain that in the period contemporary with these essays, particularly after the end of the Second World War, it was Greenberg's type of response that was considered to have real significance rather than Benjamin's?

It would be easy to respond to this question using the narratives of modernism itself to the effect that Benjamin was before his time or history has proved him right. But if we refrain from this kind of naive mythologizing, we can see instead that his version of events failed to fit in to the political, social and aesthetic process of change that the art world was undergoing in the middle of the twentieth century. The approaches of Benjamin and Greenberg correspond to two powerful trends in the art world and visual culture of that time, which might be called critical utilitarianism and autonomous individualism, respectively. These trends reflected two diametrically opposed attitudes to the function of the visual arts in modern society that could not be contained within the same institutional framework.

In his analysis of the political function of the visual arts, Benjamin made a telling distinction between Fascism's 'aestheticisation of political life' and the response of Communism, which was to 'politicise art'.[18] His analysis is based on a vision as to how art should be integrated into modern socialist society as a clearly defined function of its workings, not simply as a tool for the powers that be, but because of its critical potential for the enlightenment and activation of the masses. Here Benjamin is radicalising and developing further an aspect of the progressive utilitarianism of the Russian avant-garde in the years following the Revolution, whose manifestos called for the casting off of all forms of bourgeois culture and Art in what we have described as one of the most radical attempts to break away from the regime of authenticity. In terms of realpolitik, the problem with Benjamin's view was that it presupposed a situation in which art had been institutionalised within the socialist state; whereas, that same state had, in fact, liquidated critical utilitarianism. Benjamin's essay was published two years after Socialist Realism had been made the official doctrine of the Soviet Union and in the same year that the Moscow show trials were first held. Apart from its political and historical drawbacks, it also failed to conform to every legitimate form of political discourse in the bipolar structure that obtained after the Second World War, and, within which, critical utilitarianism in the Benjamin mould seemed to be an ideological formulation of modern art whose time had passed and that no one could possibly support.

In contrast, Greenberg's view appeared to be entirely in keeping with the political landscape of the post-war West. Far from presupposing a subversive Utopian vision, it amounted, instead, to an apology for the individualised and autonomous existence of high art in capitalist society. And these were the very aspects that proved crucial to the institutionalisation and normalisation of the avant-garde in Western Europe and the United States. There was an additional element in his essay that turned out to be of decisive importance for this process: it established a link between the contemporary world and the historical one. According to this interpretative matrix, the once radical and revolutionary avant-garde could be adapted to the already existing institutional structure of the art world: it was depoliticised, made to fit within a chronology and its ideological connotations were partially realigned in terms of freedom and individualism (as opposed to antagonism, activism and collectivism). Even though radical art might still be perceived as difficult, offensive and politically questionable, the idea of the autonomy of the work of art so long cherished by the avant-garde now served a new ideological purpose: to legitimate a particular type of action and representation in a purely aesthetic context, cut off from any obvious political connection.

The aesthetics of disparity that developed as a defence against various repressive regimes during the 1930s thus emerges as the model applied in the West during the post-war period: a disparity that concerned not only the relationship between Art and mass culture, but also the Cold War bipolar structure of two antithetical ideological systems. This was also the context in which the cluster of aesthetic social and ideological concepts of the historical avant-garde was labelled (and thus transformed into) modernism.

There can be no question that the process of institutionalisation and normalisation modernism underwent after the Second World War saw modern art assume a new ideological function in the West, with the result that one type of definition became possible, while another did not. In this context, ideological does not necessarily mean 'false consciousness' but should be understood rather as a 'socially necessary illusion' and as an 'interaction between philosophical theories and political power'.[19] A new form of socially necessary illusion was needed to make possible the problematic encounter between culture and counterculture—an encounter in which certain accepted ideas were legitimated, generalised and historicised, while others were excluded. In this respect, the World Fair held in Paris in 1937 signalled, as did the essays by Benjamin and Greenberg, a distinct historical shift in the situation of modern art, both within the domains of established culture and within the avant-garde. The nature of this shift must be understood to make possible an interpretation of the institutionalisation of modernism in the political and social context of the post-war period and the Cold War.

Although the notion of the avant-garde of modern art was, of course, not abandoned, the social function and descriptive significance of the term—as characterising a countercultural identity within contemporary discourse—were largely transformed into a historicising narrative of the heroic and tragic alienation of modern art. The myth of the artist as a misunderstood genius, struggling to create his or her own truth in the face of the ignorance of the surrounding world, became a central trope in the popularisation of the historical avant-garde in particular. This trope has been described by Donald Preziosi as crucial not only to the ideological formulation of the identity of modernism in public contexts, but also to interpretive practice in art criticism and art history as a whole. He exemplifies this state of affairs with reference to the 1956 film *Lust for Life* about the life and work of Vincent van Gogh:

The artist-hero ... is also revealed as a filter or aesthetic mediator, refracting the prose of the world into poetry; he is a distillator of the Essential from the world in which we live. In this refractive regime, the artwork is framed as a record or a trace of the artist's originality and individuality. Indeed, the film indicates that the measurable difference or distance between painted image and encatalyzing scene is isomorphic with the artist's degree of difference from the mundane world of the ordinary mortal – an iconic sign of artistic genius. As that distance changes, so too does that genius change and grow. Vincent's life is presented as a journey of growth from realism to naturalism to abstraction: a quest for the essential or higher reality increasingly different from the ordinary.[20]

This is an extremely condensed, and perhaps somewhat exaggerated, description of the process entailed in the post-war normalisation of the art and culture of the avant-garde in which the genre (popular artist biographies), the originator (a vast Hollywood production) and the intercultural identification (Kirk Douglas *is* Vincent van Gogh) constitute a circulation of levels of meaning to a much broader target group. The date of the production of the film and of its premiere are indicative both of this state of affairs and the way in which key aspects of what constituted the ideology of modernism at this time had become public property. However, what is really interesting here is the paradoxical meeting between elite culture and popular culture. This film about van Gogh brought about a popular-cultural dissemination of certain modernist myths at the same time that modernism was being legitimated as an aesthetic of disparity, whose boundaries were clearly defined in opposition to the cultural industry.

This example is also rather telling in relation to the difficulty involved in incorporating the countercultural identities of the avant-garde within the dominant culture's system of norms. This triumph of the avant-garde was not, according to Serge Guilbaut, a total or even particularly popular victory, but amounted rather to a 'typical avant-garde victory, that is to say, fragile and ambiguous, since it was constantly threatened by opposing tendencies in the world of art.'[21] There was, in fact, a fierce debate after the end of the Second World War about how the relation between art and society could and should be perceived, with particular reference to the function of modernist art in modern society. While this debate took place all over the world, its nature was, of course, determined by the specific situation that characterised each particular domain, ranging from the ideology of individual political parties to more general issues to do with modernity, democracy, tradition and humanism.

The Criteria of Normalisation

An exhibition entitled *documenta* opened in the West German city of Kassel on 15 July 1955. This exhibition was inaugurated slightly more than two months after the Allied occupation officially came to an end and the Federal Republic became a fully sovereign state. The choice of location was not a matter of chance. Kassel had been one of the cities worst affected by Allied bombing raids.[22] The former capital of the kingdom of Westphalia was situated at the centre of Germany and had also been chosen because it could represent any German city, a fairly important, but by no means exceptional, industrial town in the state of Hessen. Undergoing reconstruction on an extensive scale at the time, Kassel had a certain historical importance but lacked any symbolic resonance with the Third Reich. With the drawing of the new boundary between the two Germanies, it had also acquired a new political significance as an outpost to the East, because it lay only 30 kilometres from the border with the GDR.[23] The exhibition was mounted in the bomb-damaged Museum Fridericanum, which had not yet been restored.

The driving force behind the exhibition was Arnold Bode; he was assisted by a committee made up of representatives from government and industry, as well as individuals with art-historical and museal expertise. *Documenta's* patron was the West German president Theodor Heuss, and it was organised in collaboration with an honorary committee made up of prominent West German politicians and envoys from the Western nations.[24] In addition to West Germany, the participating countries were France, Italy, the Netherlands, Switzerland, Great Britain and the United States. *Documenta* thus became a national demonstration—sanctioned at the highest level—of the reestablishment of the ties between Germany and the Western democracies.

The exhibition comprised 570 works by 148 artists and was divided into two levels: history and the present. The ideologue behind this form of presentation was the art historian Werner Haftmann, who had published a comprehensive historical survey of twentieth-century modernist painting in the preceding year.[25] The focus of the show was an exhaustive survey of the tradition of modernism in art and architecture, to which a smaller exhibition of contemporary, especially nonfigurative, art was added.

Documenta may have been a temporary exhibition, but it highlighted many aspects of the problems facing the modern art museum. The exhibition was also entitled 'the Museum of One Hundred Days'; a label that has served to define it ever since: creating, as it did, an institutional framework for the presentation and interpretation of modern art by virtue of its sheer scale and its authoritative interpretation of the relationship between the contemporary and the historical. Although not aimed at creating a permanent collection, the selection—the temporary collection—made a significant impact on the contemporary art world and its perception of the historical. The various *documenta* exhibitions, like the biennales in Venice and São Paulo, have come to be seen as an index of how different trends succeed one another and how ideological positions become established within the institutionalised awareness of modern art.

It was no coincidence that the exhibition acquired this particular structure. The historical section was not simply an art-historical survey but, in its particular context, made reference to *Entartete Kunst*, the peripatetic exhibition mounted by the Nazi regime that opened in Munich in 1937.[26] *Documenta* could be seen as a means of reclaiming history, and as a result of its officially sanctioned status, the exhibition came to exemplify the way art and culture were viewed by the new German democracy. Wilhelm Lehmbruck's sculpture 'Knieende' (1911), for instance, was given a prominent location; it was the same sculpture the Nazis had been so keen to ridicule eighteen years earlier.[27] Great pains were taken, however, to ensure that the exhibition did not take on the stamp of official doctrine. Screens with photographs of the participating artists were set up in the exhibition halls, as if to display the individual behind the work. This could be seen as a direct response to the demonisation of the modern artist by the Third Reich: he would be on show here as a heroic figure and an autonomous agent who, despite difficult or even inhuman circumstances, had created the masterworks of our time.

Two contrasting but synergistic interpretive matrices in modernism's own historiography were being fixed in place here: on the one hand, a historical understanding of the development of modern art as an evolutionary process governed by an immanent logic and, on the other, an accentuation of the responsiveness, initiative and energy of the individual in modern society. A fundamental paradox may be perceived in this bipartite matrix with the supra-individual, contextless and incomprehensible nature of progress appearing to conflict with the reflexive individuality of modernity. Furthermore, a state of tension between both these narrative starting points—evolutionism and individualism, respectively—characterises large parts of modernist historiography.

But the emphasis on the creativity of the individual was not without risks of its own. This notion comes close, after all, to what modernism's most vehement critics had once used as a springboard for discrediting or entirely eliminating avantgardiste counterculture: the artist as a Bohemian and a transgressor of boundaries, outside the norms of society but in touch with areas beyond the normal or the natural or, to put it another way, the myth of the modern artist as a genius bordering on madness, who possesses the capacity to establish a mystical connection to the primeval, primitive sources that have been lost in modern civilisation. This is the context in which Walter Grasskamp described the interest in primitivism, exoticism and the art of the sick as the 'perilous sources' of modernism.[28] The prime example of this entire area of concern—and its watershed—was *Entartete Kunst*, which made direct comparisons between radical modernism and photographs of deformed human beings, images created by the mentally ill and works from primitive cultures, all with the aim of demonstrating the decline of modern art and decadence of the modern artist. The comparisons drawn by the Nazis should, however, be considered the culmination of a long process of heaping suspicion on modern art.[29]

The problem that arose for the champions of modernism after the war was how to deal with these associations with the irrational.

A connection with those perilous sources was something many artists and critics were keen to embrace, but it was that very connection that risked reactivating the suspicions of the general public towards what might be perceived as humbug or incomprehensible ravings. In the case of *documenta,* this also involved taking a stand in relation to recent history. One of Haftmann's fundamental theses, which existed as a subtext in 1955 but would characterise the next *documenta* of 1959 to a much more considerable extent, was that abstraction served as a *lingua franca* of the visual arts.[30] This made it possible to interpret contemporary art on the basis of the same universal explanatory model—irrespective of individual, national or cultural peculiarities—as a distinctive mode of existential expression for the modern age. But the formalist and existential model also had a diachronic dimension. In addition to the screens displaying artists' photographs at *documenta* 1955, there were others showing art from all four corners of the world and from all of history. Therefore, modern art was linked at an abstract level to history, with the result that modern art's potential aesthetically and politically subversive content was transferred to a world of formal, universal and archaicising correspondences that went beyond any historically and culturally specific context, transcending time and place.[31]

Two ideological tropes can be discerned behind these trends in the presentation of the exhibition: individualism and evolutionism. Whereas the accentuation of the individual involved rehabilitating the identity of the modern artist, the evolutionist trend was concerned with neutralising the dubious ideological and potentially revolutionary associations of modern art. The spatial borders these images were provided with contributed further to this neutralisation inasmuch as the white walls and the aestheticising hang asserted the autonomy of the individual work and its purely visual qualities— the price being that every link to the surrounding world appeared to have been sundered.

At *documenta,* this form of presentation had an obvious ideological function: reestablishing modernism/history and demonstrating the freedom of movement (intellectual and physical) of the individual in the Western democracies. It also called attention to the need for a democratic state to engage not only with art that was contemporary, but also with that of the avant-garde. Although the exhibition may be seen as an official legitimation of modernism, it also involved an aestheticisation of the position of the avant-garde, with every manifest or latent form of political connotation being dressed up in art. A number of fundamental ideological values were presented here that continually recur (although in different ways) in the artistic discourse of the western world after the Second World War: restoration, individuality, freedom and modernity. And the form this took clearly coincided with the cultural and political goals of the federal chancellor Konrad Adenauer and the policy of the victorious powers: to reestablish both the political and economic system and the structure of the cultural values of the democratic state, so as to integrate the German Federal Republic into the Western democratic hemisphere.[32] In a nutshell, the avant-garde had to be depoliticised if it were to be made useful for political ends.[33]

While the process of normalisation may be considered global in extent within the Western (or non-Communist) hemisphere, its nature and effects varied between different nations and regions. Although the bipolar structure of the Cold War provided a similar stimulus for the association of modernism with individuality, freedom and modernity in all the Western countries, culturally specific differences could be concealed in the interpretation of these values. Irrespective of the regionally and culturally determined variations, it was the story of the victor that was being written here. Worth noting in this regard is the extraordinary efficiency with which the modern institutions carried out their classification: one and the same historical scheme appeared to lie behind a multiplicity of different reproductions, thus establishing a genealogy of modernism that effectively ruled out ambivalence of any kind through various forms of exclusion and neutralisation.

This shift was not, however, unquestioned, and it did not take place over a single night. Just as we saw in the development of modernism and the time frames concerned, it involved the combination of a diffuse process with a critical juncture. Neither did this process of normalisation take place in silence: it was the subject of much debate after World War Two, particularly within the circles of avant-garde art itself. An example from the beginning of the 1960s is found in German cultural critic Hans Magnus Enzensberger's description of what he called the dilemma or self-contradiction of the avant-garde:

> Every avant-garde of today spells repetition, deception, or self-deception. The movement as a doctrinairely conceived collective, as invented fifty or thirty years ago for the purpose of shattering the resistance of a compact society, did not survive the historic conditions that elicited it. Conspiring in the name of the arts is only possible when they are being suppressed. An avant-garde that suffers itself to be furthered by the state has forfeited its rights. . . . It deals in a future that does not belong to it. Its moment is regression. The avant-garde has become its opposite: anachronism.[34]

It is true that the problem he was formulating applied to the legitimacy of radical art in his own time. And the dilemma could be said to have been that of the state as much as that of the avant-garde: the difficulty faced by the latter in legitimating its newly acquired position can be linked with the problem confronting various authorities in legitimating an art that, in essence, rejected the very legitimacy of the authorities in question. Enzensberger was not, however, the first—and certainly not the last—to make this observation about the dilemma of the avant-garde. In fact, the idea of the problematic position of the avant-garde, its death and possible resurrection, was a recurrent trope in the diagnoses by the art world of its own contemporary period ever since the 1960s.

Another example is provided by the literary critic Leslie Fielder, who referred to the death of the literary avant-garde at the beginning of the 1960s, although not in terms of loss or a necessary resurrection, but rather as a natural part of a progression in which the antagonistic strategies of yesterday become a form of entertainment for the middle class, with the result that any attempt to resist the establishment through new ways of violating taboos is almost immediately transformed into the kitsch of the cultural industry. William Burroughs' desert island is transformed into a densely populated suburb.[35]

To radical parts of the American art world in particular, the avant-garde appeared to be an antiquated historical remnant of a Europe that had vanished, an irrelevant anachronism as far as contemporary artistic practice was concerned. In 'Notes on Camp', Susan Sontag provides a telling description of how various types of social, sexual and aesthetic subcultures transgress the boundaries that separate them from one another and from the various levels (high as well as low) of the normative culture in a way that appears almost to exclude the very idea of an avantgardiste and openly antagonistic counterculture.[36] The interpretive horizon established by postmodernism at the end of the 1970s was clearly associated with the trope about the death of the avant-garde: the idea of a radical pluralism appearing to have replaced the idea of an antagonistic avant-garde as the leading trope of the narrative of contemporary art. At the same time, several of the leading actors of the art world attempted in various ways to define other forms of (neo-)avantgardiste positions so that the potential for contemporary art to criticise institutions not be entirely lost in the economic, institutional and mass-medial expansion of the market-oriented ideologies.[37]

The fact that the issue remained so obviously topical in the 1980s and 1990s is one of the clearest indicators of how comprehensive the significance the notion of modernism as institution and narrative has been for the interpretation of modern and contemporary art. In this context, the dilemma of the avant-garde appears to be a dilemma of critical categories and historical narratives: the extent to which the interpretation of the contemporary period is still determined by the discursive criteria of modernism. The issue also has much to tell us about the extraordinarily crucial role played by the notions of antagonism and critical alienation in the modernist conception of modern art. An artist or critic of the 1850s would presumably have been utterly astonished by the entire discussion. It also raises a number of additional questions. In particular, how are we to understand what happens when representatives of the most critical margins of the culture move in towards the heartlands of the official institutions and establish themselves there? This is, of course, a matter that has been the subject of countless analyses and theories, but how is this movement and the kind of institutional change involved to be understood from a historical perspective?

The Issue of the Function of Modern Art

Just as it did before the war, the reaction against modernism occurred at both ends of the political spectrum in the post-war period. The principal demand made by the Marxist camp as a whole was that art be committed, but what this meant in practice depended on the particular degree of ideological orthodoxy. Europe's Communist parties, which were intimately linked to the Soviet Union at the time, advocated the subordination of art to the directive on Socialist Realism. This viewpoint naturally met with greater sympathy in countries where the Communists benefited from a considerable measure of popular support, such as in France and Italy. The artistic doctrines of the Communist Party in France provided a powerful and controversial alternative stance, not only as a result of the party's significant status among French opinion-makers, but also because after the war a number of well-known artists and intellectuals such as Pablo Picasso, Fernand Léger and Jean-Paul Sartre had allied themselves with the Communist Party (the PCF) to varying degrees. The problem was, however, that after 1948, the French Communist party chose increasingly to follow the official Soviet party line, which meant that Socialist Realism became an absolute aesthetic doctrine as far as the art world was concerned. An artist such as André Fougeron, who has been more or less forgotten, was lauded in these circles as a modern master. In contrast, the idea of creating a contemporary social modernist art as championed by Léger, in particular, was roundly condemned.[38]

For less dogmatic Marxists, however, the requirement that art be committed did not necessarily imply criticism of modernism as such. One significant example is Jean-Paul Sartre, who summarised his view of the relationship between commitment and freedom on the part of the writer or the artist in *Qu'est-ce que la littérature?* (1947):

> Thus, whether he is an essayist, a pamphleteer, a satirist, or a novelist, whether he speaks only of individual passions or whether he attacks the social order, the writer, a free man addressing free men, has only one subject – freedom. . . . Thus, however you might have come to it, whatever opinions you might have professed, literature

throws you into battle. Writing is a certain way of wanting freedom; once you have begun, you are committed, willy-nilly.[39]

But this description, which out of context might have been taken from simply any bourgeois or ecclesiastical text, reveals its ideological (Marxist) stance somewhat later when Sartre maintains that '*actual* literature can only realize its full *essence* in a classless society'.[40] Nevertheless, there is a yawning gulf between Sartre and the more dogmatic defenders of Socialist Realism. He makes no direct requirement of the writer or artist to adapt his language and idiom according to any fixed political dogma; neither does the artist, in his view, have to be in the vanguard of the struggle to make socialism victorious or subordinate his work to this one overriding goal. Instead, he understands the political function of literature to be dependent on the social context in which it is inscribed. The strict adherence of the European Communist parties to the Moscow line meant, however, that the appeal of their alternative artistic approach was extremely limited: Socialist Realism was scarcely an acceptable option for the majority of Europe's more progressive artists during the post-war period.

There was a very different reaction to both modernity and modernism from the champions of conservative values. Art academies, such as the Académie des Beaux-Arts in Paris and the Royal Academy of Arts in London, still maintained an extremely conservative, anti-modernist stance, which was not without influence on contemporary cultural life. Furthermore, modernism continued to be regarded in conservative, church and political circles as ideologically and politically suspect. The symbolic position a defender of freedom assigned to modernism in certain contexts was portrayed by them as a particularly dangerous lie, because they considered its aesthetic and world view to have arisen from the same nihilistic quagmire as the ideas of the revolutionary and authoritarian regimes.[41]

In the United States, the questionable ideological connotations of the avant-garde led to a ferocious dispute about the country's official cultural policy. This was exemplified in 1948 when the Institute of Modern Art in Boston abandoned its previously modernist-oriented exhibition policy and published an officially anti-modernist statement. It was modernism's obscure, arcane and extremist tendencies that were objected to. The museum was intent on emphasising a humanist middle way: a position that Serge Guilbaut has shown to have been impossible in practice in the extraordinarily fraught and politicised climate of the debate for and against modernism.[42] The political overtones of this polemic were further heightened at the beginning of the 1950s by the anticommunist campaigns waged by Senator Joseph McCarthy that led to the notion of what was American or un-American, determining both what was possible in the discourse of the visual arts and the capacity of the political establishment to provide financial support for contemporary art. To advocate radical modernism in such a situation meant having to walk a veritable rhetorical tightrope, as we shall see.

The European debate followed a somewhat different pattern. Within conservative and ecclesiastical antimodernist circles, modernist art was portrayed as expressing a complete lack of respect for humanism, tradition and established norms on the part of individuals and society. Pope Pius XI had condemned the use of modernist art in the building of churches as early as 1932, and the Catholic church, which took an unfavourable view of both the deformation of human and religious figures and the absence of narratives in art, reiterated its condemnation after the Second World War, when abstract and nonfigurative motifs were used in some instances in the decoration of churches.[43] Although this negative attitude towards modernism was far from universally prevalent, it served to articulate the scepticism that had long characterised the Catholic sphere. Both the religious and political opposition to modernism could thus be said to have aesthetic, ideological and ethical origins.

One of the most controversial examples of this antimodernist rhetoric was Hans Sedlmayr's *Verlust der Mitte*, published in 1948.[44] In this work, the author describes modern art as a symptom of a disease with which modern society has infected culture: a falling away from the path of truth and eternal values. Sedlmayr considered it his task as a historian to present a diagnosis of this spiritually deadly affliction. He portrays a historical course of events, beginning in the French revolution and culminating in the modernist art of the contemporary world, in which mankind, society and art have lost their meaning, their essential centre. A culture that had once been so coherent has splintered into fragments: modernist art merely reflects the chaos and dissolution, the inhuman isolation and alienation modern life has brought with it. Modernism patently distorts the perception of human nature in his view, which results in a demonisation of the human being; all these -isms express the same fundamental decline in their affirmation of chaos, disease and fragmentation. Modernism is a path that leads away from everything worthy of the name of art and spirituality; it is an art of the devil.[45]

Sedlmayr's almost apocalyptic vision of how modernity inevitably leads to the decline of civilisation can no doubt be inscribed in that shared intellectual construct we touched on earlier concerning the relationship of the modern age to tradition (antiquity), but it also bears witness to the more specific influence of Oswald Spengler's *Der Untergang des Abendlandes* (1922), a work that was highly controversial in its time.[46] In Sedlmayr's argument, the historical analysis of modernity is interwoven with a normative, and ahistorical, evaluation of the eternal nature of true art. But his own position, as an Austrian who was only too ready to put his services at the disposal of the Nazi German forces of occupation, renders his arguments if not empty, then at least dubious.[47] He completely fails to mention the attempts to solve the problem of the loss of the centre in the modern era that had been made only a few years earlier as part of the cultural and political practices of the Third Reich. Neither does he hesitate to compare modernism with a mental illness, even if he hastens to add that this is not the same as saying that modernist artists are mentally ill.[48] Implicit in his diagnosis is an *a priori* thesis that permits no deviation: all the artistic utterances of modernism are and have to be symptoms of the fundamental illness of society (modernity).

Sedlmayr's proposed way out of this state of affairs and his prognosis for the future are, however, much vaguer than his diagnosis of contemporary society. One problem is the contradictory character of his approach, as it is based on an evolutionist explanatory model, on the one hand, while resembling, on the other, some basic features of a superficially Marxist reflection theory:

Art should evolve towards an ever-greater degree of ideal beauty but is inevitably dragged down to the very opposite of such an ideal as it reflects the insanity of contemporary Western society. Such an approach results not only in an inferior historiography, but also undermines any form of active intervention, unless one is willing and capable of changing the direction of contemporary social conditions as a whole. Human beings appear locked in the iron cage of the modern era with no means of extricating themselves. Unlike the various alternative proposals and programmes that have had an actual impact (against all the odds in some cases) on modern cultural life—from William Morris' critique of the design culture of the nineteenth century to Clement Greenberg's defence of the avant-garde—Sedlmayr fails to start from a concrete formulation of the problem. His sweeping rejection of both modern art and modern society was little more than a gesture of resignation. As the crisis of modern art was perceived in terms of an essentially spiritual crisis by this devout Catholic, any change could only be brought about, in his view, through a renewal of the spiritual climate and of religious art.[49] But what would a renewal of this kind be like? The book provides no guidelines of any kind in this respect and comes across instead as an agonized and bitter elegy to a degenerate present that is fundamentally and irretrievably lost.

Sedlmayr's work resulted in an extensive debate that demonstrated the existence of significant groups in the Western democracies that shared his doubts—or rather his despair—about the contemporary world and were explicitly opposed to the normalisation process of modernism. But the problem for the forces of reaction from both the Marxist and the conservative camps was that they lacked any viable, or even conceivable, visual codes in the cultural policy climate that developed after the war. Moreover, the effects of recent history, which had witnessed the elimination of the avant-garde by Nazi Germany, and the contemporary political situation created by the Cold War meant that the privilege of defining the problem had slipped away from the antimodernist forces.

As a counterweight to works such as Sedlmayr's historiography, Werner Haftman wrote what was, in its time, the most comprehensive history of modernism, published in 1954 under the title *Malerei im 20. Jarhhundert*. Haftmann's survey started with Impressionism in the 1870s and worked its way through all the -isms of the twentieth century, right up to the author's own time. The chronological pattern is reminiscent of the historicisation of modernism in the interwar years as presented in survey works and exhibitions, such as the scheme Alfred Barr employed to organise *Cubism and Abstract Art* at the Museum of Modern Art in 1936 or the linear sequence Christian Zevros set out in *Histoire de l'art contemporain* in 1938.[50] The number of subjects, topics, questions and cross-references is so large in Haftmann's work, however, that its structure has been broken down into a series of interrelated essays, whose reading may seem at times like a labyrinthine journey through a wild and untamed landscape. But it is the same issue that formed the basis of Sedlmayr's work—modernity entailed a fundamental change in the way human beings perceived reality—that allows both the overall structure and the individual analyses to cohere.

This notion, however, meets with a completely different response in Haftmann's work, whose rhetoric inverts Sedlmayr's alienation from the modern era by putting modernism in a clearly defined relationship with history:

> Modern painting is indeed the most striking expression of the universal process by which one cultural epoch with a long history yields its place to another. It bears witness to the decline of an old conception of reality and the emergence of a new one. The view of the world that is being superseded today is that which was first shaped by the early Florentine masters with their naïve enthusiasm for the concrete reality of the visible world, which they set out to define.[51]

Instead of reinforcing nostalgia and bitter lament, the notion of the decline of the old culture and its art is transformed here into a progressive argument in favour of the relevance and value of modernist art. Although the rapid shifts of the modern age may appear alienating, and although modern art can seem obscure and strange, this is nothing new in itself. The reference to the Italian Renaissance in particular is, of course, no accident but a calculated way of linking the once revolutionary potential of the most elevated and classical of epochs to the freshness and originality of contemporary art. Then, as now, art can be understood as a reflection of the way the wider culture perceives the world, and this is what makes modernist art so significant today: it is an authentic expression of its own time and demonstrates the way in which the perspectives of ages past have been replaced by new ones. To cling to antiquated aesthetic ideals amounts to not only a false and fundamentally reactionary form of nostalgia, but also a refusal to see the changed reality of the contemporary world and its future direction.

And yet, even though it presented an impartial historical analysis and an alternative interpretation, the publication of Werner Haftmann's book formed only an indirect argument within an ongoing debate. His art-historical arguments gained a much greater public hearing the following year when he organised *documenta* together with Arnold Bode—an exhibition whose selection has been described as an illustration almost of Haftmann's survey work.[52] Indeed, this show made a much more explicit contribution to the debate—and one whose message could not fail to be heard. What it exemplifies so strikingly is that it was not the approaches and actions of various individuals that were of crucial significance for the changed status of modernism after the war, but the response of official institutions and public bodies. Because the originator in this case was the state and not a number of subcultural groups at the margins of the bourgeois public sphere, *documenta* signalled very clearly that a new order had been established.

This example also demonstrates something else; namely, the frontline had shifted by this time. It no longer separated the defenders of tradition and innovation, respectively, but was now drawn between east and west. The bipolar structure of the Cold War established a matrix for interpretation, understanding and evaluation that transcended every interest or conflict in specific areas of activity, a matrix to which the normalisation of modernism may largely be related. However, the Cold War was not in itself the sole cause of this process. The Second World War should be considered a far more important cause of the rapid course of events that took place during the post-war period. It was then that all the energy dammed up by the war, which had proved such a fatal setback to the normalisation of modernism already initiated during the 1930s, was liberated. Moreover, the increasingly reactionary tone of American domestic politics was quite clearly an attempt to uphold aesthetic, cultural and ideological values that were in direct conflict with the theory and ideology of modernism. What the Cold War context demonstrates was the possibility of legitimating the avant-garde by means of a rhetoric that inscribed these phenomena in specific ideological images.

The Aesthetic and Ideological Criteria of Normalisation

The Dictates of the Antitheses: The Cold War Cultural System

Jürgen Habermas has characterised a fundamental change within the public life of the early twentieth century as a paradoxical interplay between the state and civil society, with society becoming increasingly 'statified', while the state was being 'societalised' to an ever greater degree.[53] According to Habermas, the cause of this change lay in an escalating need for state regulation within the private realm at the same time that social issues were increasingly becoming an issue for the state. When applied to the art world, this abstract formula can be understood in terms of a more obvious interaction between the private and public sectors, determined in particular by the establishment and expansion of the radical art world and its supporters. In contrast with the image of constant flux evoked in analyses of the cultural field, such as those of Pierre Bourdieu, what Habermas makes apparent is how official institutions, in public or private ownership, become increasingly important as norm-constructing actors in the contemporary radical or avantgardiste art world.

The new official and institutional interest in modernist art after the War had ramifications beyond cultural policy; it also served ideological, political and symbolic functions: for the ideological entrenchment of the modern democracies in a rational and progressively-oriented modernity, for enhancing the image of a particular nation as progressive and open, for the restoration of value structures and historical connections that had been crushed by

---

How to cite this book chapter:
Hayden, Hans. 2018. The Aesthetic and Ideological Criteria of Normalisation. In: Hayden, H. *Modernism as Institution: On the Establishment of an Aesthetic and Historiographic Paradigm* Pp. 164–187. Stockholm: Stockholm University Press. DOI: https://doi.org/10.16993/bar.e. License: CC-BY

repressive regimes, for establishing a democratic alternative to the dictatorships in Eastern Europe. While none of these causes need exclude any of the others, national and regional differences in the rhetoric relating to the establishment of the modern art museums and their exhibition programmes can be clearly identified. We are not invoking a turning point that was uniform and universal when referring to the normalisation of modernism, but pointing rather to a diffuse process with considerable regional differences. One country can, however, be singled out as playing a key role in the post-war international art world, a role, moreover, that would be of crucial importance in historical terms for the process of normalisation: the United States of America.

Before we consider the details of how this process was legitimated in several different contexts, it may be worth attempting to provide a backdrop to the cultural life of Western Europe and the US after the Second World War and how the Cold War created a potent incentive for the Western powers to define a more distinct cultural policy. This subject has all but become an art historical genre of its own ever since Serge Guilbaut published *How New York Stole the Idea of Modern Art* in 1983, and it is aptly summarised in his subtitle 'Abstract Expressionism, Freedom, and the Cold War'. Guilbaut's book in particular, albeit in tandem with many other works within this genre, has unquestionably served to enrich our understanding of the complexities of art history and cultural policy in the post-war period.[54] However, the intense focus on the dynamics of the Cold War by some experts and authors has established what is, in my view, a rather determinist and conspiratorial narrative whose subtext appears concerned with delegitimising Abstract Expressionism as no more than an instrument of—or conceivably the invention of—the American intelligence service. Another recurring trope in this genre is how and when New York took over the role of international art centre from Paris. Although this, too, is an interesting question, it is only of secondary relevance to this study. My starting point is understanding how the rhetorical function of avant-garde art in a geopolitical context became a crucial impetus for its institutionalisation after the Second World War.

Obviously, the Cold War was of major significance in this regard as well. The escalation of the confrontation between the US and the Soviet Union after 1945 meant that it was vitally important for both sides to maintain the intactness of their respective hemispheres. Reconstruction and the military balance of power were considered issues of vital importance from political, economic and military perspectives, as well as social and cultural ones.[55] The ideologised nature of the situation led to the active involvement of both the Soviet and American sides in ensuring that the border between the two systems was not a grey zone, but a clearly demarcated frontline so that all global conflicts would be interpreted within the framework of the bipolar structure of the Cold War.[56] The rhetorical logic of the structure calls to mind Zygmunt Bauman's description of modernity's system of segregating and classifying the world: a structure that acknowledges the existence of thesis and antithesis, of friends and enemies, but not of a third category outside the system—it refuses to recognise the existence of the Stranger.[57] In the structure of the Cold War, the Stranger not only posed a threat to the entire set-up, but also risked undermining the efforts of the two blocs to gain absolute legitimacy within their respective spheres.[58] The polarity between the US and the Soviet Union consolidated a way of thinking that could be applied in almost every different context: political, economic, cultural and military.

At one level, this involves the major discursive field Friedrich Engels once called ideological powers: the reproduction of norms by public institutions. More specifically, it also concerns the need at a particular historical stage to produce condensed, uniform and normative ideas about, and in, a complex and ambivalent situation so that it could be simplified, explained and mediated to the public in the form of concentrated ideological representations. These reproductions ranged from obvious ideological manifestos to vaguer notions, images and metaphors. It is this discursive production of ideological images that is of interest here, images that, irrespective of whether they were produced in the East or West, could be said to inhabit the borderland between interpretations of a real situation and mystical illusions. The Western images served as the very real boundaries for the representation and interpretation by the official art world of both history and the present.

One example of an interpretive approach of this kind can be found in the work of Stephen Kotkin, who has described the socialist society that developed in Russia after the 1917 revolution as an ideological model that, while highly flexible in many practical respects, was based on the absolute tenet that socialism was the radical antithesis of capitalism.[59] The ideological stance of the Bolsheviks brought with it a tendency to make their own thesis universal, with every single truth having to be based on a correct (scientific) analysis of the aims of history. While their analyses, and political orientation, were frequently subject to change, the Communist party had an absolute monopoly over every analysis and every change. This fundamental principle of anti-Capitalism interlaced all the various processes and details of society and life as a whole, with the habits and behavioural patterns of the individual considered just as significant as the planning of economics, politics and the various social institutions:

> The story of socialism was nearly indistinguishable from the story of people's lives, a merged personal and societal allegory of progress, social justice, and overcoming adversity – in short, a fable of a new person and a new civilization, distinct because it was not capitalist, distinct because it was better than capitalism.[60]

The politicisation of the Soviet state entailed extraordinarily extensive efforts to create a new social identity and a comprehensive model for perceiving and conceptualising the world that would encompass all the different parts of society, from culture and the mass media to the teaching of Marxist-Leninism at the very beginning of school. This was a system for the total political indoctrination of society, which involved a colossal attempt to force people to learn to speak—and think—Bolshevik, as Kotkin puts it.[61]

The art world was, of course, also integrated into this system of blanket control. After the revolution, a range of interpretations and definitions existed of what the art of the socialist state should be, from an academic classicism to various forms of Constructivism and Futurism. By the beginning of the 1930s, it had become increasingly obvious that the state favoured the realist and classicist wings. The bringing together of all the various artistic institutions under the aegis of the Union of Artists in 1932 was a crucial step towards subordinating all cultural activities to party control.[62] The institutional structure was further centralised after the Second World War when all art affairs were brought under the control of the Soviet Council of Ministers and administered by a hierarchical structure of central and local committees. A central Soviet art academy was founded in Moscow in 1947 that became the long arm of the regime in the art world, as it assumed responsibility for education, exhibitions, commissions and prizes.[63] The post-war Soviet art world was completely dominated by official institutions and quite beyond the reach of any critical margin; neither was there any real possibility for disseminating alternative forms of representation within a private sector—other than in extreme secrecy.

After intensive discussions among Soviet cultural workers and party functionaries at the beginning of the 1930s, the necessity of Socialist Realism was officially proclaimed in a speech by Stalin's cultural commissar and subsequently Politburo member Andrei Zhdanov at the first Soviet Writers' Congress in 1934.[64] Socialist Realism was not simply a matter of a specific idiom; it was also a method and a concept for the way the visual arts were to function in society: as the engineers of human souls, artists and writers were to refashion the mentality of the people in the spirit of socialism. The artist was supposed to describe reality in its revolutionary development, which meant a break with the individualised and unrealistic romanticism of earlier periods and which heralded the beginning of a new kind of revolutionary romanticism that was a source of inspiration while remaining firmly rooted in the material basis of real life. The visual arts' repertoire of stylistic devices and methods was thus combined with a determination of its function based on the decree prescribing realist form and socialist content: the visual arts were to be figurative and narrative in epic fashion and their content should reflect and praise the political goals of the party.[65] As Boris Groys has suggested, Stalin's arts policy could in fact be understood as a radicalisation and transformation of the basic tenet of the constructivist avant-garde: art should both represent and become part of the changed lifestyle and circumstances of the new man in the overall aesthetic-political plan of the Soviet state.[66] The aesthetic was to be totally subordinate to the political, and if the political leadership judged that the aesthetic was failing to fulfil its function, it would have to be made to conform to the goals of policy. To this end, aesthetic parameters were developed that defined acceptable visual language for the arts in various contexts—a specific aesthetic code—that was largely aimed at developing the propaganda value, clarity, legibility and rhetorical power of art as an antithesis to the 'cosmopolitanism' and 'formalism' of Western modernism.[67]

In reality, the situation for artists and intellectuals in Eastern Europe differed between each country, and it was also a situation that changed over time. As recent research has emphasized, this situation was tremendously complex: the cultural production behind the iron curtain could embrace both Socialist Realism and modernism, but it cannot be understood only as a reflection of ideals derived from the Soviet Union, nor merely as peripheral and unmatched attempts to imitate modernist movements in the West.[68] However, the logic of the Cold War demanded—on both sides—an idea of two separate and fundamentally different systems and cultural expressions. The intimacy of the connection between political and cultural discourses within a single dominant hegemonic order marked an essential difference between Soviet and Eastern European cultural life on the one hand and that of America and Western Europe on the other. However, the bipolar structure of the Cold War also created a new need for the US to coordinate different representations within the framework of a single overarching ideological ideal. For the culture of post-war America, the result was both continuity and change in this regard: ideas and identities that had developed and become established earlier in the twentieth century became more clearly defined while also acquiring new or partially new meanings.

The increasing need for greater clarity in defining the frontline against the Soviets created one very particular problem: how could a society characterised by a pluralist approach construct a clear and coherent alternative to the distinctiveness of Soviet discourse without abandoning the democratic freedoms and multiplicity that were the very cornerstone of the Western way? With the lessons of President Woodrow Wilson's failures after the First World War in mind, the goal of the Truman administration was to establish a new stability in the period immediately following the end of the Second World War by setting up a variety of institutions aimed at creating an open global market and foreign policy order. Truman, however, was being pressured not only by the growing geopolitical ambitions of the Soviet Union, but also by domestic opinion, particularly from a Congress that was under the control of the Republicans. A significant measure of political freedom of manoeuvre could be achieved by creating a situation that linked the foreign and domestic policy issues closely together while also associating the problem of the reconstruction and stability of Western Europe with an increasingly pronounced anti-Communist rhetoric. The historian Richard Freeland has described how a series of actions were initiated between 1947 and 1948 with the aim of mobilising the American public so as to create this freedom of manoeuvre by rhetorical and political means.[69] Various measures were targeted specifically at oppositional individuals and groups, actively linking the issue of freedom with the question of loyalty. Freedom was not to be understood as an absolute civil right but must always be interpreted within the framework of patriotic loyalty to the political interests of the US. A specific myth of what it meant to be American—a uniform and ideologised image—had to be established as an integral part of the post-war ideological discourse of the United States. And because the Cold War was a symbolic war to a very considerable extent, propaganda was its foremost weapon. The cultural sphere, too, would have to be extensively mobilised as part of the production and reproduction of this myth.

And yet it would be mistaken to see the Cold War as the sole cause of the changes in American cultural and social life after the Second World War. The historian Alan Brinkley has shown how a wealth of different factors interacted to bring about these developments: the unparalleled degree of economic growth above all, the ideological assurance that unfettered capitalism was the best means of achieving a just society, the importance of the expanding middle class and its increasingly homogeneous self-identity. In tandem with the bipolar structure of the Cold War, these factors clearly made the creation of an illusion of unity in the ethnic, political and social heterogeneity of American society essential:

The architects of the Cold War came to view a diverse and rapidly changing world through the prism of a simple ideological lens, smoothing out the rough spots and seeing a uniformity of beliefs and goals that did not in fact exist. The architects of postwar middle-class culture looked at a diverse and rapidly changing society in the United States through a similarly limited and self-referential perspective. They constructed and came to believe in an image of a world that did not exist.[70]

The disjunction between these official images and the perceived commonplace reality of American citizens also provides a key to understanding the differences between the American and Soviet discourses. Although American ideology was repressive at times and sought to limit the freedom of thought and action of the citizenry, it would, of course, have been impossible for a democratic state to establish a distinct doctrine for cultural policy in the same way as had been done in the Soviet Union. The existence of a sub- and countercultural critical margin could, in fact, be considered a distinguishing feature of American and Western European culture, even though the official image that prevailed during the Cold War served to underpin and strengthen conservative ideas within a range of areas.[71] The political and cultural discourses of the West were not based on a single hegemonic perspective despite the obvious attempts by various reactionary groups, particularly in the US, to influence and restrict public debate.

The pluralism of American society did, however, pose many kinds of dilemmas for successive administrations that had to create a clearly defined line against an enemy able to produce an image without any cracks and without any critical opposition. The constitutional and institutional structure of the United States was entirely different in kind. Prior to 1965, there was no single authority in the US with responsibility for art affairs, neither was there any federal budget for such matters, although both the Department of the Interior and the intelligence services considered them part of their own area of interest.[72] In contrast with the extraordinarily top-down and centralised structure of the art and cultural spheres of the Soviet Union in the 1940s and 1950s, the American authorities had to rely on various private institutions, social networks and secret contacts. The degree of awareness that an open and democratic society had to impose certain limits on the conduct of psychological warfare also varied considerably within different administrative and security organisations.[73] There was quite simply no consensus in the political debate about what foreign and cultural policy direction the US should follow.

The American response to the ideological and cultural agenda of the Soviet Union and the massive resistance to avant-garde and 'un-American' art from influential parts of the political establishment may be seen as constituting two major fields of force in the official promotion and normalisation of modernism, irrespective of whether the aim was to spread a particular type of culture or to use the latter for political ends.

This state of affairs made it essential to employ elaborate strategies within fields where explicit diktats would have been impossible. The opposition to modern art and culture in general and to avant-garde movements in particular within large parts of the political sector meant that contacts had to be more or less secret both to maintain the liberal notion of a free art world and to produce an alternative image to that presented by the authoritarian cultural policy of the Soviet Union. The key institution in this context was the Museum of Modern Art and its International Council.[74] The ownership structure of MoMA—in the form of a private foundation—in combination with the membership of its board made it the centre of a remarkable and influential network of contacts that consisted of individuals in key positions in American politics, the security services and trade and industry.[75] MoMA was, therefore, linked by professional and social ties to the pragmatic forces in American politics that wanted to retain the ideological offensive as well as to an internationally oriented cultural policy. With financial aid from private funds and the partially concealed backing of the American Department of the Interior, MoMA launched its international programme for artistic exchanges with other countries in 1952. It was also responsible for American participation at various international art events, such as the biennales held in Venice and São Paulo.[76]

Employing and exporting visual art for propaganda purposes naturally posed a particular dilemma for a democratic nation. For one thing, direct indoctrination was likely to be counterproductive and would not be taken seriously by European intellectuals. For another, visual art and art exhibitions, no matter how wide-ranging, constituted a rather blunt propaganda weapon when compared with the public dissemination of popular culture through the daily and weekly press, comics, popular music, advertising, radio, television, film. And although modernism was established within the framework of the cultural policy of the United States and the Western European states, nonfigurative art as such proved to be an extremely diffuse instrument of propaganda in comparison with Socialist Realism: just where exactly in a painting by Jackson Pollock could freedom and democracy be seen?

The Production of Identity as *Realpolitik*

A key issue for the ideological function of every art genre and mass medium is the relation between rhetorical clarity and critical autonomy. The role of the visual arts in the democratic states was not primarily a matter of images but rather their use and involved an ideologised context for the interpretation of works of art, rather than explicit presentations of an ideological content in particular works. Here, as in so many other respects, the Cold War created an intricate and very peculiar logic for the interpretation of matters both large and small.

The position of 'leading nation of the free world' that the US attempted to occupy after the end of the Second World War required not only extensive economic and military spending, but also the investment of cultural and intellectual capital. Within the art world, this was a struggle that could be said to have been waged on several different fronts: against the Soviet Union primarily, but also against the art and cultural life of old Europe (France in particular) and against the reactionary tendencies of domestic opinion. If a powerful alternative to the Eastern bloc was to be successfully promoted, it would have to be legitimated both within the cultural spheres of the European states and to opinion at home. The key to the success of the international establishment of the American art world as a vital centre of the arts—and to the successful dissemination of the image of American art by the authorities after the Second World War—was not primarily a matter of conspiracies or the promotion of particular artistic idioms, it had to do instead with the establishment of a dynamic institutional structure whose principal strengths lay in its flexibility, its financial position and the mobility it afforded between the private and the public spheres. The part played by Europe in this game was not one of passive submission it had more to do with a shared interest on the part of certain key actors in disseminating the image of modernist art—and nonfigurative art in particular—as the free world's response to Socialist Realism.[77] A rich and varied artistic life developed in several different places in Europe after the War, which meant that the post-war European art scene also had a significant role to play in the normalisation process of modernism.

An important aspect of this process was the necessity of legitimating and reproducing specific values with which modern art could be associated. However, as we saw earlier, this also brought a two-pronged dilemma: for the dominant culture in having to embrace parts of a counterculture as a bearer of its norms and for the avant-garde, which would lose its *raison d'être*, its countercultural position, as a result. The problem was not entirely confined to the post-war period but may be understood in historical terms, at least in part, as a process involving the gradual establishment and consecration of the various avant-garde movements. What was different about post-war normalisation was that it did not simply entail a gradual and retroactive form of acceptance; it actively involved the institutionalisation and official sanctioning of certain values peculiar to the avant-garde.

This process was freighted with different ideological values in different nations and was legitimated by them in different ways. As we have seen, *documenta* served as an extraordinarily significant paradigmatic manifestation of modernist art in West Germany, a country whose historical situation created an entirely different impetus for the normalisation of modernism than that of the US. A central theme of this exhibition was the issue of the restoration of the democratic system of values and the creation of a national identity within the framework of that system. And yet German official art policy could also be described—as Benjamin Buchloh has done—as being determined by a collective political and psychological loss of memory.[78] When considered in these terms, the years between 1933 and 1945 emerge not as a period that had been the object of systematic analysis and description but rather as a gulf across which restoration formed a bridge to a recent history (parts of the progressive culture of the Weimar republic, in particular) that could serve as a sounding board for the new democratic republic.

The issue of restoration also played a crucial role in France after the war. Although the situation here was less chaotic than in Germany once hostilities had ended, the nation had nevertheless been wounded economically, socially and culturally.[79] The country's problem of cultural restoration took on a different ideological connotation than in the German Federal Republic. The making of extensive cultural policy initiatives was also made more difficult by political instability and the weakness of France's economic position.[80] There was, however, a pronounced awareness on all political sides of the importance of culture for social life and national identity. This was particularly evident in the efforts made as part of French art and cultural policy during both the Fourth and Fifth Republics that revolved around the same symbolic theme permeating so much of French post-war policy as a whole: affirming the role of the nation as a great power in political, military and cultural terms, while keeping up the image that the continuity of the great French tradition had never been broken. What was reestablished was, in essence, the same image that was promoted by the World Fair held in Paris in 1937; although, now the French government played a much more active part in the mediation and legitimation of modern art.

An example is provided by the exhibition programme of the Museée Nationale d'Art Moderne, which emerged after the war as the central institution and the major actor in the official French art world.[81] Its hallmark throughout the post-war period was an emphasis on the Frenchness of the development of modern art.[82] The contemporary art it promoted was in the main the work of those artists active within what was known as the Nouvelle Ecole de Paris, such as Jean Bazaine, Roger Bissiére, Alfred Manessier and Bernard Buffet. This could be referred to as a kind of modernist *juste-milieu* painting, whose primary significance lay in that it codified key values of official French cultural policy in purely iconographic terms, thus creating continuity with tradition. The aim of the museum was not to exhibit what was local or national but to set for the international art world a standard whose national character may to a very large extent be considered both nationalist and universalist.

This is not to say that French art or the Parisian art world after the Second World War lacked vitality or dynamism. On the contrary, the 1950s were an extremely lively period in the areas of art and art debate. Alternatives to the official line were provided by less formal networks that linked together galleries, periodicals and private art schools and in which a new generation of artists and critics could operate.[83] It is evident, nonetheless, that the establishment of a particular image of the relationship between French contemporary art and historical national development occurred as an interaction between the public and private sectors: through coverage by the mass media, as a result of the reports by leading critics and their assessments, by means of exhibitions at private galleries, and through the publication of survey works and monographs. A measure of change, dynamism and mobility within the institutional structure of the official art scene should also be taken into account; this created greater scope for various types of nonfigurative art during the 1950s, particularly those works that went under the name of *abstrait chaude* (lyrical abstraction) or *art informel*.[84] Although it is clear that the discursive practice of the visual arts in France, as in the rest of the Western world, was shaped by an interplay between the private and public spheres, the existence of much stricter boundaries between the two than in America, for instance, made the French art world exceptional, with the French government all but entirely in control of international exchanges and presentations.[85]

However, it would be a mistake to interpret this situation as though the image of France as a cultural great power had been turned into nothing more than illusion. As Kathryn Boyer has shown, the French government devoted significant financial resources to retaining the initiative at both the national and international levels. The French authorities also proved successful at disseminating the image of a continuous French tradition on the international art scene. The official international art programme was organised by the Association Française d'Action Artistique, which managed to arrange an average of twenty-two exhibitions per year between 1949 and 1965 that toured various places all over the world.[86] Although these exhibitions were made up of both older and more recent French art, the emphasis was on the older material, and among the exhibitions of twentieth-century art that were shown, there was a marked preponderance from the first half of the century when the Fauvist and Cubist traditions were dominant.[87] One of the association's most important commissions was organising the French pavilions at the prestigious biennales held in Venice and São Paulo. The arts policy of the French state met with great success at these events, and France was able to assure its international position by winning the top prizes at these biennial exhibitions on an annual basis during the 1950s.[88] It is evident, moreover, that the Venice Biennale in particular was characterised by a retrospective spirit in the years following the Second World War that was demonstrated in thematic displays of early modernism and also influenced the awarding of its prizes.[89]

The problem of restoration played a subordinate role in the US, which meant that American rhetoric was formulated in somewhat different terms. The issue here was not a matter of establishing an image of an unbroken tradition but of asserting the dynamism and progressive modernity of American culture. The nucleus of this rhetoric involved the reproduction of an image of the vitality of American art, with the aim of gaining acceptance for it and ensuring its power to convince in contexts beyond direct American control. But the American self-image had to be adapted in order to be successfully exported and legitimated in a European intellectual milieu. Serge Guilbaut has described the necessary adaptation as occurring in two stages: first, from nationalism to internationalism and second, from internationalism to universalism.[90] Establishing a position within an international context involved getting rid of the stamp of provincialism that had marked the (socially committed) art of the 1930s. Once the required level had been reached, where the leading role of Paris was beyond dispute, an aesthetic approach based on values specific to American art had to be formulated, and these values had to be perceived as universally applicable.[91] What the French were keen to portray as a natural and self-evident continuity involved a kind of representation based on exactly the same shared intellectual construct that certain actors within the American art world were simultaneously attempting to establish for their own ends. For the most part, this struggle over interpretive privilege could be said to have been a struggle over the right to define what was universal.

The reproduction of this new self-image was quite clearly one aspect of the larger process of the production of national identity at this time, while also forming part of a greater plan, as some have maintained, directed by the powers that be to export American culture to the wider world. Although if there were a plan, it could only have been successfully enacted owing to an aspect of the situation that appears to have been more random and difficult to control: the export of the new cultural self-image of the US began at the same time the domestic avant-garde (the New York School) was making great advances and entering its productive heyday. The US was at this time definitely capable of manifesting a level of artistic production fully comparable with that of any European nation, although it lacked breadth and the deep historical roots found in France in particular. The war years had led to an exodus of leading European figures to the United States in the art field as well, just as the American art world was establishing what was to some extent a new institutional structure.[92] But the absence in the US of a dynamic cultural tradition of modernist art brought with it specific problems for this process of legitimation. Unlike France, there was no cosmopolitan and bohemian avant-garde to point to as a historical marker of national identity. On the contrary, this very type of identity—and its politically subversive, cosmopolitan and, therefore, 'un-American' values—seemed highly suspect to large parts of the political and cultural establishment. Bringing together culture with subculture proved more problematic in the US than in most European countries.

A solution that proved viable was formulated by Alfred Barr, when describing the symbolic role of modern art in his brief survey *What is Modern Painting* (1943): '[T]he work of art is a symbol, a visible symbol of the human spirit in its search for truth, for freedom and for perfection.'⁹³ In the context of its time, this was a defence of the freedom of art against the oppression of Stalin and Hitler, although in the political context of the post-war period, the same argument could be used against both the cultural policy of the Eastern bloc and conservative opinion at home. At the height of McCarthyism, Barr formulated a defence of modern art as the expression of a free democratic society in more explicit terms in 'Is Modern Art Communistic?' (1952) when he asserted that the conformity and lack of freedom represented by Nazi Germany and the Soviet Union reflected the particular intolerance of these regimes to the creativity, freedom and individuality of modern art.⁹⁴ The fundamental theme of both these essays was that the artist serves as a symbolic representative whose art and identity, even though they may exceed the boundaries of the acceptable according to the social and moral codes of everyday life, must be understood and accepted by any society that calls itself free.

By assigning to modernist art an extraordinary symbolic significance, not as a representation of sound American values but as a litmus test of how free and democratic a society actually is, Alfred Barr was, in fact, employing, and inverting, the very rhetoric adopted by reactionary opinion in order to suppress the avant-garde. He was evidently aware of the need for counterreactionary arguments in the debate on modern art with just as much aggression and force as the opposing side could ever mobilise.

What was also evident in the US was the development of an image of a particularly American synthesis of historical modernism, an art that even though it could be located in a historical context was nevertheless genuinely modern. Moreover, a particular set of values was being identified as typical of American art: violent, spontaneous, new, vital, big, brutal, unfinished.⁹⁵ Hence, it was viewed as different from the art of France, which was described as weak, conservative, feeble, cultivated, mannered and charming. This rhetoric, with its peculiar gender-stereotyped metaphors, presents a snapshot of what Laura Cottingham has tellingly described as 'the masculine imperative' of modernism.⁹⁶ The image it produced was of American culture offering a revitalising, masculine energy capable of injecting new life into the old, stagnant and feminised cultural tradition of Europe. An obvious example is provided by the mythologising approach at this time to Jackson Pollock—as a representative of the contemporary modern artist—in both the art world and in the public sphere.[97] This mythologising served to inscribe the contemporary artist in a historic context of the heroic but misunderstood geniuses of modern art, albeit with the crucial rhetorical difference that genius was now accepted and legitimated by the system of norms that pertained in the democratic states. In its particular political context, this rhetoric appeared essential to distinguish what was specifically American from an alien and politically subversive European heritage. The myths of Romanticism were readopted, as it were, and refashioned into a progressive and aggressive narrative of the genuinely modern, the genuinely American.

This rhetoric did not, however, bring any automatic benefits to American artists in terms of support, sales of work and financial gain, other than ensuring their ability to operate on a public stage. During the post-war period, the New York art world consisted of fairly loosely connected networks of artists, critics, collectors and intellectuals who set up particular social milieux and who embraced similar aesthetic approaches and issues.[98] There is no sense in which the group known as the New York School was a favoured elite of artistic functionaries in the service of the state, although a great deal of space was subsequently devoted to them in the international programme of MoMA.[99] Neither was it a question of culture being integrated into the official political discourse, as was the case in the Eastern bloc in particular, but also to some extent in the official art world of France. As Serge Guilbaut has shown, the production of value and meaning by the American art market was based right from the outset, and to a much greater extent, on ideas and identities that had become established among critics, gallery-owners and artists in the avant-garde art scene of New York. These were later subsumed within an overarching symbolic representation whose subject was modern art in a free and democratic society.

As we have seen, a crucial aspect of the rhetoric of normalisation has to do with the individualisation of works of art, and this led to the avant-garde being understood as consisting of a number of individuals with personal visions, rather than as a collective counterculture. Abstract Expressionism possessed a specific quality in this regard, which meant it could be used as part of a wider geopolitical rhetoric. As so interestingly described by the secret service agent Donald Jameson,

> We recognized that this was the kind of art that had nothing to do with socialist realism, and made [S]ocialist [R]ealism look even more stylized and more rigid and confined than it was. And that relationship was used in some exhibits.[100]

According to this argument, the freedom in a painting by Jackson Pollock lay in its stylistic differences from Socialist Realism; this is not then a matter of iconographic identification but rather a rhetorical use of the painting (and the particular phenomenon of Abstract Expressionism) in a larger political context.

There is a strange irony to this rhetorical game in that the Soviet approach to art was defined as an antithesis to the capitalist view; whereas, the American rhetoric provided an antithesis to this antithesis, as it were. This was a calculated strategy on the part of America and Western Europe that intended to allow them to make use of representations from the private art and cultural worlds as part of their official rhetoric. But in order to do so, a very peculiar interpretive model had to be applied.

The Model of Indirect and Symbolic Interpretation

The rhetorical individualisation of the avant-garde was of decisive importance for the process of normalisation beyond the borders of the United States as well. At *documenta* 1955, the various ideological connotations of the historical avant-garde were neutralised by the concept of a supra-individual formal evolution in which the struggle for freedom of the individual as such was emphasised (irrespective of his or her personal deviations in political or social terms) as a vital symbol of the open and democratic society. The notion that the value sphere of the visual arts constituted an isolated preserve clearly set off from the surrounding world was interwoven into this approach. This necessitated the depoliticisation of modern art in order to be able to use it politically and the recoding of avant-garde art as a private form of expression without any representative function beyond its own aesthetic existence. The problem lay in defining parameters for the interpretation of nonfigurative art capable of satisfying both sides: allowing art to retain (the semblance of) its avantgardiste legitimacy while ensuring that it appeared to be a legitimate representation of the cultural norm systems of the Western democracies.

This was not a question of various authorities acting repressively when it came to selection and interpretation, as in Abstract Expression serving as a representation of the ideology of the Cold War or the decreeing of a direct prohibition of certain kinds of interpretation, but involved instead the overlayering of different contexts for the interpretation of contemporary art. And, as previously mentioned, this was a transformation that first took place in the art world. The isolationist viewpoint was expressed most explicitly by Clement Greenberg, who wrote in 'Avantgarde and Kitsch' (1939) that avant-garde art had to cut itself off from society and create a distinct separation between itself and the arenas of politics and popular culture: a culture that was vital, progressive and advanced had to be a culture of disparity. Greenberg was far from alone in promoting an approach of this kind. More existentialist-minded or psychoanalytically oriented critics and historians, such as Harold Rosenberg, the German Werner Haftmann, the Englishman Herbert Read and the Frenchman Michael Tapié also emphasised—independently of one another—individual expression as a manifestation of 'personal mythology', 'inner necessity', 'metaphysical anguish' and 'universal creativity' that transcended the confines of the contemporary political and social worlds.[101] A general and universalising intellectual construct may be seen to underpin these mutually differing positions and diverse definitions that served to distinguish modern art from other social and intellectual spheres and whose rhetoric and scope extended, in principle, beyond specific national contexts.

How did this shared intellectual construct actually function in practice in the interpretation of a particular *oeuvre* or an individual image? An example that can shed light on this question is the promotion of Jean Fautrier. His breakthrough came with a series of paintings called *Les otages* (The Hostages), which were begun in 1943 and shown for the first time at the Galerie René

Drouin after the end of the war in 1945. The peculiar technique he employed attracted much attention. The paintings were executed in a series of different layers and types of material: on a piece of paper thinly painted in earth colours, Fautrier built up a thick cake of distemper and gypsum at the centre of the painting. Drawn around the coarsely applied painting materials was an amorphous outline that suggested the shape of a human face. In context, this outline creates not only the shape of a head, but also an illusion of volume in relation to the background that accentuates the plasticity of the colour elements and their function as symbols of incarnation. Fautrier scratched and painted a number of strokes, cutting through the outline and the paint, which may be interpreted in many ways but are, in context, highly suggestive of extreme violence: a face being demolished by a series of slashes and cut into pieces. Or was this simply an example of the deformation of the surrounding world by modern art? The question, in the context of the post-war period, was how these images were actually to be understood.

In *Un art autre* (1952), Michel Tapié declared that the value of Fautrier's work and of *art informel* lay in that it transposed the viewer to a situation that could not be understood by traditional yardsticks. He or she was forced by the enigmatic quality of the image into new existential considerations beyond the norms and truth claims of convention.[102] André Malraux, however, who took part in the Resistance movement with Fautrier, saw a more obvious association between the subject matter and a specific historical situation: 'Les otages' served as 'hieroglyphs of grief', as ideograms of the horrors of war, portrayed in a way that conveyed an immediate experience beyond language.[103] This much more specific interpretation was based on the allusion in the title of the series to oppression and to the associations with violence evoked by the demolished face, in which the colours not only accentuate a difference between its various parts, but also conjure up an image of greenish decomposition and of a devastating blood-drenched wound. Serge Guilbaut has provided an account of the way in which these and similar interpretations situated Fautrier and other practitioners of *art informel* in a specific context:

Fautrier took a very gruesome topic, one quite literally unrepresentable: the Holocaust. His task was ambitious but quite difficult if he cared not to exploit and sentimentalize such a painful topic. . . . Fautrier, who painted extraordinary powerful dead rabbits à la "Soutine" before the war, found, with the horror of the camps still very present, a way to talk about the unspeakable by withdrawing from direct discourse and replacing it with allusions, connotations. The physical, painful, difficult constructions of layers of transparent, thin papers on the canvas, the pulverization of white paint, the transformation of painting material, became a metaphor for the suffering many still felt in France. . . . What is special in Fautrier is that he makes these connotations barely visible, transforms them, buries them under an avalanche of technical virtuosities. We are here at the edge of the Inform, at the edge of figuration, when the drawing, the image, when the corpse, the stump, the flattened face, all in an advanced state of decomposition, tend to subside, to be transformed into soil, into *matière* (matter). But this one is of course an archeological *matière*, with signs of history buried in it, in order to jolt the casual viewer into recalling elements themselves buried in one's memory.[104]

The key problem in both these interpretations touches on the question of representation or, rather, on a borderland of representation. For how could what was essentially unportrayable (the Holocaust) ever be portrayed? And how could the portrayal of such a subject be legitimated in an artistic context (*art informel*) that repudiated not only the realist tradition, but also the very idea of the representative function of the visual arts? This problem resembles the one that confronted Picasso in his efforts to combine the expansive movement of Futurism with Symbolism's introspective preoccupation with the language of pictorial art; it could be said to lie at the very heart of the entirety of the modernist discourse of the twentieth century. For Fautrier's part, the answer lay in the absence of conventional representations of a subject or theme, which meant that the image operates in the disjunction between the apparent and the possible by employing metaphors, allusions, connotations and associations.

Although the interpretation was still based on a preunderstanding (the historically specific horizon of the interpreter), the work, as such, continued to remain open to a multiplicity of differing interpretations. The limited, though nevertheless extant, iconic sign functions of the image and the title, in particular, obviously provided a measure of guidance. Had Fautrier given his series of hostage pictures a more neutral title ('nr 1' to 'nr 33', for example) the horizon of interpretation would in all likelihood have been different. But an interpretation that treats the title seriously comes up against the question: is the subject here—in a quite literal sense—a realistic representation of the formation of a wound as a result of external violence? In that case, its significance would be fixed to a particular historical experience: the factual outcome of being a hostage of the Nazi occupation forces and/or their fellow-travellers. Or is it rather a matter of also understanding the image as a metaphor of the split in personality caused by the individual having to adapt to the demands of the occupying forces and, therefore, by a form of internal violence? The theme of the hostage would also then describe the condition of internal exile and the complex of lies, collaboration, submission and oblivion in which so many people found themselves while suffering oppression. And can the latter interpretation be said to represent not only the experience of the horrors of war, but also to evoke (on a deeper metaphorical level) a more universal image of the alienation and the sense of fragmented identity that so characterise modern society? Or is it the case instead that Fautrier's paintings should be seen as a continuation of the great French tradition, with their exquisite handling of light and materials being understood as a modern version of the sensibility of a Chardin or a Watteau? Is this actually a form of art suited to the drawing-room walls of the comfortably-off middle classes?

The communicative and linguistic problems posed by Fautrier's hostage pictures are typical in many regards of the way modernism, and the radical art of the post-war period in particular, is able to refer to the external world. A more explicitly realistic representation of the subject matter could not have been legitimated within avant-garde discourse but would have been consigned to the non-position of Socialist Realism or the trivial art and kitsch culture of the bourgeoisie. A picture entirely lacking any form of mimetic representation could, it is true, have been interpreted indirectly or on a metaphorical level as a statement critical of civilisation, but it would then have lost any connection at all to the surrounding world in terms of its subject matter. This demonstrates how the visual arts are characterised by a multifaceted discursive logic at a particular time and in a specific social and political situation. However, the very vagueness of Fautrier's critique of civilisation could also be identified as one of the factors that made it possible to subsume modernist art within the dominant system of cultural norms: it was not explicitly antagonistic to the ideological norms of the society that surrounded it, neither was it a call to political activism, but it involved, in most cases, an individual reaction to a particular situation. It is possible to refer here to forms of absence and alienation that were different from those that characterised the avant-garde of the early twentieth century in a new era, whose hallmarks were a tangible sense of trauma, the extinction of utopias and the impossibility of collective experience. The key words in this regard are individualism and doubt, in contrast to the collectivism and antagonism of the historical avant-garde.

In fact the absence of any explicitly political and propagandist content was a precondition for any use of modernist art as propaganda, because the acceptance of the avant-garde served as a rhetorical device for freedom and individualism, which meant its idiom could serve as an antithesis to Socialist Realism and because it would have been impossible in the art worlds of the Western nations to employ propaganda directly and still be taken seriously. The same goes for American Abstract Expressionism to a very considerable extent. Jackson Pollock may serve as an example of the difficulty involved in fixing any obvious or even possible meaning, which explains the very diverse metaphorical interpretations of his paintings that have been produced over the years: as a Gothic, morbid, extreme and supremely American exponent of the medium-specific efforts of modern art (Clement Greenberg); as an example of the attempts of Communism to infiltrate American society and create chaos within it (George Dondero); as a portrait of the complex social and psychological situation of the modern urban man (Rudolf Arnheim); as a means by which contemporary art could free itself from the material constraints of painting and develop art as process rather object (Allan Kaprow).[105]

Kirk Varnedoe has described how Pollock's works constitute a historical turning point in the history of modern art, because his work always involved oppositions in a way that made any definitive assignment of meaning impossible, thus illustrating the openness of aesthetic interpretation.[106] But in my view, this both exaggerates and diminishes the significance of Pollock's contribution. It exaggerates in the sense that neither Jackson Pollock, nor American Abstract Expressionism as such can be put forward as the sole exponents of this openness; informal art and the critical debate in Europe played at least as important a role in the establishment of the post-war changes in the definition of art and interpretation. And it diminishes because the ramifications of this issue extended far beyond matters of aesthetics or philosophy. For if it is not possible to say where in a painting by Jackson Pollock or Jean Fautrier freedom and democracy are being expressed, neither is it possible to say where their potentially transgressive or politically subversive message lies.

The deliberately radical opening-up of the possible interpretive horizons of the work that informal and Abstract Expressionist art introduced had implications that were aesthetic, political and social. It was not only the meaning of the work that seemed vague, arbitrary and subjective in this light, but also its ideological position. The strategy that was characteristic of the established institutions in their interpretation of avant-garde art could be called the model of indirect and symbolic interpretation. This meant that the propaganda value of the visual arts in the West was to be found on a more subtle level, with the paintings and exhibitions playing a subordinate role: it was the demonstration of the place of avant-garde art in the norm systems of the free world instead that was crucial. And this is a key point for the process of normalisation, because what is being institutionalised here is a context for the understanding of modern art that is, in essence, open to both a cultural and a countercultural pattern of interpretation at one and the same time.

The Modernist Metanarrative

Between History and the Present

The establishment of modernism in the system of cultural norms of the Western world and the new role of New York as the centre of the art world are largely bound up with questions of power, of ideological representations and of interpretive privilege. This situation was, in essence, not unlike that of the late eighteenth century when the academic system expanded and Paris increasingly eclipsed Rome as the most vital city on the art scene. In both cases, these shifts determined the circumstances of contemporary artists and the historiography of later generations. For here, as ever, it is the victor who writes the history.

The American artist Mark Tansey has produced a wonderfully ironic painting of the triumph of American art over the French, entitled *The Triumph of the New York School* (1984). The work was executed as a traditional academic historical painting—with obvious Socialist Realist features—in terms of its subject matter and idiom as well as its vast scale. At the centre of the picture, André Breton is being obliged to sign the treaty of surrender in front of Clement Greenberg. Behind Breton stand the aging representatives of the once mighty French avant-garde; visible on the American side are the exponents of Abstract Expressionism.[107] Note, too, the difference between the equipment of the two sides, with the French troops apparently reliant on their cavalry, while the Americans have access to modern tanks. The subject of the work is, in other words, the outright victory of modernity over tradition, portrayed in the traditional academic style. The

---

How to cite this book chapter:
Hayden, Hans. 2018. The Modernist Metanarrative. In: Hayden, H. *Modernism as Institution: On the Establishment of an Aesthetic and Historiographic Paradigm* Pp. 188–241. Stockholm: Stockholm University Press. DOI: https://doi.org/10.16993/bar.f. License: CC-BY

backdrop against which the treaty of surrender is signed is a panoramic view of the landscape—the art world—that has been laid waste by the battles.

This is at once a penetrating, problematic and disquieting rendering of the historical image. The irony in Tansey's painting is directed not so much at the representatives of Abstract Expressionism as at the historiographic view, which accentuates both the masculine metaphors of the battlefield and the conspiratorial metaphors associated with espionage in portraying how a particular view of art became established. The cultural logic of the Cold War does, of course, provide an essential context for understanding the normalisation of modernist art after the Second World War. But the context created by more local and national social and aesthetic considerations that serve to define a range of specific situations in which individual artists operated and expressed themselves is just as crucial. In this way, a much more multifaceted complex of factors is revealed than those suggested by the signing of a treaty of surrender. What Tansey's picture, like much of the research on this subject produced in recent years, fails to say is that the real victory was not won on the battlefield but in the historiography.

Another image should be introduced here as a supplement to Mark Tansey's painting: a little drawing by Alfred Barr from 1941.[108] He called it 'Torpedo moving through time', and it outlines a diagram for an ideal permanent collection at the Museum of Modern Art. The drawing was part of an argument in an ongoing debate about whether MoMA would build its own permanent collection or if the museum should serve as a transit museum and a branch of Metropolitan Museum of Art.[109] What Barr tried to accomplish was to give a graphic form to the idea that MoMA must be built around a permanent collection that would constitute a canon of international modern art as well as a historical foundation for contemporary art and design. The upper torpedo is drawn along a time-axis reaching far back into the historical past and is almost entirely dominated by the French traditions. Once the torpedo in the lower part of the image has moved forward nine years, a new and much more uniform pattern emerges. Jacketed in the French and European tradition, the torpedo is now equipped with a high-explosive warhead consisting of American contemporary art.

The martial metaphor obviously implies that this is something more than a schematic image of an ideal museum collection: it demonstrates both that a shift in the American awareness of the front line of contemporary art had taken place at this time, with Barr considering that the US had taken over the initiative, and that MoMA should be more actively engaged in supporting this change. But it also demonstrates something far more important: the existence of a focal point between the historical and the contemporary, around which the gradual shifts in art taking place in the present create new historical perspectives and patterns. For, on one level, the institutionalisation of modernism after the Second World War brought about a radical change in the practice of the individual artist, such that every formulation of the new was already inscribed in tradition from the outset.

Institution and Narration

The post-war period is portrayed in art-historical handbooks as a time when a new generation of artists emerged. A generation characterised by various aesthetic movements and -isms: Abstract Expressionism, *art informel*, Cobra, Tachisme, Action Painting, *art autre*, *art concret*, Color Field Painting. The story told here is of the establishment of new forms of nonfigurative and abstract art on both sides of the Atlantic that became a key part of the prevailing value system of the official art world. At the same time, the history of modernism was also being written in the form of exhibitions and texts of different kinds and with various levels of ambition: from the megaexhibitions (the biennales held in Venice and São Paulo, *documenta* in Kassel) and ambitious historical surveys presented at the major museums to minor retrospective exhibitions at private galleries; from historical and theoretical specialist studies and general handbooks to reviews, newspaper articles and pamphlets. This took place in parallel with a comprehensive institutional change in the art scene of the Western world that saw an increasing number of galleries and magazines promoting radical modernist art to an ever-larger audience. At the same time, the pioneers of the historical avant-garde were being appointed to positions at the leading art schools and academies in Europe and the US, whose students were now able to acquire knowledge about the theory and practice of the historical avant-garde first-hand.

An enormous and continually expanding amount of propositions and statements were being produced about modernism both past and present. This expansion can be described in both qualitative and quantitative terms, as exemplified in Diana Crane's in-depth study of the New York art world of the period:

> During the fifties and sixties, the New York art world could be described as an extensive social network in which many participants performed more than one role: artists served as critics; critics as curators and vice versa; art editors as curators; curators as collectors; and curators as trustees of museums and as backers of art galleries. Groups of artists were linked to groups of sponsors or "constituencies" whose members were able to obtain a sense of new developments and trends through their participation in this network.[110]

Many other critics and historians have described this complicated interplay of roles and the changing of roles within the art world as social networks, such as Irvin Sandler who, in *American Art of the Sixties,* characterises the New York art scene in terms of a number of coteries that functioned as distinct, although not *per se* closed, groups, each of which was defined by a specific orientation.[111] What is perhaps most interesting about such an analysis is that it points to a degree of mobility in the field that was both social and intellectual.

Although the jostling for position might lead to refinements of artistic style and aesthetic statement, these positions were far from as rigid as the posthumous categorisations of art history. The result of this flexible and complex system was that both the private and public sectors were able to play an active role in the economic make-up of the art world, as Diane Crane has shown:

> Beginning in the middle sixties, federal and state governments, corporations and foundations began to give more support to the arts in general. For example, support for the arts by the National Endowment for the Arts, which was created in 1965, increased

from $1.8 million in 1966 to $131 million in 1983. Corporate spending increased from $22 million to $436 million. Support by all the state governments increased from $2.7 million in 1966 to $125 million in 1983, while foundation support increased from $38 million in 1966 to $349 million in 1982. Museums received the largest share of both corporate, federal and state funds.[112]

This economic expansion is, of course, only one index among many of a complicated process of institutionalisation in which the distribution of capital had not only a financial aspect but also major social and symbolic dimensions. And although Crane provides a fairly stereotypical description of how the impact of this expansion affected the establishment of different styles, she has a point in that idioms and aesthetic approaches can also be inscribed and analysed in this economic and social context. And, given this context, the promotion, evaluation and interpretation of a particular artistic trend can never be considered innocuous or refer solely to a sphere of exclusively aesthetic considerations.

Although Diane Crane's study reflects the circumstances of the American art world in the main, the model of unrivalled expansion and of a complex pattern of interaction between the private and the public spheres can also be applied to Europe and other areas within the Western hemisphere. We can recognise a type of rhetoric at work here that we encountered earlier, one in which the regional, the arbitrary and the hierarchical have been embedded in a notion of the universal. It is an idea whose origins clearly lie in a European (and Eurocentric) canon of aesthetic, ideological and epistemological representations irrespective of how this canon would subsequently be transformed and expanded.

From the 1980s onwards in particular, this expansion has led to an increasingly evident globalisation of the art world. This has been portrayed on occasion as no more than the incorporation of new territories within that world, with its growing expansion into a worldwide network. But just as the promotion of a particular type of art cannot be described as an innocuous or purely aesthetic matter, neither should the globalisation of the art world be understood as an evolution of a flat (nonhierarchical) structure. As Charlotte Bydler has shown in *The Global Art World, inc.* (2004), the art world should be seen as both a horizontal network and a hierarchical categorisation of various institutions and centres. A limited number of professional actors operate in this world who are able to set the agenda as a result of their access to key institutions across a range of core nations and are, therefore, also able to define what is possible within the discourse; these actors shape the idea of the globalisation of art on the basis of institutions, languages and a history of European origin.[113] The rhetoric surrounding the phenomenon of globalisation is reminiscent of that which underpinned ideas about modernisation, with the centrifugal motion outward from an inner nucleus leading to both the universal and the global being defined on the basis of a norm, a canon and an interpretive horizon, all of which originate in a particular geographic and historical position. And although Bydler is describing the situation at the beginning of the twenty-first century, and even though this structure has become extraordinarily more complex and the ways of regulating and defining the discourse of the order ever more subtle, and thus harder to analyse, mechanisms that were in operation in the European art world from the end of the nineteenth century can clearly be recognised.

The expansion under discussion here has, in any case, meant that a wealth of different styles, media and aesthetic approaches have been established and presented within key institutions. And yet it is also clear that the art world of Western Europe and America, until the end of the 1950s at least, was, as we have seen, characterised by a rather one-sided—not to say doctrinaire—interpretation of the meaning of modernism in aesthetic, medial and historiographic terms. At a more overarching level, what normalisation means in this context is the establishment of an interpretive privilege, such that the position of modern art shifted from being challenged to being possible and, ultimately, to constituting the only apparent possibility—the historically normal.

A key institution in this regard is the museum of modern and contemporary art. This type of museum was not an innovation purely of the twentieth century but can be traced back to the establishment of the Musée du Luxembourg by the French state in 1818, which served as an annex to the Musée du Louvre. The relationship between these museums, known as the Louvre-Luxembourg system, meant that works were deposited in the collections of the contemporary museum until the centenary of the artist's birth had been reached, when they were either transferred to the central collection of the Louvre or, in the case of those works that were no longer considered of major significance, were sent to museums and institutions in the provinces.[114] The flexibility of this system made it initially appear ideal for several of the twentieth century's museums of modern art. However, it is precisely because this system was not implemented that it is possible to refer to the modern museums that were set up in the middle of the twentieth century as constituting a new type of museum. This new museum combined to some extent the functions of the Musée du Luxembourg and the Salon in nineteenth-century Paris, serving as a normative and sanctioned arena for contemporary art while establishing a similarly normative and sanctioned historical collection.

The international prototypes for this kind of museum were the Museum of Modern Art in New York (1929/1939) and the Musée National d'Art Moderne in Paris (1939/1947). The way these two institutions operated was, however, rather different. While the latter represented the continuity of the modern museums with the official art world of the nineteenth century as a result of its conservative, hierarchical and centralising approach, the unrivalled collections and the progressive and historically informed exhibition programme of the former meant that it would become the paradigm for the modern art museum as a new type of institution. The causes behind the emergence of this new type of museum could, of course, vary, ranging from a pragmatic realisation of the lack of scope for modern art in major art historical collections or a reactionary aspiration to be able to separate the great tradition from the decadence of the contemporary to a more aggressive pursuit of a specific site at which to present and study the art of the present and its history. This shift and the process of establishment may be understood in general terms as reflecting the institutional change introduced by modernity, as part of which, older institutions continued operating but with somewhat altered functions and a different basis of legitimation. There could thus be continuity between premodern and modern institutions, with the particular transformation of their significance and function serving as an index of their new roles and grounds of legitimation. The expansion of modern art museums around the world after the Second World War meant that this type of institution not only assumed the normative functions of the Academy, but also helped to shape the understanding of modern art and its history to a considerable extent.

* * * *

The creation of the museum for modern art involved the establishment not only of a new type of museum, but also of a particular narrative structure in the post-war public sphere that served as a normalised matrix for the interpretation of contemporary art and its recent history. The historical selection was defined with such a degree of specificity that the word modern combined a period of time (the twentieth century) with a particular aesthetic trend (modernism).[115] In the modern epochal museum, a specific and all-inclusive historical interpretive matrix was devised and entrenched that every other form of representation had to relate to and be measured against: antimodernism, regional variants and deviations, postmodernism. A pattern of interaction between narrative and institution emerges here that served as a code for the historically normal.

To assert that the modern museum formed a narrative specific to itself might seem to be a massive exaggeration, because a range of different narratives and interpretations were demonstrably in evidence in the post-war period: the Tate Gallery was not telling exactly the same story as the Museum of Modern Art, the Solomon R. Guggenheim Museum was not the same as the Musée National d'Art Moderne, the Stedelijk Museum was not the same as the Hamburger Kunsthalle, Moderna Museet was not the same as the Louisiana Museum for Moderne Kunst, and so on. And if the various survey works covering the art history of the twentieth century published from the mid-1950s onwards are also taken into account, then an even greater range of variation becomes evident.

But it is possible to refer to the existence of a common pattern behind these variations, which can appear so self-evident and internalised it may be difficult to pick out. Carol Duncan has described the uniformity of the selections and narratives of the modern museums, in Europe as well as in the USA, as a function of their task of presenting generally accepted values and forms of knowledge to the public.[116] She distinguishes a hierarchy among different museums in this respect with the Museum of Modern Art providing the paradigm, not only in terms of the composition and presentation of its collection, but also in terms of the standard narrative of modernism. This narrative is not, however, presented solely by museums of modern art around the world, but also in various texts, articles, books and survey literature. It also provides the foundation for an oral mediation of the history of modern art in the teaching carried out in art schools and at university. There can be no disputing the fact that the standard narrative of modernism now serves as the normalised matrix for the understanding of modern art.

As the fundamental problem in this regard is the understanding of the normal as a historically specific construction, one way forward would be to compare the normalised account with other narratives produced about twentieth-century art. The universal history of art might be compared, for example, with its regional and national variants. Or a comparison might be drawn, as James Elkins has done, between the narratives and selections presented by survey literature published in Western Europe and the US with their counterparts in Eastern Europe and the Soviet Union.[117] One significant example is the nine-volume Soviet work *Vseobsjtjaja istorija iskusstv* (The Universal History of Art), which was published by the Institute for the Theory and History of the Visual Arts at the Art Academy in Moscow in 1956.[118] Both in terms of narrative and selection, the earlier parts resemble what has become the standard version in the major surveys published in the West during the twentieth century, but a deviation starts to emerge in the seventh volume in the treatment of nineteenth-century art— what are considered to be the origins of the modern period, that is. Instead of one great line emerging from the development of French art, the narrative is structured around various national schools, with the emphasis placed on Russia and Eastern Europe. It may, of course, be objected that Elkins exaggerates the unusual nature of this type of structure, which actually has historical precedents and which is interesting precisely because it demonstrates a kind of narrative that preceded the now-established evolutionary progression from romanticism/realism to modernism.[119] The seventh volume describes the developments in art during the nineteenth century in the capitalist countries, structured according to national schools and applying an inclusive global perspective in which all the continents are represented, while the eighth and final volume deals with the corresponding developments in the socialist countries, with a considerable emphasis on the Soviet Union.

The historical account and the selection provided in *Vseobsjtjaja istorija iskusstv* not only portray a different twentieth century and a different modern art to the one presented by Western European and American survey works, they also reveal, as Elkins emphasises, an interesting structural agreement:

> The gaps are complementary: "our" texts, nominally unbiased, are sometimes perfect casts of Eastern models. . . . The Russian "universal history" shows with uncanny exactitude how America's apparently nonjudgmental survey texts are not only deeply biased towards the West (we knew that) but are in parts virtually capitalist manifestoes, excluding each and every one of the movements that the Russian text includes.[120]

The two different narratives thus provide a specialised example of the discursive logic of the Cold War: an art-historical microcosm that is more or less directly related to the macrocosmic structures of the official ideologies. But Elkins misses a crucial aspect when describing these two opposed but complementary structures: the Soviet survey work actually devotes a whole volume of over 900 pages to capitalist art. This is an inclusive approach almost entirely absent from the Western European and American surveys, and one is forced to ask oneself why that should be the case. The answer obviously has nothing to do with a greater willingness on the part of the post-Stalinist regime to permit the publication of alternative opinions in the public sphere. It should be remembered that this project was launched by the Soviet art academy at a time when all the bodies representing the art world had been centralised in a rigid hierarchical structure under the direct control of the Party, so it can hardly be a question of a mistake or of a particular volume managing to slip through the net of the censor without the authorities reacting. *Vseobsjtjaja istorija iskusstv* represented the official view of the history of art in a way that was quite different from any corresponding work or collection in the West. So why then was the enemy included in this picture?

One possible answer could be drawn from what has been said previously in this study. As we have seen, the normalisation of modernism in the US and parts of Western Europe was dependant on the putatively nonpolitical function of art, which meant that the deideologisation of the avant-garde was essential if it was to be used for ideological ends; this was made possible by the application of what I have called the model of indirect and symbolic interpretation. This allowed for an interpretation of the visual arts that was simultaneously cultural and countercultural, with the result that certain fundamental tropes—freedom, individuality, authenticity, modernity, universality—could be used for the legitimation of radical art by both camps. The situation in the Soviet Union and Eastern Europe was the exact opposite. One of the basic principles of Socialist Realism was that the visual arts were subordinate to the control of the party and they formed part of the fabric of the Socialist state. The function of art was clear: every representation could and had to be interpreted on the basis of an explicit political context (the doctrine of realistic form and socialist content). And because the dialectic of materialism formed the scientific foundation of this approach, a particular synthesis had to be formulated in relation to any given antithesis. This led to a narrative structure that is entirely different from that of the West, with triumphing over its antithesis (capitalism) providing the immanent driving force of history, although in so doing it necessarily demonstrates the existence of its antithesis in the historiography of art as well (modernism).

And yet the dialectic is more complicated than that. For if one surveys the selection of images in the volume dealing with the art of the capitalist countries, one finds reproduced both a familiar modernist canon and a different image that affords considerable scope for a more socially critical, realistic and, possibly Socialist, art. Although Jackson Pollock, Mark Tobey, Robert Motherwell and Franz Kline appear in the chapter on art and architecture in the US, Abstract Expressionism does not exactly dominate the presentation; it gets seven lines in a chapter of just over thirty pages. What does dominate is the Social Realism of the interwar years and artists such as George Bellows, Kent Rockwell, Robert Minor, William Gropper, Andrew Wyeth, Alton Pickens and Ben Shan. The text starts by drawing a distinction between two trends in American society that are mutually opposed: the democratic humanism of progressive realism is set against the official, reactionary, 'late-bourgeois' culture of decadence.[121] This distinction provides the matrix on which the interpretation of every artistic and architectural creation is then based. As part of this scheme, Abstract Expressionism inevitably falls within the latter category as the style that embodies those artist-charlatans who shamelessly, and quite literally, are making a fast buck out of the sensation-seeking American public. Although artists such as Pollock and Kline are concerned with developing the appearance of existential and authentic expression in their work, this does not reflect anything real in practice, apart from the decline of bourgeois culture.[122]

The rhetoric of this presentation makes two antithetical positions—one of which is rejected—admirably clear, but it also identifies a trend of critical, popular and progressive culture within the stronghold of capitalism that may represent a potential for revolutionary change among the peoples of capitalist countries. The volume on capitalist art does not constitute an end in itself as part of the historical presentation but fulfils its particular function only when considered in relation to the concluding volume on Socialist art. The latter volume's appendix of illustrations ends with a lithograph from Cuba portraying the people's militia on the march; this individual portrayal could be interpreted in the light of the larger image mediated by the work as a whole of the triumphal march of Socialist Realism into the future.

So what do these parallel historical narratives tell us that we did not already know: that two different ideological systems produced apparently incompatible narratives at a particular time? What the comparison sheds light on in particular are their respective ideological and rhetorical starting points, the structures, tropes, techniques and narrativesthat are presented in each account as the historically normal and have been concealed to a greater or lesser extent. This applies especially to the putatively open, impartial and universal criteria of the Western form of historiography, in which the notion of modernism as modern art is a premise that has been taken for granted rather than an evaluation. Moreover, a form of historiography is involved in both cases that has had an enormous influence on assumptions about the present. This is particularly true of the modern museums—both the Eastern and Western varieties—which have become the key institution for the intersection of history's diachronic line with the synchronous field of the contemporary period.

The place where these movements come together is not an innocuous position, for this is the very point where the struggle for interpretive privilege is waged unceasingly both by history and the present. It is also at this point that the issue of which historical image is produced becomes decisive in determining what form of contemporary art is legitimate and possible. Here, interpretation is not so much a matter of a number of individual statements based on different personal preferences, but rather a pattern for what may be legitimately formulated as part of the discourse.

Alfred Barr's Diagram

The narrative pattern of modernism could be likened to a matrix for legitimate statements that extends both beyond and below individual narratives and constitutes their tacit foundation. Although this kind of proposition is all well and good at a sufficiently abstract level, the issue here is its implications in more concrete terms. Instead of setting out a wealth of different examples drawn from exhibitions, catalogues, survey works, specialist studies and monographs from Western Europe and the US, I propose to concentrate on a single one: the exhibition *Cubism and Abstract Art* held at the Museum of Modern Art in New York in 1936 and Alfred Barr' schematic rendering of the development of abstract art that was published on the front cover of the catalogue.

The exhibition comprised over 400 works in various media that filled all four storeys of the museum's then temporary premises on 53rd Street: painting, sculpture, photography, architecture, furniture, posters, stage sets, typography and film. Most of the space was, however, given over to painting and sculpture, with the greater part of these works being made up of loans from European collections. *Cubism and Abstract Art* formed part of an ambitious attempt by Alfred Barr to chart and present the history of modern art up to the present day; it was followed somewhat later by a companion exhibition *Fantastic Art, Dada, Surrealism* (1936–37).[123] These exhibitions not only provided two of the most comprehensive surveys of the various movements and history of modernism, but also came to be seen after the Second World War as a paradigmatic formulation of modern art.[124]

One of the factors contributing to their importance was they made no attempt to avoid the radical and potentially subversive aspects of modernism. They presented what was at that time a clearly defined picture of the trends considered significant, even though Barr expressly stated that the aim was to present a historical study in 'a retrospective' rather than 'a controversial spirit'.[125] However, taken together, the exhibitions created a public and critical commotion that laid bare the existence of a yawning gulf between the avant-garde and the US public of the period, and it also contributed in no small measure to the proliferation of myths surrounding 'misunderstood modernism'.[126] Although it may not have been the first or the largest of its kind, what made *Cubism and Abstract Art* such a special exhibition was its character of an art-historical genealogy in which history was placed in an active relationship with the present. This difference also emerges from a comparison with *Les Maîtres de l'Art Indépendant* at the 1937 Paris World Fair. Where the French exhibition focused on a number of significant individuals, in *Cubism and Abstract Art*, the individual was subordinated to the historical process. The concept was made abundantly clear by the cover of the catalogue, which was adorned with Alfred Barr's controversial diagram of the development of abstract art.

This image had a decisive influence on the way the history of modern art has been viewed in the post-war period and proved far more influential than the exhibition itself—or any other exhibition, for that matter. Its significance lies not in its didactic aim of providing the public with an introduction to the course of art history, but rather in the way it formulates a developmental logic of the history of modernism in more general terms. Sibyl Gordon Kantor's meticulous biography of Alfred Barr reveals that he had two crucial qualifications for producing this diagram. He had been thoroughly schooled in art history at Harvard and Princeton, where, through his teacher and mentor Charles Rufus Morey, he became acquainted with what was at the time the most advanced research in formalism, in the work of Alois Riegl and Heinrich Wölfflin in particular.[127] As part of his preparations for his dissertation, he set off on an extensive European study trip in 1927–28 that took him to London, Amsterdam, Dessau, Berlin, Moscow, Paris and other places. There, Barr came in contact with some of the leading and most progressive representatives of European modernism, especially at the Bauhaus and its Russian counterpart VKhUTEMAS. This allowed him to acquire a rather unusually comprehensive grasp of the range and radicalism of modernism, not only in the visual arts and architecture, but also in other media. As a result, the idea of modernism as a coherent, supra-individual and transnational epochal style would be of crucial importance for Barr.[128] And it was this synthesis of first-hand information and historical analysis that served as the bedrock of the exhibition and which gave Barr's notion of (modernism as) modern art such a wide-ranging and enduring import. For this flow-chart of the development of abstract art, with its various interconnections, interrelationships and influences, also provided a formulation of the main direction of modern art: an evolution towards an ever purer and increasingly visual (medium-specific, self-reflexive) idiom.

The starting-point for the diagram was specific and, at that point, controversial: the Post-impressionism of the late nineteenth century, with the emphasis on Cézanne, Gauguin, van Gogh and Seurat.[129] Also displayed in the diagram are five rectangles of developmental influences outside the self-enclosed universe of the visual arts of the Western world that may be brought together under the headings of primitivism (Japanese prints, the art of the Middle East and 'negro sculpture') and modernity (the machine aesthetic and modern architecture).[130] The rectangles are differentiated graphically from the structure of the diagram, and their contents appear as isolated monads of underlying influences; whereas, the various stylistic movements are bounded by open semi-circles, which suggest that they constitute distinct but integrated components of the system as an organic whole. Apart from the abstract effects of the rectangles, the development appears to be a perfectly isolated evolutionary sequence in which a veritable hodgepodge of movements and trends pours out of the sources of Syntheticism and Post-impressionism. Cubism occupies a central place, indicated by the size of the font, and leads on to the trends, which form geometrical abstract art. To the left of the main Cubist channel, all the influences of the late nineteenth century run together into Fauvism, which in turn leads on to an alternative line towards nongeometrical abstract art. Barr himself emphasised that the two strains making up contemporary abstract art (the biomorphic and the geometric) were refinements of the late nineteenth century trends towards subjectivism (van Gogh, Gauguin) and objectivism (Cézanne, Seurat), respectively.[131] This allows one to detect a further level of abstraction in the diagram, consisting of two ideal straight lines below the confusion of various individual movements and styles. As Michael Auping has insightfully pointed out, this systematic approach appears to be a mirror image of the two tendencies in human consciousness, localised in the left and right hemispheres, respectively, of the brain: emotional creativity and rational logic.[132]

The diagram can be difficult to analyse today because it seems so familiar. Few who have taken a foundation course in art history or read a handbook on twentieth-century art can have avoided having this diagram and its underlying tropes imprinted on their awareness: the main movements, the various influences and interrelationships, the autonomy and inherent essentialism of the developmental process, creative originality its ultimate driving force. And yet it was a historical accident that made Barr's diagram so applicable and, therefore, so significant: its description of two different trends towards abstraction appears to be an almost prophetic account of the post-war situation and the issues it faced.

A somewhat peculiar aspect of the selection of the diagram, which may not appear obvious at first, is that Barr chose to include so many movements in the process instead of refining it by highlighting one or two significant strains (the route, for example, from Cubism through Orphism, Purism, Suprematism and Constructivism to the then contemporary Concrete Art). What he formulated instead was the pursuit of abstraction as an underlying impulse—a *Kunstwollen,* as it were—in modern art that, like the preoccupation of the Florentine Renaissance with the doctrines of perspective and proportion, was manifested everywhere and had occurred time after time.[133] This pursuit emerged as an essential form of expression that lay behind modernism's medley of movements, practices and idioms. At the same time, the thematic approach of the exhibition became a means of charting, characterising and presenting modernism as a whole to the American public. In this respect, the diagram served as a blueprint, or a concealed matrix, not just for the development of abstract art, but also for the understanding of modern art as a whole.[134]

Barr himself could hardly be said to possess any exclusive copyright to this narrative or its fundamental criteria. The major significance of the diagram lies rather in the way it codifies and systematises theoretical propositions and identities that were produced by the historical avant-garde. It bears comparison with the curious text published in 1925 by El Lissitsky and Hans Arp under the title *Die Kunstismen 1924–1914.* This was not a historical survey in the accepted sense but a selection of movements, artists, quotations and images that began in the contemporary period and led backwards, while a line was simultaneously being drawn in graphic terms from 1924 into the future where a question mark was waiting.[135] The aim of bringing together the historical and the contemporary at a rhetorical question mark about the future course of modern art could be interpreted as providing a form of guidance for the general public, as a historical legitimation of contemporary radical art and as the creation of a genealogy within avant-garde discourse. The book also clearly demonstrates the level of historical awareness to be found in the avant-garde at this time and how the variety of -isms could be presented in a chronological sequence in order to distinguish a general development that transcended individual styles. While Barr, for his part, does not deviate noticeably from this catalogue of -isms and, indeed, formulates what is in many respects the same image of the situation of modern art, he does so not as an artist or critic but as an art historian.[136] It is here, too, that a major difference lies, specifically in an institutional context: where El Lissitzky and Hans Arp were attempting to formulate a historical context within and for avant-garde discourse as a private initiative, Barr was speaking from his position as the head of a public art museum. His proposition was inscribed, in other words, as a legitimate representation in the context constituted by the official exhibitionary complex.

There is an additional similarity between Barr's diagram and *Die Kunstismen* that is crucial: they both make generalisations that transcend the national and the culturally specific. Although the nationalities of the artists were indicated in the catalogue to *Cubism and Abstract Art*, this information had no bearing on the image of a universal development that the diagram presented. To this end, movements and artists with a more local impact were excluded, as were works that were created before or after those deemed of significance to the major evolutionary line.[137] Barr was not, however, describing a determinist development; instead, every artist was faced with a choice: whether he or she wanted to be part of the progressive, forward movement of the modern era or to stand outside it.[138] Evident here are the two diverse and paradoxically interacting interpretive matrices referred to in relation to the historiography of *documenta* held in Kassel in 1955: the understanding of the development of modern art as both a supra-individual, essentialist process and a narrative about the autonomous efficacy and capacity for reflection of the individual in modern society. These two narrative structures might appear essentially opposed to one another, but it is in fact more a matter of the one determining the other. While the development of modern art could be understood as supra-individual, it was dependent on the choice of the individual, because as we all know, there are different kinds of choices, heroic as well as cowardly ones. In the political context of the post-war period, the individual artist could, as we have seen, be presented as a symbolic representative of the free man, the corollary being that the very existence of a real freedom of choice—and the creative action of the individual in this situation—was the factor that led art (and society) forward.

To refer in this instance to a range of different narratives and tropes, or like Carol Duncan to distinguish a standard modernist narrative, would be to miss the point to some extent.[139] For it is possible, in my view, to distinguish a more fundamental pattern that links together the various normative attributes and the individual narratives; this pattern establishes the standard, so to speak, behind the standard narrative. This pattern involves a narrative of the art world and history that is not primarily concerned with the experiences and statements of the individual, but it provides instead an underlying matrix that defines the parameters for the possible within every particular interpretation. While the pattern under discussion takes the form of a narrative, it functions rather as a metanarrative.[140]

* * * *

The normalisation of the modernist metanarrative could be described in terms of a number of stages, in which the typical (modernism as a vital movement in the discourse) becomes presented over time as the ideal type (modernism defines the discourse), only to be transformed a few years later into an archetypal assumption (modernism's definition of the discourse as an underlying presupposition). As an archetype, this notion remains below the surface; it need not be legitimated and explained in terms of its historical premises but has become instead a self-evident premise on which to base the understanding of the visual culture of modernity. And it is as an archetype that the notion of the modernity of modernism is also introduced at this point as a self-evident premise in the interpretation of modern art: modernism is no longer just a crucial part of the visual culture of modernity, modernism *is* the modern.

This change brought with it both an expansion and restriction of the field and range of avant-garde visual culture. A key trope, formulated in various ways in the programmes of movements such as Bauhaus, De Stijl and VKhUTEMAS, was that the visual arts have to be abandoned as an autonomous value sphere in favour of an all-inclusive and socially integrated environmental design. In *Painting as Model* (1990), Yve-Alain Bois has interpreted these efforts in relation to the view of history taken by the modernist movements, and by De Stijl in particular:

De Stijl was a typically modernist movement, whose theory was grounded on those two ideological pillars of modernism, historicism and essentialism. On historicism, because on the one hand De Stijl conceived of its production as the logical culmination of the art of the past, and on the other because it prophesied in quasi-Hegelian terms the inevitable dissolution of art into an all-encompassing sphere ("life" or "the environment"). On essentialism, because the motor of this slow historical process was an ontological quest: each art was to "realize" its own "nature" by purging itself of everything that was not specific to it, by revealing its materials and codes, and in doing so by working toward the institution of a "universal plastic language". None of this was particularly original, although De Stijl's formulation of this modernist theory developed quite early on.[141]

These two pillars also serve as the basis of Barr's programme—both for the exhibition *Cubism and Abstract Art* and for MoMA as an institution—as evidenced in its inclusive approach, in which a wealth of different media were represented, and its formalist focus on, and understanding of, the development of the various media as linear and autonomous processes. Barr had learnt the lesson of Bauhaus in this regard: every medium has to be developed according to its particular characteristics, while all media start from the same basic course in the aesthetics of form. And yet this is also the very point at which the disparate clusters of forms and movements of the historical avant-garde are circumscribed, classified and legitimated as modern art—and by extension as modernism. The open-ended question mark of the fragmentary image is being transformed into the definitive full stop of the historicising system.

Barr's diagram should not, however, be seen as the absolute origin of the historiography of the post-war period. Instead, through its codification and systematisation of certain aspects of the theory, practice and historiography of the historical avant-garde, it provides a condensed and explanatory image of how the history of modern art can be written. Its entrenchment in the identity of the avant-garde is of crucial importance in this regard, because it was the actors of the art world itself who wrote the history of modern art after the war. Moreover, the diagram does not simply constitute a specific image or narrative but should be considered rather as a manifestation of a particular discursive order. In this regard, it needs to be read in relation to the purely physical presentation and staging of the modernist programme by the modern museums after the Second World War. This staging not only involved the placing of artefacts of different kinds in an alien context, but also the recoding and incorporation of artefacts as material and discursive objects within the specific sign system of the modern art museum: the white cube.

In *The Power of Display* (1998), Mary Anne Staniszewski has convincingly described how revolutionary Barr's exhibition praxis actually was; this may be difficult to understand today because it has set the pattern for the normal to such a considerable extent. He abandoned the remaining vestiges of the Salon-hang with its tightly-packed collections of pictures and placed each work at eye level against a neutral background, with the works being hung in chronological sequences that emphasised their individuality and unicity, while also situating them in an overarching ahistorical and timeless unity.[142] The point is not, however, as Staniszewski maintains, that this exhibition aesthetic constitutes a decontextualisation but rather that it introduced a recontextualisation through the creation of a new set of relationships in which the unique visual and aesthetic qualities of the work were emphasised while the object was simultaneously liberated from its historic, cultural and medial connotations. In 'Inside the White Cube' (1976), Brian O'Doherty describes how the modern exhibition space also constitutes not only part of the modernist aesthetic, but also of its particular ways of reading and its historiography:

> The history of modernism is intimately framed by that space; or rather the history of modern art can be correlated with changes in that space and in the way we see it. We have now reached a point where we see not the art but the space first. . . . An image comes to mind of a white, ideal space that, more than any single picture, may be the archetypical image of twentieth century art; it clarifies itself through a process of historical inevitability usually attached to the art it contains. . . . The work is isolated from everything that would detract from its own evaluation of itself. This gives the space a presence possessed by other spaces where conventions are

preserved through a closed system of values. Some of the sanctity of the church, the formality of the courtroom, the mystique of the experimental laboratory joins with chic design to produce a unique chamber of esthetics.[143]

The objection I would make to one aspect of Doherty's account is that what is peculiar to the white cube is not that it appears obvious to an observer but that it demonstrates a remarkable combination of being entirely visible and completely invisible at the same time. However, the crucial point is his identification of this apparently neutral space as a primary discursive technology for the constitution of meaning and value. The white cube serves at one and the same time as the material and immaterial surface of the modernist institution: the space in which the possible transformations of the art world occur and are legitimated and where the parameters for the interpretation of contemporary art are determined.[144]

In this sense, the white cube could be said to constitute the fundamental parergon of the modernist aesthetic: an aspect of the discursive order that is both invisible and fully observable and which, to the extent that it is detected at all, can be construed from the structure of the space and the forms of presentation. This bears comparison with Michel Foucault's description of the way rooms in eighteenth century schools were structured as 'the internal discourse of the institution', the ideas, that is, about children's sexuality that lay behind the particular differentiation of spaces and functions.[145] And yet the white cube and the modern museum, as the institutionalised spaces of modernism, amount to something other and something more than a mere differentiation of function. They provide, as Brian O'Doherty maintains, a frame for the interpretation of historical and contemporary art.

One obvious example is the way in which different media were incorporated in the exhibition on *Cubism and Abstract Art*; despite the use of informative texts and documentary photographs, all the images, texts and objects were fully integrated within the aestheticising and evolutionist matrix of the diagram.[146] The price for being able to include such a broad spectrum of different media in the collections of MoMA was that every object, irrespective of its genre or original function, was selected and interpreted on the basis of the same template: aesthetic artefacts in the neutral white cube of the museum. As Douglas Crisp points out in *On the Museum's Ruins* (1993), this did not just mean that revolutionising or revolutionary movements in the history of modernism were tamed, but that what were in medial terms cross-boundary projects, such as those of Soviet Constructivism and German Dadaism, whose various experiments with montage, live performances, new sculptural materials, product design and spatial installations were intended to transcend the conventions of the traditional concept of art, were fitted into and classified in the separate medial compartments they had been attempting to demolish: painting, sculpture, photography, design and architecture.[147] Here, the once so revolutionary idea of a visual culture that participates in the social and political transformation of modern life—transcending the medial and aesthetic boundaries of bourgeois society—is neutralised and adapted to an autonomous abstract order, beyond the reach of the turbulence of the political and social world and its occasionally violent upheavals.

The relationship between modernism and modernity was not a means in this instance to situate the artefact in its historical context or to provide a stimulus to critical analysis of the institutionalised order of the different media; it formed a tacit precondition for the authenticity of modern art. This could be considered perhaps the most radical and definitely the most significant innovation of the formalist aesthetic. During the first half of the twentieth century, formalism developed from one of the leading ideas of studio discussion and the discourses of art education into an essential, although never dominant, tendency in the discourses of the artistic manifesto and of art criticism, and, ultimately, from the 1930s onwards, into a key starting point for the presentation and interpretation of historical and contemporary modern art in the modern museum. The modernist metanarrative thus emerges from, and transforms, perceptions, identities, theories and forms of legitimation that became established in the discourse of the avant-garde but is, as a result of its institutional base, far more wide-ranging and authoritative than the individual representations of that discourse. For unlike the narrative structure set up by the formation of an individual or professional identity, the metanarrative operates primarily in historiography, without itself becoming the object of historical study, with various individual statements being woven together while being simultaneously adapted to an overarching interpretive matrix.

Such underlying patterns can no doubt be discerned in all kinds of narratives and statements. The existence of metanarratives need not be understood as something suspect or conspiratorial. There is, however, one aspect of this underlying interpretive matrix that is extremely problematic, and that is its invisibility. It is actively at work in the writing of history but presented as natural. In this sense, the modernist metanarrative calls to mind Roland Barthes' definition of myth as a secondary semiological system (a metalanguage), which begins at the point an already extant linguistic meaning comes to an end.[148] The myth is, in other words, a distinct narrative form that, irrespective of substance and content, constitutes a certain way of reading and produces a particular kind of understanding:

> Myth does not deny things, on the contrary, its function is to talk about them; simply, it purifies them, it makes them innocent, it gives them a natural and eternal justification, it gives them clarity which is not that of an explanation but that of a statement of fact. . . . In passing from history to nature, myth acts economically: it abolishes the complexity of human acts, it gives them the simplicity of essences, it does away with all dialectics, with any going back beyond what is immediately visible, it organizes the world which is without contradictions because it is without depth, a world wide open and wallowing in the evident, it establishes a blissful clarity: things appear to mean something by themselves.[149]

Myth thus creates an understanding based on a particular pre-understanding, but nevertheless it transcends this by excluding part of the meaning and by transforming a historically specific import into a statement of a universal kind, presenting the historically specific as the natural, that is. An obvious example is the white cube, which parades itself quite openly in public while nevertheless remaining hidden by its putatively neutral and innocuous universality. Its existence has to be pointed out if the viewer is to discover what has been right in front of him or her the whole time as an unquestioned and natural background to the exhibition. And its existence has to be problematised and historicised in order to understand that this neutrality is actually permeated by aesthetic, social and ideological norms: a metanarrative that defines the discursive order in which every single object acquires its legitimacy and meaning.

The metanarrative cannot, of course, be compared with myths in the general sense, even though a set of myths has been produced within its field (about artists, art works, creativity, presence, originality, alienation, the transgression of boundaries). But unlike the retrospective nature of myth, the metanarrative points forward and should therefore be understood as both an ideological and an epistemological narrative, a formulation of the world that encompasses a range of different ideas and representations but produces a specific order whose evaluations and selections are presented as self-evident, neutral and universal and which actively excludes or obscures competing forms of thought.[150] In this regard, it functions as an underlying framework that is taken for granted rather than as an explicitly articulated norm.

Like Fredric Jameson, one could interpret modernism as a periodising category whose metanarrative serves as a spectral and allegorical subtext that incorporates the individual work and determines the parameters for its possible meanings.[151] We are faced here with a reflexive relationship that is both the end of its own teleological explanation and yet remains open-ended towards the objects that can be included, with the selection serving as the subtext and the subtext representing a narrative about the *telos* of progress and history. A context is thus established in which the fragmentary and contradictory elements of history are integrated within a coherent and unified system. This discursive system is manifested both by the neutral exhibition space and the linear narrative, and it defines a specific course through modern art that leaves no room for question marks or alternative routes.

Endnotes

1. Robert B. Pippin, *Modernism as a Philosophical Problem. On the Dissatisfactions of European High Culture*, Oxford/Cambridge (Mass.) 1991, p. 45.

2. Mary Kelly, "Re-viewing Modernist Criticism" (1981), in Brian Wallis (ed.), *Art After Modernism: Rethinking Representation*, New York 1984, p. 95.

3. Charles Jencks, *The Language of Post-Modern Architecture*, London 1987 (1977), p. 9.

4. Andreas Huyssen, *After the Great Divide. Modernism, Mass Culture, Postmodernism*, Bloomington/Indianapolis 1986, p. 197.

5. See Igor Golomstock, *Totalitarian Art in the Soviet Union, the Third Reich, Fascist Italy and the People's Republic of China*, (Trans. Robert Chandler), London 1990, p. ix.

6. James D. Herbert, *Paris 1937: Worlds on Exhibition*, Ithaca/London 1998, p. 87.

7. The reconstruction that follows is based on the catalogue for the exhibition *Les Maîtres de l'Art Indépendant, 1895–1937*, Paris 1937. Concerning the selection of artworks, see also Dawn Ades, "Paris 1937. Art and Power of Nations", *Art and Power. Europe Under the Dictators 1930–45*, Hayward Gallery 1995–1996, London 1995, p. 59. The criterion on which this selection was based was that the artists in question should either be French citizens or they should have lived and worked in France for a long time.

8. Herbert, p. 100.

9. Ibid, p. 103.

10. Ibid, p 124.

11. For a brief survey of the *Exposition International du Surréalisme*, see Bruce Altshuler, *The Avant-Garde in Exhibition. New Art in the 20th Century*, New York 1994, pp. 116–135.

12. Walter Benjamin, "The Work of Art in the Age of Mechanical Reproduction" (1936), *Illuminations* (ed. Hannah Arendt, trans. Harry Zorn), London 1999 (1955), p. 215.

13. Ibid, pp. 227–228.

14. Ibid, p. 231.

15. Greenberg (1939), 1988 a, p. 22.

16. Ibid, p. 17.

17. Ibid, p. 10.

18. Benjamin (1936), 1999, p. 235.

19. Terry Eagleton, *Ideology. An Introduction*, London/New York 1996 (1991), pp. 2 and 6.

20. Donald Preziosi, *Rethinking Art History. Meditations on a Coy Science*, New Haven/London 1989, p. 22.

21. Serge Guilbaut, *How New York Stole the Idea of Modern Art. Abstract Expressionism, Freedom, and the Cold War*, Chicago/London 1983, p. 3.

22. See Harald Kimpel, *Documenta. Mythos und Wirklichkeit*, Köln 1997, pp. 94–95. On the night of 22 October 1943, 83% of the city's housing and 63% of its industry were destroyed in a massive bombing raid. In 1939, Kassel had a population of 216,000 inhabitants, by the end of the war, this had shrunk to only 71,000.

23. Ibid, p. 128.

24. *Documenta. Kunst des XX. Jahrhunderts*, München 1955, unpaginated (p. 5). The foreign delegates included the ambassadors of France, the United States and Great Britain, and the Swedish envoy Herr Kumlin.

25. Werner Haftmann, *Malerei im 20. Jahrhundert*, München 1954.

26. This exhibition, which comprised over 650 works, was shown in eleven cities from 1937 to 1941 and attracted around 1.2 million visitors. Some of the works would subsequently end up in the hands of highly placed party functionaries who made them part of their own collections, some were offered at auctions at which collectors and museums from all over the world made acquisitions. What works were left were finally burnt in a manner reminiscent of the book-burnings of 1933. For an in-depth analysis and documentation

of these exhibitions and their political context, see Stephanie Barron (ed.), *Degenerate Art. The Fate of the Avant-Garde in Nazi Germany*, Los Angeles County Museum of Art, New York 1991 and Walter Grasskamp, "Degenerate Art and Documenta I: Modernism Ostracized and Disarmed", in Daniel J. Sherman & Irit Rogoff (eds.), *Museum Culture: Histories, Discourses, Spectacles*, London 1994, pp. 163–194. The double standard revealed by the fact that some of the works were included in private Nazi collections speaks volumes about the real political and rhetorical function of the exhibitions (and the bonfires of art): rather than being concerned primarily with the establishment of aesthetic norms, the aim was to use avant-garde art in a fairly simple and populist fashion as a cautionary tale on the degenerate culture of the Weimar period that was targeted at domestic opinion. And if Joseph Goebbels actually felt a certain sympathy for German Expressionism or Herman Göring appropriated a couple of works by Gauguin was completely irrelevant as long as this remained a private matter and was kept outside the sphere of political rhetoric.

27. See Hans Belting, *Art History after Modernism*, Chicago/London 2003 (1995), p. 39.

28. Grasskamp, pp. 168–169.

29. See John M. MacGregor, *The Discovery of the Art of the Insane*, Princeton 1989, pp. 161–163 and pp. 238–239.

30. Kimpel, pp. 258–274.

31. This approach characterised almost every survey exhibition and handbook about modernism after the Second World War. One example can be found in Herbert Read's *The Philosophy of Modern Art* (London 1951, p. 13), where he asserted that there was no art form from the cave paintings of the Palaeolithic period to contemporary Constructivism that could not be derived from Man's universal, biological and predestined creativity. Another, and at the time, incredibly influential example was André Malraux' *Psychologie de l'art. Le musée imaginaire*, in which he maintained that photography and the new and more sophisticated techniques of reproduction were throwing wide the doors to a museum of the imagination that would allow images from various times and places to be compared

and so facilitate a new understanding of their stylistic equivalency (Malraux, *The Psychology of Art. Museum without Walls*, (Trans. Stuart Gilbert), New York 1949 (1947), p. 24). So the formal analogies were more to do with stirring the imaginative capacity and associations of the viewer rather than engaging his or her historical and contextual knowledge. While based on a formalist/psychologising model, the approach set up in this way went beyond the classification, chronology and teleology of traditional handbooks and seemed at certain points to amount to a free intertextual flow of images.

32. Dennis L. Bark & David R. Gress, *A History of West Germany. Vol. I: From Shadow to Substance 1945–1963*, Oxford/Cambridge (Mass.) 1989, pp. 248–250.

33. Guilbaut, 1983, p. 143.

34. Hans Magnus Enzensberger, *The Consciousness Industry. On Literature, Politics, and the Media*, (Trans. John Simon), New York 1974 (1962), pp. 40–41.

35. Leslie Fiedler, "The Death of the Literary Avant-Garde" (1964), *The Collected Essays of Leslie Fiedler*, vol. II, New York 1971, p. 459.

36. See Susan Sontag, "Notes on Camp" (1964), *Against Interpretation and Other Essays*, New York 2009 (1966), pp. 275–293.

37. An important example is the attempt by Jean-François Lyotard to establish the postmodern as an intellectual and ideological position in opposition to the market-oriented anything-goes realism of contemporary eclecticism. This involved demarcating a boundary to the modernist on the one hand, while establishing a continuity with (certain aspects) of history on the other; his response to the question of the implications of this position is formulated as a paradox: 'A work can be modern only if it is first postmodern. Thus understood, postmodernism is not modernism at its end, but in a nascent state, and this state is recurrent.' (Jean-François Lyotard, "An answer to the question, What is the Postmodern?" (1982), in *The Postmodern Explained*, Minneapolis 1997 (1988), p. 13). A position that was similarly critical of institutions was adopted by the editorial committee of the periodical *October* during the 1980s and 1990s. For Hal Foster and Benjamin Buchloh, the neo-Marxist interpretation of

postmodernism as institutional critique meant that the established use of the concept of the avant-garde could be redeployed not only to define a potentially radical position in the field, but also as a means of identifying certain artistic practices as radical in both aesthetic and political terms, practices that could be distinguished from the manipulations of visual culture by the consciousness industry while nevertheless defining a certain historical continuity with (a selection from) the visual logic of early modernism. In this regard, both Foster and Buchloh were attempting to surmount Peter Bürger's exclusively negative assessment of the NeoDadaism and Pop Art of the postwar period by bringing about a reinterpretation of the concept of the *neo-avantgarde*. In their work, this concept has come to mark a radical boundary within the pluralist domain of contemporary art by describing various artistic strategies as being the antitheses of what are perceived as uncritical, market-driven, commodity-fetishised and reactionary trends in the contemporary world (see e.g., Hal Foster, *The Return of the Real. The Avant-Garde at the End of the Century*, Cambridge (Mass.)/London 1996, in particular the essays 'Who's Afraid of the Neo-Avantgarde?', pp. 1–32, and 'The Art of Cynical Reason', pp. 99–124, and Benjamin Buchloh, *Neo-Avantgarde and Culture Industry. Essays on European and American Art from 1955 to 1975*, Cambridge (Mass.)/London 2000, pp. xxiv-xxv). The concept of the neo-avantgarde functions here as a mediating historical link between a selection of the trends of the early twentieth century (Dadaism and Constructivism in particular) and a more restrictive selection of the art of the present, where the emphasis is on the possibility of a countercultural, institution-critical and transgressive attitude that is simultaneously within and outside the established institutional order. In order to legitimate a genealogy of this kind, Bürger's definition of the *neo-avantgarde* (as an aestheticisation of the subversive attitude of the historical avant-garde) has to be repudiated in favour of a definition that allows us to realise how the radical art of the 1960s was actively engaged with a historical context and how this has also brought about a transformation of the institutional-critical position in our own time (Foster, 1996, p. 4).

38. Serge Guilbaut, "Postwar Painting Games: The Rough and the Slick", *Reconstructing Modernism: Art in New York, Paris and*

Montreal 1945–1964, (ed. Serge Guilbaut), Cambridge (Mass.)/London 1990, p. 43 ff.

39. Jean-Paul Sartre, *What is Literature?*, (Trans. Bernard Frechtman), Cambridge (Mass.) 1988 (1947), pp. 68–69.

40. Ibid, p. 137.

41. This type of criticism was a potent force, particularly in the cultural life of West Germany, which found itself obliged in various ways to process, interpret and understand the barbarism that had been unleashed by its own society (see Hermann Glaser, *Kulturgeschichte der Bundesrepublik Deutschland. Bd. 2: Zwischen Grundgesetz und Grosser Koalition 1949–1967*, München/Wien 1986, pp. 263–266).

42. Serge Guilbaut, "The Frightening Freedom of the Brush: The Boston Institute of Contemporary Art and Modern Art" (1985), in Marcia Pointon (ed.), *Art Apart. Art Institutions and Ideology Across England and North America*, Manchester/New York 1994, pp. 233–234. Guilbaut describes how its manifesto and subsequent change of name from Institute of Modern Art to the more neutral Institute of Contemporary Art were an attempt to establish a liberal middle course between the modernist and conservative camps. These efforts were, however, immediately identified by both sides as a movement away from liberalism and towards conservatism. The same applied to the exhibition 'American Painting in Our Century' in 1949, which was immediately kidnapped by conservative actors and enrolled in the campaign against modernism as being un-American, foreign, subversive and potentially Communist (pp. 238–241).

43. See Helen Fuchs, *Glasmåleri, modernitet och modernism. Studier i glasmåleriets (konst)historia*, (Diss. Lunds universitet 2005), Lund 2005, pp. 101–118 for a discussion about various positions within the Catholic church in relation to modernist and abstract art.

44. Hans Sedlmayr, *Verlust der Mitte. Die bildende Kunst des 19. und 20. Jahrhunderts als Symbol der Zeit*, Salzburg 1948.

45. Ibid, p. 133.

46. There are a number of interesting points of agreement between Sedlmayr's account and the critique of Enlightenment that Max

Horkeimer and Theodor Adorno formulated in their *Dialektik der Aufklärung* (1947), even though they were working from diametrically opposed ideological positions. Their analyses of the causes of the decline of the modern era also diverge: where Sedlmayr sees fragmentation as the root of all evil, Horkheimer and Adorno consider that the Enlightenment and modernity become totalitarian as a result of their pursuit of uniformity. Moreover, for Adorno, the authentic (modernist) work of art appeared to remain virgin territory within the modern; whereas, for Sedlmayr, the only conceivable (though scarcely credible) salvation lay in the one healthy vein still accessible in our time: the omnipresent longing for wholeness.

47. Hans Sedlmayr held the position of professor of art history at the Technische Hochschule in Vienna from 1936 to 1945, at the Ludwig Maximilian Universität in Munich from 1952 to 1963 and at the University of Salzburg from 1963 to 1969. He became a member of the Austrian Nazi party as early as 1932, while it was still illegal to do so, and several years before the *Anschluss*. There are certainly points of contact between Sedlmayr's critique of culture and modernity and some of the cultural policy doctrines of Nazism, particularly where the aggressive description of the decline of modern art comes close to the notion that contemporary culture is degenerate. There are no explicit links made in Sedlmayr's book between this phenomenon and ethnic or racial causative factors, which would have made the book impossible to publish in Austria only three years after the end of the war. Instead, the decline is described in the more general terms of a critique of civilisation. The generality of its approach no doubt meant that *Verlust der Mitte* could play a crucial role in the post-war cultural debate; that very quality, however, also allows it to be considered in many ways as a typical representative of the antimodernism of the time. For a discussion of Sedlmayr's role in the art world of Nazi Germany, see Jonathan Petropoulos, *The Faustian Bargain. The Art World in Nazi Germany*, New York 2000, pp. 169 and 204; Friedrich Stadler, "The Emigration and Exile of Austrian Intellectuals" *The Cultural Exodus of Austrian* (eds. Friedrich Stadler & Peter Weibel), New York 1995, pp. 14–26.

48. Sedlmayr, pp. 165–168.

49. Ibid, p. 242.

50. See Alfred Barr, *Cubism and Abstract Art*, The Museum of Modern Art, New York 1936 (the catalogue cover) and Christian Zevros, *Histoire de l'art contemporain*, Paris 1938. Both of these are based largely on the same chronology of various -isms presented in schematic form, from the pioneers of Post-impressionism via Fauvism and Cubism to the present. It is worth noting that both accord considerable space to Marcel Duchamp, even though his ready-mades were excluded.

51. Werner Haftmann, *Painting in the Twentieth Century. Vol. 1: An Analysis of the Artists and Their Work*, (Trans. Ralph Manheim), New York 1976 (1965), p 10.

52. Kimpel, p. 258.

53. Jürgen Habermas, *The Structural Transformation of the Public Sphere. An Inquiry into a Category of Bourgeois Society*, (Trans. Thomas Burger & Frederick Lawrence), Cambridge (Mass.), 1989 (1962), pp. 141–143.

54. In a brief historical survey, Nancy Jachec describes how this research can be divided from the beginning of the 1970s into three generations that deal with this theme from rather different angles of approach ("Transatlantic Cultural Politics in the late 1950s: the Leaders and Specialists Grant Program", *Art History*, vol. 26, Sept. 2003: 4, pp. 533 and 552, n. 1–3).

55. At the end of the Second World War there was good reason on all sides to fear a global economic depression similar to the one that had convulsed Europe following the First World War. American policy was therefore primarily oriented towards establishing structures for an open world economy based on the free exchange of goods, capital and technology (Melvyn P. Leffler, *A Preponderance of Power. National Security, the Truman Administration, and the Cold War*, Stanford 1992, p. 16). Under the leadership of both Truman and Eisenhower, the US conducted an active and expansionist European policy whose goal was to reconstruct the free world around American leadership. The European Recovery Program (known as the Marshall Plan) was put into effect between 1948 and 1952 to counteract the chaos of the situation in Europe. This plan entailed

making enormous loans to several Western European states and, in tandem with political, social and economic reforms, laid the foundations for a remarkable economic recovery during the 1950s. The US set up various monetary and financial institutions, such as the World Bank and the International Monetary Fund; it also initiated the GATT agreement, a multilateral treaty that proved to be of great importance for the control of tariffs and international trade. The Truman administration made full use of its very powerful position after the war to ensure that a regulatory apparatus for international contacts was in place that would function irrespective of the various bilateral agreements in existence and despite the protectionist efforts of individual states. The attempts made by the US to ensure the economic, political and military stability of Western Europe may be understood in this context, as may the scale of American influence over this new order. But the provisions of the Marshall Plan were also offset by American demands that were both economic and political in nature and increasingly tied improved trade to the issue of military support (for an analysis of these links, see Leffler, pp. 182–219). These requirements covered issues as diverse as the abolition by the recipient countries of protectionist import regulations, the integration of Germany into the western hemisphere and the need to exclude national Communist parties from direct participation in government (Jean-Pierre Rioux, *The Fourth Republic 1944–1958*, (Trans. Godfrey Rogers), Cambridge 1987 (1980/1983), p. 134). The former meant that the European market was opened up to American goods, while the latter facilitated the forming of a stable front against the East, particularly in France and Italy where the Communist parties enjoyed powerful popular support. In parallel with the Marshall Plan, the official American foreign policy stance promoted in 1947 and known as the Truman Doctrine involved a more general and long-term plan of action to maintain the independence of the nations of the West and acquired an institutional framework with the founding of NATO in 1948. The rhetoric underpinning this doctrine served to further entrench the image of a new world order that was based on a fundamental conflict between two incompatible ideological systems (John Lewis Gaddis, *The United States and the Origins of the Cold War, 1941–1947*, New York/London 1972, p. 317). With the formation of Cominform in 1947, the Soviet Union was able to exert a much firmer grip on its Eastern European satellites, with the result that the circumstances of political, social and cultural life were, to all intents and purposes, dictated by Moscow and the Eastern sphere was moulded into a monolithic bloc (see Fernando Claudin, *The Communist Movement. From Comintern to Cominform*, (Trans. Brian Pearce & Francis MacDonagh), Harmondsworth 1975 (1970), pp. 466–467. In practice, the Cominform ceased to function after the death of Stalin, and its military and foreign policy roles were assumed by the Warsaw Pact in 1955.

56. Richard Crockatt, *The Fifty Years War. The United States and the Soviet Union in World Politics, 1941–1991*, London/New York 1995, p. 75.

57. Zygmunt Bauman, *Modernity and Ambivalence*, Cambridge 1991, pp. 53–55.

58. Attempts were made to establish viable positions outside the bipolar system of the Cold War, such as the Bandung Conference in 1955 at which some Afro-Asian countries that had recently gained their independence from their respective colonial masters attempted to set up an independent group outside the conflict between East and West and beyond the influence of the Northern hemisphere (that of the US and Europe) under the name of the Third World, a term that had been coined a few years earlier. But every such attempt was almost immediately redefined within the overarching order of the bipolar system (see Cary Fraser, "An American Dilemma. Race and Realpolitik in the American Response to the Bandung Conference 1955", in Brenda Gayle Plummer (ed.) *Window of Freedom. Race, Civil Rights and Foreign Affairs 1945–1988*, Chapel Hill 2003, pp. 120–124).

59. Stephen Kotkin, *Magnetic Mountain. Stalinism as a Civilization*, Berkley 1995, p. 152.

60. Ibid, p. 360.

61. Ibid, pp. 180–181 and pp. 226–236.

62. Boris Groys, *Gesamtkunstwerk Stalin. Die gespaltene Kultur in der Sowjetunion*, (translated from Russian by Gabriele Leupold), München/Wien 1996 (1988), p. 39. The party and the state were thus able to acquire a concerted grip not only on culture, but also

on the entirety of the industrial, economic and social structure of Soviet society. The proclamation of the first Stalinist Five-Year-Plan entailed the abolition of the previously formulated New Economic Policy and, in practice, of every form of critical margin, whether this involved separate and mutually competing organisations and schools or the private art market. The party took an even firmer grip on the art world in 1936 with the formation of the KPDI, the Committee for Art Affairs (see Matthew Cullerne Brown, *Socialist Realist Painting*, New Haven/London 1998, p. 220). This gradual process may be considered from the perspective of Igor Golomstock's description of the way various totalitarian regimes have shared a fundamentally similar attitude towards the function of art in society; he portrays this as a seizure of power in five stages: (1) the state declares that art and cultural affairs as a whole constitute an ideological weapon and a resource in the struggle for power, (2) the state acquires a monopoly over the art world of the country, (3) the state sets up a comprehensive apparatus for the control of the art world, (4) the state selects one among the various artistic movements still in existence to be given official sanction, and (5) the state declares war against all the alternative trends and forms of representation (Golomstock, p. xiii).

63. Brown, p. 226. The Academy of Arts of the USSR was structured along the lines of the Russian Imperial Academy of Arts, which was established in 1757 and abolished in 1918. The organisational model for control over the art world was thus derived from the academic systems of the eighteenth and nineteenth centuries, although with the major difference that the Soviet model possessed an absolute hegemony over all forms of representation, making critical margins and alternative approaches impossible.

64. Andrei Zhdanov, "Soviet Literature – The Richest in Ideas. The Most Advanced Literature" (1934), in H. G. Scott (ed.), *Soviet Writers Congress 1934. The Debate on Socialist Realism and Modernism*, London 1977 (1935), pp. 15–24. Zhdanov began his speech by praising the incomparable superiority of the Soviet state in all areas of society, the cultural in particular, stating that no previous epoch in history had come close to matching the level achieved by Soviet culture. Taking Stalin's definition of the writer as the engineer of human souls as his watchword, Zhdanov went on to say that the specific task of

art, like every other social sector, was to serve the Socialist state. There was, however, one problem: literature and art had not yet come close to fulfilling their potential and could not be said to be properly serving the state. Zhdanov was among those who were closest to Stalin at the head of the party. He played a major role in the Great Purge from 1936 to 1938 and, as governor of Leningrad, he organised the defence of the city against the German troops during the Second World War; he was also one of the figures behind the setting up of Cominform in 1947. His speech bore the stamp of an officially sanctioned doctrine and was followed by a series of condemnations of anti-Soviet (cosmopolitan) and aesthetically subversive (formalist) modernism.

65. Brown, p. 141.

66. Groys, pp. 42–43.

67. It is in this light that the relatively extensive range of the praxis of Socialist Realism—from delicate realistic depictions of everyday life to bombastic neo-Baroque tableaux of heroic achievements by the party and hagiographic portraits of the Leader—may best be understood. The rhetorical function of Socialist Realism meant that art had to be both evocative and easily understood in terms of form and content. And it was here, too, that the interpretive element and freedom of movement that the code of Socialist Realism nevertheless made possible could be found, because the universally applicable and objective character of the ideology had to be portrayed in a way that was subjectively convincing (Groys, p. 61). In every type of subject matter, artists were supposed to be guided by specific content criteria whose key categories were *partiinost* (the realisation of the leading role of the Communist party in all areas) and *ideinost* (the introduction of new ideas and ideological content), followed by *narodnost* (popular and national support) and *klassovost* (class consciousness) (see David Elliott, *Art and Power. Europe Under the Dictators 1930–45*, Hayward Gallery 1995–1996, London 1995, p. 187). The common denominator for all the various parts of this praxis was, however, that it both could and *had* to be interpreted in a political context.

68. See for instance Piotr Piotrowski, *In the Shadow of Yalta. Art and the Avant-garde in Eastern Europé 1945–1989*, (transl. Anna Brzyski), London 2009 (2005).

69. Various loyalty programmes were coordinated with campaigns to create a specific climate of opinion. There was a particular focus on the prime importance of education as a means of fostering a profound patriotic insight into the personal responsibility incumbent on every individual in the open, but continually threatened, democratic system (see Richard M. Freeland, *The Truman Doctrine and the Origins of McCarthyism. Foreign Policy, Domestic Politics and International Security, 1946–1948*, New York/London 1985 (1970), pp. 201–245. In March 1947, nine days after launching the idea of the Truman Doctrine in a speech to Congress, President Truman gave the order for a new initiative aimed at eliminating disloyal public employees, known as the Federal Employee Loyalty Program. As part of this programme, a series of campaigns were conducted in various fields, intended to establish officially sanctioned parameters for acceptable political activities. The attorney general published a list of subversive organisations, while new rules governing the conduct of public employees were also devised. Membership in, or any form of association with, these organisations disqualified an individual from employment within federal or local government and could lead to the dismissal of those already employed, which made it extremely risky in practice for a public employee to express any deviation from the officially determined political course. New and stricter regulations covering immigration were another measure that was introduced, and the authorities were given greater powers to deport subversive elements. These efforts even went so far as to attempt to initiate a loyalty programme for the press; however, this initiative encountered such resistance that it was withdrawn. Unreliable reporters could, on the other hand, be denied exit visas, and a codified system for what information could be communicated to the mass media was set up. The Freedom Train was sent around the country in 1947 as a representation of all these efforts in symbolic form. A combination of a museum of the history of the US and a campaign for greater patriotism, this train visited hundreds of communities. Freeland shows how all these measures meant that Truman was able to recapture the initiative in a number of fields where the Republicans would otherwise have carried the day, thus creating the freedom of manoeuvre in foreign policy he required (for the approval of the Marshall Plan in particular). However, they also laid the ground for the politically

charged climate of opinion that Senator Joseph McCarthy successfully exploited a few years later for his campaigns.

70. Alan Brinkley, "The Illusion of Unity in Cold War Culture", Peter J. Kuznick & James Gilbert (eds.), *Rethinking Cold War Culture*, Washington/London 2001, p. 72.

71. This applies to movements ranging from civil rights to women's rights to the sexual equality of homosexuals in the form of the early homophile groups to literary and artistic subcultures. Despite the fact these movements developed in a repressive environment, they were able to claim legitimacy precisely because they could invoke the focus of official rhetoric on the freedom of the individual in contrast to Stalinist oppression (see Joanne Meyerowitz, "Sex, Gender, and the Cold War Language of Reform", in Peter J. Kuznick & James Gilbert (eds.), *Rethinking Cold War Culture*, Washington/London 2001, p. 117).

72. Kathryn Boyer, *Political Promotion and Institutional Patronage. How New York Displaced Paris as the Center of Contemporary Art, c:a 1955–1968*, (Diss. University of Kansas 1994), UMI Dissertation Services, Michigan 1995, pp. 51–52.

73. See Frances Stonor Saunders, *The Cultural Cold War. The CIA and the World of Arts and Letters*, New York 2000 (1999), pp. 148–153.

74. Jachec, p. 536.

75. Eva Cockcroft, "Abstract Expressionism, Weapon of the Cold War" (1974), *Pollock and After. The Critical Debate*, (ed. Francis Frascina), London 1985, pp. 126–133. At this point, the members of MoMA's board of trustees included individuals such as Porter A. McCray (who worked during the war for the Bureau of Inter-American Affairs and who was made responsible for MoMA's international programme in 1952), Thomas W. Braden (Secretary of MoMA's governing body from 1948 to 1949, and from 1951, he was responsible for the cultural activities of the CIA) and, most importantly, its president Nelson Rockefeller (coordinator of the Bureau of Inter-American Affairs, Chairman of the Board of Chase Manhattan Bank and son of Abby Rockefeller, one of MoMA's original donors).

76. Saunders, pp. 262–263.

77. Jachec, pp. 550–551.

78. Benjamin Buchloh, *Neo-Avantgarde and Culture Industry. Essays on European and American Art from 1955 to 1975*, Cambridge (Mass.)/London 2000, p. xx.

79. The domestic political life scene in post-war France was dominated by three parties of roughly equal strength: the Socialists, Communists and Conservatives. The constitution was not, however, designed to aid the formation of stable governments, and twenty or so governments were formed during the existence of the Fourth Republic, which lasted from 1946 to 1958. France was able to recover economically with the help of the Marshall Plan, although at nothing like the pace of West Germany. Accepting American financial help was by no means an uncomplicated process in France, which was fully determined to reestablish its sense of national identity and its place among the great powers. One obvious price it had to pay for this financial support—and a condition of American aid—was the exclusion of the Communist party from the coalition government of 1947 (at that time it was the largest party in France with over 30% of the votes), (Rioux, p. 134). The chaotic nature of the domestic political situation pushed France into an extremely unstable position at the end of the 1950s, and this led to the creation of a new constitution. The Fifth Republic was proclaimed in 1958 and gave the president a much stronger power base. Charles de Gaulle won the first presidential election of the new republic and emerged as the strong man of France. Three issues dominated France's relations with the rest of the world at this point: European integration (the creation of a common ,market), the country's increasingly apparent intention to play an independent role in the conflict between East and West (a national defence and foreign policy course that culminated in the withdrawal from NATO in 1966) and the dissolution of its colonial empire (in which the Algerian crisis played a major role in terms of both domestic and cultural politics).

80. The importance of Paris for the international art market also diminished at this time particularly because of tax legislation that

did not favour the donation of art to public institutions, unlike the American system in which loans and donations gave rise to substantial tax reductions (Boyer, 1995, pp. 92–93). The situation in France was also affected by restrictive export rules and by the state regulation of the art trade that awarded a monopoly to particular auction houses. But the country still preserved a significant potential in this regard: the art market was extremely active once more at the end of the 1940s and eclipsed New York in terms of price. This state of affairs, however, gradually changed during the 1950s when economic growth created increasingly favourable circumstances for the American art world (Michael D. Plante, 'The Second Occupation'. American Expatriate Painter and the Reception of American Art in Paris 1946–1958, (Diss. Brown University 1992), UMI Dissertation Services, p. 454).

81. The Musée National d'Art Moderne (MNAM) was inaugurated in 1939 and housed in the Palais de Tokyo. Although a certain amount of exhibition activity did take place during the war, it did not begin presenting regular exhibitions until 1947 (Catherine Lawless (ed.), *Musée national d'art moderne. Historique et mode d'emploi*, Centre Georges Pompidou, Paris 1986, p. 87). It then assumed the position of France's official museum for contemporary art, which had been previously been held by the Musée de Luxembourg (1818–1886) and the Musée de l'Orangerie, respectively, for French art and by the Jeu de Paume (1886–1939) for international work (see Boyer, 1995, pp. 118–119). Essentially MNAM represented the officially sanctioned attitude to contemporary art, and its collections were organised on the basis of the so-called Louvre-Luxembourg system from the outset (Plante, p. 130). The exhibition programme of MNAM after the end of the war clearly signalled that the French state had abandoned the academic discourse of art for good (Eustathia P. Costopopulus, "Musée National d'Art Moderne", in Virginia Jackson (ed.), *Art Museums of the World*, New York/London 1987, p. 294).

82. The collection of the Musée National d'Art Moderne was largely comprised of art that derived from the Fauvist and Cubist traditions (Laure de Buzon-Vallet, "L'Ecole de Paris. Elément d'une enquête", *Paris-Paris. Création en France: 1937–1957*, Centre national d'art et de culture Georges Pompidou, Paris 1981, p. 252). In his

reconstruction of the collections at MNAM, Sylvain Lecombre has shown what this programme looked like in practice (*La peinture en France au lendemain de la seconde guerre mondiale: 1944–53*, Paris 1979). Although one of the museum's rooms was assigned to Surrealism, that movement's place in the hang as a whole was extremely peripheral. There was no space at all allocated to movements that had developed outside Paris. Although devoting an entire room to Picasso was not a problem because he had worked in Paris throughout his career, which could be said to have developed within a French tradition, not the slightest interest was shown in acquiring works for display by artists such as Mondrian or Kandinsky. Michael Plante goes so far as to maintain that official art policy lacked any sort of coherent vision or understanding of contemporary art beyond its nationalist credo (Plante, p. 129).

83. Harry Bellet, "1943–1959: des galleries", *Cimaise*, vol. 36, no. 199, 1989, p. 25.

84. At the beginning of the 1950s, a split occurred among the advocates of nonfigurative art between what were known as *abstrait froid* (geometric abstraction) and *abstrait chaude* (nongeometric abstraction) (see Plante, p. 158). The Salon des Réalistés Nouvelles had its roots in the nonfigurative art of the interwar years and was formed in 1939 from the circle surrounding the group Abstraction-Création, which, in its turn, had come into being as a merger of the previous Cercle et Carré and Art concret groups. There was an evident set of historical and social interrelationships underpinning the tradition of geometric abstract art. The Salon succeeded in establishing abstract art in the Paris art world by mounting extensive thematic exhibitions: *Art abstrait, concret, constructivisme, non figuratif* was shown in 1946 and consisted of 384 works; exhibitions of more than 600 works were subsequently shown annually and included not only French and European, but also American art. The latter trend, whose more radical variants are usually referred to as *art brut* or *art informel*, was centred around the Galleri René Drouin and the Studio Paul Facchetti. The growing significance of *art informel* was reflected in the increasing criticism of the impersonal idiom of concrete art and of its roots in a Utopian rhetoric of the 1930s. The critic Michael Tapié played a key role in the promotion and expansion of this movement, and his

approach went far beyond the national and retrospective pathos of the official art world: he was among the first to include American abstract expressionism in his exhibitions and considered Surrealism and Dadaism in particular as the foremost (or even the only) historical influences on contemporary art (Plante, pp. 318–319 and pp. 323–324). Tapié's vision was, then, not about continuity, tradition and the formation of national schools but much closer in fact to Werner Haftmann's thesis that nonfigurative and informal art was a response to a universal need on the part of the contemporary individual.

85. Boyer, 1995, pp. 80–86. In practice, it was a very small circle of individuals drawn from the political and cultural spheres, who were closely connected and often bound together by ties from their time in the Resistance, that determined official art policy in France.

86. Kathryn Boyer, "Association Française d'Action Artistique and the School of Paris", *Konsthistorisk Tidskrift*, vol. 70, 2001: 3, p. 159.

87. Kathryn Boyer provides an almost tragicomic description of the discrepancy between the image created by the exhibition policy of the AFAA and the reality of contemporary art (see Boyer, 2001, p. 161). Even in exhibitions whose theme was contemporary art, such as 'Peinture Français Contemporaine' (Yugoslavia, 1952), the emphasis was on the traditional: of the 61 artists whose work made up the exhibition, 49 were in the age range 50–80, and 13 of the artists exhibited were actually dead. The selection for this exhibition was not a bizarre exception but rather the rule.

88. Ibid, p. 165.

89. In the decade following the end of the war, the Gold Medal for Painting of the Venice Biennale (the Premio Presidenza del Consiglio dei Ministri) was consistently awarded to the pioneers of early modernism: George Braque in 1948; Henri Matisse in 1950; Raoul Dufy in 1952; Max Ernst in 1954; Jacques Villon in 1956 (Lawrence Alloway, *The Venice Biennale 1895–1968. From Salon to Goldfish Bowl*, London 1969, p. 137). At the time they received their awards, the average age of these artists was 73, and although they were officially awarded their medals for new work, they were long past their heyday. Rather younger artists were awarded the prize at

the biennales immediately afterwards: Osvaldo Licini in 1958; Jean Fautrier and Hans Hartung in 1960 and Alfred Manessier in 1962. This goes to show both that the jury thought it was vital to demonstrate the newly acquired official legitimacy of modernism and that the Ecole de Paris was still capable of asserting the continued centrality of its role in the international art world, even when *art informel* was increasingly made part of the equation at the end of the 1950s (a trend that would be even more clearly delineated at documenta II in 1959). It was at this point that a particular shift in meaning took place in the perception of *art informel* with the result that an artist such as Fautrier was transformed from an *avantgardiste* critic of civilisation into a representative of the French Tradition.

90. Guilbaut, 1983, pp. 174–175.

91. Mention should be made here of three influential voices that were characteristic of this change: Harold Rosenberg, who thought that political developments had undermined the distinctive cosmopolitan character of Paris and forced French culture into an increasing degree of national chauvinism (Harold Rosenberg, "The Fall of Paris" (1940), 1982, pp. 209–220); Clement Greenberg, in whose view European culture had collapsed as a result of political crises and the social foundation of its radicalism had been lost (Clement Greenberg, "The Decline of Cubism" (1948), *The Collected Essays and Criticism, vol. 2: Arrogant Purpose, 1945–1949*, (ed. John O'Brian), Chicago/London 1988 b (1986), pp. 211–215); and Barnett Newman, who in 'The Sublime is Now' (1948) felt that the European avant-garde had lost touch with the essential aims of modern art as a result of its ties to tradition (Barnett Newman, "The Sublime is Now" (1948), *Barnett Newman. Selected Writings and Interviews*, (ed. John P. O'Neill), Berkeley/Los Angeles 1992 (1990), p. 173). Although the theses of these three writers were formulated from different starting points, they share a common trope: the decline of French and European art. And, in the work of Greenberg and Newman, that trope led to another: the historic task incumbent on American art of spearheading progressive developments.

92. Henry Geldzahler describes what he considers to be some of the factors crucial to the revitalisation of American art after the Second World War: the major museums (MoMA, in particular); the

immigration of leading European modernist artists (the Surrealists, in particular) and the setting up by the Roosevelt administration of the Works Progress Administration in the 1930s (which provided artists with a degree of financial security, established new networks of contacts and gave them a partial sense at least of belonging to society) (see Henry Geldzahler, *New York Painting and Sculpture 1940–1970*, Metropolitan Museum of Art, New York 1970, pp. 17–18).

93. Alfred H. Barr, *What is Modern Painting?*, Introductory Series to the Modern Arts, Museum of Modern Art, New York 1952 (1943), p. 5.

94. Alfred H. Barr, "Is Modern Art Communistic?" (1952), in Irving Sandler & Amy Newman (eds.), *Defining Modern Art. Selected Writings of Alfred H. Barr Jr.*, New York 1986, p. 214.

95. Guilbaut, 1983, p. 176.

96. See Laura Cottingham, "The Masculine Imperative: High Modern, Postmodern" (1994), *Seeing Through the Seventies. Essays on Feminism and Art*, Amsterdam 2002 (2000), pp. 47–71.

97. With the presentation of Pollock on two pages in full colour in the issue of the magazine *Life* dated 8 August 1949, a serious attempt was being made to introduce modern art to its readership (at that time counted in the millions). The headline of the article employed a phrase of Clement Greenberg's from 1945 but turned it into a question: 'Is he the greatest living painter in the USA?' (see Clement Greenberg, "Review of Exhibitions of Mondrian, Kandinsky, and Pollock; of the Annual Exhibition of the American Abstract Artists; and of the Exhibition *European Artists in America*" (1945), 1988 b, p. 16, in which Pollock was described as 'the greatest painter of his generation and perhaps the greatest to emerge after Miró'). Despite the slightly ironic tone of the *Life* article, it largely reproduced the myth of the modern artist as a rebel in the service of freedom at the heart of American society. It was in this context that a range of mythical masculine values were assigned to Pollock's work in particular and to American painting in general and which Andrew Perchuk characterises as a 'masquerade of masculinity' that was based on a number of masculine archetypes characteristic of the post-war United States: the

rebel, the tortured soul, the alcoholic, mother-fixation, phallus worship. (Andrew Perchuk, "Pollock and Postwar Masculinity", in *The Masculine Masquerade. Masculinity and Representation*, Cambridge (Mass.) 1995, p. 31). Although these myths could be located in a more historical context of the shifting identities of the avant-garde, what is interesting is how well they fit in with the interpretive matrix applied by both specialists and popular culture to the modern artist. The prime example of the former category is the simultaneously esoteric and rebellious stance underlying Harold Rosenberg's term action painting (see Harold Rosenberg, "The American Action Painters" (1952), 1982, pp. 23–39). Another, and considerably more ambivalent, dissemination of Pollock's images in popular-cultural contexts is found in the fashion photographs by Cecil Beaton that used Pollock's paintings as a backdrop in the March issue of *Vogue* in 1951: even though the vast readership of the magazine could obviously not be ignored, the context in which the images were presented lent a decorative and feminine quality to the paintings of Pollock that would have been anathema to the avant-garde art world of the time.

98. For a description of this milieu, see e.g. Irving Sandler, *The New York School. The Painters and Sculptors of the Fifties*, New York 1978, pp. 1–45, and Dore Ashton, *The New York School. A Cultural Reckoning*, Berkeley/Los Angeles/Oxford 1992 (1972), pp. 164–208. During the 1940s and 1950s, American artists were as dependent as they had previously been on the private sphere's networks of galleries, critics, patrons and social contacts. The New York art scene was on the whole extremely stratified, from the fashionable and influential uptown galleries to the 10th Street alternative scene of small cooperative galleries, but these boundaries were not fixed, and there was considerable interaction between different strata. The established galleries in New York that focused on contemporary avant-garde art in the 1940s and 50s included the Samuel Kootz Gallery, the Sidney Janis Gallery, the Egan Gallery, the Stable Gallery, the Betty Parsons Gallery and the Leo Castelli Gallery (see Geldzahler, p. 19). The alternative galleries were important as meeting places and also served as hothouses nurturing the new artists and movements who might in time move uptown (see Joellen Bard, *Tenth Street Days. The Co-ops of the 50's*, The Association of Artist-Run Galleries, New York 1977,

p. iii). They were also situated in the neighbourhood where several established artists had their studios, which created social and aesthetic interaction between different groups, established and not. The artists, collectors, gallery-owners and curators also moved freely between these different strata, which facilitated an exchange of critical ideas and social contacts that encompassed both the private and public spheres. Moreover, New York's artists possessed a form of capital that eclipsed the art scenes of every other city: access to the superior collections of international and American modernist art in its museums (see Plante, p. 39). The specialist niches of the different museums also complemented one another. MoMA possessed an unrivalled collection of European modernism, the Museum of Non-Objective Art focused on Abstract art outside Paris (German, Russian, Dutch) and the Whitney Museum of American Art focused on American art.

99. This is a common perception whose origins are found in Eva Cockcroft's article 'Abstract Expressionism, Weapon of the Cold War' in *Artforum* 1974, where she maintained that the politics of the Cold War were the direct cause of the establishment of Abstract Expressionism in the 1950s (Cockcroft, p. 126). However, when the exhibitions exported to Europe as part of MoMA's international programme are considered, they were not exclusively made up of Abstract Expressionism, but also included other less experimental movements that attracted less publicity at that time. This is also borne out by one of the first peripatetic exhibitions under the auspices of the MoMA International Program, *Twelve Contemporary American Painters and Sculptors*. This was a presentation of contemporary trends in American art that opened at the Musée National d'Art Moderne in Paris and was then shown in a range of European cities between 1953 and 1954, including Stockholm. The Swedish catalogue to the same exhibition *Tolv nutida amerikanska målare och skulptörer* (Liljevalchs konsthall, exhib. catalog. nr. 206, Stockholm 1953) makes clear that the show focused on figurative art by artists such as Edward Hopper, Ben Shan and Stuart Davis, while sculptures by Alexander Calder and David Smith were also exhibited, as were a few paintings by Arshile Gorky and Jackson Pollock. And even if artists from The New York School appeared with increasing frequency in MoMA's international exhibitions from the mid-'50s

onwards (reaching their high point in the major retrospective exhibition *Jackson Pollock 1912–1956,* which toured Europe from 1958 to 1959), this need not indicate anything more conspiratorial than the fact that these artists were deemed increasingly significant in the American art world during the same period and that Abstract Expressionism was also regarded with greater interest in Europe as a result of the growth in importance of European *art informel* at the time. The appearance of being biased in favour of a particular style or school in the exhibitions that were sent abroad would also surely have undermined their most crucial ideological value: the progressive image of individualism and freedom.

100. Saunders, p. 260. The statement is drawn from an interview with Jameson carried out by Saunders in 1994.

101. See Rosenberg, (1952), 1982, p. 31; Haftmann, pp. 434–435; Read, 1951, p. 13, and Read, 1974 (1959), p. 222; Michel Tapié, *Un Art autre*, Paris 1952, unpag. (text page 33).

102. Tapié, unpag. (text pages 33–34).

103. André Malraux, "Les otages" (1945), *Oevres complètes IV : Écrits sur l'art I*, Paris 2004, pp. 1199–1200.

104. Guilbaut, 1990, pp. 56–59.

105. See Greenberg, "The Present Prospects of American Painting and Sculpture" (1947), 1988 b, p. 166; the attacks by the Republican Congressman George Dondero on Pollock and Abstract Expressionism made at the end of the 1940s are quoted in Saunders, p. 253 f.; Rudolf Arnheim, "Accident and The Necessity of Art", *Journal of Aesthetics and Art Criticism*, vol. 16, September 1957: 1, p. 30; Allan Kaprow, "The Legacy of Jackson Pollock", *Art News*, vol. 57, October 1958: 6, p. 56.

106. Kirk Varnedoe, "Comet: Jackson Pollock's Life and Work", *Jackson Pollock*, The Museum of Modern Art, New York 1998, p. 17.

107. In Arthur Danto, *Mark Tansey: Visions and Revisions*, New York 1992, p. 136, a key is provided that reveals the names of those represented by the various figures: with Salvador Dalí, Henri Rousseau, Juan Gris, Guillaume Apollinaire, André Derain, Henri Matisse, Pierre Bonnard,

Fernand Léger, Pablo Picasso, Marcel Duchamp and André Breton on the French side and Joseph Cornell, Jackson Pollock, Arshile Gorky, Clement Greenberg, Barnett Newman, Ad Reinhardt, David Smith, Willem de Kooning, Harold Rosenberg, Mark Rothko and Robert Motherwell on the American side.

108. See The Museum of Modern Art Archives, New York, Alfred H. Barr Jr. Papers, 9a: 15.

109. For a detailed account of the discussions about MoMA's collections in the 1930s and 1940s, see Kirk Varnedoe, "The Evolving Torpedo: Changing Ideas of the Collection of Painting and Sculpture of the Museum of Modern Art", *The Museum of Modern Art at Mid-Century: Continuity and Change*, New York 1995, pp. 12–73.

110. Diana Crane, *The Transformation of the Avant-Garde. The New York Art World, 1940–1985*, Chicago/London 1987, pp. 34–35.

111. See Irvin Sandler, *American Art of the Sixties*, New York 1988, pp. 105–123.

112. Crane, p. 6.

113. Charlotte Bydler, *The Global Art World, Inc. On the Globalization of Contemporary Art*, (Diss. Uppsala universitet 2004), Acta Universitatis Upsaliensis, Figura Nova Series 32, Uppsala 2004, pp. 32–36.

114. Costopopulus, p. 293.

115. One indication of the powerful connotations of the adjective modern is the controversy surrounding the change of name undergone by The Institute of Modern Art in Boston in 1948 to the (then) more neutral sounding The Institute of Contemporary Art (see Guilbaut 1994, pp. 233–234).

116. Duncan, p. 103.

117. James Elkins, *Stories of Art*, New York/London 2002, pp. 89–97.

118. Like Elkins, I have studied this work in the German translation published in the GDR at the beginning of the 1970s, see Ulrich Kuhirt (ed.), *Allgemeine Geschichte der Kunst VII, Die Kunst des 20. Jahrhunderts: Kapitalistische Länder*, Leipzig 1972 (1965),

and *Allgemeine Geschichte der Kunst VIII, Die Kunst des 20. Jahrhunderts: Socialistische Länder*, Leipzig 1970 (1966). Unlike the original Russian publication, this edition was published in eight volumes. I have been unable to compare the two editions, although in light of the changes undergone by the Soviet Union and its Eastern Europeans satellite states after the death of Stalin, it seems obvious that certain revisions must have been carried out, particularly in the field of art and architecture. This is not simply a matter of the emergence of new and different examples, but rather that art and architecture, in particular, were de-Stalinised at the end of the 1950s, and various local variants of Socialist Functionalism were developed (see Anders Åman, *Architecture and Ideology in Eastern Europe during the Stalin Era. An Aspect of Cold War History*, Cambridge (Mass) 1992 (1987), pp. 211–229).

119. See e.g., Richard Müller, *Gechichte der Malerei im XIX. Jahrhundert: I-III*, München 1893–94, which is structured around national schools and also places great emphasis on domestic art (in this instance the German tradition).

120. Elkins, p. 97.

121. A. D. Tjegodadzjev, "Die Kunst der Vereinigen Staaten von Amerika", in *Allgemeine Geschichte der Kunst VII, Die Kunst des 20. Jahrhunderts: Kapitalistische Länder*, Leipzig 1972 (1965), p. 427.

122. Ibid, p. 433.

123. See Alfred Barr (ed.), *Fantastic Art, Dada, Surrealism*, Museum of Modern Art, New York 1947 (1936).

124. The MoMA exhibitions were not, however, unprecedented; *Sonderbund: Internationale Kunstausställung* in Cologne in 1912 and *The Armory Show* held in New York the following year were two exhibitions that, in terms of their scale, eclipsed the surveys presented by MoMA. With its 634 works, the Sonderbund exhibition was probably the most comprehensive exposé to that point of the various movements of modern art and the development of its tradition from van Gogh, Cézanne, Munch, Gauguin and Signac (Dirk Teuber, 'Die Ausstellungen im Spiegel der Kölner Presse', in Wulf Herzogenrath

(ed.), *Frühe Kölner Kunstaustellungen. Sonderbund 1912, Werkbund 1914, Pressa USSR 1928*, Köln 1981, p. 151). The Armory Show of 1913 with its nearly 1200 works was almost twice as large (Milton W. Brown, *The Story of the Armory Show*, New York 1988 (1963), p. 42). But it lacked the same focus on the modernist tradition and was made up of *juste-milieu* and academic art.

125. Barr, 1936, p. 9.

126. In *The Museum of Modern Art. The First Ten Years* (New York 1943, pp. 57–59). A. Conger Goodyear describes the negative critical response and how *Cubism and Abstract Art* was preceded by a controversy involving the American customs authorities who refused to allow nonfigurative sculpture to enter the country because it conflicted with their definition of sculpture as works of art. Barr, himself, writes about conservative American opinion in the catalogue, exemplifying it with the alternative editions of posters for the *Pressa* exhibition held in Cologne in 1928 that were distributed in Europe and the US: the former being highly stylised and Constructivist in its design, while the latter was considerably more conventional (Barr, 1936, p. 10). Although *Fantastic Art, Dada, Surrealism* (strangely enough) did not run into difficulties with customs, it was condemned by a largely unanimous body of critics. Other opinion-forming organisations also criticised this exhibition for reasons that ranged from its being a Communist conspiracy to it representing merely humbug and madness.

127. Sibyl Gordon Kantor describes how, through Morey, Barr learnt methods for incorporating disparate and complex historical material within schematic models that were organised on the basis of stylistic development (*Alfred H. Barr Jr. and the Intellectual Origins of the Museum of Modern Art*, Cambridge (Mass.)/London 2002, pp. 19–26).

128. Ibid, p. 155.

129. Their crucial significance for modern art had already been emphasised in Barr's first exhibition at MoMA, in which he traced various influences forward in time, so that the art of van Gogh, for example, was presented as the archetype of expressionism (Alfred Barr, *First Loan Exhibition: Cézanne, Gauguin, van Gogh, Seurat*, Museum of Modern Art, New York 1929, p. 18).

130. The influence on modern art of the machine aesthetic and primitivism, respectively, were among the themes chosen by Barr for his unfinished doctoral dissertation (Kantor, p. 147).

131. Barr, 1936, p. 19.

132. Michael Auping, "Fields, Planes, Systems: Geometric Abstract Painting in America Since 1945", *Abstraction – Geometry – Painting. Selected Geometric Abstract Painting in America Since 1945*, Albright-Knox Art Gallery, Buffalo 1989, New York 1989, pp. 14–15. According to Auping, the two trends distinguished by Barr have their direct origin in Wilhelm Worringer's polarisation of the visual arts into two primary tendencies: logic, order/structure (Abstraktion) and feeling/transgression (Einfühlung); in its day, this polarisation proved enormously influential among art historians, art critics and artists. These are linked in the final chapter with what Worringer considered to be two fundamental veins running through contemporary art: immanence and transcendence (see Wilhelm Worringer, *Abstraktion und Einfühlung, Ein Beitrag zur Stilpsychologie*, München 1921 (1908), pp. 161–179).

133. Barr, 1936, p. 11.

134. This interpretation is reinforced by the fact that the line of text placed below the scheme in the first edition (which was worded the Development of Abstract Art) was absent in subsequent editions of the catalogue (cf. the editions of 1936 and 1966).

135. El Lissizky & Hans Arp, *Die Kunstismen – Les Ismes de L'art – The Isms of Art 1924–1914*, Baden 1990 (1925), p. 1.

136. The greatest difference in terms of the selection lies in Barr's emphasis on Fauvism and Orphism (not referred to in *Die Kunstismen*) and in his tracing of the historical roots back to the late nineteenth century, whereas modern art is seen by El Lissizky and Arp as a contemporary phenomenon to a greater extent.

137. Barr, 1936, p. 9.

138. From a historiographic perspective, this combination of determinism and individualism would appear to resemble the problem that confronted Alois Riegl when formulating his notion that every era is governed by a particular *Kunstwollen*: how is one to

understand the unique and ingenious features of a work if all art is governed by an underlying, culturally determined developmental process? The answer he provided in *Das holländische Gruppenporträt* was that while the actions of the individual are determined by the surrounding environment, a choice is nevertheless always available within specific parameters. These parameters are not, however, static but undergo change depending on cross-cultural connections and the results of individual efforts, such that the most significant art is that which succeeds in moving development forward and thus fulfils the *Kunstwollen* of its time. One example is Rembrandt, who unmistakably formed part of the long Dutch tradition in his late group portraits but succeeded nevertheless in infusing that same tradition with new vigour through his contacts with Italy and as a result of his genius (Alois Riegl, *The Group Portraiture of Holland*, (Trans. Evelyn M. Kain & David Britt), Los Angeles 1999 (1902), pp. 253–254).

139. Duncan, p. 103.

140. In *La condition postmoderne,* Jean-François Lyotard employed the concept of metanarratives (*meta écrits*) in order to identify and deconstruct the ideological narratives that, in his view, underlie modernity's all-inclusive production of knowledge and meaning; here, it is the Enlightenment ideas of a continual evolution of reason and a belief in the direct significance of the accumulation of knowledge for human emancipation, in particular, that are metanarratives used to legitimise specific social, political and economic interests (Jean-François Lyotard, *The Postmodern Condition: A Report of Knowledge* (Trans. Geoff Bennington & Brian Massumi), Minneapolis 1993 (1979), pp. xxiv-xxv). Confidence in these major narratives has, however, been eroded, and they need to be replaced, according to Lyotard, by a more fragmentary, relativistic and antitotalitarian understanding of the world based on local language games. My use of the term is, however, both more specific and less polemical than Lyotard's. The aim here is to identify and analyse critically an underlying structure, not to question the necessity of ideological frameworks. This divergence is not simply a matter of political conviction, but also of an epistemological doubt as to whether it is even possible to avoid employing some form of metanarrative in the writing of history.

141. Bois, 1995, p. 102.

142. Mary Anne Staniszewski, *The Power of Display. A History of the Exhibition Installations at the Museum of Modern Art*, Cambridge (Mass.) 1998, pp. 62–66.

143. Brian O'Doherty, *Inside the White Cube. The Ideology of the Gallery Space*, Santa Monica/San Francisco 1986, p. 14 (originally published as three separate articles in *Artforum* in 1976).

144. For a historical presentation and analysis of this context, see Malin Hedlin Hayden, *Out of Minimalism: The Referential Cube. Contextualising Sculptures by Anthony Gormley, Anish Kapoor and Rachel Whiteread*, (Diss. Uppsala universitet 2003), Acta Universitatis Upsaliensis, Figura Nova Series 29, Uppsala 2003, pp. 59–71.

145. Michel Foucault, *The History of Sexuality. Vol 1: An introduction*, (Trans. Robert Hurley), London 1990 (1976), p. 28.

146. Staniszewski, p. 74.

147. Douglas Crimp, *On the Museum's Ruins*, Cambridge (Mass.)/London 1995 (1993), pp. 263–269.

148. Roland Barthes, *Mythologies*, (Trans. Anette Lavers), London 1973 (1957), pp. 114–115.

149. Ibid, p. 143.

150. Eagleton, pp. 5–6.

151. Jameson, 2002, p. 111.

PART III
TRANSFORMATION/TRANSMEDIA/ TRANSFUSION

Gropius wrote a book on grain silos,
Le Corbusier one on aeroplanes,
And Charlotte Periand brought a new object to the office every morning;
But today we collect ads.[1]

Alison Smithson and Peter Smithson,
'But Today We Collect Ads' (1956)

[T]he work itself functions as a general sign and it is normal that it should represent an institutional category of the civilization of the Sign. The Text, on the contrary, practices the infinite deferment of the signified, is dilatory; its field is that of the signifier and the signifier must not be conceived of as 'the first stage of meaning', its material vestibule, but, in complete opposition to this, as its deferred action. Similarly, the infinity of the signifier refers not to some idea of the ineffable (the unnamed signified) but to that of a playing...'[2]

Roland Barthes, 'From Work to Text' (1971)

Realities Around and Underneath the Sign

Approaches in Post-war Visual Cultures

A photograph of a television set in a fastidiously furnished room—the image is a 1958 advertising poster for Philips, showing an interior whose furnishings and subdued colours evoke an unmistakable sense of the fifties.

The selection of paints and materials in shades of blue and grey contrasting with light-coloured wood and black metal seems both carefully coordinated and in tune with the times. The light shines at an angle from behind, as if thrown by a ceiling lamp. Like every other advertising image, the primary function is to sell a product. At the heart of the image is a television set. Its centrality is emphasised by the way the restricted depth of field places the focus on the set, while making the room and foreground appear more diffuse. The sharpness of the television picture, a rather crucial part of the sales pitch, tells us that this is a photomontage. A game of football is being played. The dramatic quality of the image on the screen (will it be a goal?) is clearly being contrasted with the cosiness and emptiness of the domestic setting (come in and sit yourself down). And unmistakable is perhaps the most astonishing function of the new medium: you can watch the whole world from your living room—if you buy a television.

This image may not seem particularly radical in design terms when compared with many other examples of late 1950s advertising, but that does not mean it lacks interest. It depicts what was, at the time, an extremely modern home with cutting edge

---

How to cite this book chapter:
Hayden, Hans. 2018. Realities Around and Underneath the Sign. In: Hayden, H. *Modernism as Institution: On the Establishment of an Aesthetic and Historiographic Paradigm* Pp. 245–271. Stockholm: Stockholm University Press. DOI: https://doi.org/10.16993/bar.g. License: CC-BY

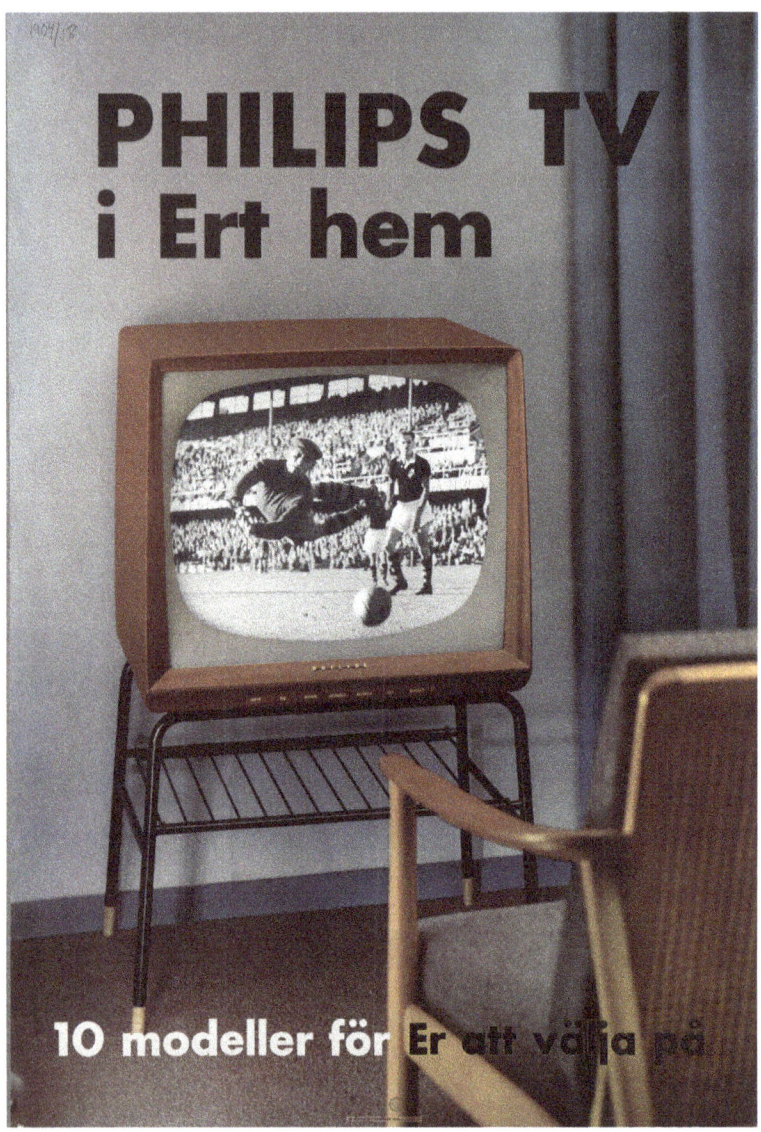

Figure 7. Advertising poster for Philips TV, 1958, Photo and copyright: The National Library of Sweden, License: CC BY-NC-ND.

technology blending seamlessly into the everyday environment. No longer concealed in a bulky cupboard with shutters, a model that was still available, the television set—a trim, modern piece of furniture in wood and steel—demonstrates its function for all to see. The home is fairly anonymous, without any distinct social markers: it is the home of anyone and everyone who wants to keep in step with the contemporary world. It is not only the domestic setting that is modern, but also the rhetoric of the advert.

The text fills a vital function in this image. It is written in the same font as the Philips logo. The message is worded as a personal address, stressing notions of home and freedom of choice, in addition to the trademark. The function of the text could be described as providing an anchorage of the image, to use Roland Barthes' term: it defines the genre of the image and identifies its component parts; it indicates how it should be read and the correct level for interpretation. Considered as a whole, however, the rhetoric of the image amounts to something considerably more powerful. Instead of stating explicitly 'Buy Philips TV', the tacit message is woven into a complex totality of different visual and verbal codes, within which the indirect but personal form of address plays a key role. What is being offered is not just the chance to buy a particular television set, but also the chance to acquire a modern lifestyle, the underlying message being that the product is an integral part of that acquisition. An interlinked chain of connotations permeates the image: modernity, topicality, technology, cleanness, security, hygiene, light, living standards. This chain of connotations is entirely consistent with the values that characterised the normative structure of post-war European society, with the addition that this particular value (Philips television) is not automatically provided but has to be bought in store. The rhetoric is based around the offer of an opportunity and a choice: this may not be what your home looks like, but it could be. The modernity of the rhetoric lies in that it not only wants to persuade viewers to buy a particular product, but also it also aims to get them to convince themselves of the necessity of purchasing it.

As a reflection of a characteristic 1950s home, the advert is somewhat deceptive: this is not what most people's homes actually looked like. But one of the most important functions of advertising is not to reproduce (passively) already-existing norms and ideas but (actively) to influence and change them to some extent, to generate positive values around a product.[3] Modernity is being promoted here as a sales pitch, linking new technology with modern furnishings and, implicitly, with modern living standards. Although the advertisement creates a distorted picture of the domestic setting typical of the period, the gulf between historical reality and the heightened setting also makes visible a key function of the message of the image: the reproduction of an ideal. Here, the modern is not being portrayed as a utopia of advanced technology but instead as a cosy reality, as a blend of modernity and normality.

A number of different perspectives on the modernity of the post-war period converge in this image. The most obvious is the increased importance of technology, although the issue here is not technological discoveries and innovations as such but their introduction and effect within and upon broader strata of the population. A stabilised and steadily growing economy was leading to higher living standards and creating ever-greater scope for private consumption; this allowed both older and more recent innovations to be made available to larger and larger swathes of the population. As a result of the growth in demand, there was an expansion of supply and increasing competition, both of which were evident in almost every sector of the economy. Technology should be interpreted here in relation to a larger social, economic and political context, as clearly exemplified in the rapid diffusion of television through post-war society and the enormous impact it made.[4] Seen from a different perspective, this also involved a change in the nature of the news and advertising media. Here, the advertising image reflects both developments in photography (colour images) and improved reproduction techniques and the breakthrough of the televisual medium and the increasing importance of advertising.

These developments did not distinguish the post-war period from the early history of modernism in any fundamental sense. From the beginning of industrialism, various forms of pictorial codes and representations aimed at a broad audience had emerged in which technological innovations combined with new social and cultural patterns to change visual communication in a comprehensive manner. But the process occurred significantly more rapidly during the 1950s, and its impact on the individual appeared much greater as a result. This was a quantitative change that also entailed a qualitative one when considered as a whole. The visual landscape was transformed not only by new buildings, but also by illuminations, shop windows, advertising, logos, symbols and posters. Various forms of advertising acquired greater importance as a result, as did the design of goods and packaging. These changes not only introduced more advanced forms of communication between originator and recipient, but also they meant that the functional and exchange values of goods coalesced to a greater extent with their 'sign value'.[5] The expansion of the media altered the way images were used in both the public and private spheres, and this created in turn new patterns of consumption and communication.

The interconnections between technology, economics, ideology and visual culture appear to be obvious here. Indeed, during the 1960s and 1970s, cultural critics and various academic disciplines increasingly focused their attention on the comprehensive nature of this change. One key example is the characterisation by Marshall McLuhan of the media as 'extensions of Man'—the notion that the technological revolution within the media was of crucial significance for the way human beings perceive both themselves and the world around them, and this applied to television in particular: 'What electric implosion or contraction has done inter-personally and inter-nationally, the TV image does intra-personally and intra-sensuously'.[6] This example provides a potent demonstration of McLuhan's thesis on the reciprocal relationship of technology and society: when a new technology emerges in a particular society, it also contributes to defining that society irrespective of whether the technology is print or television.

McLuhan's inspired formulation of this relationship was also interpreted more critically, as for example by Hans Magnus Enzensberger, who described the interconnections between technology, economics, ideology and culture with the term 'the consciousness industry'.[7] According to Enzensberger, the explosive development of this industry after the Second World War could be seen as a new phase following from the exploitation of raw materials by industrialism, a phase in which the power structure of a society is determined by whoever controls both financial capital and the intellectual capital of the consciousness industry. In the mid-1970s, McLuhan's analysis also provided the foundation to some extent for Jean Baudrillard's description of how the worldview of the urban individual after the Second World War was increasingly constituted by a hyper-real play of signs, in which the boundary between immediate and mediated experience, between the real and the simulated, appeared to implode.[8] Both McLuhan and Baudrillard saw technology not as an isolated force of production (in the Marxist sense) but as a medium and, as such, one that was of crucial significance for the change in human consciousness. Both also perceived how technology in their contemporary periods had introduced a radical turning point in the way human beings related to the world around them, such that its medium/mediation is the reality we can understand and participate in. A rhetoric is being formulated that stipulates not only that the world *can* be observed in your living room, but also that the world *is* what you observe in your living room.

* * * *

A key aspect of the changes in visual culture after the Second World War was the constitution of a strict relationship between the art world and the world around it, in the sense that it focused to such a considerable extent on the work's transcendence of the surrounding world through the agency of the originator and the creative process. When considered in terms of the requirement for medium specificity, this transcendence involved an ever-more explicit exclusion of large parts of the contemporary social, political and medial culture. The institutionalisation of modernism, therefore, also entailed the establishment of an aesthetic of disparity.

It may seem odd that this aesthetic acquired such a dominant position in the 1950s. It became established at a time of heightened visual modernity, when the codes and forms of the visual cultures had been subject to an expansion, without historical parallel, in advertising, television, film, logos, the daily and weekly press, comics, record covers, product design and posters. This was the social context that Guy Debord described as 'the society of spectacles'.[9] Irrespective of whether one shares this rather misanthropic form of conspiracy thinking, it provides an apt description of the condensed visual and communicative codes that characterise the urban landscapes of modernity and of the post-war period in particular in Western Europe and the United States. And in the midst of this enormous visual transformation and expansion, at the heart of the burgeoning and variegated forest of signs, conventions, codes and signals, advanced modern art was presented as a more or less isolated preserve—more clearly, perhaps, during the post-war period than at any previous time.

This aesthetic of disparity is not a new phenomenon as such but simply a consequence of the mechanics of the modern art world (a system with the capacity to produce value by making distinctions) and of its basic form of legitimation (authenticity). What is evident during the 1950s, however, is that two types of distinction were emphasised as being of definitive importance in the contemporary art world: between Art and art and between art and the rest of the world. This aesthetic did not, of course, constitute an entirely uniform theory; its foundations lay in a cluster of theories, whose least common denominator was the axiom concerning the authenticity of the work of art (of the form/of the symbol) and its ontological boundary towards the outside world. And this applied irrespective of whether the work/form was shown in isolation in a gallery, as public adornment in an urban space or as part of a larger environmental design. The potential relation between the world of art and other worlds was seen as a one-way communication from art to the outside world but never, in principle, in the other direction.[10]

Perhaps the most paradoxical aspect of the aesthetic of disparity, superficially at least, is its preoccupation with oil painting as the primary medium of modern art. It would be legitimate here to refer to the transformation of an ancient institution so that it could survive into the modern era. A number of crises in painting run through the whole history of modernity in parallel with a progressive accentuation of the key importance of the medium, particularly within the theory and historiography of modernism. Oil painting in traditional terms could no longer be defended as a form of representation in the modern era: from Paul Delaroche's declaration of the death of painting after Daguerre's public presentation of photography in 1839, followed by a series of similar declarations (listing various causes of death) from within the various forms of the modernist avant-garde of the twentieth century and on to the postmodernist variant (based on different theoretical premises) of the same theme.[11] A return to the comparison between the prognoses for contemporary art put forward by Walter Benjamin and Clement Greenberg at the end of the 1930s, which offered two diametrically opposed interpretations of the meaning of this crisis, provides us with a telling example. Note how the latter's accentuation of the primacy of painting precisely because of its ambivalent, and therefore potentially critical, relationship with the technology of the modern era ensured its place as the privileged interpretation.

If the institutionalisation of modernism (and the premise of the significance of oil painting) is considered from a longer historical perspective, this process is neither an unusual or remarkable one; rather, it is a fairly self-evident function of the fact that a particular group acting within a discursive context will acquire the interpretive privilege through its control of key representations and institutions. It is, in fact, this alteration of the political, cultural and institutional landscape that lays the foundation for the creation of a new discursive order to reproduce and normalize a specific image of modern art and to establish the boundaries for what is possible and legitimate within the discourse. An interesting diagnosis of the relationship between authentic art and popular culture within this order was provided by Theodor Adorno and Max Horkeimer in their ferocious settling of accounts with what they called 'the culture industry' in *Dialektik der Aufklärung* (1947):

> Light art has accompanied serious art as its shadow. It is the social bad conscience of serious art. The truth which the latter could not apprehend because of its social premises gives the former an appearance of objective justification. The split between them is itself the truth: it expresses at least the negativity of the culture which is the sum of both spheres. The antithesis can be reconciled least of all by absorbing light art into serious or vice versa. That, however, is what the culture industry attempts. The eccentricity of the

circus, the peep show, or the brothel in relation to society is as embarrassing to it as that of Schönberg and Karl Kraus.[12]

Despite the fact that their diagnosis is a swingeing critique of the state of affairs in Western capitalist society, written in exile in Los Angeles in the final phase of the Second World War, their identification of a necessary boundary between the authentic and the popular provides a telling portrayal of the aesthetic of disparity that was established after the war in the institutions of the art world. An apparently paradoxical pattern of centrifugal and centripetal forces at work in the post-war art world can be discerned here: an increasingly specialised, closed and metaphysical aesthetic was promoted to an ever-expanding mass audience in ever more sectors within the field of officially sanctioned culture, and as part of which, the avant-garde art world was increasingly becoming an integrated part of the cultural industry of modern society. Adorno and Horkheimer were no doubt correct in maintaining that the split was the truth but in a rather different way than they intended: the split was presented as a normative order within a field; whereas, the two fields separated by the split were actually being incorporated within the system of norms of the established cultural sphere.

What the order described here actually calls to mind is the bipolar opposition of the Cold War: the creation of a boundary between two opposed camps that refused to acknowledge the existence of a third. In a maxim that would subsequently become celebrated, the American artist Ad Reinhardt summed up the essence of this aesthetic of disparity: 'The one thing to say about Art is that it is one thing. Art is art-as-art and everything else is everything else.'[13] This deliberately tautological and rather thought-provoking definition presents the work of art as entirely concrete in the sense of being autonomous, as a sign whose ontology, value and meanings cannot be related to anything outside itself. The distinction is not dialectical in the sense that it leads on to a synthesis; instead, it establishes absolute boundaries for the space—the value sphere, the art world, the economy of signs— within which the dialectic can be enacted. Ad Reinhardt's radical dramatisation of the interface between art and the world around it leads to a conceptual endpoint that he could only relate to by repeating the same subject matter and the same aesthetic and intellectual gesture throughout the last years of his life: producing image after image whose rectangular surfaces had been meticulously painted with a black cross on a black background.[14]

This rather extreme radicalisation of an idea involved pushing it towards a limit, however, where the parameters of its own logic were transgressed and it became inverted. In his reinterpretation of Reinhardt's strategy, Joseph Kosuth produced equally meticulously executed pictures of a black square on which various definitions drawn from dictionaries were depicted. In this way, a path was opened out through the image from the lowest circle of hermetic distinction. The projection of text onto image also served to expose the closed aesthetic to critical and metalinguistic illumination, which reveals that the absolute criteria of distinction here are, in fact, arbitrary. Kosuth's strategy also introduced a threat from within to the polarisation between Art and the surrounding world by grafting a third element—an outsider—on to the territory of Art that would, in the long term, pose a much greater threat to the absolute boundary than the enemy ever could.

This strategy was not unique but may be considered part of a pattern within—or, if you prefer, a function of—the aesthetic of disparity and its drive to refine the essence of every medium (on the basis of a particular and predetermined logic). This led to a situation in which each thesis at its most refined was predestined, in the words of John Perreault, to give birth to its own antithesis:

> Paradoxically, the closer an artist gets to the mythological "essence" of his particular medium the faster the medium becomes something else. Frank Stella's shaped-canvases become a kind of flat sculpture for the wall. Cage's "music" becomes theatre. Concretist poems become graphic art. Prose becomes poetry or music. Film becomes a kind of projected painting. Architecture as it tries more and more to be simply architecture becomes sculpture. And sculpture as it strives for "sculptureness" becomes architecture or merely interior design. This paradoxical "media transportation" indicates perhaps that just as there is no ideal gameness that relates all Games, there is no ideal art or essence of painting or sculpture, no "nature".[15]

The strategy in question is of key importance because it demonstrates a trend in post-war modernism that, as a result of its introspective linguistic critique, reached paradoxically outwards to encompass areas that were taboo. And in the modernist discourse that would be aimed, above all, at the refinement of each and every concept; this absolute focus on the medium-specific, the self-reflexive and the primacy of the visual surface inevitably meant that its opposite was put in play. This apparently paradoxical motion—inward to the core and then on outward through the core—is a trope that many critics and historians have drawn attention to. In the work of Michael Fried, it served as the definitive argument in what were, ultimately, his attempts to delegitimate minimalism.[16] The same motion has been used in the work of critics such as Rosalind Krauss and Hal Foster to explain the transition from modernism to postmodernism in terms of certain artists exceeding the bounds of the possible in the idioms and aesthetics of modernism as a result of their refinement of a particular logic.[17] What we are referring to here is a general aspect of the logic that Thierry de Duve described in the transition from painting to the readymade in the 1910s, where the search for absolute purity in the work of artists such as Malevitch, Kupka and Mondrian led inevitably to the zero point of painting—a transition that would, in the long term, provide the impetus for Marcel Duchamp's transgression of the very boundaries of the idiom.[18]

My point is not, however, to identify one transgressive act as a critical juncture in the modern history of the visual arts, but to demonstrate how this particular movement can be interpreted as part of a historical continuity, as a function of the modernist language game that is almost inevitably inscribed in a dialectic, rather than linear, process and, furthermore, to show that this dialectic extends beyond the absolute boundaries and schematic classifications on which the historiography of modernism is based.

The Reactivation of an Old Relationship

In his introduction to *New York Painting and Sculpture: 1940–1970*, the major retrospective exhibition held at the Metropolitan Museum of Modern Art in 1970, Henry Geldzahler insisted that Pop Art was only a transitory episode in the art history of the post-war period, whose real importance—apart from a few significant *oeuvres* at the beginning of the 1960s—was that it repaid, so to speak, the debt owed by art to visual mass culture.[19] The notion that there should ever have been a debt to repay makes this a particularly interesting observation. It is a way of considering the matter that completely inverts the relationship for which Clement Greenberg and Theodor Adorno, each in their own way, had argued so persuasively and which few representatives of leading art institutions would have even recognised only a few years before.

At much the same time, Richard Hamilton, who was one of the artists to make a serious attempt to introduce mass culture as visual material in his art at the end of the 1950s, described this peculiar state of affairs as follows:

> The surprising thing is that it took until the mid-fifties for artists to realise that the visual world had been altered by the mass media and changed dramatically enough to make it worth looking at again in terms of painting. Magazines, movies, TV, newspapers and comics for that matter, assume great importance when we consider the percentage of positively directed visual time they occupy in our society.[20]

Although this description may be accurate, it needs to be modified to some extent. As we have seen, there is a long tradition underpinning the distinction between Art and other visual cultures that had been institutionalised in academic discourse. But we have also seen that the distinction between high and low was far from clear in the aesthetic practices of early modernism. On the contrary, as Thomas Crow has maintained, the problematic but intensive exchange between both these levels can be seen as a characteristic and constant feature of the aesthetics of the avant-garde, from Manet's 'Olympia' onwards.[21] The interaction between modernism and modernity served in this regard to establish an ambivalent relationship between art and the world around it, with the idea of Art's autonomy and distinctiveness in relation to the surrounding culture making possible the interpretation of its specific position within that culture. But Hamilton is no doubt right that an intensification of the exchange between popular and elite cultures did characterise parts of the visual arts of the late 1950s, albeit on the periphery of the art world. In some surveys this phenomenon is sometimes reduced to no more than an additional branch on the genealogical tree of the metanarrative, to a mere change of style (with Pop Art replacing Abstract Expressionism), but one that would nevertheless provide a major stumbling block to many of those writing about the development of modern art during the 1950s as a linear progression towards abstraction as a universal idiom, an inner necessity or the logic of history.

One aspect of this change in perspective was a radical reformulation of the function and boundaries of the serious visual arts, without the abolition of any fixing of those boundaries as a result. Another involved the establishment of a different relation to the historical models of the avant-garde. When considered as a whole, this meant that a shift in discursive—the interpretive privilege—was taking place. A situation emerged in which the dialectic was no longer isolated within a specifically defined field but was also oriented outwards, and thus involved various outsiders from the world beyond the sanctified precincts of Art: popular culture, the mass media, product design, handicraft and other forms of applied art. This could, but need not, be interpreted as modernism being challenged and its boundaries breached. Instead of referring to a critical juncture, the new phenomenon might be considered a reactivation of some of the aesthetic and medial strategies of the avant-garde that had been excluded from the historical narrative of modernism following the Second World War, with this change of position occurring initially at least within the framework of the order of modernist discourse.

It is important that the introspective, structural and linguistic elements of this change are borne in mind as they tend to get lost in the projections by the cross-boundary art genres of everyday objects, hybrid forms, popular cultural references and spectacular stagings. The problem resembles to a considerable degree that which confronted Picasso when executing *Guitar and Wine Glass*: how to operate at the dividing line between an introverted (symbolic) linguistic critique and an expansive (futurist) cult of the contemporary without renouncing either side. This is an issue

Robert Rauschenberg touched on in a subsequently celebrated pronouncement published in connection with the exhibition *Sixteen Americans* held at MoMA in 1959:

> Any incentive to paint is as good as any other. There is no poor subject. . . . Painting relates to both art and life. Neither can be made. (I try to act in the gap between the two.) A pair of socks is no less suitable to make a painting with than wood, nails, turpentine, oil and fabric. A canvas is never empty.[22]

This statement describes in a nutshell how the relationship between modernity and art has been dealt with, transformed and rediscovered time after time since Baudelaire's day: the modern notion of beauty is focused at a point between the eternal and the transience of the everyday. The split that Theodor Adorno and Clement Greenberg took for granted as an absolute constant emerges as arbitrary in Rauschenberg's words, or perhaps rather as a fruitful position from which the artist is obliged to relate to two incompatible areas, each of which, ultimately, can never be attained.

But even though this issue already had one hundred years of history behind it by the end of the 1950s, each individual artist's interpretation of the problem would, of course, be determined by his or her particular situation. Where Baudelaire described Constantin Guy's depictions of different individuals as representatives of the social types of the modern era, where Picasso employed the fractured syntax of the music-hall theatre and newspaper references as allusions to the existence of the surrounding world and as a means to experiment with figurative language, Rauschenberg made objects, images and texts from the everyday world—topical, public, controversial, banal, extravagant, discarded, private, obsolete, forgotten—into the material for new aesthetic experiences. These were entities that functioned simultaneously as slices of contemporary modernity and as archaeological excavations of conscious and unconscious segments of modern experience.

Although the problem that confronted Rauschenberg is reminiscent of the one Picasso faced, the two problems are not identical.[23] It is not the image of a linear tradition that is relevant here, but the understanding of how a specific problem is established and transformed by a great many pivotal moments in history. The historical dimension in particular serves as an important dividing line, with the very idea of the tradition of the new creating a sense of alienation and a reference point to which every artist and generation of artists after the Second World War has had to relate. And yet it is at this very point that one can see how extraordinarily challenging in historical terms—and rhetorically awkward—the introduction of new art forms has proved within the parameters of avant-garde discourse, whose *raison d'être* is not only a countercultural position, but also the formulation of a direction towards/away from: into the future, away from history. What is evident is that this problematic issue was dealt with in a number of different ways and with varying degrees of success during the post-war period and that the extent to which it was successfully tackled proved to be a decisive factor in establishing a position in the field.

Two exhibitions exemplify this. Held in New York at the beginning of the 1960s, both attracted attention at the time; although, they were accorded extremely different levels of significance. In the summer and autumn of 1960, *New Form–New Media* was shown in two versions at the Martha Jackson Gallery. It presented the work of a motley collection of some seventy artists from the United States and Europe and showed contemporary and historical examples alongside one another in two sections, with the aim of throwing into international and historical relief what was described as a new American art form: assemblage, junk-art, happenings, environments, ready-mades, collages.[24] In the catalogue, Lawrence Alloway describes the existence of a historical link between Neo-Dadaism and the Dadaist and Futurist traditions that was reflected, all their differences notwithstanding, in an essential accord, namely their dependence on the urban environment and their close connection to popular culture.[25] Allan Kaprow emphasised the untidiness, the unfinished surface, the impression of immediacy and the indifference to traditional concepts of beauty as common denominators.[26] Although the overall impression of the selection and content of the exhibition as presented in Alloway's and Kaprow's texts was of confronting the viewer with a new form of art that deviated in aesthetic terms from the then-current norms pertaining to serious Art, this was nevertheless anaesthetic with obvious historical references.

The raw, amorphous and perhaps offensive idiom the exhibition displayed did not in itself constitute a generic difference from the set of technical, aesthetic and medial connections on which the interpretation of Abstract Expressionism and informal art was frequently based. It would hardly have posed a problem, in terms solely of theory and form, to show one of Willem de Kooning's pictures of women from the mid-1950s as part of the exhibition. But an inclusion of this kind would have erased one of the exhibition's most important rhetorical distinctions: between established and independent culture.

This rhetoric was largely concerned with social distinctions, rather than purely aesthetic ones; the primacy of the latter would have made the explicit historical connections the source of legitimacy for the contemporary works. But this use of history would have laid the exhibition open to the kind of criticism that rejected assemblage art as a mere plagiarism of long-since exhausted gestures (the negative implication of the term 'neo-Dada').[27] Or, as Thomas Hess put it, the new forms of art amounted to no more than a collection of romantic souvenirs from the barricades (the street, history).[28]

Another major thematic exhibition of new trends in contemporary art was shown two years later in November 1962: *The New Realists* at the Sidney Janis Gallery.[29] It comprised an international selection, including artists from France, Italy, Great Britain, Sweden and the United States. American artists predominated in numerical terms but were, for the most part, represented not by the relatively well-known (and in some cases already established) neo-Dadaists but by a younger generation of artists, such as Roy Lichtenstein, Claes Oldenburg, James Rosenquist, Steven Segal, Andy Warhol and Tom Wesselmann.[30] This exhibition created a different context from the one held at Martha Jackson Gallery. In part, this was a matter of the location (the Sidney Janis Gallery was one of the most established galleries in New York and represented the elite of the Abstract Expressionists), in part it involved the visual style of American Pop Art (far removed from any possible accusation as to romantic souvenirs); above all, however, the change had to do with a difference in rhetoric: a new *avant-gardiste* front line was defined here, whose historical context was constituted not by a vanished modernist past but by international and domestic New Realism and neo-Dadaism.

In his foreword, Sidney Janis referred to a historical transformation, with New Realism supplanting Abstract Expressionism in the role of principal pacemaker in the contemporary art world.[31] John Ashbery described New Realism as a transgression of the causality of historical relationships; his point being that Dadaism, in its time, had reactivated a trend that had always existed in art and that New Realism was currently creating a situation in which the images and objects of everyday life could be employed without serving as metaphors.[32] That interpretive construct national→international→universal was evidently once more in play and utilised here in a context that set out a clear demarcation from both Abstract Expressionism and causal historical comparisons. In this respect, the selection drew attention to a new internationalism, with the United States most definitely in the vanguard as a result of the aggressively visual style of Pop Art.[33]

The signals sent out by the exhibition were summarised most trenchantly in the exclamation by the *New York Times* critic Brian O'Doherty that '"Pop" goes the new art!' and by Harold Rosenberg's phrase in *The New Yorker* that the exhibition had struck the art world of New York 'like an earthquake.'[34] After a meeting of the Abstract Expressionists who were associated with the Sidney Janis Gallery, Philip Guston, William Baziotes, Robert Motherwell, Adolph Gottlieb and Mark Rothko decided to leave the gallery with only Willem de Kooning choosing to stay. Their fury could, as Calvin Tomkins has pointed out, be readily understood: after decades of hard work to reach a position of legitimacy and a relatively stable income, everything they stood for—the serious, autonomous, spiritual, existential—appeared to have been turned upside-down in the course of a single evening at the opening of the show.[35] The exhibition thus achieved what every avant-garde must: to define clear boundaries while simultaneously identifying something new. But unlike most of the previous manifestations of the avant-garde in history, this was accorded a form of institutional legitimacy almost immediately: first through a symposium at the Museum of Modern Art in mid-December, at which a number of leading critics and curators discussed the meaning and content of the new art, and subsequently as a result of a series of exhibitions of Pop Art held throughout the United States and Europe.[36]

The key aspect of *The New Realists*—and what distinguishes it from previous exhibitions—was that it made evident a new context, both in rhetorical and real terms. Although this context could be inscribed in a historical continuity, history here was not a static backdrop of linguistic expressions and stylistic props but served, instead, as a legitimising subtext whose orientation pointed forward toward an aesthetic context in the contemporary world. The relation between past and present appears, in fact, to be an extraordinarily—boomerang-like—dynamic that has proved important both for artistic production and the rhetorical legitimation of that production and, subsequently, for its historical interpretation. Once again, the historical pivot is in action here; where artists such as Picasso or Duchamp had established certain pictorial incentives in a particular period, these had now been dislocated by artists such as Rauschenberg or Warhol, and this had, in turn, given rise to various artistic and theoretical reinterpretations of history. The postmodern semiotic readings of Cubism by Rosalind Krauss, Jeffrey Weiss and Yve-Alain Bois would, in fact, be all but inconceivable without this dislocation.

Even specialised surveys suffer under the yoke of the obligatory classifications, with particular categories, such as Pop Art, being described in terms of their birth, rise, maturity, descent and inheritance on the basis of an evolutionist and anthropomorphic narrative.[37] The key issue here, however, is not the abstraction from empirical data, which is, of course, essential to any historical interpretation, but its implementation: a far-reaching, complex and contradictory process is reduced to a number of fixed categories that are defined in turn in relation to a nucleus of *oeuvres*/works. A label, such as 'Pop Art', serves in this system as a term covering all the possible phenomena that have some kind of connection with a particular stylistic idiom, with proximity to that nucleus constituting a crucial criterion for the art-historical importance of the phenomena. In her 1966 survey *Pop Art,* Lucy Lippard listed only five artists as forming part of the core—The New York

Five—who were presented on a falling scale in terms of the degree to which their work was in accord with the principles of Pop Art: Andy Warhol, Roy Lichtenstein, Tom Wesselmann, James Rosenquist and Claes Oldenburg.[38] These then defined retroactively a specific order in which other artists could be included or from which they could be excluded, depending on the degree of stylistic similarity.[39] Related artistic works in other countries were inevitably deported to the periphery—as precursors, variants, copies, deviations—irrespective of the extent to which they fit into the paradigm set out by the category's coordinates.

The interpretation of individual *oeuvres* was similarly adapted to and determined by the internal logic of the categories. As, for example, at the beginning of the 1960s when Jasper Johns and Robert Rauschenberg ceased to be classified as Neo-Dada or as an odd variant of second generation Abstract Expressionism and were labelled instead as pre-Pop, with certain qualities and features of their art becoming emphasised at the cost of others in order to make it better suited to the definition of Pop Art and its narrative.[40] What we are dealing with here is a self-perpetuating category that reduces both the overarching context and the individual *oeuvre*.

This does not, of course, mean that we should simply abandon the term Pop Art completely; it is of both historical and historiographical relevance. An analysis of this concept can provide a powerful indication of the significance of the categories in the establishment of a particular perspective, the drawing up of a chart and the normalisation of a selection. Indeed, the term Pop Art demonstrates a particularly interesting history of changes to artistic and historical reception and production: from its introduction (the end of the 1950s), its cultural transposition and establishment (1962–63), its rapid institutional sanction (1963–64) and historicisation (1965–68) to its historical revision (late 1970s and onwards).[41] A similar—and no doubt, interesting—historical account could also be written about the other stylistic and epochal terms of the 1950s and 1960s, but the problem remains: how are we to name the transformation within the order of modernist discourse that took place during this period? And how should we actually understand the role played by Pop Art in that transformation?

This is a question that has elicited different responses over the last four decades. One example is found in Henry Geldzahler's previously cited catalogue essay for *New York Painting and Sculpture 1940-1970*, held at the Metropolitan Museum of Art in New York in 1970:

> It seems today that Pop Art was an episode, an interesting one that has left its mark on the decade, and will continue to affect the future, but not a major modern movement which continues to spawn new artists. In fact, just about everything new and original in Pop Art was stated by a few artists in the first years of its existence. Since then no artists of first importance have been recruited and no second generation has come along.[42]

A quite different assessment is provided by Rosalind Krauss in her lecture to a symposium on 'Theories of Art after Minimalism and Pop' at Dia Art Foundation 1987:

> [W]e are deluding ourselves if we think that we are dealing with a period of art that succeeds or comes after pop. For as far as we are concerned there has been no "after pop"; its terms, no matter how third-hand, no matter how degraded or sad, have been rehearsed and re-rehearsed throughout almost everything that has happened within dominant aesthetic practice in the past two decades.[43]

How are we to understand the fact that two individuals, who both possess such a thorough knowledge of the contemporary art world, can arrive at such different viewpoints? One explanation may be the different dates at which these assessments were made; perhaps the significance of Pop Art was not as obvious in 1970 as in 1987. Another, and in my view more likely, explanation is that they are not talking about the same thing. One would, after all, quite simply have to agree with Geldzahler that Pop Art as a style had already seen its heyday by the mid-1960s. Neither does Krauss contradict this; on the contrary, there is an air of resignation in her words at all the different varieties and hybrids that have evolved and been promoted in the art world ever since. But what she actually seems to be referring to is not a stylistic concept but a discursive order: the fact that the change of the rules provoked by Pop Art was still (in 1987) a dominant issue in the order of the discourse.

If the transformation we have referred to here was largely a matter of establishing a new relationship between art and the world around it, the question is not so much how this relationship was expressed directly in the image, but how it influenced language, roles and definitions within the discourse of the visual arts. Just as modernism cannot be seen as a direct or essential artistic translation of modernity, Pop Art cannot simply be understood by analogy to mass culture. In my view, what is interesting about both instances is what happens in their mediation: between the present and the past, between high and low, between visual language and adjacent linguistic systems—between the art world and other segments of society.

Trespassing on Common Culture

A remarkable exhibition opened at the Whitechapel Art Gallery in London on 9 August 1956 entitled *This is Tomorrow*. The exhibition had been initially intended to serve as an exposé of British Constructivism; however, it subsequently encompassed trends that were more cross-boundary in media terms.[44] It was made up of twelve pavilions in which different groups had created separate interiors, installations and hangs that alluded in various ways to the futuristic theme of the exhibition. This theme was further underlined in the press release, which emphasised the diversity of the exhibition, ranging from orthodox abstract order to extravagant games with the various signs, images and objects of mass culture.[45] The fact that the exhibition was opened by a full-scale model of Robby the Robot (from the film *Fantastic Planet*) only served to enhance the spectacular nature of this compilation and provoked countless newspaper headlines and considerable public interest.[46]

The visitor was steered through a labyrinthine installation of twelve separate variations on the futuristic theme that, when taken together, presented a fragmentary and contradictory vision of the future. In a press release, Lawrence Alloway, who was in charge of publicity for the exhibition, described the aim of the show as demonstrating the various ways architects, painters, sculptors and other visual artists could collaborate to create interrelated works.⁴⁷ It also formed part of the ongoing debate in the twentieth century on the relationship of the various forms of art to architecture and the environment, while also providing a rather radical (for its time) cross-boundary approach to the possibility of a fusion of different media and professional skills.

The aims of the exhibition met with an interesting and fairly well-informed contemporary reception, although its mixed composition and rebellious attitude were variously dismissed as a rehash of the glory days of the Bauhaus and of Dadaism in the 1920s. Pierre Rouve, for example, adjudged what he perceived to be the twofold front the exhibition was attempting to erect against both realism and modernism a failure in that it was too dependent on both Dadaist gestures and formalist models.⁴⁸ In more recent decades, however, much of the formalist and Dadaist duality has been missing from the received image of the show inasmuch as only one of the pavilions has entered the history books: that of Richard Hamilton, John McHale and John Voelker. On display was a remarkable mixture of the high and the low— collages of films and media, a full-length portrait of Marilyn Monroe, a jukebox, a four-metre-high image of Robby the Robot, perspective projections and reconstructions of Marcel Duchamp's rotoreliefs—in a setting that called to mind a mixture of an ethnographic museum and an amusement park. As exemplified in this pavilion, the exhibition has gone down in history as the first manifestation of Pop Art.

But the really interesting thing about *This is Tomorrow* is that it provided an anthology of some of the various possible approaches to contemporary visual culture and to that of 'tomorrow' found in the mid-1950s, on the borderland between Art and environment, and very much outside the accepted art-historical categories. It also took an approach to the reception of visitors that was distinctly different from accepted practice, which had institutionalised the white cube as the ultimate representative space of modern art. This was made explicit in the press release: 'Visitors are not expected to merely look at pictures on the walls or sculptures on stands. Visitors are invited to enter strange houses, corridors and mazes. This is modern art to entertain people, modern art as a game people will want to play.'⁴⁹ Modern art—and the presentation of modern art—were thus being characterised as an interactive game rather than in terms of the isolation of the individual work for elevated, aesthetic contemplation.

If a single theme is to be posthumously identified as crucial to the exhibition, this would have to be the mediation of various linguistic, social and technological systems as visual forms of expression. The exhibition was organised by individuals who were associated with a small and only loosely connected set within the Institute of Contemporary Arts (ICA) called the Independent Group. This group was formed in 1952 and consisted of individuals operating in many different fields: Richard Hamilton (industrial designer, visual artist), John McHale (graphic designer), Eduardo and Freda Paolozzi (visual artists), Nigel Henderson (photographer), Reynes Bantham and Lawrence Alloway (art critics), Richard Lannoy (gallery assistant), Alison and Peter Smithson (architects). The aim of its meetings, seminars and exhibitions was to examine the whole range of representations that characterised society, culture and 'the consciousness industry' in post-war Great Britain: mass media, comic albums, advertising, design, trademarks and logos, science fiction and pulp-fiction, systems of communication and technology, architecture and town planning, social interactions, the visual arts and art history.[50] This enterprise involved a kind of ambivalent archaeology of the then-contemporary world, in which the surface of mass culture appeared to be at least as important as the social unconscious and in which an ironic detachment was coupled with undisguised fascination. The aims of the group were, as Lynne Cooke has observed, not to produce art but to analyse and visualise different types of contexts and processes.[51] In this perspective, their efforts should, perhaps, best be understood as ancestral to the visual culture studies of recent decades. *This is Tomorrow* then becomes part of a larger pattern rather than serving simply as a model for the Pop Art of the early 1960s.

The positioning of the exhibition in art history, as an early prototype of Pop Art, is frequently underlined (and illustrated) by Richard Hamilton's collage *Just What Is It That Makes Today's Homes So Different, So Appealing?* (1956). This collage served as one of the posters for the exhibition and was also reproduced in the catalogue. When placed beside a work by one of the American pop artists from the beginning of the 1960s, the correspondences can be striking (at least if they are compared as though based on photographs of the same scale), and, indeed, this image has been canonised as 'the first Pop Artwork' in many contexts.[52] The connection is emphasised in particular in Lawrence Alloway's introduction, as well as in the subsequent historicisation of the term Pop Art, in which some of the activities of the Independent Group were reformulated as an aesthetic programme.[53] But a stylistic comparison of this kind conceals a number of fundamental differences between Hamilton's poster and later Pop Art. One might observe to begin with that this is a very small picture (26 x 25 cm), entirely lacking the visual impact of the often enormous canvases of American Pop Art. If it is related to anything in the art history of the twentieth century, it would be the German Dadaist photo-montage of the 1920s, and yet even that comparison misses the mark. For, despite the absurd heaping together of references and visual signs, the aim of Hamilton's collage is not, fundamentally, the creation of antiaesthetic or poetic values but the provision of information. He was not working from an idea about paradoxical metaphors or dynamic composition; instead, he saw the image as a visual form of exhibition index in which a number of words or phenomena had to be included: man, woman, humanity, food, newspapers, cinema, TV, telephone, comics (picture information), words (textual information), tape recording (aural information), cars, domestic appliances, space.[54] These phenomena were put together with a dry humour such that the sheer pleasure of the play with perspectives and references could work in tandem with the aim of conveying as clearly as possible the theme of the exhibition as a whole.

The way the image heightens and concentrates the phenomena and visual codes it presents appears, however, to clash with the futuristic theme of the exhibition. It bears comparison here with the advertising image for Philips TV of the same period. Hamilton's collage not only contains quotations from contemporary advertising, but also it is obviously based on a comprehensive analysis of the codes and rhetorical devices of contemporary commercial culture. Here, too, we are dealing with a form of presentation that thematises and makes display of a distinct notion of modernity, but, unlike in the Philips image, this value has not been provided with a veil of normality. The setting is actually distorted in a rather obvious way that alienates what is familiar without concealing the identification of its own visual rhetoric. In this respect, the alienation of the familiar would seem to be one of the most important informative aims of the image. This was a deliberate strategy on the part of (the industrial designer) Hamilton, as he believed that the future could only be conceptualised by an expansion of the visual experience of the present.[55] Seen in this light, rather than functioning as a stylistic model for a new art form, Hamilton's collage emerges as an allegory of the contemporary culture of consumption and its ideals and as a visual index of the attitudes and intellectual frames of reference that characterised the Independent Group—at once curious, affirmative, ironical and critical. The polemic against the preoccupation of historical modernism with technical innovations, functional structures and the fetishisation of more attractive everyday goods is all too evident here: the future is to be found in what surrounds us, in what is used up and discarded, which has hitherto been all but ignored by the representatives of elite culture.

The point of identifying this connection is to make it possible to see the operations of the Independent Group as an aspect of a larger shift in interest that took place in the modern discourse of the visual arts. Although not the accepted focus of the group's sphere of ideas, contemporary radical visual art did, of course, play a very important part. But, here, the basis for the reception of contemporary Art was not exclusivity but the perspective of mass culture. A few years after the exhibition, Lawrence Alloway put forward a definition of this perspective in 'The Long Front of Culture' (1959):

> Acceptance of the mass media entails a shift in our notion of what culture is. Instead of reserving the word for the highest artefacts and the noblest thoughts of history's top ten, it needs to be used more widely as the description of "what a society does". Then, unique oil paintings and highly personal poems as well as mass-distributed films and group-aimed magazines can be placed within a continuum rather than frozen in layers in a pyramid. . . . Acceptance of

the media on some such basis, as entries in a descriptive account of society's communication, is related to modern arrangements of knowledge in non-hierarchic forms ... The mass media are crucial in this general extension of interpretation outwards from the museum and library into the crowded world.[56]

The approach set out above is based on the social and communicative functions of culture, with interpretation playing a dual role: the understanding of sophisticated art within the framework of mass culture and the establishment of a nonhierarchical aesthetic based on a continuity between mass culture and elite culture. This could also be said to apply in large part to *This is Tomorrow*, which was, moreover, put together within the framework of an established and serious institution (the ICA).[57]

Hal Foster has analysed this interface between cultural and linguistic spheres in connection with Richard Hamilton's visual art (its overlapping of commercial and modernist representational styles, and between verbal and visual codes) in terms of a new regulatory apparatus or a new symbolic order, transcending the horizons of industrial society and formalist aesthetics.[58] It is this point that is of such particular interest: the reception (within the Independent Group) opened up, as it were, new sections of the archive (history/the present) that, in their turn, shifted the focus and laid new foundations for the production of art. This involved a way of using information from a set of different fields not simply as visual material in images but as a means of employing knowledge to reformulate the visual and conceptual codes of modern art. Although their projects and methods differed in other respects, this approach provided a common denominator for both Hamilton and Rauschenberg. Here is the point at which the surrounding world reenters art at the same time linguistic critique and the relation to history are reactivated. The point, in both cases, is nevertheless dependent on the grid in which it is set: the field called art.

This shift does not, as it turns out, actually contradict Ad Reinhardt's precept 'Art is art-as-art and everything else is everything else.' Lawrence Alloway's definition of a continuity between elite culture and mass culture and all the different variants of this formulation over the last fifty years have not led to an implosion of the value sphere of the visual arts. Irrespective of the extent to which this activity was legitimised by a form of rhetoric that undermined the difference between art and everything else, it was the transformation in question that was crucial: of the surrounding world in the social and linguistic space of the visual arts, of the social and linguistic space of the visual arts by the reestablishment of a connection to the world around them.

What this shift highlights is the problematic nature of one of the parts of Ad Reinhardt's formula, namely 'as-art'. For this part of the phrase would—entirely counter to Ad Reinhardt's intention—emerge as being vulnerable to extremely diverse interpretations that have established a somewhat different order in the discursive practice of the modern visual arts.

Open Aesthetics

Paradigmatic Reinterpretations

In his study *Opera aperta* (1962), Umberto Eco analyses a trend in post-war music, literature and the visual arts that has brought about a radical reformulation, in his view, of the perception of the work of art and its communicative function. What is new is an interest in open, variable and (deliberately) incomplete structures that leave some of the constituent factors of the work free to be supplemented either by the executor, by the viewer or by chance:

> This difference can be formulated in elementary terms as follows: a classical composition, whether it be a Bach fugue, Verdi's *Aïda*, or Stravinsky's *Rite of Spring*, posits an assemblage of sound units which the composer arranged in a closed, well-defined manner before presenting it to the listener. He converted his idea into conventional symbols which more or less oblige the eventual performer to reproduce the format devised by the composer himself, whereas the new musical works ... reject the definitive, concluded message and multiply the formal possibilities of the distribution of their elements. They appeal to the initiative of the individual performer, and hence they offer themselves not as finite works which prescribe specific repetition along given structural coordinates but as "open" works, which are brought to their conclusion by the performer at the same time as he experiences them on an aesthetic plane.[59]

The traditional view of the work as a structurally closed/completed organic whole was being challenged here. The open work, in Eco's sense, involves the inscription of a multiplicity of alternatives within the structure of the work such that its openness is both

How to cite this book chapter:
Hayden, Hans. 2018. Open Aesthetics. In: Hayden, H. *Modernism as Institution: On the Establishment of an Aesthetic and Historiographic Paradigm* Pp. 272–306. Stockholm: Stockholm University Press. DOI: https://doi.org/10.16993/bar.h. License: CC-BY

communicative and structural in nature. This also entails changes to the fundamental criteria that govern the interpretation of the work by the executor, encompassing both variations in the aesthetic character of the piece (tempo, dynamic, emphases) and its structural framework and form. Eco exemplifies this new category of works with compositions, such as Karl Heinz Stockhausen's *Klavierstück XI* of 1956, which consists of nineteen groups of notes and the interpreter is free to determine the internal arrangement according to which the sequence should be played. It is the dimension of choice, and the open structure in particular, that constitutes the new type of work and distinguishes it from previous traditions in which the work was considered to be an organic whole whose structure was fixed by the score.

Experiments with variability were not an entirely new invention in the 1950s and can actually be traced far back into the past. It was at this time, however, that the open form became of central importance to various composers in different parts of the world. Among those who went furthest in terms of variability and the dismantling of the structure of the work as a whole was John Cage. One of his early principles was to break with both the harmonics of the Western tradition and twelve-tone serial music in order to experiment with different types of sound in rhythmic sequences where time was the structuring factor.[60] Initially, it was the prepared piano, which emphasises the percussive mechanics of the piano, that served as the typical instrument for these endeavours, whose most radical implication was, in principle, any sound at all could be used in a composition. Perhaps Cage's clearest declaration of intent is found in the celebrated piece 4'33 of 1952 (partly inspired by the silence in Robert Rauschenberg's *White Paintings*), whose three movements consist of a single notation: tacet. As a result, all the ambient sounds in the venue became incorporated in the piece, without any hierarchies operating between them. In this instance, it was not only the soloist who participated in the variability of the piece, but also the audience and the space to a considerable extent.

However, it would be a mistake to refer to an absence of structure, because the framework of the composition was precisely specified: the duration (four minutes and thirty-three seconds), the division into three movements (which it was up to the interpreter to mark in some way) and the space (the concert venue). The structure—and aesthetic—Cage was attempting to demonstrate was one that made possible an opening up of the score and the performed work, and that could involve any and all kinds of sounds, such that the world would pass through the work, so to speak, allowing the audience to become aware of their environment by employing a different form of attention and sensibility. Cage's aesthetic with its radical emphasis on the importance of the accidental for the work differs in many ways from the considerably stricter structure of a composer such as Stockhausen. And Cage's exploration of the possibilities of time and silence also took the idea of the open work beyond Eco's modified communicative sequence (originator→work→interpreter) to create a situation in which the work was no longer to be understood as an autonomous and uniform structure but as a communicative process outside the direct control of the originator. For Cage, silence and chance meant that the composer had to abandon the idea of his own intentions in relation to the work in order to accentuate its particular quality of indeterminacy.[61]

Instead of understanding the work as a specified hierarchical structure with a fixed centre, Cage employed a metaphor from the natural world to demonstrate the possibility of an open structure that transcends all hierarchies: a person studying a leaf cannot determine a particular viewpoint from which the constitution or essence of the leaf can be defined.[62] It is interesting to note how this organic metaphor is employed to contravene the notion of the work as an organic whole: the structure of the work is no longer seen as developing out of a predetermined centre; the work no longer appears to be a transcendence of the presence of the originator; the work no longer has any set boundaries but can (and must) change over time. There can be no doubt that here we have arrived at a point in twentieth century Western aesthetics where the premises of the regime of the authentic are being seriously challenged. The reason that this challenge should occur, become possible even, within the aesthetic/ideological context of the 1950s was because, in contrast to the utilitarian visions of the Soviet Constructivists, it did not entail abandoning Art as an autonomous sphere (for it to be subordinated to society's forces of production) but involved, instead, a change to the linguistic systems and discursive framework (the art world) of serious art.

Umberto Eco (who never mentions Cage by name) does not deal with these revolutionary aspects in his study but takes as his paradigmatic examples of the new open type of work contemporary European composers (Stockhuasen, Boulez, Pousseur) and a somewhat older European literary tradition (Joyce, Mallarmé, Brecht). In these instances, variability was not a matter of abandoning a view of the work as an organic whole but of focusing instead on works whose structural coordinates were, although variable, based on a predetermined set of permutations within an overall framework. This becomes all the more apparent when Eco broadens the discussion of the open work to include the visual arts as well. In the latter case, he refers exclusively to (European) *art informel* whose openness was considered to exist primarily on a communicative level:

> This sort of painting is, therefore, still a form of communication, a passage from an intention to a reception. And even if the reception is left open – because the intention itself was open, aiming at a plural communication – it is nevertheless the end of an act of communication which, like every act of information, depends on the disposition and the organization of a certain form. Understood in this sense, the "informal" is a rejection of classical forms with univocal directions but not a rejection of that form which is the fundamental condition of communication. The example of the informal, like any open work, does not proclaim the death of form; rather, it proposes a new, more flexible version of it – *form as a field of possibilities*.[63]

According to Eco, informal art is open because it encompasses a greater number of interpretive possibilities. In a work by Jackson Pollock or Jean Fautrier, the spontaneous and arbitrary execution means that the structure of the painting cannot be perceived as conveying meaning in itself but demands a dialectical relationship with the viewer. This communicative and semantic openness served, as we have seen, as a crucial aspect of the understanding and legitimation of contemporary avant-garde art after the Second World War, which was open in principle to a pattern of interpretation that was both cultural and countercultural. Eco, for his part, observes that the interpretation of contemporary nonfigurative art must necessarily be ambivalent and that this semantic ambivalence is transformed into a fundamental criterion for a new category of artworks (open works).

This was not an entirely original innovation on Eco's part but should be seen as a codification of ideas that were circulating in the art world of the time. European informal art in particular was interpreted by some critics in considerably more radical terms than is apparent from the classification and downgrading of this kind of art in more recent times as market-oriented and as mannered high-modernism. A similar argument can be found in the lecture given by Marcel Duchamp at the Convention of the American Federation of Arts in Houston in 1958 entitled 'The Creative Act'. There, he maintained that the act of artistic creation had two principal poles, those of the artist and the viewer, that were both of equal importance for a work to come into being. This meant that he did not consider the work as finished once the artist had signed it, but rather its existence, in terms of its aesthetic meaning, entailed an uncompleted historical process:

> The creative act takes another aspect when the spectator experiences the phenomenon of transmutation; through the change from inert matter into a work of art, an actual transubstantiation has taken place, and the role of the spectator is to determine the weight of the work on the aesthetic scale. All in all, the creative act is not performed by the artist alone; the spectator brings the work in contact with the external world by deciphering and interpreting its inner qualifications and thus adds his contribution to the creative act.[64]

Duchamp is thus placing production and reception on an equal footing in the presentation of the work of art as an aesthetic object. This text also reflects a somewhat Romantic idea of interpretation as transubstantiation: a ritual transformation of substances, such as the wine and the bread into the blood and body of Christ as part of Holy Communion. This idea recurs somewhat later in Ulf Linde's analysis of Duchamp's *The Large Glass* 'La mariée mise à nu par ses célibataires, même': by an odd coincidence (a draught), the world of the bachelors (the viewers) can be connected with that of the bride (the artist's) in an upward movement (a transubstantiation) straight through two horizontal glass structures (the bride's clothes, the work of art). The work does not emerge as a work of art until the moment the viewer succeeds in establishing a connection, when he or she is capable 'of permeating it with his or her own life without demanding higher truths'. [65]

Today, some forty years later, these ideas of the polyvalence of meaning and the significance of reception seem not only familiar concepts, but also as forming two of the accepted postulates in the contemporary discussion of interpretive theory. It may, nevertheless, appear somewhat remarkable that Umberto Eco should employ *art informel,* and Abstract Expressionism in particular, as examples of what this new type of art might mean. For this was the very period in which completely different forms of art were being established that deliberately employed communicative openness as a starting point for cross-boundary medial experimentation. What may appear today as a confusing use of categories may, itself, be an interesting example of how possible contexts, transgressions and shifts can be formulated before these categories become fixed in the historical record.

* * * *

A significant example of what continuity and historical cross-fertilisation could mean in practice—subsequent historical categorisations notwithstanding—can be found in Allan Kaprow's article 'The Legacy of Jackson Pollock', published in *Art News* in 1958. He maintained that while Pollock may have created wonderful paintings, in so doing he also succeeded in eradicating painting by violating the boundaries of the genre: in the use of his technique (drip-painting instead of brushstroke), by exceeding the formal framework of painting (all-over-ness instead of the organic whole of the planar image) and by the enormous scale and spatial structure of the paintings that blurred the boundary between the space of the painting and that of the viewer. The real inheritance left by Jackson Pollock was not that he established a certain style or a specific aesthetic approach but that he identified (indirectly) a new route for the visual arts that could take them beyond painting:

Pollock, as I see him, left us at the point where we must become preoccupied with and even dazzled by the space and objects of our every-day life, either our bodies clothes, rooms, or, if need to be, the vastness of Forty-Second Street. Not satisfied with the *suggestion* through paint of our other senses, we shall utilize the specific substances of sight, sound, movements, people, odors, touch. Objects of every sort are materials for the new art . . . Pollock's near destruction of this tradition [of painting] may well be a return to the point where art is more actively involved in ritual, magic and life than we have known it in our recent past.[66]

This provides an interesting insight into the way the problem of modern art was reformulated during the second half of the 1950s, when the categorisation of various movements and approaches had not yet been fixed. In his own artistic practice, Kaprow moved from a direct interpretation of Pollock's working method (action-collage) to the use of the gallery space as a means of expression (environment). When he showed his spatial installations, he realised that each visitor both influenced and became part of the artwork, with the result that the experience of an installation involved something other and greater than simply a communication of visual impressions:

> We simply enter it, are surrounded by it, become part of it, passively or actively according to our talents for 'engagement', in much the same way that we have moved *out* of the totality of the street or our home where we also played a part.[67]

This led Kaprow to engage more actively with the development of forms that could transcend the boundaries between artistic media as well as those between the viewer and the work (happenings).[68] A link to painting can still be found, albeit at a metaphorical level, in *18 happenings in 6 parts*, which was staged at the Reuben Gallery in New York in 1959: in one scene, an artist is sitting on a red chair; he lights and blows out nineteen matches; he gets up slowly, without making any gestures, in order to move over to each of the four laminated walls in front of which containers of paint and brushes have been placed and 'solemnly paint'.[69] This could be seen as an at once ironic, symbolic and utterly concrete representation of the change in the status of painting, from being the essential form of expression to becoming one sign among all the others in the cross-boundary and wide-open reference system of the visual arts.

Although, as Benjamin Buchloh has pointed out, Kaprow's declaration of the death of the tradition of painting because of Pollock was based on a twofold misconception: on the one hand, it involved an overestimation (that would subsequently be reproduced in countless historical surveys) of the significance of the stylistic and medial rupture, while on the other, his focus on the magical and ritual functions of art meant that he considered these categories transhistorical and universal (which would have implied a continuity with aspects of the aesthetics of Abstract Expressionism).[70] In contrast with Buchloh, I consider the first misconception to be the more important. It manages to situate in historical terms both the context in which an open aesthetic emerged and the polysemous diversity that was the hallmark of the art scene of the 1960s. At much the same time that happenings, Pop Art and Minimalism were being treated as serious trends within contemporary art, Pollock was being posthumously canonised, Barnett Newman and Ad Reinhardt were being taken seriously as artists, Mark Rothko, Robert Motherwell and Willem de Kooning were continuing their successful careers and a new wave of radicalised abstract art (colour field, hard edge, post-painterly abstraction, op-art, shaped canvas) was being established, all of which meant that a critic, such as Clement Greenberg, could acquire renewed topicality. This was not solely an American phenomenon; the same pattern was repeated in Western Europe. The rather modest introduction of Neo-Dadaism and Pop Art at *documenta III* in 1964 and their relaunch on a much larger scale at *documenta IV* in 1968 occurred against a background that accorded equal prominence to contemporary nonfigurative painting.[71] Instead of accepting Kaprow's interpretation of Pollack uncritically, we could see it as forming part of the process of legitimation of a radical alternative that existed on the fringes of New York's established art world at the end of the 1950s and had profound effects on the European art scene by the mid-1960s.

In this respect, Kaprow's own artistic process calls to mind that of many other American artists of the same period, for whom

John Cage's lectures at the New School of Social Research in New York provided the nexus for various intermedial experiments.[72] Cage's class was, however, only part of a network of artists, dancers, musicians, actors and writers who participated in one another's performances, attended one another's openings and, most importantly, exchanged ideas between the different artistic genres in every conceivable direction.[73] It was this medial cross-fertilisation in particular that provided a radical antithesis to the powerful medium-specific trend of the art world of the late 1950s. If Clement Greenberg's type of exclusionary criteria could be said to characterise the established end of the American art world in the late 1950s, the process of redefining traditional forms of art became a fundamental criterion of the subcultural context, one of whose cornerstones was provided by Cage's inclusive and open aesthetic.

This medial cross-fertilisation also altered the way in which history was read. Knowledge of the Dadaist tradition was, of course, significant in this regard, both as a catalyst and as an example of the existence of other sources and alternative strains within modernism. It also helped to shape the situation in which a radical reevaluation of the particular significance of Marcel Duchamp for twentieth-century art took place.[74] His *oeuvre* was interpreted in a manner that transcended the historical context (and, on occasion, even his own wishes) and led to the emergence of a reactivated and, to some extent at least, new image of Duchamp. John Cage has described at some point his way of seeing Duchamp's *The Large Glass*; this does not involve a historical reconstruction or an intrusive close reading (as exemplified in the interpretations by André Breton and Ulf Linde) but a form of observation whose lack of pretension reveals an entirely different horizon of interpretation:

> Looking at the Large Glass, the thing that I like so much is that I can focus my attention wherever I wish. It helps me to blur the distinction between art and life and produces a kind of silence in the work itself. There is nothing in it that requires me to look in one place or another, in fact, requires me to look at all. I can look through it to the world beyond. . . . So he's telling us something

that we perhaps haven't yet learned, when we speak as we do so glibly of the blurring of the distinction between art and life. Or perhaps he's bringing us back to Thoreau: yes and no are lies.[75]

Sometimes this attitude has been considered an eclectic, uncritical or unoriginal recycling of historical sources, such as in the dismissal of the cross-boundary experimentation of the late 1950s with the pejorative label of Neo-Dada in the critical writing of Thomas Hess and others, or, as in the work of Peter Bürger, as the rejection of the workings of the neo-avantgarde as a market-oriented institutionalisation and aestheticisation of the institution-critical (and fundamentally anti-aesthetic) attitude of the historical avant-garde.[76] In its polemical eagerness to present a situation as black and white, this kind of dismissal ignores the complexity of the process in which the redefinition of a discursive order can both activate and be activated by a historiographic reformulation. It was not the change to historical knowledge itself that was crucial to the establishment of an open aesthetic but the real and active reinterpretation of this knowledge that took place in artistic and theoretical practice. Seen in this light, the historical avant-garde emerges as a far more complex, contradictory and ambivalent source than the institutionalisation of the post-war period and the historiography of modernism would have it appear. If the late 1950s is to be considered a critical juncture in the history of modern art, which seems appropriate in many ways, the change involved is one that occurs as part of a continuity.

But even if the subcultural arts circles of New York at this time displayed a multiplicity and a concentration without parallel in the contemporary world, their cross-boundary ambitions were far from unique. Quite the opposite, as similar activities could be witnessed elsewhere in the United States, Europe and other parts of the world, with artists seeking in various ways and (initially) independently of one another to discover new forms while also searching for alternative historical sources and attempting to define different aesthetic problems. And it is in this particular regard that Umberto Eco's argument becomes of serious interest in relation to the visual arts. Moreover, the distinctions he draws can be made considerably more useful for our purposes if their scope is broadened from the definition of a new type of work (the open artwork) to the identification of a fundamental change in aesthetic approach (the open aesthetic). The point of this operation is to make possible a discussion of underlying attitudes, rather than a comparison based on form or stylistic similarity, so as to explicitly transcend an essentialist view of the work as a closed structure of meaning and encompass all artistic media, while also describing an international phenomenon irrespective of the formation of national schools, derivations of influences, normative examples and distinctions between the centre and the periphery.

The aim here is not to establish a new historical category for the inclusion and exclusion of ideas, works and names. It is, rather, to identify and clarify an underlying context: to interpret and understand a number of disparate historical phenomena, documents, images and other representations on the basis of what might be described as a specific discursive order. The open aesthetic does not entail a definitive historical rupture in this respect but rather a shift of the focus within the discourse of modernity. What this opens up is, in fact, the 'as' which precedes 'art' in Ad Reinhardt's phrase—a displacement of the conceivable boundaries within which artistic practice and interpretation are possible and legitimate. This open 'as' serves to characterise a change in attitude, which affects both the way the work is seen (as artwork), its meaning as a work of art and the relationship of the originator as well as the observer to the work. This is a shift that may be described in the words of Hal Foster as a transition from emphasising the work as quality to understanding it as interest.[77] That is, it is a shift away from a focus on normative critique, presence and essence in order to move beyond established (stylistic, aesthetic, medial) categories and to emphasise the communicative situation of the work. This does not mean that the extremely disparate contexts the open aesthetic describes lacked norms in the form of discursive rules for the possible and acceptable, but rather that those norms were not to be derived from a fixed, essentialist or teleological relation to the specific nature of the medium, the logic of history or the authentic style of the individual.

The Play of Opposites

American theatre and dance historian Sally Banes' book *Greenwich Village 1963* (1993) is that unusual thing: a monograph of a single year as observed from a single place. The reason she chose this particular geographic and temporal location was its crucial importance, in her view, to an entirely new direction in the cultural life of the United States:

> In 1963 what we now call the Sixties began. For political historians that year is memorable for the nuclear test ban treaty, the historic civil rights March on Washington, U.S. help in overthrowing the Diem government in Vietnam and the increase of American advisers there twentyfold, President John F. Kennedy's visit to the Berlin Wall, the deepening Sino-Soviet split, and the assassination in Dallas, among other events. But in 1963 another kind of history and another kind of politics were being made, in Greenwich Village, New York City. This was a political history that had nothing to do with the states, governments, or armies, or with public resistance. It had, instead, to do with art and its role in American life. For it was not only the policymakers in Washington who were shaping American postwar culture, but also, importantly, groups of individuals setting forth models of daily life for a generation – gently loosening the social and cultural fabric by merging private and public life, work and play, art and ordinary experience. . . . There was a feeling – so unlike the early 1990s – that all things were possible. . .and permitted.[78]

This might be thought a flagrant example of the kind of revolutionary dramaturgy we referred to earlier, with a pivotal moment being fixed upon as the introduction to an era. But Banes' book is more interesting than that. What she actually does is break up traditional types of linear and/or evolutionist narratives by allowing a multiplicity of diverse periods, contradictory styles and ambivalent attitudes to intersect at a singular, albeit composite, focus. The focal point she describes could be considered the culmination of a process over many years in the art and cultural worlds of New York in which forms of expression that had operated as subcultural manifestations in relation to the established culture, remaining in hiding as it were, were gradually rising to the surface and increasingly coming to define the discursive order of cultural life.

A counterpart in the art world to Banes' list is the extraordinarily rapid impact of Pop Art on New York and the United States at the end of 1962 and during 1963. This much discussed period can be read to advantage through Banes' study, particularly in order to restore to Pop Art a feature it later lost as a result, for the most part, of its institutional internalisation: its close connection with a subcultural scene and with a diverse arrangement of social, political, sexual, aesthetic and medial groups. Pop Art may be considered a product of this cultural melting-pot, whose once so-obviously transgressive tendencies had both social and aesthetic aspects. Susan Sontag attempted to convey something along these lines in 'Notes On Camp' (1964), whose argument recreates the historical backdrop vital to an understanding of how alien Pop Art and its specific sensibility must once have appeared to its contemporaries before it was fixed, classified and made the object of theory as an idea.[79]

An interesting aspect of this institutional transformation of living culture is that it expresses a relationship of a more general kind between two different interpretive positions: the way in which a phenomenon occurs within a particular temporal and discursive framework and then undergoes a transformation when that framework is exchanged, for example, when an object is shifted from serving a particular contextual function to becoming a museum exhibit. The issue may also be formulated directly with reference to the work of art, in which case it concerns the relation between the signifier and the signified: what happens, that is, to the surrounding world when it is transformed, manipulated and encapsulated within the borders of the work. Although this is an ancient and incredibly complex question within the history of art, it emerged in various ways as an issue of acute importance for many of the avant-garde movements of the twentieth century, when it was sometimes formulated in terms of an attempt to bridge the divide between art and life. This divide has taken on an almost metaphorical significance at times, with the prescription for bridging it set out in diametrically opposed ways: from a metaphysical conviction of the immediate communicative capacity of the image

(Kandinsky) to the idea of abandoning the individual work in favour of a universal form of plastic representation (Mondrian).[80] The issue may already have been overplayed by the beginning of the 1960s, but the solutions proposed by Cage, Rauschenberg or Warhol were radically different from those provided by any of the artists practising in Europe of the 1910s.

It is not only the change itself that is interesting, but also the problematic issues with which the open aesthetic confronts the interpreter. How, for example, should one interpret the sounds that happen to occur in a particular performance of John Cage's 4'33? Can such a question even be put in relation to this work? Are we not, in fact, confronted in this instance with an aesthetic that in its most radical extension makes any interpretive activity impossible?

The answer to these questions is fundamentally semiotic in nature and concerns whether it is even possible to distinguish a particular phenomenon as a sign, whether a sound, a movement or a material item or sediment when inscribed into a particular conventional space (the art world, the work of art) is transformed from substance into form, thus becoming a sign that can be interpreted. But even if the problem is rarely as complicated as in the case of 4'33, it is nevertheless one the viewer is forced to confront in relation to large parts of the work created by arts practitioners from the 1960s onwards. The interesting question here is not whether something is a work of art, but how meaning is generated within the framework of the open aesthetic and how meanings may be transformed by institutional relocations.

* * * *

When Öyvind Fahlström's *Dr. Schweitzer's Last Mission* (1964–66) was shown for the first time at the Venice Biennale of 1966, it attracted a great deal of international attention. Fahlström was among the preliminary favourites for the major painting prize (Premio Presidenza del Consiglio dei Ministri), which was ultimately awarded to the Argentinian Julio Le Parc. The work had been produced for display at the institution that had established itself in the post-war period as the foremost international shop-window of the art world and, hence, as the gatekeeper for the established order of the discourse. It was bought that same year by the gallery owner Sidney Janis in New York, who sold it to Moderna Museet in Stockholm in 1970. It would be futile to attempt to distinguish between sensibility and concept when faced with a work that was so evidently produced within the framework of the established institutions of the art world, because the sensibility of the open aesthetic had become the very concept the institutions of the art world were busy producing and reproducing at this time.

It is the very normality of the Venice Biennale of 1966 that is so interesting here in that it demonstrates that a significant change had taken place on the international art scene and that the open aesthetic had become a self-evident part of the institutionalised establishment. The exhibition lacked even a vestige of the heroism that characterised other aspects of the turbulent political and cultural history of the 1960s, such as the legendary Biennales held in 1964 and 1968.[81] In a similar vein, *Dr. Schweitzer's Last Mission* could be said to represent a type of structure, concept and aesthetic that was normal for the more radical end of the institutional and economic structure of the art world—the part that ended up in the history books. Although the position adopted by Fahlström's works at this time makes them typical of the serious art of the 1960s, this does not mean they are mediocre or uninteresting, quite the contrary. Indeed, *Dr. Schweitzer's Last Mission* provides a striking example of the aesthetic and linguistic interface that encompassed large parts of the visual arts of the 1960s.

The work is made up of 68 parts in different materials that are hung in a three-dimensional space. The relationships between the visual elements are not fixed but determined by the person responsible for the exhibition, which means that the design of the work can (and should) vary between each display. The 68 painted elements of the work are hung in a clearly defined area that should indicate its spatial extent. The viewer was originally supposed to be able to move freely within this real space, but this is no longer permitted today. The structure of the work is not predetermined, and the fixed (hard) shapes of the visual elements have pronounced contours, which makes them appear to be discrete signs in the syntax of a pictorial language.

A peculiar relationship to several of the components that are of traditional importance in the history of art may be discerned here. First, Fahlström did not execute the workmanship himself but delegated it to the artist, and his then-wife, Barbro Östlihn—a circumstance that was openly declared initially but subsequently toned down.[82] Second, the space of the work seems most peculiar. The various pictorial elements are set within a frame that constitutes a fixed temporal situation; they are parts of a narrative (although a fragmentary one) and therefore also encompass an element of time. This means that they exist at once as a space, a narrative and a relationship between part and whole. *Dr. Schweitzer's Last Mission* is not fundamentally different from the paintings of previous eras in this regard. But the fact that the dividing line between the pictorial space and the space of the viewer is blurred makes the medial identity of the work less than clear. Can this be called painting at all? Yes, if it is the artist who says it is. In structural terms, however, this is a painting located in the borderlands between painting, the multiple and the installation that simultaneously challenges and extends the specific boundaries of the medium.

In terms of its scale and subject matter, the work could be described as a modern variant of history painting—*une grande machine* (a great machine)—however, that evidently produces a very different history than the allegorical stagings of academic discourse. Fahlström's particular status as artist and critic should be taken into consideration when attempting to understand this approach. From the beginning of the 1950s, he had been a driving force in Swedish cultural life in terms of introducing new types of visual art, literature, poetry, music and film. At the same time that Umberto Eco was publishing *Opera aperta*, Öyvind Fahlström was summarising a number of cross-medial features he believed he could discern in the radical art of the day: the participation of the observer in the execution of the work; the ever increasing importance of chance; a nonnormative and value-relative approach to art; open and unfinished forms; a nonhierarchical approach to material, methods and genres; an anti-symbolic and antiexpressionist view of objects as physical and visual facts.[83] Although Fahlström could never match Eco in terms of analytic acuity, he clearly possessed an unusual overview of the front line of contemporary culture, as well as an ability to transform his theoretical and empirical insights into images. Indeed, *Dr. Schweitzer's Last Mission* appears almost to be a visual manifesto of the changes in the aesthetic position of contemporary painting. To borrow Craig Owen's specifically postmodern definition of allegory—the superimposition of texts, the fragments, the movement outward from the work, the active role of the viewer—*Dr. Schweitzer's Last Mission* could be said to constitute an allegorical reflection on the contemporary period and its art.[84] One layer of meaning refers to a peculiar hodgepodge of allusions to espionage, surveillance, violence, the Cold War balance of power and other more quotidian aspects of high and mass culture, while another seems to speak of the possibilities of painting as an artistic medium.

The corollary of this twofold perspective is that the individual pictorial elements are, of course, important for the understanding of the work. The question is simply in what way they are important. Several years before, Fahlström had described in the essay 'Manipulating the World' (1962) how he conceived of the way in which the pictorial elements would function in variable paintings:

> These elements, while materially fixed, achieve their character-identity only when they are put together; their character changes with each new arrangement. The arrangement grows out of a combination of the rules (the chance factor) and my intentions, and is shown in a "score" or "scenario" (in the form of drawings, photographs or small paintings). The isolated elements are thus not paintings, but machinery to make paintings. Picture organ. The finished picture stands somewhere on the intersection of paintings, games (type Monopoly and war games) and puppet theatre.[85]

What is being established here is a structure that appears to make traditional hermeneutics implode: should you manage to extricate yourself from the forest of individual pictorial elements and the almost endless permutations of references, meanings, cross-references and connotations, you discover that the structure as a whole has been changed by a new hang. And yet this artwork, like every other, can be interpreted. The ambivalence between the apparent and the concealed, the familiar and the unknown, is actually a fundamental aesthetic principle in Fahlström's work, particularly when fairly simple pictorial elements, which a contemporary viewer would presumably have been able to identify immediately, are contrasted with mysterious combinations of fragments and transformations of the familiar. The combination of a great diversity of discrete pictorial elements with the existence of an explanatory text—*Minnesanteckningar (till 'Dr.Schweitzers sista uppdrag') [Memoranda (to 'Dr Schweitzer's Last Mission')]* of 1964—could be seen as actually inviting a close reading: together, they serve to encourage an iconographic interpretation. The arrangement makes for an almost embarrassing correspondence with Marcel Duchamp's *The Large Glass* and its relationship to the Green Box.[86]

In Jean-François Chevrier's view, the various pictorial elements in Fahlström's work may be seen as conventional character types that possess the obvious meaning of hieroglyphs (in which a hand means a hand).[87] While the comparison is interesting, the conclusion drawn seems peculiar to say the least. In hieroglyphic script, each sign can convey a multiplicity of meanings both on its own and in relation to other signs. These meanings are, however, determined by a conventional set of rules, which gives the script a linear syntax that can be translated into other written languages. Since premodern times, hieroglyphs have also been associated with occult knowledge and mysticism, and it is this aspect of tradition that makes the comparison interesting: allowing the original cultural significance of the character types to be transformed into different, alien and possibly hidden meanings. Instead of functioning as hieroglyphs (signs in a conventional written language), the pictorial elements allude to the hieroglyphic (with its mystical connotations in Western cultural history). A work such as *Dr. Schweitzer's Last Mission* is one that both opens and closes itself at the same time.

An illustrative example is provided by the pictorial element that serves as a key to understanding the title of the work. Here we have a portrait of Fahlström that can be put together with a picture representing a scene (inscribed in the silhouette of a woman) in which the weeping doctor and missionary, Albert Schweitzer, looks up at the night sky and a passing rocket (or missile). The iconicity of the individual visual signs does not constitute a problem here; a little historical knowledge makes it possible to identify the various individuals and objects. But how is one to interpret the individual pictorial elements and their variable reciprocal relationships in particular? It has been pointed out that here, as in several other parts of the work, it is possible to see how various elements have been put together as pairs of opposites that are based on similarity and/or paradoxes.[88] An example is provided by the contour line between the two detachable pictorial elements. They form the silhouette of a woman who is kissing a man and, at the same time, a portrait of the artist. Together, they create a scenario full of mystery. The dividing line connotes both closeness and separation. How are we to understand the scene of a weeping Dr Schweitzer? Is he a witness to truth—a good man who was awarded the Nobel Peace Prize in 1952—weeping over the arms race or the madness of the modern age? Or is he an outdated remnant of the old colonial order bemoaning the changes taking place in the present? And what does he have to do with Fahlström, who is looking at us while being kissed by a woman who has been reduced to a silhouette? Should we understand the way the artist gazes at us in terms of an established convention by which an individual in a historical scene gazes out of the pictorial space in order to establish a connection with the viewer? In that case, the gaze would seem to be encouraging the viewer to reflect on something. The question then is what should we reflect on?

* * * *

Naturally, more general themes could be attributed to the various images. The iconic significance of each individual pictorial element cannot, however, be related to a fixed iconographic scheme.[89] The open structure actually communicates nothing more than its own situation, which is that of being a situation: the artist who leaves the work unfinished, the work that establishes a structure of meaning that highlights the establishment by the work of structures of meaning, the viewer who tries in vain to decipher a final and inherent meaning.

Fahlström wrote about this state of affairs in a 1961 article in which he characterised the concrete poetry of the day, which can also be read as a draft of his own poetics: 'The basic mistrust of symbolism (allegorical and surrealistic alike) leads to an affinity for everyday materials and subjects, worn banalities lacking in overtones. . .'[90] A fundamental tenet of Fahlström's poetics is to avoid providing any kind of key. Applied to the visual arts (to *Dr. Schweitzer's Last Mission*), this provides an explanation of a possible way of reading that goes beyond those established by art-critical and art-historical praxis during the twentieth century: at once iconography and formalism and an existential, sympathetic interpretation (Einfühlung). At this point, any notion of the work as an organic whole, of the idiom as a complete and nonreducible structure, of the subject as a linear narrative and its signs as representations of a coherent world-image, seems to disintegrate. Fahlström's use of images, texts and objects calls that of Rauschenberg to mind inasmuch as they both simultaneously separate and link together material with the aim of displacing accustomed conventions so as to create a polysemous field of association. The very argument used by Branden Joseph to describe the strictly iconographic interpretation of Rauschenberg's work as meaningless also appears to apply to Fahlström's work. While it would not be impossible to establish an iconographic scheme, a scheme of that kind could be established at any point and have any direction.[91] Here it is the absence of a key that emerges as a crucial insight into how to understand this poetics and the ways of reading it (a leaf possesses no absolute and privileged viewpoint from which it can be defined and understood).[92]

The iconographic interpretation of Fahlström's work may, in fact, be seen to fulfil a twofold function: it draws attention to particular meaning-saturated fields of association as a result of its strongly logocentric tendency to fix a specific meaning, while simultaneously demonstrating the openness of that meaning by failing to connect together the individual signs into a uniform programme. For the viewer who refuses to take up the challenge of a close reading posed by the work, the arbitrariness of its meaning and its subversive potential remain concealed under the noncommittal surface of the visual spectacle. This pursuit of a poetics based on a way of reading that transcends both form and content could be compared with changes in other artistic media of the same period. An example Fahlström himself often referred to was so-called Concrete Poetry.⁹³

Öyvind Fahlström described the new function of poetry in his manifesto *Hätilaragulprfåtskilaben. Manifest förkonkretpoesi* (1954):

> Poetry is not only for analysis; it is also structure. Not just structure with the emphasis on expression of ideas, but also concrete structure. Let's say good-bye to all systematic or spontaneous depiction of private psychological, contemporary cultural or universal problems. Words are symbols, of course, but that's no reason why poetry shouldn't be experienced and *written* on the basis of *language as concrete matter*.⁹⁴

Here, language is no longer seen as a conventional system of references (to the objects, ideas, feelings and perceptions of the surrounding world) but as linguistic material to play with: unexpected new word formations in order to evoke new associations, systematic reductions of words and sentences in order to expose new structural connections, distortions of words and syntax, experiments with the sonic qualities of words and with visual and typographically embellished interweavings of words and sentences in complex ideograms (sound-image-poems). In a work such as *Dr. Schweitzer's Last Mission,* Fahlström can be seen to be actively employing a poetics derived from the concrete poetry and abstract sign painting (signifigurations) of the 1950s, a poetics that he had transformed in the variable paintings of the 1960s with their explicit iconic references to the surrounding world.⁹⁵ Even though the aesthetic devices and referentiality of the sign had changed, the code remained the same, so to speak.

The concrete aspect of this poetics is reminiscent of the efforts of many other artists, poets, composers and writers at this time. An example can be found in John Cage's description of Robert Rauschenberg's combine-paintings, with particular reference to the use/reuse of objects and motifs:

> This is not a composition. It is a place where things are, as a table or as a town seen from the air: any one of them could be removed and another come into its place through circumstances analogous

to birth and death, travel, housecleaning, or cluttering. . . . There is no more subject in a *combine* than there is in a page from a newspaper. Each thing that is there is a subject. It is a situation involving multiplicity. . . . Of course there are objects. . . . And object is fact, not symbol.[96]

Everything on the canvas, from the concrete objects to the paint, appears to be physical and material facts, recorded and selected in order to be used in a specific context (a work of art). A very different approach to painting and the image is being described here that is strongly reminiscent of Leo Steinberg's concept of the flatbed picture plane: a place that no longer takes its orientation from that of the upright human body but is organised instead as a horizontal surface filled with objects, signs and images, whose reference is not to (natural, optical) perception but to a (cultural, interpretive) coordination and confrontation of information with signification.[97] The paradigmatic model would be the groaning desk rather than the open transparent window or the vertical opaque surface of the nonfigurative image. Irrespective of whether the canvas then hangs on a wall or lies on the floor (or is transformed into an installation or a happening), this way of organising and reading the work appears to be radically different from that of older traditions, a way of reading that is neither illusory nor symbolic.

A similar nonsymbolic and nonpsychological aesthetic is also found among the practitioners of the *nouveau roman,* such as Alain Robbe-Grillet, who wrote in the foreword to *Dans le labyrinth* (1959)

> Yet the reality in question is a strictly material one; that is, it is subject to no allegorical interpretation. The reader is therefore requested to see in it only the objects, actions, words, and events which are described, without attempting to give them either more or less meaning than in his own life, or his own death.[98]

The long descriptions of passages of time, objects and interiors that Robbe-Grillet presents have no symbolic or metaphorical function but serve instead as an inventory of the sensory perceptions the narrator receives from a particular place and time. Roland Barthes has also described this aesthetic in the following terms:

The novel becomes a direct experience of man's surroundings, without this man's being able to fall back on psychology, a metaphysic, or psychoanalysis in order to approach the objective milieu he discovers. The novel here is no longer of a chthonic, infernal order, it is terrestrial: it teaches us to look at the world no longer with the eyes of a confessor, a physician, or of God – all significant hypostases of the classical novelist – but with the eyes of a man walking in his city with no other horizon but the spectacle before him, no other power than of his own eyes.[99]

The horizon of the narrative is the observation of a passage of time by an individual human being at ground level that offers no possibility of an overarching understanding of its logic or causal connections. There is an explicit aversion in the *nouveau roman* towards any kind of transcendent humanism, towards all finished metaphysical or psychological constructions. The world and its objects are not presented through sentimental or anecdotal fiction, by means of mysticism or riddles; they are neither absurd nor meaningful. The structure of the narrative in the work of an author such as Robbe-Grillet resembles a construction that simulates the experience of the various aimless moments of the everyday, without reference to any privileged and hierarchical viewpoint but in which the viewer is given an active, co-creative role, rather than passively receiving a finished presentation of the world.[100]

It is, however, not necessarily the depiction of everyday life—in the sense of observable, true-to-life references to the surrounding world—that is important here but, rather, the view taken of the concrete function and value of language/matter. Neither does this involve some naive form of realism but a metarealism that highlights the descriptive or interpretive activity itself (on the part of the artist and the viewer), instead of providing a simple inclusion and or description of the individual objects, images and signs located in the work.

Examples of similar aesthetic motives can be found in a range of artistic genres at this time. A nonfigurative artist such as Frank Stella may be considered a counterpart to Rauschenberg. In the mid-1960s, Stella characterised his own art and aesthetics as follows: 'My painting is based on the fact that only what can be seen there *is* there. It really is an object. . . . [Y]ou can see the whole idea without any confusion. . . What you see is what you see.'[101] A statement of this kind may appear on first reading to be a noncommittal and all but mystifying tautology in imitation of Ad Reinhardt. But the attitude it reveals is one that is prepared to take the focus of modernism (and Abstract Expressionism in particular) on the visual beyond the boundary of the material: paint and idiom are no longer seen as conveying anything (a content) apart from their own physical existence; the composition (the balancing of shapes) has been discarded in favour of a presentation of a symmetrical pattern, and the originality of the brushstroke has been abandoned in favour of a neutral application of industrial pigment to an untreated canvas. The pigment and the canvas emerge as concrete and real objects in the concrete and real physical space of the viewer. This is, in other words, an aesthetic that transgresses an earlier modernist nonfigurative tradition (in terms of both its metaphysical implications and its belief in the work as an organic whole) while pointing forward to some of the movements of the 1960s (the visual facticity of Pop Art and the material objecticality of Minimalism). Absent as well is any trend towards representative vision.

The point of referring to all these highly diverse examples is not to indicate the existence of an implicit programme or a least common denominator for all the different art forms of the 1960s. Rather, it is to demonstrate the considerable extent to which what we have referred to as the open aesthetic involves the multivalent transformation of visual signs in movement through the context called art: the dual aspect of the goat as physical object and linguistic sign in Rauschenberg's *Monogram*; the visuality and materiality of paint and canvas in Stella's paintings of the early 1960s. We are confronted here, perhaps more clearly than anywhere else, with a realisation that the interpretation of the visual arts also has to transcend appearance and stylistic criteria. In the case of *Dr. Schweitzer's Last Mission,* realism has as much to do with form (the variable and spatial structure of the work) as content (the references to the surrounding world). For this is painting that has, as Pontus Hultén put it, 'abandoned the wall' and been transformed into 'theatre, games, psychodrama'.[102] Or to put it another way: painting whose realism serves as the concrete existence of the work and of its interaction with the viewer in a real space-time. The absence of a key here is not a metaphor for freedom in general or an escape manoeuvre from responsibility but a crucial means of understanding the content and function of the piece. Having served as a fixed and inherent meaning, content now emerges as an indication of one fragmentary context among many others to which the text can be related. The meaning of the work is altered as a result, from encompassing the content of the sign to pointing out its function.

The interpretation of *Dr. Schweitzer's Last Mission* is not aimed at deciphering what the work means but at an attempt to understand how it means. In my view, this is the truly radical content of Fahlström's piece; this is what it encourages us to contemplate. The particular dialectic between the presence of boundaries and the transgression of boundaries can be considered one of the fundamental subjects of *Dr. Schweitzer's Last Mission*. The existence of a certain traditional order is a precondition for playing with the rules and boundaries of the medium. Similarly, the openness of meaning also appears to be a game that presupposes the existence of a traditional view that holds that meaning is fixed as essential and intrinsic in every work of art. Several years previously, Fahlström had formulated an ideal (based on contemporary concrete poetry and aleatory music) that radicalised the remnants of traditional composition still to be found in the visual arts:

> The open form: one prefers an imperfection of form, a more or less consciously incomplete, unsurveyable and unforeseeable form, fluid and present, as opposed to the anecdotal/thematic/aphoristic form, which piles up past moments like steps to perceived goals, peripetia and climaxes. A form that does not mark a beginning or an end and that can be entered and exited at any time and place.[103]

The open structure is intimately connected with the communicative and meaning-generative aspects of the work, with the relation to the viewer being one of the work's constituent factors. Seen in this light, *Dr. Schweitzer's Last Mission* emerges as a dramatisation of the changing view of the ontology and meaning-function of the work of art at this time, as a staging of the artwork as a meaning-producing machine, in which the traditionally static structures of form and pictorial space are transformed at a metaphorical level into an open space of meaning—into an arena of possibilities and possible readings—in which the viewer is able to move, both figuratively and literally, searching for connections and associations, choosing the direction of travel and selecting focal points, but never fixing either a stable relationship between the parts and the whole or an accepted core of meaning.

However, the structure that Fahlström establishes is far too strict and far too compelling simply to be characterised by an expression as vague as 'an arena of possibilities'. At issue is rather a game of opposites. It is no accident that he refers to games and games theory on many different occasions. A game implies the existence of a set of rules and the necessity of interaction, which indeed appear to be two key themes in his work. And yet even this particular combination may also seem much too static to describe the radically variable elements in Fahlström's work. The crucial aspect of the reference to rules here is not the fixing of a set of rules as such but the dialectic between the establishment of those rules and their dissolution. An example is provided by one of his earlier paintings, *Performing K.K. no. 2 (Sunday Edition)* of 1963–64. In this work, he took George Harriman's comic character 'KrazyKat' as his starting point and transformed the already absurd storyline into a subversive and almost hallucinogenic narrative structure. Fahlström appears to have transferred the structure of his earlier nonfigurative sign paintings to one of the most regulated genres of the visual arts in modern society: the comic. A crash, a dislocation, occurs here between two different logical systems, with the image operating in the field of tension between a particular fundamental structure (a conventional understanding of the linear structure of the narrative) and the dissolution of the structure (in execution and interpretation).

In a 1966 article, Fahlström described how the relationship between the freedom provided by the variation and manipulation of the components exists in direct proportion to the rigidity of the rules and the invariability of the components.[104] At issue here is an aesthetic that is far removed from free association, amorphous form-experiments and spontaneity. In this context, the word 'game' means a combination of rules and interaction.

This combination was formulated by Fahlström in a way that suggests that the work/sign could have both an aesthetic and a political dimension. In a situation in which every structure, every convention and every rule appear to be arbitrary, they can—to the extent the possibility is conceived of—be changed or manipulated. This is not, however, a matter of creating art for political purposes or as a form of agitation but about setting up instead a potentially subversive linguistic approach that has been arrived at through the various experiments of modernism. As in previously cited examples, it is the direction that is crucial here: the movement through linguistic analysis, through the examples of history, in order to arrive at life through the image.

A mediation of this kind also serves to illuminate the hierarchical structure existing between the value sphere of the visual arts and other cultural domains. Benjamin Buchloh has described this unequal relationship as a double negation that is institutionally inscribed in the concept of the art:

> Every time the avant-garde appropriates elements from the discourse of low, folk, or mass culture, it publicly denounces its own elitist isolation and the obsolescence of its inherited production procedures. Ultimately, each such instance of "bridging the gap between art and life", as Robert Rauschenberg famously put it, only reaffirms the stability of the division because it remains within the context of high art. Each act of cultural appropriation, therefore, constructs a simulacrum of double negation, denying the validity of individual and original production, yet denying equally the relevance of the specific context and function of the work's own practice.[105]

Buchloh's analysis is entirely correct in describing a movement that values the destination of the individual element rather than its origin, such that the grafting onto the artwork of the surrounding world leads inexorably to a transformation. This is a function, as it were, of the kind of semiotic formation of meaning that the art world makes possible, in which every fragment of the outside world constitutes undifferentiated substance until it undergoes transformation in the work of art and becomes form.

But the occasionally radical use of visual material within the open aesthetic cannot be described as unambiguously as Buchloh would have it in terms of visual and semantic colonisation. The transformation constitutes a zone of its own on the boundary between the art world and the wider one, with the fragments left dangling between them. The angora goat in Rauschenberg's *Monogram* is transformed into a visual sign in this work, while also retaining something of its origins (the angora goat and the stuffed angora goat, respectively). The selection of visual elements is of major significance because the transformation works in both directions. This becomes particularly clear in a work such as *Monogram* because the goat occupies such a prominent visual place; indeed, within the art world's system of norms its goatness was once perceived as an extraordinarily aggressive sign. Here, as in the previous history of modernism, the circulation of signs involves a multiplication of voices and a multiplication of meaningful contexts.

The movement we are referring to here both opens up and closes down the possible production of meaning and value in the world of art and in the wider world. It may be entirely correct, as Buchloh writes, that this process takes place within the framework of Art as its institutional and authoritative focal point. Nevertheless, a distinction must be drawn between the movement taking place in the present (and actively challenging the validity of the distinction) and the historicisation of that movement, in which the provocative gesture is archived and codified together with other similar gestures and where the potential connection between serious art and popular culture is transformed into a purely art-historical context. In complete contrast with what Buchloh writes, Rauschenberg denies the very possibility of bridging the gulf between art and life. And it is for this very reason that he realises the necessity for operating in this breach.

This seems to be one of the clearest formulations of the artist's linguistic and existential dilemma in the modern era of differentiation and fragmentation, in which the boundary to a once natural unity has been forever breached with no possibility of return. It is a formulation that seems to confirm that Art *is* art as art (and that everything else is everything else) while also expressing disbelief that the artist will ever be able to (re)gain access to that unity. Authentic art—like authentic life—appears to be a beautiful but fragile illusion to which we are continually drawn back but which vanishes as soon as someone reaches out a hand to grasp it. Rauschenberg's phrase conveys not a trace of nostalgia but rather the reverse: an active desire to explore this particular divide. While he quite clearly commits a form of violence against the origin and meaning of the individual objects and pictorial fragments, so, too, do every interpretation and every quotation. As I see it, the ethical dilemma is not to be found in the forms of appropriation that constitute artistic practice but rather in the tendency of the historiography of the post-war period to read this practice in terms of much more rigid narratives and structures of meaning. To point out once again the gulf between art and life, and to reemphasise its value, would be to revitalise the subversive and transgressive values that the avant-garde once produced, irrespective of whether we are referring to European art of the 1910s or American art of the 1960s.

As in Octavio Paz's definition of modernity, art never appears as itself in this context but always as another. And to the extent that the idea of this gulf has been realised and institutionalised as a discursive order, art, like modernity, is condemned to pluralism. This is the radical interpretation, as it were, of Rauschenberg's definition and of modernism as the aesthetic of openness.

The open aesthetic does not, in practice, entail a break with the self-reflexive and self-critical aesthetic of modernism. The realism of a work by Cage, Rauschenberg, Stella, Fahlström or Robbe-Grillet only exists in the sense that the surrounding world has re-entered the centre of the work through a filter of linguistic forms and historical reflections; this involves language, medium, memory, convention and history just as much as the world outside the work. But unlike the theories of early modernism, the open aesthetic provides an approach that distrusts the romantic view of the symbol, of organic unity and essential expression, whether these apply to the ontological status of the sign or to the communicative function of the work. The metalevel actualised here and in many other places in the visual arts of the 1960s could, in fact, be considered to have been a precondition of the comprehensive aesthetic dislocation within the discourse of the visual arts. The phenomenon could be likened to the growing historiographic interest that always seems to surround shifts in the discursive order of the historical and aesthetic disciplines: in order to go beyond the boundary of the possible and legitimate, that boundary (its historical and theoretical determinants) has to be made visible and analysed.

The transgression of these parameters may be considered in light of the much more radical shift from work to frame that Craig Owens has described as a key aspect of the transition from modernism to postmodernism:

> Rather, postmodernism approaches the empty space left by the author's disappearance from a different perspective, one which brings to light a number of questions that modernism, with its exclusive focus on the work of art and its "creator", either ignored or repressed: Where do exchanges between readers and viewers take place? Who is free to define, manipulate and, ultimately, to benefit from the codes and conventions of cultural production? These questions shift attention away from the work and its producer and onto its *frame* – the first by focusing on the *location* in which the work of art is encountered; the second, by insisting on the *social* nature of artistic production and reception.[106]

Fahlström's work and his aesthetic may be seen as a historical symptom of such a major shift; however, this misses a crucial point: these transgressions entail a dislocation within and throughout the order of modernist discourse. At issue here are an artistic practice and an aesthetic attitude that clearly diverge from certain fundamental values in the theoretical canon of the modernist narrative and that (to some extent) violate the boundaries of what was previously referred to as the regime of authenticity. Under consideration here are various expressions and representations of an attitude that could be described as a post-romantic modernism. This is what the emphasis of the open aesthetic on the communicative function of language and the shift from work to frame during the 1950s and 1960s meant—a shift that subsequently led to a number of theoretical and discursive changes that might very well be characterised as a postmodern condition).

Endgame

Instead of considering medial critique (modernism) and institutional critique (avant-garde, postmodernism) as different in kind, as some theoreticians have done, both practices could be recognised as two sides of the same coin: a linguistic critique that is fundamentally to do with communication and relates in various ways (antithetically and synthetically) to an institutionalised social context. This was the insight that compelled an art critic such as Arthur Danto to begin theorising on the meaning of the art world and of aesthetic identification after viewing and attempting to understand Andy Warhol's Brillo-boxes in 1964. The basic problem in this regard is no different from that of the reception of Picasso's work in 1912 or Pollock's in 1948, apart from the fact that Warhol (to some extent) and Fahlström (to a considerable extent) formulated the problem of language/discourse at a highly conscious level. In Fahlström's case, the course taken by the dialectic of the work moves through a thorough exploration of the grammar of the visual language in order to expand far beyond any notion of a closed framework. And yet it seems all the more essential to make that framework—its boundaries—visible in order to understand and analyse the meaning of the space that makes this movement possible or, in other words, the discursive space that *Dr. Schweitzer's Last Mission* seems to identify by means of its complex structure and that also provides this work with its particular sign function as art.

If we return at this point to the comparison previously drawn between Clement Greenberg and Walter Benjamin, a reversal has evidently taken place. The (avant-garde) aesthetic of disparity that Greenberg championed from the end of the 1930s became the possible narrative for modern art in the political, social and economic context of the post-war period, in contrast with Benjamin's thesis on the profound change to the work of art in the age of mechanical reproduction. However, the discursive order that made one statement possible but not the other has shifted since that time. Detached from its original political connotations, Benjamin's text has been recoded as a possible interpretation of the pluralism and cross-boundary artistic practices of recent decades. Particularly, his idea that the aura of the work of art (the very idea of the aura of the work of art) had been abandoned because the mass (re-)production provided by film and photography has become widespread within and without the art world. It would not be farfetched to maintain that today the photographic code has replaced painting as the predominant sign system of the art world. But does this mean that we now find ourselves beyond the reach of the regime of authenticity—that it is no longer possible to make a distinction between Art and art?

It is quite clear at a theoretical level that this particular distinction has come in for massive criticism and, ultimately, been delegitimated, both in the practices of the visual arts and those of art criticism and philosophy. However, it would be naive to regard pluralism as a value-nihilist state purely on the basis of a changed theoretical position. Despite the fact that the distinctions and positions of the art world have undergone various radical changes during recent decades, and despite the fact that the structure of the system itself has become extraordinarily more complex, its practitioners still find themselves within a particular institutional and economic framework that converts, distributes and accumulates various types of values—aesthetic, symbolic, ideological and economic. The circulation of capital and values within this domain depends as much today as ever before on the power and capacity to make distinctions.

The complicated machinery that Pierre Bourdieu describes in *Les règles de l'art* and elsewhere has not broken down in any sense, but the pattern of movement and the distinctions operating in this field are shaped and formulated in a somewhat different way today. Within the framework of this machinery, the idea of the authentic in both the descriptive and normative senses of the word still appears to be a central value. A more radical alteration of this state of affairs would presumably require not only a number of critical philosophical and artistic deconstructions, but also a completely different institutional and economic system.

And it is here that we return to the point where we began: wonderment at the alienated effect evoked by Thomas Struth's photographs. This effect is, in large part, based on the peculiar activity the image dramatises as photograph and as work of art: that people and societies, now more so than ever before, place such a high value on the idea of Art and the transformations that take place within the world of art that they are prepared to invest enormous quantities of money and time to make this activity possible. This activity is one that also involves a most peculiar encounter between different types of quantifications. A building that cost hundreds of millions to erect and maintain is visited annually by hundreds of thousands of people who look at images and objects whose collective value reaches into the billions. In this building, the images are hung individually so that each visitor can encounter a unique work (a work the artist considered himself at one time to be one with) in order to contemplate its singular meaning and the personal address it makes. Unfettered mass distribution and isolated unicity are the simultaneous hallmarks of the situation. The space stipulates a real encounter with a physical object, whose transformation into Art and Meaning occurs in an entirely different symbolic or ritual sphere—to the extent, that is, that anyone still believes it is possible for transformation to take place (literally and figuratively) at all.

This situation brings to mind the space Michel Foucault described with the term heterotopia: a kind of place that exists in the midst of society but which is regulated on the basis of different perceptions than those governing the rest of society; it is completely real and yet unreal at the same time.[107] The cemetery is one such space, as are the theatre, the park, the library, the cinema—and the museum. The heterotopic place brings together different spaces and attitudes that are mutually incompatible; it embraces different perceptions of time, implying a system of openings and closures that both isolate the functions of the space and relate them to the surrounding world. Foucault likens this type of place to a mirror in which I am observing an image of myself in a placeless place:

> From the standpoint of the mirror I discover my absence from the place where I am since I see myself over there. Starting from this gaze that is, as it where, directed toward me, from the ground of this virtual space that is the other side of the glass, I come back toward myself: I begin again to direct my eyes toward myself and to reconstitute myself there where I am. The mirror functions as a heterotopia in this respect: it makes this place that I occupy at the moment when I look at myself in the glass at once absolutely real, connected with all the space that surrounds it, and absolutely unreal, since in order to be perceived it has to pass this virtual point which is over there.[108]

Thomas Struth's photographs convey something of this strange feeling of finding oneself dangling in the discontinuity between different moments of time and different levels of reality. The distancing effect of the photograph makes it possible for us to observe observation, but that effect is also at work in the fact that a work of art is making visible the constitution and existence of art in modern society. What Thomas Struth is doing is demonstrating the romantic foundations of the white cube: that moment in which the sublime content of the work is meant to be conveyed to the viewer directly and immediately. And he portrays this moment in a manner that recalls the rhetorical apparatus a Romantic such as Caspar David Friedrich initiated in his work by showing a number of individuals who turn their backs on us, the viewers, in order to observe the sublime for themselves.

This may be understood not only as an ironic game with conventions and traditions, but alo as an allegory of how the linguistic and epistemological gulf that characterised the visual arts of the modern era also characterises our own age. The presentation of Jackson Pollock's painting in the neutral space of the museum presupposes an individual experience of the aura and sublime effect of the authentic work. And yet Struth's images could also be said to perform a deconstruction of this unarticulated context by portraying it in a piece that is both a clinical form of documentation and an aestheticising artwork—a work that serves as a sign of the impossibility of an origin of the sign or of the fixing of its meaning, a sign that demonstrates how the search for the meaning of the sign always leads on to another sign and never to anything originally signified. In this context, Thomas Struth's image can be seen as a sign that stages a radical deconstruction of the possible authenticity of the sign/the work of art.

While this interpretation may be legitimate, it would appear to be a particularly pessimistic proposition about the communicative function and value of the visual arts (and, by extension, of human language). Although what seems truly remarkable in light of such radical scepticism is the actual existence of any communicative function and value. What Thomas Struth's picture is bringing to the fore is, in fact, that problematic section of Ad Reinhardt's formula 'Art is art as art and everything else is everything else': the phrase that designates something 'as art'. Poststructuralist scepticism could be described in this regard as a form of secularisation and emancipation. Art, like every other value and every other meaning, cannot be understood as something simply god-given but rather as a social construction, at once utterly real and unconditionally unreal. The hopeful aspect of this situation is that an understanding of this part is being established that transcends the authoritative sanction of the unified modernist narrative, whose formula has been dissolved and fragmentised in such a way that the definition of modern art has reacquired that once so open question mark.

This is also a key implication of a differentiation of the canon: to make it possible to revisit an *oeuvre*, such as that of Jackson Pollock's, from outside the singular narrative of modernism and, perhaps, even to believe in it once again. Although this would involve a diametrically opposed form of belief to the truths mediated by the theory and historiography of modernism—a belief characterised not by historical necessity or blind faith in the authenticity of the work but by a deep ambivalence between absence and meaning.

Endnotes

1. Alison & Peter Smithson, "But Today We Collect Ads", *Ark*, November 1956: 18, p. 49.

2. Roland Barthes, "From Work to Text" (1971), *Image, Music, Text*, (transl. Stephen Heath), London 1977, p. 158.

3. Kjell Nowak & Gunnar Andrén, *Reklam och samhällsförändring. Variation och konstans i svenska populärpressannonser 1950–1975*, Kulturindikatorer svensk i symbolmiljö 1945–1975: rapport nr. 3, Lund 1981, pp. 12–23.

4. The advent of television took place in stages: principles developed in the late nineteenth century found application in a range of inventions during the early twentieth century that made possible the construction of apparatuses for the transmission and reception of images by the end of the 1920s. The British Broadcasting Corporation began transmissions on a regular basis by 1936, while transmission on a smaller scale were also initiated in other European countries and the United States at the end of the 1930s. But it was not until after the Second World War that television became a mass medium when nationwide networks of transmitter stations were constructed in a large number of countries. The development and expansion of television may also be considered to have taken place in direct relation to the economic development of the various countries and, therefore, with the ability of the population to invest in what were fairly expensive apparatuses (for an exhaustive history of the development of the medium of television, see R. W. Burns, *Television. An International History of the Formative Years*, History of Technology Series 22, London 1998).

5. Jean Baudrillard, *The Consumer Society. Myths and Structures*, (transl. Chris Turner), London 1998 (1970), pp. 76–78.

6. Marshall McLuhan, *Understanding Media. The Extensions of Man*, New York 1965 (1964), p. 322.

7. Hans Magnus Enzensberger, *The Consciousness Industry. On Literature, Politics, and the Media*, (transl. John Simon), New York 1974 (1962), p. 4. The term 'consciousness industry' may be

considered an extension of Theodor Adorno's and Max Horkheimer's critical concepts of the culture industry and enlightenment as mass deception.

8. Jean Baudrillard, *Symbolic Exchange and Death*, (transl. Ian Hamilton Grant), London 1995 (1976), pp. 70–76.

9. Guy Debord, *Society of the Spectacle*, (transl. Ken Knabb), London 2005 (1967).

10. This is the substance of a discussion conducted within relatively radical modernist circles during large parts of the twentieth century that, superficially at least, was about the relationship of free art to applied art and architecture, but, at a deeper level, concerned the fundamental grammar of modern form—irrespective of medium. Although an aesthetic of this kind seemed to cross the boundaries between various media, it actually involved coordination through specialization with questions of form, function and aesthetics being raised within separate spheres that were assumed to exist at a remove from the rest of society and from the expanding medial and mass culture.

11. An interesting and, in its time, extraordinarily significant analysis of this subject is found in Crimp 1995 (1993), pp. 84–105. For an analysis of Paul Delaroche's declaration and various historical misconceptions about its significance, see Stephen Bann, *Parallel Lines. Printmakers, Painters and Photographers in Nineteenth-Century France*, New Haven/London 2001, pp. 104–109.

12. Max Horkheimer & Theodor Adorno, *Dialectic of Enlightment. Philosophical Fragments*, (transl. Edmund Jephcott), Stanford 2002 (1947), pp. 107–108.

13. Ad Reinhardt, "Art as Art" (1962), in Barbara Rose (ed.), *Art-as-Art. The Selected Writings of Ad Reinhardt*, Berkeley/Los Angeles 1991 (1975), p. 53.

14. In the mid-1950s, Ad Reinhardt set out twelve technical rules for contemporary art. These may be considered a manifesto for his own version of the aesthetics of disparity as a radicalisation of modernism's tradition of defining itself by establishing taboos: no textures, no brushwork or calligraphy, no sketches or drawings, no forms, no design, no colours, no light, no space, no time, no size or scale,

no movement, no object, no subject, no matter, no symbols, images or signs (from Ad Reinhardt, "Twelve Rules for a New Academy" (1957), in Rose, pp. 205–206). But unlike the taboos of early modernism that were aimed at the academic and realist traditions, Ad Reinhardt's target was the tradition of historical modernism. His list was thus concerned with the refinement of modernism through self-criticism.

15. John Perreault, "Minimal Abstracts" (1967), in Gregory Battcock (ed.), *Minimal Art. A Critical Anthology*, Berkeley/Los Angeles/London 1995 (1968), p. 262.

16. Michael Fried, "Art and Objecthood" (1967), *Art and Objecthood: Essays and Reviews*, Chicago/London 1998, p. 148–172.

17. See e.g. Rosalind Krauss, "Sculpture in the Expanded Field" (1979), *The Originality of the Avant-Garde and Other Modernist Myths*, Cambridge (Mass.)/London 1991 (1985), p. 287, and Hal Foster, *The Return of the Real. The Avant-Garde at the End of the Century*, Cambridge (Mass.)/London 1996, pp. 53–54.

18. Thierry de Duve, *Pictorial Nominalism. On Marcel Duchamp's Passage from Painting to the Readymade*, (transl. Dana Polan with the author), Minneapolis/Oxford 1991 (1984), pp. 154–163.

19. Geldzahler, p. 37.

20. Richard Hamilton, "Roy Lichtenstein", *Studio International*, vol. 175, 1968: January, p. 23.

21. Crow, 1996, p. 3.

22. Robert Rauschenberg, "Statement", *Sixteen Americans*, Museum of Modern Art, New York 1959, p. 58.

23. In his 1963 introduction to the *Robert Rauschenberg* catalogue at the Jewish Museum in New York, Alan R. Solomon linked Rauschenberg's work to that of Picasso ("Robert Rauschenberg", in Steven Henry Madoff (ed.), *Pop Art. A Critical History*, The Documents of Twentieth Century Art, Berkeley/Los Angeles/London 1997, pp. 20–21). However, Solomon's argument was based on the premise that Rauschenberg could not be directly linked to the antiaesthetics of Dadaism, and this led him to overemphasise the

correspondences between Rauschenberg's combine-painting and Picasso's collage.

24. Martha Jackson, "Foreword", *New Form – New Media*, Martha Jackson Gallery, New York 1960, (unpag.). The exhibition was a collaboration between several different galleries, and the contemporary artists shown included George Brecht, John Chamberlain, Bruce Conner, Jim Dine, Jean Dubuffet, Dan Flavin, Red Grooms, Robert Indiana, Jasper Johns, Allan Kaprow, Yves Klein, Louis Nevelson, Claes Oldenburg, Robert Rauschenberg, Richard Stankiewicz, Antonio Tapies, Bob Withman, while those in the historical section included Hans Arp, Alberto Burri, Alexander Calder, Joseph Cornell, Henry Moore and Kurt Schwitters.

25. Lawrence Alloway, "Junk Culture as Tradition", *New Form – New Media*, unpaginated.

26. Allan Kaprow, "Some Observations on Contemporary Art", *New Form – New Media*, unpaginated.

27. The same could be said of the first thematic survey of American and European neo-Dadaism that was displayed in the exhibition *The Art of Assemblage* at the Museum of Modern Art in 1961. While this exhibition attracted a great deal of attention, its aim—of mounting a historical exposé—resulted in the new art being situated, once again, in a strictly historical context. This was important for the legitimation of new forms of art and the dissemination of information (about the present and the past), but the exhibition failed to provide any rhetorically applicable context in which to view that present.

28. Thomas B. Hess, "Mixed Mediums for a Soft Revolution", *Art News*, vol. 59, Summer 1960: 4, p. 62.

29. This exhibition may be considered a companion piece to *Le Nouveau Réalisme à Paris et à New York* at the Galerie Rive Droite in Paris in 1961, although there were differences in both the selection and the rhetoric of the two shows that would later prove significant. As the title indicates, the latter was an exhibition focused on the group of artists known as the *Realistes Nouveaux*, who had been grouped together the previous year under a manifesto by the critic Pierre Restany and who had been absent from Martha

Jackson's show. The aim was to show similar radical trends on both sides of the Atlantic: with France being represented by such artists as Arman, César, Raymond Hains, Yves Klein, Niki de Saint-Phalle and Jean Tinguely and with the United States being represented by Lee Bontecou, John Chamberlain, Vardea Chryssa, Jasper Johns, Robert Rauschenberg and Richard Stankiewicz. In his foreword to the catalogue, Restany presents a report on the situation of contemporary art that bears the stamp of the ideas in his New Realist manifesto, where a new feeling for nature and for the world around us has led to the development of an art that attempts to examine in an immediate way the urban landscapes of the present, its industrial products, mechanical methods of production and popular culture (Pierre Restany, "La réalité dépasse la fiction", *Le Nouveau Réalisme à Paris et à New York*, Galerie Rive Droite, Paris 1961, unpag.). This new sensibility is presented as an existential and universal undercurrent in the contemporary avant-garde (irrespective of nationality)—a notion underlined by placing side by side the works of French and American artists based on their visual correspondences. Similarly, in *New Form – New Media,* the exhibition's combination of continuity (with an older Romantic tradition) and newness (an almost sociological approach to the surrounding world) served as an attempt to explain and legitimise/legitimate the present in terms of history, although the selection was aimed to a far greater extent at what was then contemporary and its possible future importance. The problem here was that although this offered an effective rhetorical approach, the institutionalised French art world was too inflexible to respond to it (see Boyer, 1995, pp. 117–138).

30. See *New Realists*, Sidney Janis Gallery, New York 1 November – 1 December 1962, unpaginated. The artists taking part were (from Great Britain) Peter Blake, John Latham, Peter Philips; (from France) Arman, Christo, Raymond Hains, Yves Klein, Martial Raysse, Daniel Spoerri, Jean Tinguely; (from Italy) Enrico Baj, Gianfranco Baruchello, Tano Festa, Mimmo Rotella, Mario Schifano; (from Sweden) ÖyvindFahlström, P. O. Ultvedt; (from the United States) Peter Agostini, Jim Dine, Robert Indiana, Roy Lichtenstein, Robert Moskowitz, Claes Oldenburg, James Rosenquist, Steven Segal, Harold Stevenson, Wayne Thiebaud, Andy Warhol and Tom Wesselmann.

31. Sidney Janis, "On the Theme of the Exhibition", *New Realists*, unpaginated.

32. John Ashbery, "The New Realists", *New Realists*, unpaginated.

33. The difference between American and European art was noted by the participating French artists, in particular, who were extraordinarily upset at being presented side by side with their American colleagues, which made their own art seem a great deal more dated, conventional and traditional and thus incapable of pointing the way forward (see Altshuler, 1994, pp. 215–218).

34. Brian O'Doherty, "'Pop' goes the New Art", *The New York Times*, 4 November 1962, Section 2, p. 23; Harold Rosenberg, "The Art Galleries: The Game of Illusion", *The New Yorker*, 24 November 1962, p. 162.

35. Calvin Tomkins, *Off the Wall. Robert Rauschenberg and the Art World of Our Time*, Harmondsworth 1981 (1980), p. 185.

36. See "A Symposium on Pop Art", in Madoff, pp. 65–81. Peter Selz (curator, MoMA), Henry Geldzahler (curator, The Metropolitan Museum of Art), Hilton Kramer (art critic), Dore Ashton (art critic), Leo Steinberg (art critic, art historian) and Stanely Kunitz (poet, art and literary critic) took part in the symposium held at MoMA on 13 December 1962, when a front line was clearly staked out between those who defended Pop Art (Geldzahler, Steinberg) and those who rejected it outright (Kramer, Kunitz), with Ashton and Selz (the latter in the role of moderator and host) adopting a more neutral position between the two. For a description of the rapidity of the triumph of Pop Art as seen through ten key exhibitions, see Constance W. Glenn, "American Pop Art: Inventing the Myth", in Marco Livingstone (ed.), *Pop Art*, Royal Academy of Arts, London 1991, pp. 30–39.

37. Marco Livingstone's standard work *Pop Art. A Continuing History* (London 1990), which frames this movement under the headings of Pre-pop, Foundations, Classic, Maturity and Legacy, provides a clear example of this. In essence, a traditional evolutionist scheme of art history is being applied here, which means that the same type of narrative is used to determine the presentation of Hellenism, the Baroque and Pop Art.

38. Lucy R. Lippard, *Pop Art*, London 2004 (1966), p 69.

39. One obvious example is provided by Madoff's anthology *Pop Art. A Critical History* (1997), in which the contributions are subdivided under headings such as Pre-Pop: American Precursors, English Currents, Focus: The Major Artists (Lichtenstein, Oldenburg, Rosenquist, Warhol) and From Center to Periphery: Other Figures. Reproduced from the work of Lucy Lippard, this pattern, rather than losing its force, subsequently remained fixed, as is made clear by the selections presented in survey literature, such as Marco Livingstone's *Pop Art. A Continuing History* (1990), and in specialist studies, such as Hal Foster's *The Return of the Real* (1996), where a single artist, such as Andy Warhol, is used essentially to represent the entire phenomenon of Pop Art.

40. The concept of Neo-Dada was used for the first time in 1957 by Robert Rosenblum in a review of a group exhibition at the Leo Castelli Gallery (see Kirk Varnedoe, *Jasper Johns. A Retrospective*, Museum of Modern Art, New York 1996, p. 386, note 112). For the negative implications of the term Neo-Dada, see Susan Hapgood, Maurice Berger & Jill Johnston, *Neo-Dada. Redefining Art 1958–1962*, The American Federation of Arts, New York 1994, pp. 11–12. For what would prove to be—in historical terms—a highly influential critical intervention against Neo-Dadaism (Jasper Johns, first and foremost) and the lack of originality in its banal approach to history, see Thomas B. Hess, "In Praise of Folly", *Art News*, vol. 58, Mars 1959: 1, p. 60. Irrespective of the various premises underpinning this critique, it can be traced back to the insidious use of the prefix 'neo' linked to a historical phenomenon (Dadaism/avant-garde): in making something new by virtue of the past, a cardinal sin is committed against the temporal orientation of avant-garde logic; this requires that the new emerges from the contemporary and thus, at a rhetorical level, turns its back on the past. An example of the way in which this art could, theoretically, be incorporated within (and rejected by) Abstract Expressionism is provided by Clement Greenberg's "After Abstract Expresionism" (1962), *The Collected Essays and Criticism, vol. 4: Modernism with a Vengeance, 1957–1969*, (ed. John O'Brian), Chicago/London 1993 (1986), pp. 126–127, where Greenberg describes a trend in American and European nonfigurative art that he

calls homeless representations, lingering figurative and illusory elements, that is, with Jasper John's art being described as the swansong of this trend: as a beautiful but doomed finale. The term pre-pop was introduced in a different context in which Pop Art was celebrated and classified as a new contemporary idiom, with Rauschenberg and Johns being considered its forerunners because, while they had obvious links with Pop Art, they could not be included within it. Segregating classifications and distinctions of this kind were already being made in American art criticism in 1962–1963, when Pop Art was rapidly becoming a phenomenon that was impossible to ignore; the term pre-pop, however, was more usually employed with the aim of establishing a diachronic context. Initially, this was in the exhibitions and survey works that dealt with Pop Art as a historical phenomenon. One example is Lucy Lippard, who uses the term to distinguish Pop Art from previous attempts to reproduce popular cultural references in art (see Lippard, p. 75); another would be its use in order both to establish a historical connection with an older form of modernism and to isolate Pop Art as a distinct new stylistic and historical category (e.g., Livingstone, 1990, pp. 9–11), in which artists such as Johns, Rauschenberg and Larry Rivers are accorded a kind of transitional position between the traditional and the new.

41. The term Pop Art is usually said to have been introduced by Lawrence Alloway, either in 1954 (without a source being indicated) or in 1958 in the article "The Arts and the Mass Media" (*Architectural Design & Construction*, February 1958, pp. 84–85.), but it was not, in fact, used here. The term was, however, evidently current in the circles of the Independent Group in London at the end of the 1950s and can be found, for example, in a subsequently frequently published letter from Richard Hamilton to Peter and Alison Smithson of 1957 (see Madoff, pp. 5–6). The term took on a renewed, if slightly altered, topicality in the New York art world at the end of 1962, when a new international phenomenon was celebrated in the exhibition *New Realists* at the Sidney Janis Gallery, New York (1/11–1/12 1962), which showed work by artists from England, France, Italy, the United States and Sweden, who were grouped together by John Ashbury in his foreword on the basis of their shared interest in everyday objects. The term Pop Art had not yet become

established, and the initial conceptual confusion felt by the New York art world is clearly evident in the article by Barbara Rose "The New Realists, Neo-Dada, Le nouveau réalisme, Pop Art, The New Vulgarians, Common Object Painting, Know-nothing genre" (*Art International*, vol. VII, January 1963: 1, pp. 22–28). In December 1962 "A Symposium on Pop Art" concerning the rapid emergence of this phenomenon was held at MoMA, while the first survey exhibitions of Pop Art were held in museums shortly afterwards: Walter Hopp's *The New Painting of Common Objects*, Pasadena Museum of Art (25/9–19/10 1962) in the United States; and, in Europe, Alan Solomon's *The Popular Image*, Institute of Contemporary Arts, London (24/10–23/11 1963) and Pontus Hultén's *Amerikansk popkonst*, ModernaMuseet, Stockholm (29/2–12/4 1964). The first monographs on Pop Art were published a year or so later, e.g. John Rublowsky, *Pop Art*, New York 1965, Mario Amaya, *Pop as Art*, London 1965, and Lucy Lippard's *Pop Art* of 1966, which was long considered the standard work on the movement. That same year, the institutional and historical position of Pop Art was consolidated at the 33rd Venice Biennale, as it would be again two years later at Documenta IV, Kassel in 1968 (a state of affairs that was strongly criticised in the powerfully politicised cultural climate of that year). The Pop Art phenomenon took on a new topicality towards the end of the 1970s as a critical tool for the interpretation of the contemporary scene (see e.g. Andreas Huyssen, "The Cultural Politics of Pop", *New German Critique*, vol. 4, Winter 1975, pp. 77–98) and, subsequently, when the early work of Andy Warhol, in particular, was considered by certain theorists to define the core of the aesthetics of Pop Art and its relation to postmodernism, as for example in Fredric Jameson, "Postmodernism and Consumer Society" (1981), in Foster 2002, p. 127–144) and (where it is treated much more thoroughly in theoretical and historical terms) in Hal Foster's *The Return of the Real*, 1996, pp. 127–168.

42. Geldzahler, p. 37.

43. Rosalind Krauss, "Theories of Art after Minimalism and Pop", in Hal Foster (ed.), *Discussions in Contemporary Culture*, no. 1, Dia Art Foundation, Seattle 1987, p. 60.

44. For a description of the origins (and a plan) of this exhibition, see Graham Whitman, "This is Tomorrow: Genesis of an Exhibition", *Modern Dreams. The Rise and Fall of Pop*, Cambridge (Mass.)/London 1988, pp. 35-39.

45. Collaborative exhibition of painters, sculptors and architects: Draft proposals", Whitechapel Art Gallery Archives, London, WAG/EXH/2/45/1.

46. In an internal report compiled while the exhibition was ongoing, Lawrence Alloway wrote that visitor numbers for "This is Tomorrow" were reaching 1,000 people a day, the highest figure seen at the Whitechapel Art Gallery after the end of the War, apart from for the major Turner exhibition of 1951, and that the exhibition had attracted a great deal of attention in the press, newsreels and on television, including a forty minute feature on the BBC (see "Progress report", Whitechapel Art Gallery Archives, London, WAG/EXH/2/45/1).

47. Lawrence Alloway, "Robot opens exhibition on design in the future", *This is Tomorrow*, Immediate Release at the Whitechapel Art Gallery, 8th August – 9th September 1956, unpaginated, Whitechapel Art Gallery Archives, London, WAG/EXH/2/45/1.

48. Pierre Rouve, "Divorce of Two Minds", *Art News and Review*, 18 August 1956, p. 17.

49. Lawrence Alloway, "Robot opens exhibition on design in the future", *This is Tomorrow*, Immediate Release at the Whitechapel Art Gallery, 8th August – 9th September 1956, unpaginated, Whitechapel Art Gallery Archives, London, WAG/EXH/2/45/1.

50. See Brian Wallis, "Tomorrow and Tomorrow and Tomorrow: The Independent Group and Popular Culture", in *Modern Dreams*, 1988, pp. 9-17.

51. Lynne Cooke, "The Independent Group: British and American Pop Art", in Varnedoe & Gopnik, p. 200.

52. One example is Edward Lucie-Smith who writes, in an article intended as a survey of Pop Art, that it is "generally accepted" that Hamilton's collage is the "first truly Pop Art work" (Edward Lucie-Smith, "Pop Art", in Nikos Stangos, *Concepts of Modern Art*, London 1983 (1974), p. 225).

53. See e.g. Lawrence Alloway, "The Development of British Pop", in Lippard 2004, pp. 27–66. For a critical historiography of the Independent Group, see Anne Massey & Penny Sparke, "The Myth of the Independent Group", *Block*, no. 10, 1985, pp. 48–56.

54. Richard Hamilton, "Man, Machine, Motion" (1955), *Collected Words 1953–81*, London 1982, p. 24.

55. See statement by Richard Hamilton in the catalogue to *This is Tomorrow*, Whitechapel Art Gallery, London 1956, unpaginated.

56. Lawrence Alloway, "The Long Front of Culture" (1959), in *Modern Dreams*, p. 31.

57. For an analysis of the complex significance of the role played by the Institute of Contemporary Arts as stimulus, environment, meeting place and (in terms of the modernist and evolutionist credo of Herbert Read) as the antithesis of the Independent Group, see Anne Massey, "The Independent Group: Towards a Redefinition", *Burlington Magazine*, vol. 79, no. 1009, April 1987, pp. 232–242.

58. Hal Foster, "On the First Pop Age", *New Left Review*, vol. 44, no. 19, Jan-Feb 2003, pp. 93–112.

59. Umberto Eco, *The Open Work*, (transl. Anna Cancogni), Cambridge (Mass.) 1989 (1962), pp. 2–3.

60. See e.g. David Revill, *The Roaring Silence. John Cage: a Life*, New York 1992, p. 62 and passim.

61. See John Cage, "Indeterminacy", *Silence. Lectures and Writings by John Cage*, London/Hanover (N.E.) 1998 (1961), pp. 260–273, and Richard Kostelanetz, *Conversing with Cage*, New York 1988 (1987), pp. 188–189.

62. Revill, p. 189.

63. Eco, pp. 102–103.

64. Marcel Duchamp, "The Creative Act" (1958), in Gregory Battcock (ed.), *The New Art. A Critical Anthology*, New York 1966, pp. 25–26.

65. Ulf Linde, *Spejare. En essä om konst*, Göteborg 1984 (1960), p. 68. See also Walter Hopps, Ulf Linde & Arturo Schwartz, *Marcel Duchamp. Ready-mades etc., 1913–1964*, Paris 1964.; Hans Hayden,

"Contradicting Codes", *Konsthistorisk tidskrift*, vol 81, Issue 3, September 2012, pp. 166–171.

66. Kaprow, 1958, p. 56.

67. Allan Kaprow, "Notes on the Creation of a Total Art", *Allan Kaprow*, The Hansa Gallery, 25/11–13/12 1958, New York 1958, unpaginated.

68. Allan Kaprow, "A Statement", in Michael Kirby, *Happenings. An Illustrated Anthology*, New York 1965, p. 46.

69. Allan Kaprow, "18 happenings in 6 parts / the script", in Kirby, p. 55.

70. Benjamin Buchloh, "Andy Warhol's One-Dimensional Art: 1956–1966", in Kynaston McShine (ed.), *Andy Warhol: A Retrospective*, The Museum of Modern Art, New York 1989, pp. 44–45.

71. See *documenta 4: Internationale Ausstellung, 27 Juni bis 6 Oktober 1968*, Kassel 1968. For an analysis of the problems that putting together this combination of different idioms posed for the arrangers, see Kimpel, pp. 274–279.

72. See Bruce Altshuler, "The Cage Class", in *FluxAttitudes*, Hallwalls Contemporary Art Center, Buffalo 1991, pp. 17–23. Although, formally, it was experimental composition that Cage taught between 1956 and 1960, his lectures also served as a forum for information and discussion about new forms of aesthetics and alternative (read: Dadaist and Surrealist) historical sources, at which students of different genres could participate on equal terms. Among the more celebrated students were, in addition toKaprow, several of the artists who subsequently became prominent within Fluxus, such as George Brecht, Dick Higgins and George Maciunas. Perhaps the key lesson to be drawn from Cage's teachings was a way of approaching aesthetic and philosophical problems no matter what the traditions and discursive frames of reference of different artistic genres.

73. Seee.g.. Barbara Haskell, *Blam! The Explosion of Pop, Minimalism, and Performance 1958–1964*, Whitney Museum of American Art, New York 1984, pp. 22–23.

74. The change in reception within the visual arts was much more pronounced in the United States than in Europe. The growth in

interest in the United States in Dadaism and in Marcel Duchamp, in particular, can be explained in terms of the dissemination of historical knowledge to which various exhibitions and publications all contributed. As early as 1936, MoMA had mounted its major thematic exhibition *Fantastic Art, Dada, Surrealism*, which helped to some extent to put these movements on the map of modernism's historical sources and (its then) contemporary possibilities. Of course, it was also of key importance that many of the leading practitioners of Surrealism were living in exile in New York during the war years (although contacts with the local American art world appear to have been sporadic). After the Second World War, Robert Motherwell published an anthology of English translations of the texts of Dadaism (*The Dada Painters and Poets: An Anthology*, The Documents of Modern Art, no. 8, New York 1951) that proved to be a vital source of knowledge about its aesthetics for the post-war art world (for an analysis of the post-war reception of Dadaism and the importance of Motherwell's anthology, see Maria Müller, *Aspekte der Dada-Rezeption*, Essen 1987, pp. 21–24). By then, Duchamp had long been living in New York and his works were accorded ever greater prominence during the 1950s. The Sidney Janis Gallery (in New York) mounted a series of smaller exhibitions of Duchamp's work between 1952 and 1959. From 1954, Walter Arensberg's major collection of Duchamp's works was permanently on display at the Philadelphia Museum of Art. Three years later, the Solomon R. Guggenheim Museum of Art in New York mounted a retrospective exhibition of the work of the three Duchamp brothers. Two years after that, Robert Lebel published the first monograph on Duchamp in both French and English (*Sur Marcel Duchamp/On Marcel Duchamp*, Paris 1959). A considerable amount of space was also devoted to Duchamp in William Seitz's exhibition *The Art of Assemblage* at MoMA in 1961, which provided a comprehensive historical exposé of an alternative strand in the art history of the twentieth century. It would not be until 1964, however, that Duchamp was accorded (with his approval) a first retrospective museum exhibition, at the Pasadena Museum of Art, commissioned by Walter Hopps. By this time, however, his name and work had become public property on both sides of the Atlantic. The point of this enumeration is not to highlight a sequence of events that caused the rediscovery and subsequent fame of an artist, but to show the significance that the connections between historical knowledge, the accessibility of the works and a changed theoretical context had on the reception and reinterpretation of Duchamp. This is not a matter of history proving him right, but of a changed theoretical and visual discourse that meant his works could serve as paradigmatic examples in a larger institutionalised setting.

75. John Cage, in Kostelanetz, pp. 179–180.

76. Bürger, p. 58. His negative attitude towards the neo-avantgarde as a phenomenon is motivated by an ideologically-critical (Marxist) approach to the institutionalisation of modern art as a phenomenon, in that he considers it to be the essential task of modern art, irrespective of its medium and idiom, in the capitalist system to establish a countercultural position that is critical of institutions,. It is interesting to note how this line of argument resembles the condemnations of Pop Art and Neo-Realism made by the some of the champions of Abstract Expressionism, albeit from the exactly opposite ideological direction. Gilbert Sorrentino's dispute with the new art in "Kitsch into Art': The New Realism" (1962) is one example; in this article, Sorrentino launched a ferocious attack on the art being introduced by the *New Realists* exhibition at the Sidney Janis Gallery in New York in1962 and rejected Neo-Dadaism as a feeble, commercial and regressive fashion phenomenon whose primary aim was to rub up the uncultivated middle class the right way and that had abolished the essential boundary between Art and kitsch (Madoff, pp. 47–55). In doing so, Neo-Dadaism violated the specifically antiaesthetic aims of original Dadaism and set itself against the development of authentic (Abstract Expressionist) art and the tackling of real issues.

77. Foster, 1996, p. 46.

78. Sally Banes, *Greenwich Village 1963. Avant-Garde Performance and the Effervescent Body*, Durham/London 1993, pp. 1–3.

79. Susan Sontag, "Notes on Camp" (1964), *Against Interpretation and Other Essays*, New York 2009 (1966), p. 276.

80. Wassily Kandinsky likens the effect of colour on the human soul to a piano, at which the artist (the hand) influences the observer's eye (the hammer) by using a colour (a key) and transports the soul to the intended vibration (the strings of the piano). This

immediate communication constitutes what he calls 'the principle of inner necessity', through which life is realised in art (Wassily Kandinsky, Concerning the Spiritual in Art, (transl. Michael Sadler), New York 1977 (1911), p. 26). A much less specific and instrumental association between art and life is found in the work of Piet Mondrian. Although all the different artistic genres have clearly been developed from their specific preconditions, as Mondrian states in his pivotal essay "Le Neo-Plasticisme: Principe général de l'équivalence plastique" (1920), the goal of the New Art (irrespective of medium) is to create a union of all the genres that is based on a universal harmonic concord: that of the underlying laws that constitute the totality of existence, which make it possible for human beings to be universal as individuals ("Neo-Plasticism: the General Principle of Plastic Equivalence", in Harry Holzman & Martin S. James, (ed. and transl.), The New Art – The New Life. The Collected Writings of Piet Mondrian, London 1986, pp. 137–151). Direct communication between artist and observer via the work was not the issue here but rather that the authenticity of the work corresponded to the universal harmony found in both the being of the artist and that of the observer.

81. The first of these dates alludes, of course, to Robert Rauschenberg's tumultuous winning of the major painting prize. The controversial aspect of his victory was that it signalled a symbolic shift on many levels, of which the French, in particular, were all too aware: an American had been awarded the highest prize for the first time and for art that so clearly deviated from institutionalised modernism in general and from the great French tradition in particular (see e.g., Willi Bongard, "When Rauschenberg Won the Biennale", *Studio International*, vol. 175, June 1968, pp. 288–289; Laurie J. Monahan, "Cultural Cartography: American Designs at the 1964 Venice Biennale", in Guilbaut, 1990, pp. 369–416; Tomkins, , pp. 1–11; Boyer, 1995, pp. 189–202). Four years later, the Biennale was so shaken by protests and riots in the wake of the student rebellions throughout Europe that it failed to open. The protests were not simply to do with a conflict over interpretive privilege within the value sphere of the visual arts but a much broader ideological and social conflict that affected large parts of the artistic and cultural life of Western Europe, both directly and indirectly.

82. See Öyvind Fahlström, "Det extatiska huset", *Konstrevy*, vol. 42, 1966: 4, pp. 152–155, pp 191–192. In contrast with Andy Warhol's dramatic version of his transgression of the norms of craft skills and individual brushwork that obtained within the regime of authenticity—by emphasising the silkscreen technique's mechanical application of paint to a surface and by his (over-)emphasis of the role of his assistants in the production of the image—the collaboration between Fahlström and Östlihn was presented instead as a purely practical arrangement. This was an arrangement that was subsequently overlooked and largely forgotten (see Annika Öhrner, *Barbro Östlihn och New York. Konstens rum och möjligheter* (Diss. Uppsala 2010), Göteborg/Stockholm 2010, pp. 126–133).

83. Öyvind Fahlström, "Bris", *Rondo* 1961: 3, p. 26.

84. See Craig Owens, "The Allegorical Impulse: Toward a Theory of Postmodernism. Part I-II" (1980b), *Beyond Recognition. Representation, Power, and Culture* (eds. Scott Byron, Barbara Kruger, Lynne Tillman & Jane Weinstock), Berkeley/Los Angeles/London 1997 (1992), pp. 52–113.

85. Öyvind Fahlström, "Manipulating the World", (1962/1964), in *Öyvind Fahlström. Another Space for Painting*, Museud'ArtContemporani de Barcelona, Barcelona 2000, p. 170.

86. In contrast with the fragmentary notes in Marcel Duchamp's *Green Box* (RroseSélavy, *La mariée mise à nu par ses célibataires, même*, Paris 1934), Öyvind Fahlström's checklist contains somewhat clearer instructions for the reader/interpreter, particularly in terms of the playing-rules that set out how the various parts are to be deployed (see Öyvind Fahlström, *Minneslista (till "Dr.Schweizerssistauppdrag")*, Stockholm 1964, p. 1). This is, however, a set of instructions that alludes to parlour games rather than constituting a separate game of its own: the aim is to combine various divergent words and word combinations in order to open up unexpected patterns of association, rather than to serve as a conventional game.

87. Jean-François Chevrier, "Another Space for Painting: Concrete Lyricism and Geopoetics", *ÖyvindFahlström. Another Space for Painting*, Museu d'Art Contemporani de Barcelona, Barcelona 2000, p. 9.

88. From a draft of Lars Hjelmstedt's as yet unpublished dissertation "Tid – Tecken – Spel. Aspekter på Öyvind Fahlströms konst" (Konstvetenskapliga institutionen vid Uppsala universitet). In my interpretation of Fahlström, I am greatly indebted to Hjelmstedt, who is indisputably one of the leading experts on Fahlström's art and whose conversation and dissertation have over the years introduced me to this remarkable *oeuvre*. Hjelmsted has always been extraordinarily generous in sharing his ideas, writings and sources. My interpretation is, however, based (in part at least) on different premises than those of Hjelmstedt.

89. Lars Hjelmstedt, "Kraftzacken och språkspiralen. Om Öyvind Fahlströms signifigurationsteori", *Ord och bild*, vol. 107, 1998: 1–2, p. 102.

90. Fahlström,1961, p. 24 and p. 26. Quotations from *Öyvind Fahlström. Another Space for Painting*, Museu d'Art Contemporani de Barcelona, Barcelona 2000, p. 118.

91. Branden W. Joseph, *Random Order. Robert Rauschenberg and the Neo-Avantgarde*, Cambridge (Mass.)/London 2003, p. 162. The absence of concealed symbolism and iconographic programmes in Rauschenberg's visual art had already been noted at the end of the 1950s and has become an art-critical commonplace ever since (see e.g., Nicolas Calas, "ContiNuance. On the Possibilities of a New Kind of symbolism in Recent American Art", *Art News*, vol. 57, February 1957: 10, pp. 38–39).

92. In this respect, the argument may recall that deployed by Susan Sontag in her celebrated essay "Against Interpretation" (1964), in which she rejects any system for the analysis of images—particularly those systems that analyse the contents of images (iconography), thus displaying "an overt contempt for appearances" and so amounting to "the revenge of the intellect upon the world" (Susan Sontag, "Against Interpretation" (1964), *Against Interpretation and Other Essays*, London 2009 (1966), pp. 6–7). Despite *Dr. Schweitzer* being made up of a multiplicity of representative images, its contents seem just as open to the subjective understanding of the viewer—or just as abstract—as a painting by Jackson Pollock. There is a crucial

difference, however, that also puts Fahlström's poetics beyond the reach of Sontag's attack on interpretation: it is not interpretation *per se* or its inward movement towards the work that he is opposed to. On the contrary, he uses this very convention to examine the conventional boundaries within which this movement becomes possible. And, to counter Sontag, an iconographic or structural close-reading could also obviously be said to contribute to enriching our understanding of the areas of association the artist was working with.

93. A comprehensive collection of examples of Concrete Poetry (in a broad sense) with an exhaustive introduction is available in Mary Ellen Solt (ed.), *Concrete Poetry: a World View*, Bloomington (Ind.)/London 1968. Variants of this form of poetry emerged in different places around the world after the Second World War; its roots can be traced back both to the Symbolists, such as Mallarmé and Rimbaud, and to the onomatopoeic poetry of Dada and Futurism. At the beginning of the 1950s, the pioneers of Concrete Poetry were the Swiss Eugen Gomringer, the Brazilian Noigandres Group and the Lettriste group in France.

94. Öyvind Fahlström, "Hätilaragulpr fåtskilaben. Manifesto for Concrete Poetry" (1954), in *ÖyvindFahlström. Another Space for Painting*, Museu d'Art Contemporani de Barcelona, Barcelona 2000, p. 51.

95. See Teddy Hultberg, *ÖyvindFahlström on the Air – Manipulation the World*, Stockholm 1999, p. 150.

96. Cage (1961), 1998, pp. 99, 101 and 108.

97. Leo Steinberg, "Other Criteria" (1968), *Other Criteria. Confrontations with Twentieth-Century Art*, London/Oxford/New York 1975 (1972), pp. 82–91.

98. Alain Robbe-Grillet, *In the Labyrinth*, (transl. Richard Howard), New York 1994 (1959), p. 140.

99. Roland Barthes, "Literal Literature" (1954), *Critical Essays*, (transl. Richard Howard), Evanston (Ill.) 2000 (1964), pp. 23–24.

100. Alain Robbe-Grillet, *For a New Novel. Essays on Fiction* (transl. Richard Howard), Evanston (Ill.) 1996 (1963), p. 156.

101. As quoted in Bruce Glaser, "Questions to Stella and Judd", *Art News*, vol. 65, Sep. 66: 5, pp. 58–59.

102. Pontus Hultén, *Öyvind Fahlström, Svezia*, XXXIII Biennale di Venezia, Stockholm 1966, unpaginated.

103. Fahlström, 1961, p. 26. As quoted in *Öyvind Fahlström. Another Space for Painting*, Museu d'Art Contemporani de Barcelona, Barcelona 2000, p. 118.

104. Fahlström, "Korvar och pincetter – en löpande kommentar", *Konstrevy*, vol. 42, 1966: 4, pp. 181–182.

105. Benjamin Buchloh, "Parody and Appropriation in Picabia, Pop, and Polke" (1982), *Neo-Avantgarde and Culture Industry. Essays on European and American Art from 1955 to 1975*, Cambridge (Mass.)/London 2000, p. 349.

106. Craig Owens, "From Work to Frame, or, Is There Life After 'The Death of the Author'?",*Beyond Recognition. Representation, Power, and Culture* (eds. Scott Byron, Barbara Kruger, Lynne Tillman & Jane Weinstock), Berkeley/Los Angeles/London 1997 (1992), p. 126.

107. Michel Foucault, "Of Other Spaces" (1967/1984), (transl. Jay Miskowiec), *Diacritics. A Review of Contemporary Criticism*, vol. 16, Spring 1986: 1, pp. 22–27.

108. Ibid, p. 24.

www.ingramcontent.com/pod-product-compliance
Lightning Source LLC
Chambersburg PA
CBHW040519220526
45473CB00013B/2918